ASPEN PUBLISHERS

SO-BZW-624

Casenote™ *Legal Briefs*

FAMILY LAW

Keyed to Courses Using

Areen and Regan's
Family Law

Fifth Edition

Wolters Kluwer

Law & Business

AUSTIN   BOSTON   CHICAGO   NEW YORK   THE NETHERLANDS

Aspen Publishers
Attn: Permissions Department
76 Ninth Avenue, 7th Floor
New York, NY 10011-5201

To contact Customer Care, e-mail customer.care@aspenpublishers.com, call 1-800-234-1660, fax 1-800-901-9075, or mail correspondence to:

Aspen Publishers
Attn: Order Department
PO Box 990
Frederick, MD 21705

Printed in the United States of America.

2 3 4 5 6 7 8 9 0

ISBN 978-0-7355-6160-1

About Wolters Kluwer Law & Business

Wolters Kluwer Law & Business is a leading provider of research information and workflow solutions in key specialty areas. The strengths of the individual brands of Aspen Publishers, CCH, Kluwer Law International and Loislaw are aligned within Wolters Kluwer Law & Business to provide comprehensive, in-depth solutions and expert-authored content for the legal, professional and education markets.

CCH was founded in 1913 and has served more than four generations of business professionals and their clients. The CCH products in the Wolters Kluwer Law & Business group are highly regarded electronic and print resources for legal, securities, antitrust and trade regulation, government contracting, banking, pension, payroll, employment and labor, and health-care reimbursement and compliance professionals.

Aspen Publishers is a leading information provider for attorneys, business professionals and law students. Written by preeminent authorities, Aspen products offer analytical and practical information in a range of specialty practice areas from securities law and intellectual property to mergers and acquisitions and pension/benefits. Aspen's trusted legal education resources provide professors and students with high-quality, up-to-date and effective resources for successful instruction and study in all areas of the law.

Kluwer Law International supplies the global business community with comprehensive English-language international legal information. Legal practitioners, corporate counsel and business executives around the world rely on the Kluwer Law International journals, loose-leafs, books and electronic products for authoritative information in many areas of international legal practice.

Loislaw is a premier provider of digitized legal content to small law firm practitioners of various specializations. Loislaw provides attorneys with the ability to quickly and efficiently find the necessary legal information they need, when and where they need it, by facilitating access to primary law as well as state-specific law, records, forms and treatises.

Wolters Kluwer Law & Business, a unit of Wolters Kluwer, is headquartered in New York and Riverwoods, Illinois. Wolters Kluwer is a leading multinational publisher and information services company.

Format for the Casenote Legal Brief

Nature of Case: This section identifies the form of action (e.g., breach of contract, negligence, battery), the type of proceeding (e.g., demurrer, appeal from trial court's jury instructions) or the relief sought (e.g., damages, injunction, criminal sanctions).

Fact Summary: This is included to refresh your memory and can be used as a quick reminder of the facts.

Rule of Law: Summarizes the general principle of law that the case illustrates. It may be used for instant recall of the court's holding and for classroom discussion or home review.

Facts: This section contains all relevant facts of the case, including the contentions of the parties and the lower court holdings. It is written in a logical order to give the student a clear understanding of the case. The plaintiff and defendant are identified by their proper names throughout and are always labeled with a (P) or (D).

Palsgraf v. Long Island R.R. Co.

Injured bystander (P) v. Railroad company (D)

N.Y. Ct. App., 248 N.Y. 339, 162 N.E. 99 (1928).

NATURE OF CASE: Appeal from judgment affirming verdict for plaintiff seeking damages for personal injury.

FACT SUMMARY: Helen Palsgraf (P) was injured on R.R.'s (D) train platform when R.R.'s (D) guard helped a passenger aboard a moving train, causing his package to fall on the tracks. The package contained fireworks which exploded, creating a shock that tipped a scale onto Palsgraf (P).

🏛 RULE OF LAW
The risk reasonably to be perceived defines the duty to be obeyed.

FACTS: Helen Palsgraf (P) purchased a ticket to Rockaway Beach from R.R. (D) and was waiting on the train platform. As she waited, two men ran to catch a train that was pulling out from the platform. The first man jumped aboard, but the second man, who appeared as if he might fall, was helped aboard by the guard on the train who had kept the door open so they could jump aboard. A guard on the platform also helped by pushing him onto the train. The man was carrying a package wrapped in newspaper. In the process, the man dropped his package, which fell on the tracks. The package contained fireworks and exploded. The shock of the explosion was apparently of great enough strength to tip over some scales at the other end of the platform, which fell on Palsgraf (P) and injured her. A jury awarded her damages, and R.R. (D) appealed.

ISSUE: Does the risk reasonably to be perceived define the duty to be obeyed?

HOLDING AND DECISION: (Cardozo, C.J.) Yes. The risk reasonably to be perceived defines the duty to be obeyed. If there is no foreseeable hazard to the injured party as the result of a seemingly innocent act, the act does not become a tort because it happened to be a wrong as to another. If the wrong was not willful, the plaintiff must show that the act as to her had such great and apparent possibilities of danger as to entitle her to protection. Negligence in the abstract is not enough upon which to base liability. Negligence is a relative concept, evolving out of the common law doctrine of trespass on the case. To establish liability, the defendant must owe a legal duty of reasonable care to the injured party. A cause of action in tort will lie where harm,

though unintended, could have been averted or avoided by observance of such a duty. The scope of the duty is limited by the range of danger that a reasonable person could foresee. In this case, there was nothing to suggest from the appearance of the parcel or otherwise that the parcel contained fireworks. The guard could not reasonably have had any warning of a threat to Palsgraf (P), and R.R. (D) therefore cannot be held liable. Judgment is reversed in favor of R.R. (D).

DISSENT: (Andrews, J.) The concept that there is no negligence unless R.R. (D) owes a legal duty to take care as to Palsgraf (P) herself is too narrow. Everyone owes to the world at large the duty of refraining from those acts that may unreasonably threaten the safety of others. If the guard's action was negligent as to those nearby, it was also negligent as to those outside what might be termed the "danger zone." For Palsgraf (P) to recover, R.R.'s (D) negligence must have been the proximate cause of her injury, a question of fact for the jury.

▶ ANALYSIS
The majority defined the limit of the defendant's liability in terms of the danger that a reasonable person in defendant's situation would have perceived. The dissent argued that the limitation should not be placed on liability, but rather on damages. Judge Andrews suggested that only injuries that would not have happened but for R.R.'s (D) negligence should be compensable. Both the majority and dissent recognized the policy-driven need to limit liability for negligent acts, seeking, in the words of Judge Andrews, to define a framework "that will be practical and in keeping with the general understanding of mankind." The Restatement (Second) of Torts has accepted Judge Cardozo's view.

━━━

Quicknotes
FORESEEABILITY A reasonable expectation that change is the probable result of certain acts or omissions.

NEGLIGENCE Conduct falling below the standard of care that a reasonable person would demonstrate under similar conditions.

PROXIMATE CAUSE The natural sequence of events without which an injury would not have been sustained.

━━━

Party ID: Quick identification of the relationship between the parties.

Concurrence/Dissent: All concurrences and dissents are briefed whenever they are included by the casebook editor.

Analysis: This last paragraph gives you a broad understanding of where the case "fits in" with other cases in the section of the book and with the entire course. It is a hornbook-style discussion indicating whether the case is a majority or minority opinion and comparing the principal case with other cases in the casebook. It may also provide analysis from restatements, uniform codes, and law review articles. The analysis will prove to be invaluable to classroom discussion.

Issue: The issue is a concise question that brings out the essence of the opinion as it relates to the section of the casebook in which the case appears. Both substantive and procedural issues are included if relevant to the decision.

Holding and Decision: This section offers a clear and in-depth discussion of the rule of the case and the court's rationale. It is written in easy-to-understand language and answers the issue presented by applying the law to the facts of the case. When relevant, it includes a thorough discussion of the exceptions to the case as listed by the court, any major cites to the other cases on point, and the names of the judges who wrote the decisions.

Quicknotes: Conveniently defines legal terms found in the case and summarizes the nature of any statutes, codes, or rules referred to in the text.

Note to Students

Aspen Publishers is proud to offer *Casenote Legal Briefs*—continuing thirty years of publishing America's best-selling legal briefs.

Casenote Legal Briefs are designed to help you save time when briefing assigned cases. Organized under convenient headings, they show you how to abstract the basic facts and holdings from the text of the actual opinions handed down by the courts. Used as part of a rigorous study regimen, they can help you spend more time analyzing and critiquing points of law than on copying bits and pieces of judicial opinions into your notebook or outline.

Casenote Legal Briefs should never be used as a substitute for assigned casebook readings. They work best when read as a follow-up to reviewing the underlying opinions themselves. Students who try to avoid reading and digesting the judicial opinions in their casebooks or on-line sources will end up shortchanging themselves in the long run. The ability to absorb, critique, and restate the dynamic and complex elements of case law decisions is crucial to your success in law school and beyond. It cannot be developed vicariously.

Casenote Legal Briefs represents but one of the many offerings in Aspen's Study Aid Timeline, which includes:

- *Casenote Legal Briefs*
- *Emanuel Law Outlines*
- *Examples & Explanations* Series
- *Introduction to Law* Series
- Emanuel *Law in a Flash* Flashcards
- Emanuel *CrunchTime* Series

Each of these series is designed to provide you with easy-to-understand explanations of complex points of law. Each volume offers guidance on the principles of legal analysis and, consulted regularly, will hone your ability to spot relevant issues. We have titles that will help you prepare for class, prepare for your exams, and enhance your general comprehension of the law along the way.

To find out more about Aspen Study Aid publications, visit us on-line at *http://lawschool.aspenpublishers.com* or e-mail us at *legaledu@aspenpubl.com*. We'll be happy to assist you.

Free access to Briefs on-line!

Download the cases you want using the full cut-and-paste feature accompanying Casenote Legal Briefs on-line. Fill out this form for full access to this useful feature provided by Loislaw. Learn more about Loislaw Services on the inside back cover of this book or visit www.loislawschool.com.

Name	Phone ( )

Address	Apt. No.

City	State	ZIP Code

Law School	Year (check one) ☐1st ☐2nd ☐3rd

Cut out the UPC found on the lower left-hand corner of the back cover of this book. Staple the UPC inside this box. Only the original UPC from the book cover will be accepted. (No photocopies or store stickers are allowed.)

Attach UPC inside the box.

E-mail (Print LEGIBLY or you may not get access!)

Title of this book (course subject)

Used with which casebook (provide author's name)

Mail the completed form to: Aspen Publishers, Inc.
Legal Education Division
Casenote On-line Access
130 Turner St., Building 3, 4th Floor
Waltham, MA 02453-8901

I understand that on-line access is granted solely to the purchaser of this book for the academic year in which it was purchased. Any other usage is not authorized and will result in immediate termination of access. Sharing of codes is strictly prohibited.

Signature _____

Upon receipt of this completed form, you will be e-mailed codes so that you may access the Briefs for this Casenote Legal Brief. On-line Briefs may not be available for all titles. For a full list of available titles please check http://lawschool.aspenpublishers.com.

A. Decide on a Format and Stick to It

Structure is essential to a good brief. It enables you to arrange systematically the related parts that are scattered throughout most cases, thus making manageable and understandable what might otherwise seem to be an endless and unfathomable sea of information. There are, of course, an unlimited number of formats that can be utilized. However, it is best to find one that suits your needs and stick to it. Consistency breeds both efficiency and the security that when called upon you will know where to look in your brief for the information you are asked to give.

Any format, as long as it presents the essential elements of a case in an organized fashion, can be used. Experience, however, has led *Casenotes* to develop and utilize the following format because of its logical flow and universal applicability.

NATURE OF CASE: This is a brief statement of the legal character and procedural status of the case (e.g., "Appeal of a burglary conviction").

There are many different alternatives open to a litigant dissatisfied with a court ruling. The key to determining which one has been used is to discover *who is asking this court for what.*

This first entry in the brief should be kept as *short as possible.* Use the court's terminology if you understand it. But since jurisdictions vary as to the titles of pleadings, the best entry is the one that addresses who wants what in this proceeding, not the one that sounds most like the court's language.

RULE OF LAW: A statement of the general principle of law that the case illustrates (e.g., "An acceptance that varies any term of the offer is considered a rejection and counter-offer").

Determining the rule of law of a case is a procedure similar to determining the issue of the case. Avoid being fooled by red herrings; there may be a few rules of law mentioned in the case excerpt, but usually only one is *the* rule with which the casebook editor is concerned. The techniques used to locate the issue, described below, may also be utilized to find the rule of law. Generally, your best guide is simply the chapter heading. It is a clue to the point the casebook editor seeks to make and should be kept in mind when reading every case in the respective section.

FACTS: A synopsis of only the essential facts of the case, i.e., those bearing upon or leading up to the issue.

The facts entry should be a short statement of the events and transactions that led one party to initiate legal proceedings against another in the first place. While some cases conveniently state the salient facts at the beginning of the decision, in other instances they will have to be culled from hiding places throughout the text, even from concurring and dissenting opinions. Some of the "facts" will often be in dispute and should be so noted. Conflicting evidence may be briefly pointed up. "Hard" facts must be included. Both must be *relevant* in order to be listed in the facts entry. It is impossible to tell what is relevant until the entire case is read, as the ultimate determination of the rights and liabilities of the parties may turn on something buried deep in the opinion.

Generally, the facts entry should not be longer than three to five *short* sentences.

It is often helpful to identify the role played by a party in a given context. For example, in a construction contract case the identification of a party as the "contractor" or "builder" alleviates the need to tell that that party was the one who was supposed to have built the house.

It is always helpful, and a good general practice, to identify the "plaintiff" and the "defendant." This may seem elementary and uncomplicated, but, especially in view of the creative editing practiced by some casebook editors, it is sometimes a difficult or even impossible task. Bear in mind that the *party presently* seeking something from this court may not be the plaintiff, and that sometimes only the cross-claim of a defendant is treated in the excerpt. Confusing or misaligning the parties can ruin your analysis and understanding of the case.

ISSUE: A statement of the general legal question answered by or illustrated in the case. For clarity, the issue is best put in the form of a question capable of a "yes" or "no" answer. In reality, the issue is simply the Rule of Law put in the form of a question (e.g., "May an offer be accepted by performance?").

The major problem presented in discerning what is *the* issue in the case is that an opinion usually purports to raise and answer several questions. However, except for rare cases, only one such question is really the issue in the case. Collateral issues not necessary to the resolution of the matter in controversy are handled by the court by language known as *"obiter dictum"* or merely *"dictum."* While dicta may be included later in the brief, they have no place under the issue heading.

To find the issue, ask *who wants what* and then go on to ask *why did that party succeed or fail in getting it.* Once this is determined, the "why" should be turned into a question.

The complexity of the issues in the cases will vary, but in all cases a single-sentence question should sum up the issue. *In a few cases,* there will be two, or even more rarely, three issues of equal importance to the resolution of the case. Each should be expressed in a single-sentence question.

Since many issues are resolved by a court in coming to a final disposition of a case, the casebook editor will reproduce the portion of the opinion containing the issue or issues most relevant to the area of law under scrutiny. A noted law professor gave this advice: "Close the book; look at the title on the cover." Chances are, if it is Property, you need not concern yourself with whether, for example, the federal government's treatment of the plaintiff's land really raises a federal question sufficient to support jurisdiction on this ground in federal court.

The same rule applies to chapter headings designating sub-areas within the subjects. They tip you off as to what the text is designed to teach. The cases are arranged in a casebook to show a progression or development of the law, so that the preceding cases may also help.

It is also most important to remember to *read the notes and questions* at the end of a case to determine what the editors wanted you to have gleaned from it.

HOLDING AND DECISION: This section should succinctly explain the rationale of the court in arriving at its decision. In capsulizing the "reasoning" of the court, it should always include an application of the general rule or rules of law to the specific facts of the case. Hidden justifications come to light in this entry; the reasons for the state of the law, the public policies, the biases and prejudices, those considerations that influence the justices' thinking and, ultimately, the outcome of the case. At the end, there should be a short indication of the disposition or procedural resolution of the case (e.g., "Decision of the trial court for Mr. Smith (P) reversed").

The foregoing format is designed to help you "digest" the reams of case material with which you will be faced in your law school career. Once mastered by practice, it will place at your fingertips the information the authors of your casebooks have sought to impart to you in case-by-case illustration and analysis.

B. Be as Economical as Possible in Briefing Cases

Once armed with a format that encourages succinctness, it is as important to be economical with regard to the time spent on the actual reading of the case as it is to be economical in the writing of the brief itself. This does not mean "skimming" a case. Rather, it means reading the case with an "eye" trained to recognize into which "section" of your brief a particular passage or line fits and having a system for quickly and precisely marking the case so that the passages fitting any one particular part of

the brief can be easily identified and brought together in a concise and accurate manner when the brief is actually written.

It is of no use to simply repeat everything in the opinion of the court; record only enough information to trigger your recollection of what the court said. Nevertheless, an accurate statement of the "law of the case," i.e., the legal principle applied to the facts, is absolutely essential to class preparation and to learning the law under the case method.

To that end, it is important to develop a "shorthand" that you can use to make margin notations. These notations will tell you at a glance in which section of the brief you will be placing that particular passage or portion of the opinion.

Some students prefer to underline all the salient portions of the opinion (with a pencil or colored underliner marker), making marginal notations as they go along. Others prefer the color-coded method of underlining, utilizing different colors of markers to underline the salient portions of the case, each separate color being used to represent a different section of the brief. For example, blue underlining could be used for passages relating to the rule of law, yellow for those relating to the issue, and green for those relating to the holding and decision, etc. While it has its advocates, the color-coded method can be confusing and time-consuming (all that time spent on changing colored markers). Furthermore, it can interfere with the continuity and concentration many students deem essential to the reading of a case for maximum comprehension. In the end, however, it is a matter of personal preference and style. Just remember, whatever method you use, underlining must be used sparingly or its value is lost.

If you take the marginal notation route, an efficient and easy method is to go along underlining the key portions of the case and placing in the margin alongside them the following "markers" to indicate where a particular passage or line "belongs" in the brief you will write:

N   (NATURE OF CASE)
RL   (RULE OF LAW)
I   (ISSUE)
HL   (HOLDING AND DECISION, relates to
      the RULE OF LAW behind the decision)
HR   (HOLDING AND DECISION, gives the
      RATIONALE or reasoning behind the
      decision)
HA   (HOLDING AND DECISION, APPLIES
      the general principle(s) of law to the facts
      of the case to arrive at the decision)

Remember that a particular passage may well contain information necessary to more than one part of your brief, in which case you simply note that in the margin. If you are using the color-coded underlining method instead of margin notation, simply make asterisks or checks in the margin next to the passage in question in the colors that indicate the additional sections of the brief where it might be utilized.

The economy of utilizing "shorthand" in marking cases for briefing can be maintained in the actual brief writing process itself by utilizing "law student shorthand" within the brief. There are many commonly used words and phrases for which abbreviations can be substituted in your briefs (and in your class notes also). You can develop abbreviations that are personal to you and which will save you a lot of time. A reference list of briefing abbreviations can be found on page xii of this book.

C. Use Both the Briefing Process and the Brief as a Learning Tool

Now that you have a format and the tools for briefing cases efficiently, the most important thing is to make the time spent in briefing profitable to you and to make the most advantageous use of the briefs you create. Of course, the briefs are invaluable for classroom reference when you are called upon to explain or analyze a particular case. However, they are also useful in reviewing for exams. A quick glance at the fact summary should bring the case to mind, and a rereading of the rule of law should enable you to go over the underlying legal concept in your mind, how it was applied in that particular case, and how it might apply in other factual settings.

As to the value to be derived from engaging in the briefing process itself, there is an immediate benefit that arises from being forced to sift through the essential facts and reasoning from the court's opinion and to succinctly express them in your own words in your brief. The process ensures that you understand the case and the point that it illustrates, and that means you will be ready to absorb further analysis and information brought forth in class. It also ensures you will have something to say when called upon in class. The briefing process helps develop a mental agility for getting to the *gist* of a case and for identifying, expounding on, and applying the legal concepts and issues found there. The briefing process is the mental process on which you must rely in taking law school examinations; it is also the mental process upon which a lawyer relies in serving his clients and in making his living.

acceptance	acp	offer	O
affirmed	aff	offeree	OE
answer	ans	offeror	OR
assumption of risk	a/r	ordinance	ord
attorney	atty	pain and suffering	p/s
beyond a reasonable doubt	b/r/d	parol evidence	p/e
bona fide purchaser	BFP	plaintiff	P
breach of contract	br/k	prima facie	p/f
cause of action	c/a	probable cause	p/c
common law	c/l	proximate cause	px/c
Constitution	Con	real property	r/p
constitutional	con	reasonable doubt	r/d
contract	K	reasonable man	r/m
contributory negligence	c/n	rebuttable presumption	rb/p
cross	x	remanded	rem
cross-complaint	x/c	res ipsa loquitur	RIL
cross-examination	x/ex	respondeat superior	r/s
cruel and unusual punishment	c/u/p	Restatement	RS
defendant	D	reversed	rev
dismissed	dis	Rule Against Perpetuities	RAP
double jeopardy	d/j	search and seizure	s/s
due process	d/p	search warrant	s/w
equal protection	e/p	self-defense	s/d
equity	eq	specific performance	s/p
evidence	ev	statute of limitations	S/L
exclude	exc	statute of frauds	S/F
exclusionary rule	exc/r	statute	S
felony	f/n	summary judgment	s/j
freedom of speech	f/s	tenancy in common	t/c
good faith	g/f	tenancy at will	t/w
habeas corpus	h/c	tenant	t
hearsay	hr	third party	TP
husband	H	third party beneficiary	TPB
in loco parentis	ILP	transferred intent	TI
injunction	inj	unconscionable	uncon
inter vivos	I/v	unconstitutional	unconst
joint tenancy	j/t	undue influence	u/e
judgment	judgt	Uniform Commercial Code	UCC
jurisdiction	jur	unilateral	uni
last clear chance	LCC	vendee	VE
long-arm statute	LAS	vendor	VR
majority view	maj	versus	v
meeting of minds	MOM	void for vagueness	VFV
minority view	min	weight of the evidence	w/e
Miranda warnings	Mir/w	weight of authority	w/a
Miranda rule	Mir/r	wife	W
negligence	neg	with	w/
notice	ntc	within	w/i
nuisance	nus	without prejudice	w/o/p
obligation	ob	without	w/o
obscene	obs	wrongful death	wr/d

Table of Cases

What Is a Family?

Quick Reference Rules of Law

Baker v. State

Same-sex couples (P) v. State (D)

Vt. Sup. Ct., 744 A.2d 864 (1999).

NATURE OF CASE: Appeal from denial of marriage licenses.

FACT SUMMARY: Three same-sex couples (P) applied for marriage licenses and were denied. They (P) sought a declaratory judgment from the court that the denial was against state law and the state constitution.

🏛 RULE OF LAW
It is against the Vermont constitution to deny same-gender couples the same rights and protections that opposite-sex couples gain from marriage.

FACTS: Three same-gender couples (P) who had lived together in committed relationships sought marriage licenses from their respective town clerks, and all were refused licenses as ineligible under the state's marriage laws. The plaintiffs then sought a declaratory judgment that the State's (D) refusal to issue marriage licenses violated both the state's law and the state's constitution.

ISSUE: May the state of Vermont exclude same-sex couples from the benefits and protections that its laws provide to opposite-sex couples?

HOLDING AND DECISION: [Judge not stated in casebook excerpt.] No. Vermont may not exclude same-sex couples from the benefits and protections that its laws provide to opposite sex couples. The benefits and protections of marriage in Vermont have remained the same even while Vermont laws concerning marriage have significantly changed in the last century. [The court goes on to enumerate a number of statutory benefits and protections provided to opposite sex married couples pursuant to Vermont law.] [Decision not stated in casebook excerpt.]

▶ ANALYSIS

The court's opinion is careful to distinguish the state's Common Benefits Clause from the Equal Protection Clause of the U.S. Constitution. The latter provision reflected the solicitude of a dominant society for a historically oppressed minority and is couched in language proscribing the "denial" of rights. By contrast, according to the court, the Common Benefits Clause expresses a vision of government that affords every state citizen its benefit and gives none a particular advantage—rather, a positive injunction that all are to share the bounty equally. After this case, the Vermont legislature enacted a statute that permitted same-gender couples to enter into a civil union that afforded them all the rights and benefits of a traditional marriage. This case was one of many involving the same-sex marriage controversy and one of a few that afforded some protection to homosexual couples.

■═■

Quicknotes

DECLARATORY JUDGMENT A judgment of the court establishing the rights of the parties.

EQUAL PROTECTION CLAUSE A constitutional provision that each person be guaranteed the same protection of the laws enjoyed by other persons in like circumstances.

■═■

Braschi v. Stahl Associates Company

Companion of decedent (P) v. Management company (D)

N.Y. Ct. App., 74 N.Y.2d 201, 544 N.Y.S.2d 784, 543 N.E.2d 49 (1989).

NATURE OF CASE: Appeal from reversal of decision enjoining eviction proceedings.

FACT SUMMARY: Braschi (P) appealed from a decision reversing the lower court's ruling enjoining Stahl Associates Company (Stahl) (D) from continuing summary proceedings to evict him from the rent-controlled apartment where he resided, contending that he was a family member within the meaning of the city's Rent and Eviction Regulations.

🏛 **RULE OF LAW**
Within the context of rent control and eviction regulations, the term "family" will be interpreted to include those who reside in households having all of the normal familial characteristics.

FACTS: Braschi (P) and Blanchard lived together in a rent-controlled apartment for over 10 years until Blanchard's death in 1986. The apartment was rented in Blanchard's name. They and their families regarded them as spouses. Braschi (P) regarded the apartment as his home, receiving mail there and listing the address on his driver's license and his passport. The building's superintendent and doorman were acquainted with them and regarded them as a couple. They shared all normal household obligations, including a household budget, checking and savings accounts, and credit cards. Braschi (P) was the beneficiary of Blanchard's life insurance policy and was given power of attorney to handle his affairs during his illness. After Blanchard's death, Stahl (D) moved to evict Braschi (P) under the city's Rent and Eviction Regulations, contending that he did not qualify as a family member under the regulations. Braschi (P) successfully sought a preliminary injunction, but that decision was reversed by the court of appeals. From that decision, Braschi (P) appealed.

ISSUE: Will the term "family" be interpreted to include those who reside in households having all of the normal familial characteristics, within the context of rent control and eviction regulations?

HOLDING AND DECISION: (Titone, J.) Yes. Within the context of rent control and eviction regulations, the term "family" will be interpreted to include those who reside in households having all of the normal familial characteristics. Rent control regulations were enacted for the protection of renters. The intent of the present regulations is to restrict a landowner's ability to evict a narrow class of occupants, namely family members, other than the tenant of record. This restriction is narrow so as to further the overall objective of creating a normal free market for

housing. Thus, the definition of "family" within these regulations must be interpreted in light of these purposes and not in light of the purposes of adoption or intestacy laws. The intended protection of these regulations should not be rigidly restricted to those who have formalized their relationships by obtaining a marriage order or adoption decree. The determination as to whether one should be evicted should be based upon an objective examination of the relationship between the parties. Such an examination in the present case reveals that the relationship between Blanchard and Braschi (P) was imbued with all normal familial characteristics, and, as such, Braschi (P) should be afforded protection of the regulations. Reversed and remitted.

DISSENT: (Simons, J.) The plurality's definition of family impermissibly extends the intent of the rent regulation statute. "Family" now includes anyone with an "emotional and financial 'commitment' to the tenant enjoying rent regulation."

▶ ***ANALYSIS***

Because of the realities in the rental market today, many cities are considering adopting "domestic partner laws," which would extend rent control protections to those situated in Braschi's (P) position. Estimates have been made indicating that traditional nuclear families make up only 15% of all families. Landlords are continuing to fight the adoption of such regulations since they significantly restrict their ability to freely alienate their property.

■=■

Quicknotes

ENJOIN The ordering of a party to cease the conduct of a specific activity.

INJUNCTION A court order requiring a person to do, or prohibiting that person from doing, a specific act.

■=■

Village of Belle Terre v. Boraas

Village (D) v. Student (P)

416 U.S. 1 (1974).

NATURE OF CASE: Appeal from invalidation of a zoning ordinance.

FACT SUMMARY: Boraas (P) challenged the constitutionality of a zoning ordinance which limited residents of single-family dwellings to persons related by blood, marriage, or adoption, or to no more than two unrelated persons.

RULE OF LAW

The state police power, through zoning ordinances, is not limited to the elimination of unhealthy conditions; it can create zones where family and youth values and quiet neighborhoods can grow and prosper.

FACTS: Belle Terre (D), a small Long Island community of about 220 homes and 700 people and less than one mile square, restricted single-family dwellings to one or more persons related by blood, adoption, or marriage, living and cooking together, or to no more than two unrelated persons. Boraas (P) and five other students at Stony Brook University were leasing a house in Belle Terre (D). The six students were unrelated and were cited for violating the zoning ordinance. Boraas (P) sought an injunction invalidating the ordinance, but the district court denied it. The court of appeals reversed, and Belle Terre (D) appealed on grounds that the statute was rational and did not violate rights of travel and privacy and did not bar persons who were uncongenial to the community.

ISSUE: Is the state police power, through zoning ordinances, limited to the elimination of unhealthy conditions?

HOLDING AND DECISION: (Douglas, J.) No. The state police power, through zoning ordinances, is not limited to the elimination of unhealthy conditions; it can create zones where family and youth values and quiet neighborhoods can grow and prosper. The ordinances involve no fundamental right guaranteed by the Constitution. It is a form of economic and social legislation which does not violate equal protection if it is reasonable, not arbitrary, and bears a rational relationship to a legitimate state objective. By limiting two unrelated persons as the number that can constitute a family, Belle Terre (D) has fixed a line which must be accepted as it has not been shown to be unreasonable. The statute does not "reek with animosity" to unmarried persons because two unrelated persons, by definition, must not be married but may live together. "A quiet place where yards are wide, people few, and motor vehicles restricted are legitimate guidelines." Reversed.

DISSENT: (Marshall, J.) The zoning classification violates fundamental rights of privacy and association guaranteed by the First and Fourth Amendments. Zoning ordinances, even with legitimate aims, cannot infringe constitutional rights. While a town can limit density, Belle Terre (D) has only done so against those who are unrelated. Belle Terre (D) has not shown that the classification is necessary to protect a compelling and substantial governmental interest. Other methods, such as limiting the number of adults per household, could achieve the same goal without discriminating on the basis of constitutionally suspect criteria.

ANALYSIS

This case reveals another aspect of regulation of premarital and marital activity. Whatever the success of future challenges to such regulations, the trend, in both the judicial and legislative realm, is to far greater tolerance of nontraditional family life and "deviant" sexual behavior. While some cases have suggested that there is some constitutional protection for nonmarital sexual expression, courts have been reading such decisions narrowly. However, federal courts have indicated recognition of changing mores. In one case, it was held that engaging in purely consensual, private homosexual relations does not provide a ground for refusing to find the "good moral character" required for naturalization, 326 F. Supp. 924 (S.D.N.Y. 1971), and in another, a female who maintained a stable relationship with an unmarried man on grounds of her conscientious objection to conventional marriage could not be denied naturalization, 320 F. Supp. 1222 (D. Ore. 1970).

Quicknotes

FOURTH AMENDMENT Provides that persons be secure as to their person and private belongings against unreasonable searches and seizures.

RIGHT TO PRIVACY Those personal liberties or relationships that are protected against unwarranted governmental interference.

Penobscot Area Housing Development Corp. v. City of Brewer

Housing agency (P) v. City (D)

Me. Sup. Jud. Ct., 434 A.2d 14 (1981).

NATURE OF CASE: Appeal of denial of land use permit.

FACT SUMMARY: The City of Brewer (D) refused to grant a use permit for a home for retarded individuals in an area zoned for single-family units.

RULE OF LAW
A group of retarded individuals living in the same quarters is not a "family" for zoning purposes.

FACTS: The City of Brewer (D) defined "family" for purposes of its zoning ordinance as a domestic relationship based on birth, marriage, or other domestic bond. The Penobscot Area Housing Development Corp. (P) wished to start a home for retarded individuals in an area zoned for single-family residences. The home would consist of six to eight individuals living for an average of 1½ years at that location with rotated supervision. The City (D) denied the permit, contending the arrangement was not a "family." The zoning board of appeals affirmed, as did the superior court. Penobscot (P) appealed.

ISSUE: Is a group of retarded individuals living in the same quarters a "family" for zoning purposes?

HOLDING AND DECISION: (Nichols, J.) No. A group of retarded individuals living in the same quarters is not a "family" for zoning purposes. While "domestic bond," a term found in the definition of "family," does not require blood or marriage, it requires greater continuity than the arrangement at issue here. Specifically, the arrangement lacks a permanent authority figure, which is central to the concept of the family. Further, the fact that the average term of each resident would be 1½ years is quite unlike the concept of the family. Affirmed.

▶ ANALYSIS

It is difficult to tell whether the court here would have decided as the court did in *Carroll v. City of Miami Beach*, 198 So. 2d 643 (1967). The ordinances varied somewhat. More importantly, though, it seems that the court here placed greater value on the traditional concept of the family. It does not seem that the arrangement in *Carroll* had greater authority or greater stability.

■=■

Borough of Glassboro v. Vallorosi

Borough (P) v. Property owner (D)

N.J. Sup. Ct., 117 N.J. 421, 568 A.2d 888 (1990).

NATURE OF CASE: Action to enforce a housing ordinance.

FACT SUMMARY: Vallorosi (D) contended that a Glassboro (P) ordinance defining a family was invalid and did not apply to his living arrangement.

🏛 RULE OF LAW
Ordinances which limit occupancy of dwellings to statutorily defined families are valid where such definition uses the single housekeeping unit element.

FACTS: Glassboro (P) passed an ordinance limiting the occupancy of certain dwellings to families. The ordinance defined a family as a single housekeeping unit. Vallorosi (D) maintained a dwelling and subleased it to 10 college students, who could renew from semester to semester. They all shared the house, the cooking, the cleaning, and the maintenance. Glassboro (P) sought to evict them, claiming they did not meet the statutory requirements of a family. They defended, contending the ordinance was invalid and did not apply to them.

ISSUE: Are ordinances which limit the occupancy of dwellings to statutorily defined families valid?

HOLDING AND DECISION: (Per curiam) Yes. Ordinances which limit the occupancy of dwellings to statutorily defined families are valid if they include the single housekeeping unit element. Such ordinances promote an important governmental police function by restricting activity harmful to the community. In this case, the ordinance was thus valid. However, the college students demonstrated a cooperation in the running of the household to the extent that they were the functional equivalent of a family. Thus, no violation occurred. Affirmed.

▶ ANALYSIS

The problem with housing restrictions is that there is always the danger of abuse. Restrictions can be written so that persons with no dangerous or offensive characteristics are kept out of particular areas wishing to remain homogeneous. Thus, such restrictions must be carefully scrutinized.

Quick Reference Rules of Law

Loving v. Virginia

White man denied right to marry black woman (D) v. State

388 U.S. 1 (1967).

NATURE OF CASE: Appeal from conviction for violation of miscegenation statutes.

FACT SUMMARY: Loving (D), a white man, and Jeter (D), a black woman, both residents of Virginia (P), went to the District of Columbia to marry, as marriage between white persons and any other race was prohibited in Virginia (P).

🏛 RULE OF LAW
The freedom to marry or not marry a person of another race resides with the individual and cannot be infringed by the state.

FACTS: In 1958, two Virginia (P) residents, Loving (D), a white man, and Jeter (D), a black woman, married in the District of Columbia to evade Virginia's (P) ban on marriages between white persons and those of any other race. They returned to Virginia (P), where they were found guilty of violating Virginia's ban on interracial marriages (evading the antimiscegenation statutes), and each was sentenced to a year in prison. The sentence was suspended for 25 years on condition they leave Virginia (P) and not return for that period of time. The Lovings (D) challenged the constitutionality of the Virginia (P) statute on due process and equal protection grounds.

ISSUE: Is there a legitimate overriding purpose independent of invidious racial discrimination which justifies racial classifications for marriage?

HOLDING AND DECISION: (Warren, C.J.) No. Equal protection demands that racial classifications, particularly in criminal statutes, be subjected to the strictest scrutiny. To be upheld, it must be shown to be necessary to the accomplishment of some permissible state objective, independent of racial discrimination, which is sought to be eliminated by the Fourteenth Amendment. Virginia (P) only bans marriages between whites and others. Clearly the state intends only to protect white supremacy. While marriage is left to the states under the Tenth Amendment, their powers to regulate marriage are not unlimited notwithstanding the Fourteenth Amendment. The law deprives the Lovings (D) of due process, as the freedom to marry is one of the vital personal rights essential to the orderly pursuit of happiness by free men. Freedom of choice of marriage cannot be limited by invidious racial discrimination. The freedom to marry a person of another race resides with the individual and cannot be infringed by the state. Convictions are reversed.

▶ ANALYSIS

Marriage was first characterized as a fundamental right in a case dealing not with marriage but with sterilization. At least one state declared its miscegenation statute unconstitutional 19 years earlier than this court as a violation of equal protection limiting a fundamental right.

■━■

Quicknotes

DUE PROCESS The constitutional mandate requiring the courts to protect and enforce individuals' rights and liberties consistent with prevailing principles of fairness and justice and prohibiting the federal and state governments from such activities that deprive its citizens of life, liberty, or property interest.

EQUAL PROTECTION CLAUSE A constitutional provision that each person be guaranteed the same protection of the laws enjoyed by other persons in like circumstances.

FOURTEENTH AMENDMENT Declares that no state shall make or enforce any law that shall abridge the privileges and immunities of citizens of the United States. No state shall deny to any person within its jurisdiction the equal protection of the laws.

MISCEGENATION Marriage between persons of different races.

TENTH AMENDMENT The Tenth Amendment to the United States Constitution reserves those powers therein, not expressly delegated to the federal government or prohibited to the states, to the states or to the people.

■━■

Zablocki v. Redhail

County clerk (P) v. Father (D)

434 U.S. 374 (1978).

NATURE OF CASE: Appeal from judgment holding a marriage statute unconstitutional.

FACT SUMMARY: Redhail (P) contended a Wisconsin statute prohibiting a person with a child support obligation from marrying without a prior court order violated equal protection and due process guarantees.

🏛 RULE OF LAW
A state statute denying a fundamental right to marry must be supported by important state interests and be closely tailored to effectuate such interests in order to be constitutional.

FACTS: Redhail (P) was the father of an illegitimate child and was ordered to pay monthly child support. He subsequently applied to Zablocki (D), the county clerk, for a marriage license. He was refused on the basis of a Wisconsin statute prohibiting a person with a child support obligation from marrying without a prior court order based on the payments being current and the unlikelihood of the child becoming a public charge. Redhail (P), who was in arrears, filed a class action, contending the statute denied equal protection and due process of law. The trial court declared the statute unconstitutional and enjoined its enforcement. Zablocki (D) appealed.

ISSUE: Must a state statute denying the fundamental right to marry be supported by important state interests and be closely tailored to effectuate such interests in order to be constitutional?

HOLDING AND DECISION: (Marshall, J.) Yes. A state statute denying a fundamental right to marry must be supported by important state interests and be closely tailored to effectuate such interests in order to be constitutional. The state interest in enforcing support orders is unquestionably an important interest. However, it cannot be directly linked to a deprivation of the fundamental right of marriage. Therefore, it cannot support this statute's constitutionality. Affirmed.

CONCURRENCE: (Powell, J.) The Court's decision is correct, yet it is too broadly worded to create a usable standard to determine whether a marriage statute directly and substantially interferes with the right to marry.

CONCURRENCE: (Stevens, J.) The majority opinion reaches the correct result, yet it applies a standard different from traditional equal protection review. Such a new standard has no precedential history and should not be used.

DISSENT: (Rehnquist, J.) This statute passes the rational basis test and bears a rational relation to a constitutionally permissible objective. Viewing the statute with the presumption of validity and keeping in mind the state's specific interest in assuring the support of its minor children, this statute has permissibly achieved its goal despite burdening those few parties operating within unique and extreme circumstances.

▶ ANALYSIS

Commentators are unsure as to the exact effect of this decision. The opinion appears to invalidate all statutes which significantly interfere with the right to marry. However, there are many long-accepted regulations against polygamy, bigamy, and incest which clearly interfere with marriage but are unlikely to be held unconstitutional. Thus, it is believed the case does not provide a usable standard, as suggested by Justice Powell.

■≡■

Quicknotes

BIGAMY The criminal offense of willfully and knowingly marrying a second time while knowing that the first marriage is still undissolved.

DUE PROCESS The constitutional mandate requiring the courts to protect and enforce individuals' rights and liberties consistent with prevailing principles of fairness and justice and prohibiting the federal and state governments from such activities that deprive its citizens of life, liberty, or property interest.

EQUAL PROTECTION CLAUSE A constitutional provision that each person be guaranteed the same protection of the laws enjoyed by other persons in like circumstances.

POLYGAMY The crime of having many wives or husbands at the same time, or more than one wife or husband at the same time.

RATIONAL BASIS REVIEW A test employed by the court to determine the validity of a statute in equal protection actions, whereby the court determines whether the challenged statute is rationally related to the achievement of a legitimate state interest.

■≡■

Turner v. Safley

State Division of Corrections (D) v. Prisoner (P)

482 U.S. 78 (1987).

NATURE OF CASE: Appeal from order invalidating a prison regulation.

FACT SUMMARY: Turner (D), on behalf of the state of Missouri, contended its prison regulation severely restricting inmate marriages was constitutional.

RULE OF LAW
There is a constitutionally protected marriage relationship in the prison context.

FACTS: Missouri Division of Corrections promulgated a regulation which allowed prison inmates to marry only under compelling reasons, with the State's (D) approval. Such approval was given only where pregnancy or the danger of a child being born illegitimately arose. Safley (P) sued, contending the regulation infringed upon his constitutional right to marry. Turner (D) appealed the trial court's ruling that the regulation was invalid, contending no such constitutional right existed in the prison context.

ISSUE: Is there a constitutionally protected right to marriage in the prison context?

HOLDING AND DECISION: (O'Connor, J.) Yes. There is a constitutionally protected right to marriage in the prison context. The constitutional right to marriage is not removed by incarceration. It serves both a personal need and in some respects fulfills an inmate's religious needs. While the regulation does meet certain security needs, its scope is much too wide and presents too great an inhibition on the right to marriage. As a result, the regulation is invalid. Affirmed.

ANALYSIS

The decision to marry has been held to be a fundamental constitutional right. While this right is subject to impact by imprisonment, it cannot be unnecessarily infringed. The regulation in this case was not reasonably related to any legitimate penal interest and was thus invalidated.

Michael H. v. Gerald D.

Biological father and daughter (P) v. Presumed father (D)

491 U.S. 110 (1989).

NATURE OF CASE: Appeal from decision upholding constitutionality of presumptive paternity statute.

FACT SUMMARY: Michael H. (P) and Victoria (P) appealed from a decision upholding a decision granting summary judgment to Gerald D. (D) terminating his filiation action, contending that the legislative presumption of paternity in favor of Gerald D. (D) established by the Evidence Code was unconstitutional.

RULE OF LAW
The interest established solely by biological parenthood plus an established parental relationship is not a liberty interest accorded substantive due process protection.

FACTS: Carole married Gerald D. (D) in 1976. In 1978, she became involved with Michael H. (P). A child, Victoria (P), was born in 1981, and blood tests taken shortly after her birth indicated that there was a 98.07% chance that Michael H. (P) was Victoria's (P) natural father. During the ensuing years, although Victoria (P) always remained with Carole, they resided with Gerald D. (D), Michael H. (P), and a third man, Scott. During those periods of time where Carole and Michael H. (P) lived together, he held Victoria (P) out as his daughter. In 1982, rebuffed in his attempts to visit Victoria (P), Michael H. (P) filed a filiation action to establish his paternity and rights to visitation. A long, protracted, and confusing legal battle ensued. Finally, in 1984, Gerald D. (D), who had intervened in the action, moved for summary judgment terminating the filiation action based on the legislative presumption established by the Evidence Code that Victoria (P) was conclusively presumed to be a child of the marriage of Carole and Gerald D. (D). The motion was granted over the objections of Michael H. (P) and Victoria (P) that the legislative presumption relied on by Gerald D. (D) was unconstitutional on substantive due process grounds because it terminated a protected liberty interest created by Michael H.'s (P) biological fatherhood coupled with an established parental relationship. The decision was upheld on appeal, and Michael H. (P) and Victoria (P) appealed.

ISSUE: Is the interest created solely by the facts of biological fatherhood coupled with an established parental relationship a liberty interest entitled to substantive due process protection?

HOLDING AND DECISION: (Scalia, J.) No. The interest created solely by the facts of biological fatherhood coupled with an established parental relationship is not a liberty interest entitled to substantive due process protection. Given the fact that Michael H. (P) is most likely Victoria's (P) natural father, and there was an established parental relationship between them, the question becomes whether persons so situated have been traditionally treated as a protected family unit or have been traditionally accorded some type of societal protection. This is clearly not the case. Legislative presumptions regarding paternity were established in part because of society's aversion to declaring children illegitimate and in part to promote the peace and tranquility of states and families. In fact, the contrary is true; to protect the interests of Michael H. (P) in the present case would come at the expense of the parental and family interests of Gerald D. (D), interests that the state has traditionally protected. Victoria's (P) challenge fails for much the same reason. Affirmed.

CONCURRENCE: (O'Connor, J.) The Court should not have restricted its analysis to a single mode of historical analysis.

DISSENT: (Brennan, J.) The Court's restrictive approaches in the present case, both as to its notions of what will constitute a "tradition" and what the "interest" is at issue here, are misguided, unnecessary, and ignore precedent of this Court which has afforded liberty protection to other interests which would be considered nontraditional under the Court's present analysis.

ANALYSIS

A constitutional debate has long raged as to whether the Constitution is a living document, which adapts and changes in accord with social mores. Justice Brennan appears to be a student of this school. One can expect that given the current political climate, future judicial appointments will be more in the mold of Justice Scalia, and forthcoming decisions will continue to take a restrictive view of constitutional liberties.

Quicknotes

DUE PROCESS The constitutional mandate requiring the courts to protect and enforce individuals' rights and liberties consistent with prevailing principles of fairness and justice and prohibiting the federal and state governments from such activities that deprive its citizens of life, liberty, or property interest.

ORDER OF FILIATION Court designation of paternity for purposes of establishing a duty to support.

Singh v. Singh

Half-uncle (P) v. Half-niece (D)

Conn. Sup. Ct., 213 Conn. 637, 569 A.2d 1112 (1990).

NATURE OF CASE: Appeal of denial of motion to reopen annulment judgment.

FACT SUMMARY: After their marriage was annulled upon discovering they were uncle and niece, David Singh and Seoranie Singh remarried when they learned they were related only by half blood.

🏛 RULE OF LAW
A marriage between a half-uncle and a half-niece is void as incestuous.

FACTS: David and Seoranie Singh had their Connecticut marriage annulled when they discovered they were related as uncle and niece. Later, the Singhs discovered they were only half-uncle and half-niece, so they remarried in California. However, a Connecticut trial court denied the Singhs' motion to reopen their Connecticut annulment judgment. The Singhs appealed, arguing that Connecticut incest statutes were silent as to relatives by the half blood and extending the statute to their situation would be judicial overreaching and disrespectful to the preservation of bona fide marriages. The Singhs also argued that uncle-niece marriages, especially those of the half blood, are not the object of universal condemnation, especially under a modern approach.

ISSUE: Is a marriage between a half-uncle and a half-niece void as incestuous?

HOLDING AND DECISION: (Healey, Assoc. J.) Yes. A marriage between a half-uncle and a half-niece is void as incestuous. Early English cases interpreting incest statutes considered relationship by the half blood to be an equal bar to marriage as relationships by the whole blood. Connecticut incest statutes, which are based on the English laws, have remained unchanged as to the degree of consanguinity within which marriage is proscribed. Modernly, the Connecticut Supreme Court has held that a marriage between uncle and niece and a marriage between half-brother and half-sister violate the incest statutes. The common meanings of the words "uncle" and "niece" include half-uncles and half-nieces. Affirmed.

▶ ANALYSIS

The general rule is that a marriage which is valid in the jurisdiction in which the marriage is performed is valid everywhere. The invalidation of such marriages under incest laws of the domicile is a generally recognized exception to that rule. Courts sometimes invoke a "repugnancy standard" to refuse recognition when they find the relationship in violation of public policy.

Quicknotes

ANNULMENT To nullify a marriage; to establish that the marital status never existed.

BONA FIDE In good faith.

CONSANGUINITY The relatedness of persons based on the existence of common ancestors.

DOMICILE A person's permanent home or principal establishment to which he has an intention of returning when he is absent therefrom.

PUBLIC POLICY Policy administered by the state with respect to the health, safety and morals of its people in accordance with common notions of fairness and decency.

Back v. Back

Widow of decedent (P) v. Challenger to estate (D)

Iowa Sup. Ct., 148 Iowa 223, 125 N.W. 1009 (1910).

NATURE OF CASE: Appeal from judgment invalidating a marriage.

FACT SUMMARY: After his divorce, Back married the daughter of his ex-wife who, after his death, made application to have property set apart to her.

> 🏛 **RULE OF LAW**
> A man may validly marry the daughter of his ex-wife if the first marriage is legally terminated prior to the second marriage.

FACTS: In 1890, decedent married a Mrs. Dirke, a widow with a child from a previous marriage. They divorced in 1900, and four years later he married the daughter. Upon his death in 1906, his then-wife petitioned for a share of his estate as his widow. The trial court held the marriage incestuous under a state statute prohibiting a man from marrying his "wife's daughter." The court ruled the marriage invalid and denied the petition. Back (P), the second wife, appealed.

ISSUE: May a man validly marry the daughter of his ex-wife?

HOLDING AND DECISION: (McClain, J.) Yes. A man may validly marry the daughter of his ex-wife if the first marriage is legally terminated prior to the second marriage. Upon the decedent's divorce from his ex-wife, the relationship of affinity between him and her daughter ceased. Thus, at the time of the marriage, she was not the daughter of his wife, the statute did not apply, and the marriage was valid. Reversed.

▶ **ANALYSIS**

This case illustrates the interpretation of statutes governing consanguinity, or relationships of affinity, in determining whether marriages among people related by blood or law are incestuous. The history of incest is not clear but is thought to have its roots in both biological and sociological beliefs.

Moe v. Dinkins

Unmarried minor mother (P) v. State (D)

533 F. Supp. 623 (S.D.N.Y. 1981); aff'd, 669 F.2d 67 (2d Cir. 1982).

NATURE OF CASE: Motion for summary judgment to declare marriage statute unconstitutional.

FACT SUMMARY: Moe (P) contended a state statute requiring parental consent for minors to marry was unconstitutional.

🏛 RULE OF LAW
A state statute regulating marriages involving minors must be rationally related to a legitimate state interest.

FACTS: Maria Moe (P), a 15-year-old, and the father of her illegitimate child, Raoul Roe (P), wished to marry to cement their familial relationship and to remove the stigma of illegitimacy from their child. Maria's (P) mother refused to give her consent, preventing the marriage under New York law. Moe (P) and Roe (P) sued, contending the law unconstitutionally deprived them of equal protection. Each side moved for summary judgment.

ISSUE: Must a state statute requiring parental consent for minors to marry be rationally related to a legitimate state interest?

HOLDING AND DECISION: (Motley, J.) Yes. A state statute regulating marriages involving minors must be rationally related to a legitimate state interest. In this case, the state interests are clearly legitimate. They include the protection of minors from immature decision-making and preventing unstable marriages. Parental consent helps avoid these problems, and, therefore, the statute is rationally related to the state interests involved. Thus, the statute is constitutional.

▶ ANALYSIS

Although it has long been recognized that a person cannot be deprived of constitutional rights merely because of minority, there has been a different interpretation of such right when applied to minors. The reason for this is that children have a peculiar vulnerability and an inability to make informed decisions concerning critical issues.

■━■

Quicknotes

EQUAL PROTECTION CLAUSE A constitutional provision that each person be guaranteed the same protection of the laws enjoyed by other persons in like circumstances.

■━■

Bronson v. Swensen

Polygamist wife (P) v. County clerk (D)

2005 WL 1310482 (D. Utah).

NATURE OF CASE: Cross-summary judgment motions on the constitutionality of a Utah statute and a clause of the Utah constitution.

FACT SUMMARY: A Utah husband and wife wished to bring a second wife into their relationship. After the husband completed the application, the county clerk denied him and the second woman a marriage license because Utah prohibits plural marriages.

🏛 RULE OF LAW
The right to privacy and other individual constitutional rights do not protect polygamist marriage.

FACTS: G. Lee Cook (P) was married to D. Cook (P). Both plaintiffs claim to have a religious belief permitting plural marriage. Mr. Cook (P) desired to marry J. Bronson (P) as his second wife with Mrs. Cook's (P) consent. Mr. Cook completed a marital license application and paid the license fee but admitted on the application and verbally that he was already married. Swensen (D) refused to issue the license. The Cooks (P) and Bronson (P) now challenge the constitutionality of the Utah statutes and constitution prohibiting plural marriage as a deprivation of their constitutional rights to religious beliefs, association, and privacy.

ISSUE: Does a right to privacy or other individual constitutional rights protect polygamist marriages?

HOLDING AND DECISION: (Stewart, J.) No. The right to privacy and other individual constitutional rights do not protect polygamist marriages. The Utah statutes at issue prohibit polygamy, and the Utah constitution prohibits plural marriages as required by the Enabling Act prior to Utah joining the Union. The U.S. Supreme Court has previously rejected the argument that a prohibition on polygamy violates the free exercise of religion. That case of *Reynolds v. United States*, 98 U.S. 145 (1878), remains solid precedent. The 10th Circuit as recently as 2002 upheld the constitutionality of prohibiting polygamy. The Utah Supreme Court in 2004 upheld the constitutionality of prohibiting plural marriages. The plaintiffs cite to precedent such as *Lawrence v. Texas*, 539 U.S. 558 (2003), but that case involved the private sexual conduct of consenting adults. The prohibition of plural marriages by a state does not infringe upon the private sexual conduct of consenting adults, but rather on the issuance of a marriage license by the state. The plaintiffs simply cannot meet their burden of overcoming overwhelming precedence contradictory to their stance. Plaintiffs' summary judgment motion is denied.

▶ ANALYSIS

The nation watched with interest to see if this case would expand on the privacy right found in *Lawrence v. Texas*. Bronson's case seemed stronger than similar others because she was buttressing her privacy claims with her claim that the laws violated her religious rights and beliefs. This case also differed from prior plural marriage challenges because it was a civil rather than criminal case; the plaintiffs had not yet gone through with a plural marriage and therefore had committed no crime. Proponents of plural marriage argued that criminalizing polygamy was the same as criminalizing private sexual conduct, but the court here clearly thought otherwise. Critics of the decision have vowed to continue the fight for recognition of alternative marriages.

■=■

Quicknotes

SUMMARY JUDGMENT Judgment rendered by a court in response to a motion made by one of the parties, claiming that the lack of a question of material fact in respect to an issue warrants disposition of the issue without consideration by the jury.

POLYGAMY Having many wives or husbands at the same time, or more than one wife or husband at the same time.

■=■

Sanderson v. Tryon

Polygamous mother (P) v. Father (D)

Utah Sup. Ct., 739 P.2d 623 (1987).

NATURE OF CASE: Appeal from a child custody decree.

FACT SUMMARY: Tryon (D) contended that he was entitled to custody of his children because as a matter of law his children's mother's polygamy rendered her unfit to have custody.

> 🏛 **RULE OF LAW**
> A finding that one parent practices polygamy is insufficient by itself to deny her custody of her children.

FACTS: Sanderson (P) gave birth out of wedlock to two children. She practiced polygamy and sought custody of the children when she and their father, Tryon (D), broke up. The trial court held that her polygamous life-style rendered her unsuitable for custody and awarded such to Tryon (D). Sanderson (P) appealed, contending polygamy could not by itself serve to deny her custody.

ISSUE: May a finding that a parent practices polygamy by itself serve to deny that parent custody of her children?

HOLDING AND DECISION: (Hall, C.J.) No. A finding that one parent practices polygamy is insufficient by itself to deny custody of her children. Under Utah law, the relevant inquiry is whether custody in one parent or another is in the best interest of the child. Specific findings on this point must be made. The trial court found both parents in this case fit; however, it denied custody to Sanderson (P) based solely on her polygamous life-style. No findings were made concerning what would be in the best interest of the children. The mere evidence of polygamy did not disqualify Sanderson (P) from obtaining custody. The decree was not supported by findings concerning the best interest of the children. Vacated and remanded for further findings.

▍ *ANALYSIS*

Custody determinations focus primarily upon the best interest of the child. Polygamy would be an element in evaluating whether custody with that parent would be in the child's best interest. It may have been given a more liberal application in Utah than it would in another state.

■═■

Quicknotes

CUSTODY The granting of care and control of a child or children to a parent pursuant to an action for dissolution or separation.

POLYGAMY The offense of having several wives or husbands at the same time, or more than one wife or husband at the same time.

■═■

Goodridge v. Department of Pub. Health

Same-sex couples v. State agency (D)

Mass. Sup. Jud. Ct., 440 Mass. 309, 798 N.E.2d 941 (2003).

NATURE OF CASE: Appeal from award of summary judgment and constitutional challenge to state marriage licensing statute.

FACT SUMMARY: Seven same-sex couples (P) sought marriage licenses in Massachusetts, but the Department of Public Health (D) denied the licenses. The couples (P) challenged the constitutionality of the marriage licensing statute that denied all same-sex couples the right to civil marriage.

RULE OF LAW
The Massachusetts Constitution forbids the creation of second-class citizens and therefore may not deny the protections, benefits, and obligations of civil marriage to same-sex couples wishing to marry.

FACTS: Seven same-sex couples (P) sought marriage licenses from the Department of Public Health (Dept.) (D) in order to marry in Massachusetts. The Dept. (D) denied the couples (P) the licenses. The couples (P) filed suit claiming that the licensing statute did not specifically prohibit same-sex couples from obtaining marriage licenses, or if it is construed to do so, that the statute violated the Massachusetts Constitution on equal protection and due process grounds. The trial judge granted summary judgment to the Dept. (D) on the grounds that the Legislature has a legitimate interest in safeguarding civil marriage for the primary marital purpose of procreation and that the licensing statute accomplishes this interest in a rational manner. The couples (P) appealed.

ISSUE: Does the Massachusetts Constitution deny the protections, benefits, and obligations of civil marriage to same-sex couples wishing to marry?

HOLDING AND DECISION: (Marshall, C.J.) No. The Massachusetts Constitution forbids the creation of second-class citizens and, therefore, may not deny the protections, benefits, and obligations of civil marriage to same-sex couples wishing to marry. Strict scrutiny is the appropriate standard where a statute implicates a fundamental right, and all other statutes require rational basis scrutiny. Although the couples (P) assert that strict scrutiny is appropriate here, the marriage statute does not meet the rational basis test on either equal protection or due process grounds, so the couples' (P) argument for strict scrutiny need not be addressed. Also, the couples' (P) argument that the licensing statute may be construed to permit same-sex couples to marry is incorrect. Construing a statute requires looking to the everyday definition of words, and the everyday definition of "marriage" has always been a union

between a man and a woman. The Legislature remained silent as to the consanguinity of same-sex applicants, which also evidences its intent that only opposite-sex couples be allowed to enter into a civil marriage.

The couples' (P) constitutional claims involve equality and due process challenges. Civil marriage is a government creation through the state's police power and is a vital, fundamental social institution. Marriage provides formidable protections and benefits as well as demanding equally formidable obligations. The Massachusetts Constitution provides perhaps even greater protections for its citizens' fundamental rights than the federal Constitution and also protects its citizens from government interference in the most private aspects of a citizen's life. Choosing if and whom to marry falls within those fundamental rights and private aspects, even while the regulatory power of the state over the mechanics of civil marriage is quite broad. The United States Supreme Court protected citizens' rights to choose whom to marry in *Loving v. Virginia* when it struck down a statute which singled out one trait—race—as a basis to deprive individuals of the right to marry. The U.S. Supreme Court recognized the invidiousness of discrimination which did not allow mixed-race marriages.

The Dept. (D) puts forward three rationales for the statute's prohibition against same-sex marriage: (1) promoting procreation, (2) providing stable, two opposite-sex parent households for minor children, and (3) preserving state and private financial resources. Procreation is no longer the primary support for civil marriage. The state does not purport to test each opposite-sex couple seeking to marry for fertility or desire for procreating. Modern technology provides a variety of ways that a child may be brought into the world and into a family. The Commonwealth is always expanding its definition of "family" to include more than the traditional and no longer majority model of two parents of the opposite sex in the same home raising the children. Prohibiting same-sex couples from marrying does not increase the likelihood that additional opposite-sex couples will seek civil marriage for purposes of procreation. Children thrive in environments of love and support. A loving, supportive household with two opposite-sex parents does not necessarily provide a "more optimal" setting for child-rearing than a loving, supportive household with two same-sex parents. Finally, the State asserts that same-sex couples are not as financially dependent upon one another, thus saving state and private resources, such as tax benefits given to marital couples. This contention ignores the fact that many same-sex couples

Continued on next page.

have dependents relying on them that are no less deserving than those of opposite-sex couples.

The Dept. (D) also argues that allowing same-sex marriage will demean and undermine the institution of marriage as it has been understood for centuries. The couples (P) are not seeking to eradicate the institution of marriage or to demean the marriages of opposite-sex couples. In fact, the couples (P) are seeking to join the institution of marriage in all of its solemnity and with all of its obligations. The Dept. (D) has advanced no valid argument supporting a rational basis for the prohibition against same-sex couples wishing to marry. The only conclusion is that the purpose is based in personal prejudice, and the Constitution certainly cannot protect prejudices. Just as in *Loving*, the singling out of a trait, such as sexual orientation, to prevent access to marriage reveals invidious discrimination which cannot be allowed.

The remedy here is not to eliminate the institution of civil marriage, but to redefine the phrase. While the common law and historical definition is "a union between a man and a woman," the construction is now "the voluntary union of two persons as spouses, to the exclusion of all others." The summary judgment for the Dept. (D) is vacated. Reversed and remanded.

DISSENT: (Spina, J.) The court today wrongly acts in place of the Legislature in regulating marriage. The equal protection argument should have failed because the statute does not discriminate against either gender. A man or a woman has the right to marry any person of his or her choosing, so long as that person is of the opposite sex. Both men and women are equally treated. It is not the state's concern if a person chooses not to marry a member of the opposite sex for reasons related to the person's sexual orientation. Similarly, there is no due process restriction on a person's right to marry. Any person may marry any willing and qualified member of the opposite sex.

DISSENT: (Sosman, J.) The court supports the belief that children raised in same-sex households fare as well as children raised in households with parents of the opposite sex. While that may certainly be true, the scientific data available does not yet fully support that belief. The Legislature is entitled to wait for additional, hard data before making such a fundamental change to the marriage laws as allowing same-sex couples to marry.

▶ *ANALYSIS*

The court stayed the entry of judgment for 180 days to allow the state legislature an opportunity to respond to the opinion. The Massachusetts Legislature immediately responded by pushing through a bill that would recognize civil unions, similar to the ones recognized in Vermont. The civil unions are the legal equivalent of civil marriage, but still deny same-sex couples access to the social institution of marriage. The Supreme Judicial Court responded to the bill by issuing an opinion stating that civil unions were not

enough. Massachusetts became the first state in the union to allow same-sex couples the right to obtain licenses for civil marriages. The state is still divided, however, as parties are seeking a constitutional amendment prohibiting recognition of same-sex marriages. Also, a debate has risen over same-sex couples who are citizens of other states seeking to marry in Massachusetts. They are currently prohibited from marrying based on an interpretation of a statute from the early 1900s, but several couples have filed suit to contest the law.

■═■

Quicknotes

DUE PROCESS The constitutional mandate requiring the courts to protect and enforce individuals' rights and liberties consistent with prevailing principles of fairness and justice and prohibiting the federal and state governments from such activities that deprive its citizens of life, liberty, or property interest.

EQUAL PROTECTION CLAUSE A constitutional provision that each person be guaranteed the same protection of the laws enjoyed by other persons in like circumstances.

RATIONAL BASIS REVIEW A test employed by the court to determine the validity of a statute in equal protection actions, whereby the court determines whether the challenged statute is rationally related to the achievement of a legitimate state interest.

■═■

Wilson v. Ake

Lesbian partner (P) v. Circuit court clerk (D)

354 F. Supp. 2d 1298 (D. Fla. 2005).

NATURE OF CASE: Defendant's motion to dismiss constitutional challenges.

FACT SUMMARY: Wilson (P) and her lesbian partner, Schoenwether (P), sought to have their Massachusetts marriage recognized in Florida.

⚖ RULE OF LAW
The U.S. Constitution does not protect a person's right to enter into a same-sex marriage.

FACTS: Nancy Wilson (P) and Paula Schoenwether (P) are a same-sex couple legally married in Massachusetts. The couple sought to have their same-sex marriage recognized in their home state of Florida. Ake (D) refused to recognize the Massachusetts license because Florida does not recognize same-sex marriage. Wilson (P) challenges the constitutionality of the Federal Defense of Marriage Act (DOMA) and Florida statutes prohibiting same-sex marriage.

ISSUE: Is the right to enter into a same-sex marriage constitutionally protected?

HOLDING AND DECISION: (Moody, J.) No. The Constitution does not protect a person's right to enter into a same-sex marriage. The plaintiffs attempt to interpret the Full Faith and Credit Clause as requiring all states to recognize same-sex marriage because Massachusetts legalized same-sex marriage. Such an interpretation would result in a single state making national policy. The DOMA appropriately regulates the tension among states having two diametrically opposite laws; therefore, plaintiffs' challenge to the DOMA must fail. Plaintiffs' remaining constitutional challenges also must fail because Supreme Court precedent exists supporting the ruling that same-sex marriage is not a fundamental right for persons. Marriage as a fundamental right simply does not necessarily include the right to same-sex marriage. The plaintiffs' citation to *Lawrence v. Texas*, 539 U.S. 558 (2003), is not persuasive because the *Lawrence* court did not address same-sex marriage nor announce a new fundamental right. Finally, plaintiffs' argument that strict scrutiny should be applied in consideration of the constitutionality of DOMA fails because DOMA does not discriminate. It treats women and men equally in not allowing same-sex marriage. Thus, only a rational basis review is required. The government has a legitimate interest in encouraging relationships that allow for procreation and homes with two biological parents raising the children. Motion to dismiss granted.

▶ ANALYSIS

The couple did not appeal the dismissal of their case. Once this case was dismissed, plaintiffs in seven separate challenges

to Florida marriage laws also dismissed their cases. Florida then became one of many states in the nation to place a one-man, one-woman definition of marriage as a constitutional amendment on the ballot for 2006. Every state seeking to amend its constitution to include such a definition has had overwhelming voter support for the amendment. To date, Massachusetts remains the only state to allow same-sex marriage.

Quicknotes

FULL FAITH AND CREDIT ACT As provided in the U.S. Constitution, Article IV, any state judicial proceedings shall have such faith and credit given them in every court in the United States as they would in their own state.

RATIONAL BASIS REVIEW A test employed by the court to determine the validity of a statute in equal protection actions, whereby the court determines whether the challenged statute is rationally related to the achievement of a legitimate state interest.

M.T. v. J.T.

Transsexual male to female (P) v. Husband (D)

N.J. Super. Ct., 140 N.J. Super. 77, 355 A.2d 204 (1976).

NATURE OF CASE: Action for support and maintenance.

FACT SUMMARY: J.T. (D) alleged that his marriage was void since M.T. (P) had become a female through a sex change operation.

RULE OF LAW
A person may become a member of the opposite sex if a sex change operation successfully alters the physical structure so that he or she may function as a member of that sex.

FACTS: M.T. (P) underwent a sex change operation to become a female. The operation was paid for by J.T. (D). M.T. (P) and J.T. (D) were subsequently married. M.T. (P) separated from J.T. (D) and petitioned the court for maintenance and support. J.T. (D) challenged the validity of the marriage, alleging that M.T. (P) remained a "male" which rendered the marriage invalid under state law. M.T. (P) had had his penis removed and a vagina created surgically.

ISSUE: Where the transsexual, by virtue of an operation, physically becomes an operative member of the opposite sex, has the sex changed for purposes of the marriage statutes?

HOLDING AND DECISION: (Handler, J.) Yes. A transsexual believes himself to be a member of the opposite sex. This affects his psychological and emotional makeup. Where one undergoes an operation which physically alters one anatomically so that he or she can function as a member of that sex, he or she has successfully changed sex for the purpose of our marriage statutes. M.T. (P) can function emotionally, psychologically, and physically as a female. M.T.'s (P) marriage to J.T. (D) was valid. We find that unsuccessful sex change operations are grounds for annulment. The case herein involves no question of fraud since J.T. (D) was aware of the situation, so we do not reach this question. The order of maintenance and support is affirmed.

▶ ANALYSIS

Some states issue new birth certificates after a sex change operation. However, in *K.V. Health Div., Dept. of Human Resources*, 560 P.2d 1070 (1970), the court refused to order the issuance of a new certificate where there was no statutory authorization. Where there has been no operation or the operation has not included a change in the sex organs, the marriage will normally be deemed either void or voidable. *B. v. B.*, 78 Misc. 2d 112 (1974).

Quicknotes

ORDER FOR SUPPORT AND MAINTENANCE An order entered by the court requiring one spouse to make payments to the other for sustenance in order to maintain the person at the standard of living previously experienced.

Rappaport v. Katz

Bride (P) v. City clerk (D)

380 F. Supp. 808 (S.D.N.Y. 1974).

NATURE OF CASE: Action seeking an injunction and damages for violation of constitutional rights.

FACT SUMMARY: Rappaport (P) claimed that her constitutional rights were violated by rules regarding dress and the exchanging of rings that had been promulgated to cover weddings conducted by the city clerk, Katz (D).

🏛 RULE OF LAW

The federal courts should not get involved in supervising marriage forms and procedures in city clerks' offices, which are an area fundamentally of state concern.

FACTS: New York statute provides that a valid marriage may be entered into merely by the signature at any place, in any mode of attire or lack of it, of a contract of marriage. Insofar as marriages "solemnized" by the city clerk, Katz (D), guidelines were drawn up with the intent of keeping the solemnity of the occasion intact. Katz (D) had apparently seen couples arrive in ripped jeans, shorts, and other such attire to be married by him. In an effort to keep solemn what the law itself described as a "solemn" ceremony, a dress code was promulgated, but those who selected special ethnic, ancestral, or national dress were served and considered to be within the dress code. That code provided for a coat and tie for men and a skirt or dress for women. Another guideline for marriages performed by the city clerk was that one or two rings had to be exchanged. Rappaport (P), who wanted to wear a pantsuit instead of a dress or skirt and did not want to exchange rings, brought a federal suit seeking an injunction and damages on the ground that these guidelines put her to a choice between her statutory right to be married by the city clerk and her fundamental right to marry free of unwarranted governmental intrusion on her privacy and with free expression.

ISSUE: Should the federal courts become involved in supervising marriage forms and procedures in city clerks' offices since such involves an area fundamentally of state concern?

HOLDING AND DECISION: (Pollack, J.) No. In performing marriages, a city clerk performs a locally proscribed and directed function in an area fundamentally of state concern, so the federal court should not get involved in supervising marriage forms and procedures in city clerks' offices. The forms and the degree of decorum at weddings in the city clerk's office do not sufficiently justify provoking a federal-state conflict. Quite simply, federal judges have too much to do to become involved in this type of dispute, which is best and most appropriately resolved by the State of New York and the New York City Council, to whom Katz (D) is responsible. Complaint dismissed.

▶ ANALYSIS

After this decision came down, a New York Assemblyman introduced a bill to amend the domestic relations law to require the city clerk to solemnize a marriage without regard to the attire of the marrying parties. Of course, that would be subject to the provision that their attire did not violate the penal code.

■■■

Lester v. Lester

Wife (P) v. Husband (D)

N.Y. Dom. Rel. Ct., 195 Misc. 1034, 87 N.Y.S.2d 517 (1949).

NATURE OF CASE: Petition for spousal support.

FACT SUMMARY: Mr. Lester (D) contended he owed no spousal support because the marriage was entered into pursuant to an antenuptial agreement declaring the marriage null.

🏛 RULE OF LAW
Antenuptial agreements which purport to invalidate the marriage are unenforceable.

FACTS: Mr. Lester (D) lived with Mrs. Lester (P) for 10 years prior to participating in a marriage ceremony. Prior to the ceremony, he drew up an agreement, signed by both, indicating the marriage was to be entered into merely to appease her relatives and to curtail her threats against him. The marriage was to be void ab initio. Sometime after the marriage, Mrs. Lester (P) petitioned for divorce and spousal support. Mr. Lester (D) defended based on the antenuptial agreement.

ISSUE: Are antenuptial agreements which purport to invalidate the marriage enforceable?

HOLDING AND DECISION: (Panken, J.) No. Antenuptial agreements which purport to invalidate the marriage are unenforceable. The parties entered into an otherwise valid marriage ceremony. An agreement conflicting with the law is unenforceable. Divorce is the only legal method to terminate a marriage. Thus, a valid marriage exists until a divorce is obtained. Having entered into a valid marriage, Mr. Lester (D) was responsible for spousal support.

▶ *ANALYSIS*

Lester (D) had argued that even if the antenuptial agreement were valid, the marriage was void because he was forced into it under duress. He said Mrs. Lester (P) forced him to marry her or she would ruin his reputation. The court rejected such factual assertions, finding no duress existed. Duress is a defense to a valid marriage; however, since divorce has become increasingly less difficult to obtain, this defense is rarely used.

■=■

Quicknotes

AB INITIO From its inception or beginning.

ANTENUPTIAL AGREEMENT An agreement entered into by two individuals, in contemplation of their impending marriage, in order to determine their rights and interests in property upon dissolution or death.

DURESS Unlawful threats or other coercive behavior by one person that causes another to commit acts that he would not otherwise do.

ORDER FOR SUPPORT AND MAINTENANCE An order entered by the court requiring one spouse to make payments to the other for sustenance in order to maintain the person at the standard of living previously experienced.

■=■

Johnston v. Johnston

Husband (D) v. Wife (P)

Cal. Ct. of App., 18 Cal. App. 4th 499 (1993).

NATURE OF CASE: Petition for annulment of marriage.

FACT SUMMARY: Brenda (P) sought an annulment of her twenty-month marriage to Donald (D) on the basis that she was unaware of his severe drinking problem and that he would refuse to obtain employment.

> 🏛 **RULE OF LAW**
> In order to obtain an annulment of marriage on the basis of fraud, the fraud must go to the essence of the marital relation.

FACTS: After twenty months Brenda (P) sought to have her marriage to Donald (D) annulled. Donald (D) agreed that the marriage should be terminated but requested a judgment of dissolution. Brenda (P) testified that she was unaware of Donald's (D) severe drinking problem prior to the marriage and was upset that he refused to seek help. She also knew that he was unemployed but did not know that he would refuse to obtain work. The court concluded that Brenda's (P) consent to marry was fraudulently obtained and granted the annulment. Donald (D) appealed.

ISSUE: In order to obtain an annulment of marriage on the basis of fraud, must the fraud go to the essence of the marital relation?

HOLDING AND DECISION: (Sonenshine, J.) Yes. In order to obtain an annulment of marriage on the basis of fraud, the fraud must go to the essence of the marital relation. Donald (D) argued that the evidence was insufficient to sustain a finding of fraud. He is correct. Civil Code § 4425(d) provides that a marriage is voidable if the consent of either party was obtained by fraud, unless that party after learning of the fraud freely cohabitates with the other spouse. Here there was no fraud under this definition. Furthermore, even if Brenda's (P) testimony were true—that Donald (D) was lazy, unshaven and had a drinking problem—this is insufficient to warrant an annulment. The fraud must go to the essence of the marital relation for an annulment to be granted. Reversed and a judgment of dissolution entered.

▶ *ANALYSIS*

The court here cited to several other cases in which an annulment was not granted. These included the following circumstances: (1) concealment of "temper, idleness, extravagance, coldness or fortune inadequate to representations" (*Marshall v. Marshall*, 212 Cal. 736 (1931)); (2) a shoe salesman's false representation that he owned a shoe store (*Mayer v. Mayer*, 207 Cal. 685 (1929); and

(3) a future husband's representation that he was a "man of means" (*Marshall v. Marshall*, 212 Cal. 736 (1931).

■═■

Quicknotes

ANNULMENT To nullify a marriage; to establish that the marital status never existed.

FRAUD A false representation of facts with the intent that another will rely on the misrepresentation to his detriment.

■═■

In re Estate of Love

Decedent's son (P) v. Mother's estate (D)

Ga. Ct. App., 274 Ga. App. 316, 618 S.E. 2d 97 (2005).

NATURE OF CASE: Appeal of judgment for common-law husband in will challenge.

FACT SUMMARY: Decedent, Barbara J. Love, and Darryl Arnold held themselves out as husband and wife although they never legally wed. After Love died, her son, Bertrand Love (P), disputed the existence of a common-law marriage between Arnold and Love.

🏛 RULE OF LAW
A common-law marriage may be found when a man and woman cohabitate and hold themselves out as husband and wife, such that society views them as married.

FACTS: Darryl Arnold and Barbara J. Love moved in together approximately one year after meeting, shared a bedroom, had a joint checking account, shared household expenses, designated the other as sole beneficiaries on IRAs, purchased real estate together, incurred debt together, and generally held themselves out to society as husband and wife. After Barbara J. Love's death, Bertrand Love (P), her son, challenged Darryl Arnold's status as Barbara Love's common law husband (and apparently his entitlement to her estate as an heir). The trial court found that Darryl Arnold was in fact the decedent's common-law husband and Bertrand Love (P) appeals.

ISSUE: Are documents necessary to support the existence or the finding of a common-law marriage?

HOLDING AND DECISION: (Mikell, J.) No. Documents are not necessary to support the existence or the finding of a common-law marriage. Common-law marriage may be found when a man and woman cohabitate and hold themselves out to society as husband and wife for a given length of time. Love (D) argued that documents existed showing that decedent and Arnold did not hold themselves out as husband and wife, thus the trial court erred in finding a common-law marriage. Contrary to Love's (P) argument, however, multiple witnesses testified that Barbara Love (D) and Arnold did, in fact, consider themselves husband and wife despite not having a state-issued marriage license. Medical records were not admitted for the purpose of showing a medical condition, but rather to show that Barbara Love considered Arnold her husband. In this state, a common-law marriage must have been established prior to January 1, 1997. Reputational evidence suffices to establish such a marriage. The trial court did not err in finding the existence of a common-law marriage. Judgment affirmed.

▶ ANALYSIS

Common-law marriage is a tradition from medieval England when church officials could not always travel to outlying villages to officially wed couples. Most states today do not recognize common-law marriages no matter how long a couple lives together or holds themselves out as married. The issue does arise, however, if one partner wishes to reap the benefits of a marriage, despite the absence of a legal marriage. Probate and will contests are a common arena of dispute, such as in this case. Courts will usually then attempt to determine the true intent of the couple. Couples are advised to execute statements evidencing intent to marry to prevent contests such as these.

■=■

Quicknotes

COMMON-LAW MARRIAGE A marriage that is not solemnized but is established by an agreement to enter into a marital relationship, followed by cohabitation.

DECEDENT A person who is deceased.

REPUTATION EVIDENCE Evidence pertaining to an individual's general reputation in the community.

■=■

Quick Reference Rules of Law

McGuire v. McGuire

Wife (P) v. Husband (D)

Neb. Sup. Ct., 157 Neb. 226, 59 N.W.2d 336 (1953).

NATURE OF CASE: Action for support and attorney fees.

FACT SUMMARY: Mr. McGuire (D) was very tight with his money and refused to give his wife any funds other than to pay for groceries, though they continued to live together.

> ## RULE OF LAW
> No support payments can be granted where the parties continue to live together as husband and wife.

FACTS: Mr. McGuire (D) was exceedingly miserly with his money. He refused to give Mrs. McGuire (P) any money of her own. His sole contribution to the family's support was to pay for groceries and to keep a roof over their heads. Mr. McGuire (D) refused her any and all additional comforts. He refused to repair the car, replace the old furniture, fix the heating, buy her clothes, etc. He had more than sufficient funds to substantially raise the level of the family's life-style but refused to do so. The parties had lived like this for approximately 33 years. The trial court awarded the wife support, a new car, new furniture, and funds to visit her daughters yearly. Mrs. McGuire (P) continued to live with her husband.

ISSUE: Can support be granted to a wife who continues to live with her husband?

HOLDING AND DECISION: (Messmore, J.) No. The living standards of a family are the concern of the household, not the courts. As long as the parties remain together as husband and wife, it may be said that the husband is legally supporting the wife and the purpose of the marriage relationship is being carried out. Public policy requires that the courts not interfere in such a situation. Mrs. McGuire's (P) only alternative would be to leave her husband and then to bring suit for support. The decision of the trial court awarding support is reversed. No allowance of attorney fees shall be permitted.

DISSENT: (Yeager, J.) No precedents exist requiring separation as a condition precedent for a spouse to file an equity action for maintenance. This case is unusual in that the plaintiff wife and the defendant husband were still living in the same residence but that shouldn't deny the wife the opportunity to seek appropriate maintenance from the husband. In this case the district court did have the power to entertain the action, but should not have awarded anything beyond finances sufficient for adequate support and maintenance. A court of equity should be able to help a plaintiff who does not seek to obtain a divorce for whatever reason.

ANALYSIS

In *Miller v. Miller*, 320 Mich. 43 (1948), the court affirmed support payments to the wife even though the parties resided together in the same house. Mr. Miller took his meals alone and lived in a separate room. It was found that they had separated just as certainly as if he had moved out. This decision is, however, rare. For another example of a case denying support, see *Commonwealth v. George*, 358 Pa. 118 (1948). The wife there charged that they were separated due to the husband's occasional lengthy drunken sprees. The court held that this was insufficient since the marital relationship was continuing and denied support for the reasons mentioned in *McGuire*.

Quicknotes

PUBLIC POLICY Policy administered by the state with respect to the health, safety and morals of its people in accordance with common notions of fairness and decency.

SUPPORT PAYMENTS Payments made by one spouse to another in discharge of the spouse's duty pursuant to law, or in accordance with a written divorce or separation decree, in order to provide maintenance for the other spouse.

Graham v. Graham

Former husband (P) v. Former wife (D)

33 F. Supp. 936 (E.D. Mich. 1940).

NATURE OF CASE: Action to enforce contract.

FACT SUMMARY: Sidney Graham (P) sued to enforce a contract between him and his ex-wife calling for her to pay him a certain amount per month.

> 🏛 **RULE OF LAW**
> A contract between persons contemplating marriage to change the essential incidents of marriage is illegal.

FACTS: Sidney Graham (P) and his fiancée Margrethe (D) entered into a written contract calling for her to pay him $300 per month. The consideration for such was that Sidney (P) was to leave his job and travel with her. They married and divorced, and Sidney (P) sued to enforce the contract. Margrethe (D) contended the contract was void.

ISSUE: Is a contract that changes the essential incidents of marriage legal?

HOLDING AND DECISION: (Tuttle, J.) No. A contract between persons contemplating marriage that changes the essential incidents of marriage is illegal. A fundamental incident of marriage is the husband's right to choose the marital domicile. This contract requires Sidney (P) to travel at his wife's direction, thus forfeiting this right. The contract, therefore, changes an essential incident of marriage and is illegal.

▶ **ANALYSIS**

This case is based on § 587 of the Restatement of Contracts. Had the parties not been married, the contract clearly would have been enforceable. The problem is that the consideration for the promise to pay, the element making it enforceable as a general contract, changed the essential incident of marriage, which invalidated it in the context of a marriage.

■■■

Bradwell v. Illinois

Female applicant to state bar (P) v. State (D)

83 U.S. (16 Wall.) 130 (1873).

NATURE OF CASE: Appeal of denial of application for admission to the practice of law.

FACT SUMMARY: Bradwell's (P) application for admission to the Illinois bar was denied solely because she was a woman.

🏛 RULE OF LAW
A state, under its police power, may deny entry into an occupation or profession on the basis of sex.

FACTS: Bradwell (P), in 1872, applied for admission to the Illinois bar. The application was denied solely on the basis of her sex. Bradwell (P) appealed.

ISSUE: May a state, under its police power, deny entry into an occupation based solely on sex?

HOLDING AND DECISION: Yes. A state may, under its police power, deny entry into an occupation based solely on sex.

CONCURRENCE: (Bradley, J.) Man should be the protector and defender of woman, whose natural timidity and delicacy makes the fair sex unfit for much of civil life. The harmony of family organization, divinely created, is repugnant to the idea of a woman pursuing a career separate and distinct from that of her husband. While some women are unmarried, this is an exception to the general rule that woman's paramount destiny and mission is the noble roles of wife and mother. The rules of civil society cannot be broken to accommodate the exceptional case.

▶ ANALYSIS

This case is important for the historical perspective it supplies to the attitude of the law toward the equality of the sexes. Today, such gender-based discrimination is subjected to a medium level of scrutiny. This requires that the statute be promotive of an important government interest, or it is unconstitutional as a deprivation of equal protection.

■══■

Quicknotes

EQUAL PROTECTION CLAUSE A constitutional provision that each person be guaranteed the same protection of the laws enjoyed by other persons in like circumstances.

■══■

Orr v. Orr

Former wife (P) v. Former husband (D)

440 U.S. 268 (1979).

NATURE OF CASE: Appeal of a decision holding a state alimony statute constitutional.

FACT SUMMARY: Orr (D) contended that Alabama's alimony statute was unconstitutional because it placed alimony obligations on husbands but never on wives.

RULE OF LAW
State statutes which impose alimony obligations on only one sex are unconstitutional.

FACTS: Mrs. Orr (P) initiated contempt proceedings against Mr. Orr (D), claiming he was in arrears in his court-ordered alimony payments. Mr. Orr (D) defended by moving the court to declare the Alabama alimony statute unconstitutional on the basis that it allows courts to impose alimony obligations on husbands but never on wives. The trial court denied the motion, and Mr. Orr (D) appealed. The Alabama Court of Civil Appeals held the statute constitutional as it served the important government objective of providing wives with support and compensated women for past economic discrimination. Mr. Orr (D) was denied certiorari by the Alabama Supreme Court, and the U.S. Supreme Court granted certiorari.

ISSUE: Are state statutes which impose alimony obligations only on husbands constitutional?

HOLDING AND DECISION: (Brennan, J.) No. State statutes which impose alimony obligations only on husbands are unconstitutional. Because the statute classifies on the basis of gender, such classification must substantially relate to the achievement of an important governmental objective. Although both support of needy spouses and compensation for past discrimination are clearly important governmental objectives, this classification does not substantially relate to their achievement. Both males and females are capable of being needy spouses, and, therefore, sex cannot be a valid substitute for need. Individualized hearings can easily and inexpensively determine both the relative need of each spouse and whether the wife had in fact been previously victimized by sexual discrimination which retarded her economic abilities. Therefore, the statute violates equal protection and is unconstitutional. Reversed.

CONCURRENCE: (Blackmun, J.) Although the Court's holding is correct, it must be emphasized that society-wide discrimination is sometimes relevant in these cases.

▶ ANALYSIS

In this case, the Court recognized that gender classifications which distribute burdens and benefits unequally between the sexes often merely serve to perpetuate unwanted and invalid stereotypes. As a result of this case, it has been argued that many state statutes stating the husband has an unconditional duty to support the wife while imposing a support duty on the wife only if the husband is in need are no longer constitutionally valid.

■=■

Quicknotes

ALIMONY Allowances (usually monetary) which husband or wife by court order pays other spouse for maintenance while they are separated, or after they are divorced (permanent alimony), or temporarily, pending a suit for divorce (pendente lite).

CERTIORARI A discretionary writ issued by a superior court to an inferior court in order to review the lower court's decisions; the Supreme Court's writ ordering such review.

GENDER DISCRIMINATION Unequal treatment of individuals without justification on the basis of their sex.

■=■

United States v. Virginia

Country (P) v. State (D)

518 U.S. 515 (1996).

NATURE OF CASE: Appeal in an action challenging the constitutionality of public college admission policy.

FACT SUMMARY: Virginia (D) created the Virginia Women's Institute for Leadership (VWIL) to avoid equal protection problems with Virginia Military Institute's (VMI) (D) male-only admission policy.

> ## RULE OF LAW
> Discrimination based on sex is unconstitutional unless it is substantially related to important government objectives.

FACTS: VMI (D), a public university, had a policy of admitting only male students. VMI (D) sought to provide a military education to its students through physical rigor and adversarial methods. In 1990, a female high school student filed a complaint challenging this admission policy, and the United States (P) sued the Commonwealth of Virginia (D) and VMI (D) alleging that the male-only admission policy violated the Equal Protection Clause of the Fourteenth Amendment. The Fourth Circuit ruled against VMI (D). In response, Virginia (D) proposed a parallel program for women, the VWIL. Although VWIL purportedly would have fulfilled the same mission as VMI (D), its program offered significantly different programs and had far fewer resources. The district court ruled that the creation of VWIL satisfied the requirements of the Equal Protection Clause, and the court of appeals affirmed.

ISSUE: Is discrimination based on sex unconstitutional unless it is substantially related to important government objectives?

HOLDING AND DECISION: (Ginsburg, J.) Yes. Discrimination based on sex is unconstitutional unless it is substantially related to important government objectives. In 1971, the Supreme Court held for the first time that sex-based classifications may deny equal protection. Since then, the Court has consistently found that government laws and policies which deny women equal opportunity are unconstitutional. Although the Court has not found that sex-based classifications demand strict scrutiny, as do race classifications, the Court has held that a state must show that the sex discrimination serves an important government objective and that the means employed are substantially related to the achievement of those objectives. VMI (D) claimed that single-sex education provides important educational benefits by providing diversity in approaches. However, the history of Virginia's (D) public school policy demonstrates that the male-only admission policy was not actually created in furtherance of a state policy of diversity. Additionally, VMI (D) failed to show that its methods and goals are inherently unsuitable for women. Some women may want to pursue the type of education offered by VMI (D). The proposed VWIL is clearly inadequate and unequal in its ability to offer women a similar experience. Therefore, Virginia's (D) equal protection violation is not remedied by the proposed creation of VWIL. Reversed.

DISSENT: (Scalia, J.) Women are not a "discrete and insular minority" deserving of equal protection consideration. Furthermore, even if "intermediate scrutiny" were the correct way to analyze sex-based classifications, the majority failed to properly apply this test in the current case.

▶ ANALYSIS

Justice Scalia's dissent is accurate in pointing out the majority's failure to expressly apply the intermediate scrutiny test. However, his argument that sex-based discrimination deserves only rational basis review based on the political power of women is unpersuasive. After all, women still comprise a very small minority in the state and federal legislatures.

■══■

Quicknotes

EQUAL PROTECTION A constitutional guarantee that no person shall be denied the same protection of the laws enjoyed by other persons in life circumstances.

GENDER DISCRIMINATION Unequal treatment of individuals without justification on the basis of their sex.

INTERMEDIATE SCRUTINY A standard of reviewing the propriety of classifications pertaining to gender or legitimacy under the Equal Protection Clause of the United States Constitution which requires a court to ascertain whether the classification furthers an important state interest and is substantially related to the attainment of that interest.

■══■

Hopkins v. Price Waterhouse

Woman (P) v. Corporation (D)

920 F.2d 967 (D.C. Cir. 1990).

NATURE OF CASE: Appeal of judgment ordering former employer to award partnership to former employee.

FACT SUMMARY: Hopkins (P) was denied a partnership at Price Waterhouse (D) partly due to sex stereotyping.

🏛 RULE OF LAW
Under Title VII, a court may order an employer to award partnership to an employee where the employee shows gender discrimination contributed to the decision to deny her partnership and the employer cannot show that it would have made the same decision absent the discrimination.

FACTS: Hopkins (P), a woman, was denied a partnership by Price Waterhouse (D), partly due to evaluations of her behavior as too "macho." Hopkins's (P) supervisor advised her that if she wanted to make partner in the future she should dress, walk, and talk more "femininely." When Price Waterhouse (D) decided not to repropose Hopkins (P) for partnership, she resigned. Hopkins (P) filed a gender discrimination suit under Title VII. The district court found Hopkins (P) had proven sexual stereotyping was a factor in denying her a partnership. Thus, the burden shifted to Price Waterhouse (D) to show by a preponderance of the evidence that its decision would have been the same absent the discrimination. The court held this showing was not made and found for Hopkins (P). The court awarded Hopkins (P) reinstatement and back pay, and ordered Price Waterhouse (D) to make Hopkins (P) a partner. Price Waterhouse (D) appealed.

ISSUE: May a court may order an employer to award a partnership?

HOLDING AND DECISION: (Edwards, J.) Yes. Under Title VII, a court may order an employer to grant partnership to an employee where the employee shows that unlawful discrimination contributed to the decision to deny the partnership and the employer cannot show that it would have made the same decision absent the discrimination. Title VII has a make-whole purpose, so, since Title VII reaches partnership consideration decisions, a court has authority to order partnership as a remedy for gender discrimination. The slight infringement upon Price Waterhouse's (D) right of free association is justified by the compelling state interest in eradicating discrimination against women. The common law rule against forcing continuation of human relationships is overcome by Title VII's express grant of judicial authority to order reinstatement and hiring. Merely ordering Price Waterhouse (D) to

reconsider Hopkins (P) for partnership would be futile and unjust. Affirmed.

▶ ANALYSIS

In *Hishon v. King & Spalding*, 467 U.S. 69 (1984), the Supreme Court held Title VII can provide a cause of action if partnership is denied on the basis of gender discrimination. Gender discrimination includes discriminating against an employee or prospective employee because she is a woman, because she does not match the employer's idea of "feminine" behavior (Hopkins), or because she is held to a higher standard than are male employees (*Ezold v. Wolf, Block, Schorr and Solis-Cohen*, 751 F. Supp. 1175 (E.D. Pa. 1990)).

■═■

Quicknotes

TITLE VII OF THE CIVIL RIGHTS ACT OF 1964 Forbids an employer to fail or refuse to hire or to discharge any individual, or otherwise discriminate against any individual with respect to his compensation, terms, conditions, or privileges of employment because of such individual's sex.

■═■

Nevada Dept. of Human Resources v. Hibbs

State agency (D) v. Terminated employee (P)

538 U.S. 721 (2003).

NATURE OF CASE: Resolution of federal question due to split among Courts of Appeals.

FACT SUMMARY: The Nevada Department of Human Resources (Dept.) (D) terminated Hibbs (P) for refusing to return to work.

🏛 RULE OF LAW
Congress had the constitutional authority to allow an individual to sue a state in federal court pursuant to FMLA provisions.

FACTS: Dept. (D) terminated Hibbs (P) after he exhausted twelve weeks of unpaid leave under the Family and Medical Leave Act of 1993 (FMLA) and still refused to return to work. Hibbs (P) then sued the Dept. (D) claiming Fourteenth Amendment violations. The Dept. (D) moved for summary judgment, which the district court awarded, and Hibbs (P) appealed to the Ninth Circuit. After the Ninth Circuit reversed causing a split among the Courts of Appeal, this Court granted certiorari to address the federal question.

ISSUE: Did Congress have the constitutional authority to allow an individual to sue a state in federal court pursuant to FMLA provision?

HOLDING AND DECISION: (Rehnquist, C.J.) Yes. Congress had the constitutional authority to allow an individual to sue a state in federal court pursuant to FMLA provisions. State sovereignty is limited by § 5 of the Fourteenth Amendment, and Congress enacted the FMLA pursuant to its Article I commerce power and § 5 of the Fourteenth Amendment. The § 5 power allows Congress to enact prophylactic legislation, which deters unconstitutional conduct by legislating facially constitutional behavior. For example, gender-based discrimination is addressed under the FMLA because state laws and policies were discriminating either facially or in application based on gender stereotyping. The FMLA was specifically enacted to allow for equal family leave time for mothers and fathers or persons dealing with ill family members. Family leave policies varied widely from state to state, thus federal legislation was introduced to create "gender-neutral family leave benefits." The FMLA was to apply equally to all eligible employees, eliminating the assumption that family obligations fell only to female employees while male employees were denied leave. Congress placed many limitations on FMLA legislation, despite setting a minimum leave allowance of twelve weeks. One of the restrictions is the cause of action, limiting recoverable damages to actual monetary loss as well as limiting back pay. An appropriate cause of action may be brought by an individual against a state in federal court. Judgment affirmed.

DISSENT: (Kennedy, J.) Purposeful discrimination was not the state's intent in enacting widely varying family leave legislation. The legislation was in its infancy and adjustments are expected to have to be made. Federal legislation covering the same ground was not necessary. There is insufficient evidence of true unconstitutional discrimination. Furthermore, it is not unconstitutional for a state to not have a family leave act as nothing in the Constitution requires such legislation.

▶ ANALYSIS

The Ninth Circuit's holding that Hibbs could bring the case in federal court placed it squarely at odds with eight other Courts of Appeals. The U.S. Supreme Court unusually sided with the Ninth Circuit in this matter. An unusual decision because the Rehnquist Court often overturned the Ninth Circuit and typically held for state's immunity rights in similar challenges. The specific construction of the FMLA, however, turned the tide.

▬▬

Quicknotes

CERTIORARI A discretionary writ issued by a superior court to an inferior court in order to review the lower court's decisions; the Supreme Court's writ ordering such review.

FOURTEENTH AMENDMENT Declares that no state shall make or enforce any law that shall abridge the privileges and immunities of citizens of the United States. No state shall deny to any person within its jurisdiction the equal protection of the laws.

SUMMARY JUDGMENT Judgment rendered by a court in response to a motion made by one of the parties, claiming that the lack of a question of material fact in respect to an issue warrants disposition of the issue without consideration by the jury.

▬▬

Edwardson v. Edwardson

Former wife (P) v. Former husband (D)

Ky. Sup. Ct., 798 S.W.2d 941 (1990).

NATURE OF CASE: Appeal of order voiding antenuptial agreement.

FACT SUMMARY: Mrs. Edwardson (P) sought enforcement of an antenuptial agreement that Mr. Edwardson (D) would provide her with certain alimony and medical insurance.

RULE OF LAW
An antenuptial agreement disposing of property and maintenance upon divorce is valid if made after full disclosure and if it is not unconscionable at the time enforcement is sought.

FACTS: In an antenuptial agreement, Mr. Edwardson (D) agreed that if they divorced he would pay Mrs. Edwardson (P) $75 per week alimony and provide her with certain medical insurance for life, or until she remarried. Both parties agreed that neither party would have any other claims to alimony or any other claims against the other arising out of the marriage. In a divorce action, Mrs. Edwardson (P) sought to enforce the agreement. The trial court refused to enforce the agreement, citing Kentucky Supreme Court precedent holding that antenuptial agreements made in anticipation of divorce were void. Mrs. Edwardson (P) appealed.

ISSUE: Is an antenuptial agreement disposing of property and maintenance upon divorce valid if made after full disclosure and if it is not unconscionable at the time enforcement is sought?

HOLDING AND DECISION: (Lambert, J.) Yes. An antenuptial agreement disposing of property and maintenance upon divorce is valid if made after full disclosure and if it is not unconscionable at the time enforcement is sought. The agreement must be free of any material omission or misrepresentation. A court may modify an agreement to eliminate unconscionability while otherwise giving effect to the agreement, so long as the agreement was not procured by fraud or duress. Questions of child support, custody, and visitation are not subject to antenuptial agreements. Traditionally, antenuptial agreements contemplating divorce were said to destabilize the marital relationship and promote breakup, so the agreements were considered void as against public policy. Modernly, the notion that antenuptial agreements promote divorce has been rejected. Moreover, as divorce is legal and a commonplace fact of life, spouses should have the right to enter into appropriate agreements. Finally, the old rule was made at a time before married

women's property acts when women were decidedly second class citizens. Reversed and remanded.

ANALYSIS

The clear judicial and legislative trend is to recognize the validity of antenuptial agreements. As of 1991, eighteen states had adopted Uniform Premarital Agreement Act and courts in at least eight other states had recognized the validity of antenuptial agreements.

Quicknotes

ALIMONY Allowances (usually monetary) which husband or wife by court order pays to the other spouse for maintenance while they are separated, or after they are divorced (permanent alimony), or temporarily, pending a suit for divorce (pendente lite).

ANTENUPTIAL AGREEMENT An agreement entered into by two individuals, in contemplation of their impending marriage, in order to determine their rights and interests in property upon dissolution or death.

PUBLIC POLICY Policy administered by the state with respect to the health, safety and morals of its people in accordance with common notions of fairness and decency.

Simeone v. Simeone

Former wife (P) v. Former husband (D)

Pa. Sup. Ct., 525 Pa. 392, 581 A.2d 162 (1990).

NATURE OF CASE: Appeal of order upholding prenuptial agreement.

FACT SUMMARY: Mrs. Simeone (P) filed an alimony claim, and Mr. Simeone (D) asserted their prenuptial agreement as a bar to Mrs. Simeone's (D) claim.

🏛 RULE OF LAW
A prenuptial agreement entered into after full disclosure is binding, regardless of whether it was reasonable or fully understood by both parties.

FACTS: When married, Mrs. Simeone (P) was a 23-year-old unemployed nurse and Mr. Simeone (D) was a 39-year-old neurosurgeon with a $90,000 salary and $300,000 in assets. On the eve of their wedding, Mr. Simeone's (D) attorney gave Mrs. Simeone (P) a prenuptial agreement, which she signed without benefit of counsel. The parties disputed whether Mrs. Simeone (P) knew of the agreement in advance. The agreement limited Mr. Simeone's (D) support in the event they divorced to $25,000. Two years after they divorced, the limit was reached, and Mrs. Simeone (P) filed for alimony pendente lite (alimony payments during court proceedings to amend the terms of their divorce decree). The trial court held the prenuptial agreement barred Mrs. Simeone's (P) claim. An appeals court affirmed, and Mrs. Simeone (P) appealed, arguing prenuptial agreements were valid only if there was reasonable provision for the spouse and full disclosure.

ISSUE: Is a prenuptial agreement entered into after full disclosure binding, regardless of whether it was reasonable or fully understood by both parties?

HOLDING AND DECISION: (Flaherty, J.) Yes. A prenuptial agreement entered into after full disclosure is binding regardless of whether it was reasonable or fully understood by both parties. Inquiries into reasonableness were based on notions of women as uninformed, uneducated, and readily subjected to unfair advantage in marital agreements. Pennsylvania's Equal Rights Amendment recognizes that these assumptions are no longer valid. Inquiries into reasonableness also run counter to rules of contract law. By looking into reasonableness, courts undermine the reliability of prenuptial agreements. Moreover, if reasonableness at the time of divorce is considered, any change in circumstances could provide a basis for finding an agreement unreasonable. Courts should not interfere with the power of parties contemplating marriage to agree and rely upon what they regard as an acceptable scheme for distribution of property. Affirmed.

CONCURRENCE: (Papadakos, J.) Reasonableness should continue to be a factor in reviewing prenuptial agreements. Women are not yet treated equally in society, and prenuptial agreements remain contracts of adhesion. The law should protect the subservient party, regardless of sex, to insure equal protection of the law.

▶ ANALYSIS

The *Simeone* court held that where an agreement provides that full disclosure has been made, there is a presumption of full disclosure. The spouse attempting to rebut this presumption must prove fraud or misrepresentation by clear and convincing evidence. It would appear that it would not be enough to show that the agreement was presented at the last minute, leaving a party with little time to contemplate the ramifications and little choice but to sign or otherwise delay or cancel the wedding.

■═■

Quicknotes

ALIMONY Allowances (usually monetary) which husband or wife by court order pays to the other spouse for maintenance while they are separated, or after they are divorced (permanent alimony), or temporarily, pending a suit for divorce (pendente lite).

PRENUPTIAL AGREEMENT An agreement entered into by two individuals, in contemplation of their impending marriage, in order to determine their rights and interests in property upon dissolution or death.

SPOUSAL SUPPORT Payments made by one spouse to another in discharge of the spouse's duty pursuant to law, or in accordance with a written divorce or separation decree, in order to provide maintenance for the other spouse.

■═■

McCourtney v. Imprimis Technology, Inc.

Former employee (P) v. Employer (D)

Minn. Ct. App., 465 N.W.2d 721 (1991).

NATURE OF CASE: Appeal of denial of unemployment compensation benefits.

FACT SUMMARY: McCourtney (P), who was terminated for excessive absenteeism due to a sickly infant, was denied unemployment compensation upon a state agency's finding that she had been discharged for misconduct.

🏛 RULE OF LAW
Where an employee is terminated for persistent absences due to a sick baby, she is not disqualified from unemployment compensation if she was a good employee, her absences were excused, and she made a good faith effort to find adequate child care.

FACTS: McCourtney (P) was an excellent employee of Imprimis (D) for over ten years. She gave birth to a baby who suffered from numerous illnesses. Over the next half year, McCourtney (P) was away from work about half the time on excused absences to care for her child. McCourtney (P) was unable to find a child care service with suitable hours or an affordable price. After two written warnings, she was discharged for excessive absenteeism. McCourtney (P) applied for unemployment compensation benefits, but the Department of Jobs and Training determined she had been discharged for misconduct and was, therefore, ineligible. A Department referee upheld the finding, concluding that McCourtney (P) had some control over her absences and had violated behavior Imprimis (D) had a right to expect of its employees. The Commissioner of Jobs and Training upheld the referee's decision, and McCourtney (P) appealed to the courts. She did not challenge Imprimis's (D) right to terminate her, only the denial of unemployment compensation.

ISSUE: Is an employee's discharge for excessive absenteeism a discharge for misconduct if she stayed home to care for a sick baby after unsuccessful, good faith efforts to find adequate child care?

HOLDING AND DECISION: (Kalitowski, J.) No. When an employee is terminated for persistent absences due to a sick baby, she is not disqualified from unemployment compensation if she was a good employee, her absences were excused, and she made a good faith effort to find adequate child care. McCourtney's (P) absenteeism was motivated by a willful regard for her child's interests and not a wanton disregard of her employer's interest or a lack of concern for her job. Each of her absences was excused and due to circumstances beyond her control. She made substantial efforts to find child care. She was not required to accept services incompatible with her work schedule. The economic burden placed on employers for unemployment payments is a necessary cost of the legislature's humanitarian concern for persons unemployed through no fault of their own. Reversed.

▶ ANALYSIS

As the number of women in the workforce increases, so does the conflict between child care and employment. By 1990, thirty states had adopted some kind of parental or maternity leave laws. However, almost all of these laws only provide for leave during the first few months after the birth of a child. The issue of parental leave resulted in passage of a bill in 1991 by Congress to guarantee a minimum number of weeks of leave to care for an ill child or to attend to a newborn with the parent being able to return to his or her job, but the legislation died when it was vetoed by President Bush.

Quicknotes

GOOD FAITH An honest intention to abstain from taking advantage of another.

MISCONDUCT Conduct that is unlawful or otherwise improper.

Vaughn v. Lawrenceburg Power Sys.

Terminated employees (P) v. Employer (D)

269 F.3d 703 (6th Cir. 2001).

NATURE OF CASE: Appeal from grant of summary judgment to employer (D).

FACT SUMMARY: Keith Vaughn (P) and Jennifer Paige (P) worked for Lawrenceburg Power System (LPS) (D) and became engaged to be married. Their marriage would violate LPS's (D) anti-nepotism policy, which required the termination of employment of one employee when two employees married. Keith (P) and Jennifer (P) wed, were terminated for different reasons, then challenged LPS's (D) policy as unconstitutional.

🏛 RULE OF LAW
An employment rule may permissibly interfere with the First Amendment right to marital association if it reasonably advances a legitimate governmental interest.

FACTS: Keith Vaughn (P) was a longtime employee of LPS (D) when Jennifer Paige (P) was hired. The two began dating and soon became engaged to wed. When LPS executives learned of the upcoming nuptials, they informed the couple that one of them would need to end employment with LPS (D) pursuant to the policy manual and the anti-nepotism rule. Keith (P) and Jennifer (P) did not dispute having received the policy manual, and they were aware of the anti-nepotism policy at LPS (D). Neither one, however, wanted to quit his/her job. An LPS executive told them that they could continue to simply live together without marrying and remain LPS employees, but Jennifer (P) became pregnant with Keith's (P) child and they went ahead with the marriage plans. After the wedding, Keith (P) informed LPS executives that Jennifer (P) would terminate her employment, but he did not provide the requested letter of resignation. When Keith (P) returned to work after the honeymoon, executives called him in for a meeting and Keith's (P) employment was ended. Whether Keith (P) quit or was terminated was a disputed matter. Keith (P) and Jennifer (P) then received letters terminating Keith (P) for insubordination and Jennifer (P) because LPS (D) never received her letter of resignation. The Vaughns (P) then filed suit against LPS (D) alleging constitutional violations of their right to marital association and violations of the Tennessee Human Rights Act. The magistrate judge recommended dismissal of the Vaughns' (P) claims and the district court accepted the magistrate's report. The Vaughns (P) appeal.

ISSUE: May an employment rule interfere with the First Amendment right to marital association if it reasonably advances a legitimate governmental interest?

HOLDING AND DECISION: (Boggs, J.) Yes. An employment rule may interfere with the First Amendment right to marital association if it reasonably advances a legitimate governmental interest. The Vaughns' (P) claim that LPS's (D) rule of exogamy violated their fundamental right to marriage and further claim that the rule should be scrutinized under a strict scrutiny standard. The arguments fail, however, because LPS's exogamy rule does not place a "direct and substantial burden on the right of marriage." The Vaughns (P) were free to marry period as well as free to marry a significant portion of the otherwise eligible population of spouses. They simply could not marry the small percentage of people who were fellow employees of LPS (D). Thus, the exogamy rule should be reviewed under rational basis. Pursuant to rational basis scrutiny, the rule must be a reasonable method of advancing a legitimate governmental interest. The legitimate governmental interests at issue here are the avoidance of a conflict of loyalty between the employer and the spouse and bringing marital strife into the workplace. The anti-nepotism policy, although harsh to the Vaughns (P), is a reasonable one because LPS (D) is a small employer and cannot transfer one of the couple to another location. The Vaughns (P) argue specifically that the rule is unreasonable because it treats cohabiting couples differently from married couples. However, despite the fact that cohabiting couples may exhibit the same loyalty as married couples, it is acceptable for LPS (D) to presume that a married couple will demonstrate more loyalty to a spouse simply because of the stronger moral and legal ties conveyed by a marriage commitment rather than cohabitating. LPS's exogamy rule is a reasonable advancement of its legitimate governmental interest and therefore survives rational basis scrutiny. Summary judgment granted to LPS (D) is affirmed. [The court reversed on another issue.]

▶ ANALYSIS

Despite this case addressing the fundamental right to marital association, the court analyzed the exogamy rule under the rational basis test. Legal analysts opined that other circuits would rule differently on the standard of review, which would result in a circuit split and the potential for U.S. Supreme Court review. Other critics focused on the nepotism rule itself, which in practice tends to inhibit women's forward movement in businesses. Nepotism has existed for decades as founding fathers passed down corporations to eager sons who passed down to grandsons.

Continued on next page.

Newly devised nepotism rules may disproportionately affect women entering the same workplace as a spouse.

∎═∎

Quicknotes

LEGITIMATE STATE INTEREST Under a rational basis standard of review, a court will not strike down a statute as unconstitutional if it bears a reasonable relationship to the furtherance of a legitimate governmental objective.

NEPOTISM Favoritism shown by public officers in appointing others to positions by reason of blood or marital relationship.

∎═∎

Jones v. Jones

Divorcing wife (P) v. Divorcing husband (D)

Ga. Sup. Ct., 258 Ga. 353, 369 S.E.2d 478 (1988).

NATURE OF CASE: Interlocutory appeal of disqualification of defense counsel in action for divorce.

FACT SUMMARY: In a divorce action, counsel for Mrs. Jones (P) and counsel for Mr. Jones (D) happened to be married to each other.

RULE OF LAW
Counsel will not be disqualified simply because he or she is the spouse of opposing counsel.

FACTS: Norma Jones (P) retained Diane Zimmerman to represent her in her divorce proceeding against Larry Jones (D). Subsequently, Mr. Jones (D) retained Charles Bond as his counsel. At all times during the litigation, Bond and Zimmerman were married. Bond and Zimmerman negotiated a settlement regarding temporary custody of the Joneses' children and alimony. Zimmerman's law firm then moved to disqualify Bond, arguing that Bond and Zimmerman's marriage created a conflict of interest. Zimmerman's firm withdrew from representation of Norma (P) for other reasons. Mrs. Jones (P) new counsel pursued the motion, arguing that Zimmerman could disclose attorney-client confidences to Bond. The trial court found no evidence of impropriety or breach of confidences. However, the court disqualified Bond due to the appearance of impropriety and the threat of disclosure of confidences. Mr. Jones (D) made an interlocutory appeal.

ISSUE: Will counsel be disqualified because he or she is the spouse of opposing counsel?

HOLDING AND DECISION: (Gregory, J.) No. Counsel will not be disqualified simply because he or she is the spouse of opposing counsel. An appearance of impropriety based on status alone does not overcome a party's right to choice of counsel and, thus, is not grounds for disqualification. Marital status is of no consequence in a disqualification motion. A lawyer who opposes his or her spouse must obey ethical rules just like any other lawyer. It cannot be assumed that married lawyers will violate rules of confidentiality. As the trial court found no evidence of actual impropriety, it was an error to disqualify Bond. Reversed.

▶ **ANALYSIS**

In *People v. Jackson*, 167 Cal. App. 3d 829, 213 Cal. Rptr. 521 (1985), the defendant was convicted of assault with intent to commit rape. The defendant obtained a new trial on the ground that his defense counsel had not disclosed

that he had been dating the prosecutor during the entire time of the criminal proceedings.

Quicknotes

DISQUALIFICATION A determination of unfitness or ineligibility.

INTERLOCUTORY APPEAL The appeal of an issue that does not resolve the disposition of the case, but is essential to a determination of the parties' legal rights.

Knussman v. Maryland

State trooper (P) v. State (D)

272 F.3d 625 (4th Cir. 2001).

NATURE OF CASE: Appeal of monetary judgment to plaintiff.

FACT SUMMARY: Howard Kevin Knussman (P), a Maryland state trooper, sought to take paid leave from his job to take care of his newborn and his wife who had suffered through a difficult pregnancy. The Maryland State Police refused to qualify him as the primary caregiver for his child, thus Knussman (P) could not qualify for more than ten days paid sick leave. Knussman claimed discrimination on the basis of gender.

RULE OF LAW
Gender classifications based on stereotypes of gender roles violate the equal protection clause.

FACTS: Howard Kevin Knussman (P), a Maryland state trooper, requested paid sick leave from his employer so that he might care for his newborn and his wife who was suffering from a difficult pregnancy. The Maryland State Police (MSP) was understaffed and reluctant to grant Knussman (P) his initial request of four to eight weeks. An MSP manager, Jill Mullineaux, informed MSP employees of a new Maryland statute allowing "primary caregivers" thirty days of accrued sick leave and "secondary caregivers" ten days of accrued sick leave to care for a newborn. Knussman (P) sought classification as a primary caregiver, but Mullineaux informed him that only birth mothers would qualify. MSP granted Knussman (P) ten days as a secondary caregiver and refused his second request to be classified as a primary caregiver, thus forcing Knussman (P) to return to work. Knussman (P) filed a grievance and completed the four-stage grievance process within the MSP departments, and his grievance was denied at each stage. Knussman (P) then filed suit in federal court making a claim under 42 USCA § 1983 against Maryland (D), the MSP, and several MSP employees, including Mullineaux. The jury found that the defendants discriminated against Knussman (P) based on his gender, but that all defendants except Mullineaux were entitled to qualified immunity. Mullineaux appeals.

ISSUE: Do gender classifications based on stereotypes of gender roles violate the equal protection clause?

HOLDING AND DECISION: (Traxler, J.) Yes. Gender classifications based on stereotypes of gender roles violate the equal protection clause. Mullineaux challenges the jury's verdict as well as making a claim that she was entitled to qualified immunity. Mullineaux's actions did constitute discrimination and a violation of the equal protections clause. Mullineaux refused to classify Knussman (P) as a primary caregiver solely because of his gender.

The Maryland statute makes no reference to gender, but simply provides that a primary caregiver is granted thirty days sick leave, while a secondary caregiver is granted ten days. No assumption is made that a birth mother would be a primary caregiver. Mullineaux applied a facially gender-neutral statute in a discriminatory manner, so her actions constituted a constitutional violation. Mullineaux is entitled to qualified immunity if the law regarding gender discrimination was unclear at the time of her action. Gender discrimination based on stereotypes of gender roles was clearly not allowed at the time of her action and a reasonable person would have known that it was not allowed. Mullineaux is therefore not entitled to qualified immunity. Affirmed in part, reversed in part. [Court remanded case for redetermination of monetary award based on the excessive amount awarded to Knussman (P).]

ANALYSIS

This case was the first sex-discrimination case brought in relation to the Family and Medical Leave Act. The American Civil Liberties Union represented Trooper Knussman, fighting for and achieving the gender-neutral interpretation of the Act. Knussman continued the fight for ten years as the case wound its way through the court system; he eventually won his claim for attorneys' fees from Maryland. The state supported Mullineaux's claim that she was merely passing on information from another state agency and was attempting to perform her job in good faith. The state's responsibility, though, was to enforce the Act in a gender-neutral manner. Maryland permitted Knussman to take extended leave for his second child.

Quicknotes

EQUAL PROTECTION CLAUSE A constitutional provision that each person be guaranteed the same protection of the laws enjoyed by other persons in like circumstances.

GOOD FAITH An honest intention to abstain from taking advantage of another.

QUALIFIED IMMUNITY An affirmative defense relieving officials from civil liability for the performance of activities within their discretion so long as such conduct is not in violation of an individual's rights pursuant to law as determined by a reasonable person standard.

Griswold v. Connecticut

Director of Planned Parenthood (D) v. State (P)

381 U.S. 479 (1965).

NATURE OF CASE: Appeal from convictions for illegal contraceptive counseling.

FACT SUMMARY: Griswold (D) contended a statute prohibiting the dissemination of contraceptive information violated constitutional rights of privacy.

🏛 RULE OF LAW

Laws restricting the use of or dissemination of information about contraception by or to married couples violates the constitutional right of privacy.

FACTS: Griswold (D) and Buxton (D) were the Executive Director and the Medical Director, respectively, of the Planned Parenthood League of Connecticut. Both were convicted under a Connecticut statute prohibiting the use of or dissemination of information concerning the use of contraceptives. They appealed, contending the law violated constitutional rights of privacy.

ISSUE: Do laws restricting the use of or dissemination of information about contraception by or to married couples violate the constitutional right of privacy?

HOLDING AND DECISION: (Douglas, J.) Yes. Laws restricting the use of and dissemination of information about contraceptives by or to married couples violate the constitutional right of privacy. The right to privacy falls within the penumbra of several amendments. Regulating the use of contraceptives rather than their manufacture or sale indicates the use of the most destructive impact on the protected marital relationship. Thus, the statute is unconstitutional. Reversed.

CONCURRENCE: (Goldberg, J.) The Ninth Amendment clearly supports the penumbra theory presented here by the majority.

CONCURRENCE: (White, J.) The statute deprives married couples' liberty without due process of law.

DISSENT: (Black, J.) The absence of specific constitutional provisions precludes recognition of a right of privacy.

▶ ANALYSIS

This case reaffirmed the case of *Lochner v. State of New York*, 198 U.S. 45 (1927). That case recognized the theory that the Constitution included a penumbra of rights not specifically mentioned in the text. The right to privacy in marital relations falls within this penumbra. The right to privacy as personal autonomy serves as the basis for several other cases, such as the right to abortion.

■■■

Quicknotes

PENUMBRA An outlying, surrounding region; periphery; fringe.

PRIVACY RIGHT Those personal liberties or relationships that are protected against unwarranted governmental interference.

■■■

Eisenstadt v. Baird

State agency (P) v. Distributor of contraceptives (D)

405 U.S. 438 (1972).

NATURE OF CASE: Appeal from conviction of distributing contraceptives.

FACT SUMMARY: Baird (D) appealed his conviction of distributing contraceptives to unmarried persons on the basis that the statute prohibiting such violated the Constitution.

⛪ RULE OF LAW
A statute treating married and unmarried people differently regarding contraceptive devices is unconstitutional.

FACTS: Baird (D) was convicted of distributing contraceptive devices to unmarried persons. He appealed, contending the statute was unconstitutional because it treated married and unmarried persons differently by not criminalizing the distribution of contraceptives to married couples. The Massachusetts Supreme Judicial Court upheld the conviction on this point, and Baird (D) appealed.

ISSUE: Is a statute treating married and unmarried people differently regarding contraceptive devices unconstitutional?

HOLDING AND DECISION: (Brennan, J.) Yes. A statute treating married and unmarried people differently regarding contraceptive devices is unconstitutional. If the purpose of the statute is to promote health, it is clearly discriminatory and overboard. It also cannot be valid as a deterrent to fornication, as such is already a crime. Thus, the statute is unconstitutional. Reversed.

▶ ANALYSIS

This case has been interpreted as prohibiting the favoring of married couples over unmarried persons. However, in an appropriate factual situation, such favoring might be necessary. Classifications based on marital status do not have to pass a strict scrutiny standard, however. Because marriage is a fundamental right, statutes affecting the right to marry are held to a high standard of scrutiny.

■═■

Quicknotes

FUNDAMENTAL RIGHT A liberty that is either expressly or implicitly provided for in the United States Constitution, the deprivation or burdening of which is subject to a heightened standard of review.

■═■

Lawrence v. Texas

Constitutional claimant (D) v. State (P)

539 U.S. 558 (2003).

NATURE OF CASE: Appeal from convictions for deviate sexual intercourse and denial of constitutional challenges.

FACT SUMMARY: Two gay men (D) were arrested while engaging in a sexual act in their private home and charged with having deviate sexual intercourse. They (D) argued that the charging statute was unconstitutional but the contentions were rejected. The men (D) appealed to the court of appeals. The constitutional arguments were again rejected and the convictions affirmed. The U.S. Supreme Court then granted certiorari review.

🏛 RULE OF LAW
The Equal Protection Clause of the Fourteenth Amendment protects freedom to engage in private conduct among heterosexual and homosexual partners.

FACTS: Lawrence (D) and his homosexual lover, Garner, were engaged in sexual acts in the privacy of Lawrence's (D) home. Police officers responded to a reported weapons disturbance and observed Lawrence and Garner in a sexual act. Police arrested both men (D) and they were charged under a Texas statute with deviate sexual intercourse with a member of the same sex. The men (D) argued that the charging statute was a violation of the Equal Protection Clause of the Fourteenth Amendment and the Texas Constitution. They (D) pleaded nolo contendere to the charges. The trial court rejected the constitutional arguments, and Lawrence (D) appealed to the court of appeals. The court rejected the constitutional contentions and affirmed the convictions. Lawrence (D) appealed to the U.S. Supreme Court, which granted certiorari review.

ISSUE: Does the Equal Protection Clause of the Fourteenth Amendment protect freedom to engage in private conduct among heterosexual and homosexual partners?

HOLDING AND DECISION: (Kennedy, J.) Yes. The Equal Protection Clause of the Fourteenth Amendment protects freedom to engage in private conduct among heterosexual and homosexual partners. Consideration of the facts requires a reconsideration of *Bowers v. Hardwick*, 478 U.S. 186 (1986). The primary difference between *Bowers* and the instant case is that the Georgia statute in *Bowers* prohibited the proscribed sexual conduct between any persons, while the Texas statute prohibits the proscribed sexual conduct only between members of the same sex. Homosexual persons have the liberty to define their relationship and experience it within a private home just as heterosexual persons do, absent injury to the

individual or abuse to a legally protected institution. A traditional view of a practice as immoral is insufficient to support continued prohibition, and intimate choices made by married or unmarried persons are protected as a form of liberty. This was Justice Stevens's dissenting view in *Bowers*, and as it should have controlled then, it should control now. The judgment of the court of appeals is reversed and the case remanded.

CONCURRENCE: (O'Connor, J.) While *Bowers* should not be overruled, the majority is correct in finding the Texas statute here to be unconstitutional. Homosexuals should not be branded as criminals because of moral disapproval when heterosexuals participating in the same conduct are protected. Texas asserts no legitimate state interest here.

DISSENT: (Scalia, J.) Certain sexual behavior can and should be regulated because of moral disapproval. "Liberty" protections do not extend to certain other proscribed activities, such as heroin use and prostitution. Judgments of this kind should be made by the people and not imposed by the courts.

▶ ANALYSIS

Legislating morality is always under debate in this country because of a wide variance in the closely held values of American society. The *Lawrence* court held that private behavior among consenting adults should be protected as a liberty interest when the behavior is not harming another, but the court fell short of declaring such behavior a fundamental right. As understanding and acceptance of the gay and lesbian community increases, equal protection will become commonplace and expected, but scholars remain uncertain as to the impact of *Lawrence* on the future expansion of "fundamental" rights.

Quicknotes

CERTIORARI A discretionary writ issued by a superior court to an inferior court in order to review the lower court's decisions; the Supreme Court's writ ordering such review.

EQUAL PROTECTION CLAUSE A constitutional provision that each person be guaranteed the same protection of the laws enjoyed by other persons in like circumstances.

Roe v. Wade

Pregnant woman (P) v. District attorney (D)

410 U.S. 113 (1973).

NATURE OF CASE: Appeal from denial of injunctive relief to restrain enforcement of anti-abortion statutes.

FACT SUMMARY: Roe (P), a single woman and pregnant, sought to enjoin the enforcement of Texas statutes making it illegal to perform abortions except to save the mother's life.

🏛 **RULE OF LAW**
A state criminal abortion statute excepting from criminality only life-saving procedures on behalf of the mother, without regard to pregnancy stage or recognition of the other interests involved, violates the Due Process Clause of the 14th Amendment.

FACTS: Roe (P) was an unmarried, pregnant woman who wished to terminate her pregnancy by safe, clinical means. However, she was a resident of Texas, where abortions were illegal except to save the mother's life. Roe (P), unthreatened by her pregnancy, alleged that she could not afford to travel to a state where a safe abortion could be legally obtained. She claimed the Texas statutes were unconstitutionally vague and abridged her right to personal privacy. The district court found the statutes unconstitutional but denied injunctive relief. Both sides appealed.

ISSUE: Are anti-abortion statutes prohibiting abortion except where necessary to save the mother's life vague and violative of the right to privacy?

HOLDING AND DECISION: (Blackmun, J.) Yes. Historically, legislation against abortion is a fairly recent development in the law and reached its most severe point in the late 19th century. There are divergent views on when abortion should be necessary and when life begins. Reasons advanced for abortion laws include discouraging illicit sexual activity, to protect the health of the pregnant woman, and to protect prenatal life. It is not necessary to determine when life begins as where there is at least potential life involved, the state has an interest beyond the protection of the pregnant woman alone. A zone of privacy has been found in the Constitution, but it covers only personal rights that can be deemed "fundamental" or "implicit to a concept of ordered liberty." The right of privacy is invaded when the state would impose upon a pregnant woman a complete denial of her choice to terminate her pregnancy. Children could be distressful to a woman's life physically or psychologically. These factors should be considered by a woman and her physician. Even though there is a right to privacy, there may be appropriate occasions where state regulation in areas protected by that right may be appropriate. Thus, the right of personal privacy includes the abortion decision, but this right is not unqualified and must be considered against important state interests in regulation. Examination of the word "person" in the Constitution does not show it to apply to the unborn. "The unborn have never been recognized in the law as persons in the whole sense." The interests of the woman and the state are separate and distinct, and each grows in substantiality as the pregnant woman approaches term, and, at a point during pregnancy, each becomes compelling. In light of current medical knowledge with respect to the state's important and legitimate interest in the mother's health, the end of the first trimester of pregnancy is the point where that interest arises. It is during that period when the mortality rate from abortion is less than in normal childbirth. But after the first trimester, the state may regulate abortion to the extent it reasonably relates to protection and preservation of the mother's health. Prior to this point, the mother, with her physician, is free to determine without state regulation whether or not to terminate her pregnancy. The state's interest arises at the point of fetal viability, where the fetus can survive outside the womb. The Texas statute is far too broad. There is no distinction between procedures performed early in pregnancy and later on. It limits abortion only to saving the mother's life. Thus, during the first trimester of pregnancy, no abortion regulation is permitted. During the second trimester, reasonable regulation to protect maternal health is allowable. Only in the last trimester may there be a complete abortion ban except to protect the mother's health.

▶ **ANALYSIS**

A companion complaint, filed by John and Mary Doe, a married couple (alleging that Mary, because of health reasons, could not use contraceptive measures nor risk pregnancy, thus facing the need for an abortion), was dismissed for being too speculative. In the companion case of *Doe v. Bolton*, 410 U.S. 179 (1973), three procedural conditions of the Georgia abortion statute were invalidated under the Fourteenth Amendment. The first was that a hospital accredited by the joint committee on accreditation of hospitals was the only place an abortion could be performed; the second that there be advance approval of the hospital medical staff committee where the abortion was to be performed; and the third that two other physicians concur in writing to the performing physician's

Continued on next page.

opinion that an abortion should be performed. The Court held the scheme unreasonably interfered with the mother's privacy right.

∎══∎

Quicknotes

DUE PROCESS CLAUSE Clauses found in the Fifth and Fourteenth Amendments to the United States Constitution providing that no person shall be deprived of "life, liberty, or property, without due process of law."

INJUNCTIVE RELIEF A court order issued as a remedy, requiring a person to do, or prohibiting that person from doing, a specific act.

FUNDAMENTAL RIGHT A liberty that is either expressly or impliedly provided for in the United States Constitution, the deprivation or burdening of which is subject to a heightened standard of review.

PRIVACY RIGHT Those personal liberties or relationships that are protected against unwarranted governmental interference.

∎══∎

Planned Parenthood v. Casey

Reproductive health clinic (P) v. State (D)

505 U.S. 833 (1992).

NATURE OF CASE: Appeal from a ruling reversing in part and affirming in part a finding that certain provisions of a state statute were unconstitutional.

FACT SUMMARY: Planned Parenthood (P) argued that certain provisions in Pennsylvania's (D) Abortion Control Act violated the due process and liberty spheres of the 14th Amendment.

RULE OF LAW
Only where state regulation imposes an undue burden on a woman's ability to procure an abortion does the power of the state violate the liberty interest protected by the Due Process Clause.

FACTS: After the Pennsylvania (D) legislature enacted the Abortion Control Act of 1982, Planned Parenthood (P) challenged five of the provisions. The disputed provisions required that a woman give informed consent to an abortion, requiring a twenty-four-hour. delay to review information, mandated the informed consent of one parent for a minor to obtain an abortion, but provided for a judicial bypass of such consent, required that a married woman notify her husband of her intended abortion, defined a "medical emergency" excusing compliance, and imposed reporting requirements on facilities providing abortion services. The trial court found all five provisions unconstitutional. The court of appeals reversed, upholding all the provisions, except the one requiring husband notification. Planned Parenthood (P) appealed.

ISSUE: Does state power violate the liberty interest protected by the Due Process Clause only where state regulation imposes an undue burden on a woman's ability to procure an abortion?

HOLDING AND DECISION: (O'Connor, J.) Yes. Only where state regulation imposes an undue burden on a woman's ability to procure an abortion does the power of the state violate the liberty interest protected by the Due Process Clause. An undue burden exists, and therefore a provision of law is invalid, if its purpose or effect is to place a substantial obstacle in the path of a woman seeking an abortion before the fetus attains viability. As construed by the court of appeals, the medical emergency definition imposes no undue burden on a woman's abortion right. In addition, the informed consent requirement, along with the twenty-four-hour waiting period, cannot be considered a substantial obstacle to a woman's obtaining an abortion and does not, therefore, constitute an undue burden on that right. However, the spousal notification requirement is likely to prevent a significant number of women who may be victims of spousal

abuse from obtaining an abortion. It is an undue burden and is therefore invalid. But a state may require a minor seeking an abortion to obtain the consent of a parent or guardian, provided that there is an adequate judicial bypass procedure. Finally, all the recordkeeping and reporting requirements of the statute, except that relating to spousal notice, are constitutional. Affirmed in part, reversed in part.

CONCURRENCE AND DISSENT: (Blackmun, J.) This Court fully supported a woman's reproductive rights prior to *Webster v. Reproductive Health Services*, 492 U.S. 490 (1989). The instant case revised that support but only a single justice is needed to turn the court back to darkness.

CONCURRENCE AND DISSENT: (Scalia, J.) Abortion-on-demand is not constitutionally required although states may permit it. Applying the rational basis test, the Pennsylvania (D) statute should be upheld in its entirety. The joint opinion's undue burden standard is inherently pliable and will prove hopelessly unworkable in practice.

ANALYSIS

Many hoped that with its decision in this case the Court would overrule its holding in *Roe v. Wade*. However, the plurality stated that the essential holding of *Roe* should be retained and once again reaffirmed. While the plurality rejected *Roe*'s trimester framework for the undue burden standard, it retained *Roe*'s viability test. The Court noted that its obligation was to define the liberty of all, not to mandate the justices' own moral code. This case was unusual in that three justices—O'Connor, Kennedy, and Souter—took part in writing the plurality opinion.

Quicknotes

UNDUE BURDEN A burden which is unlawfully oppressive or troublesome.

Ayotte v. Planned Parenthood

Party not identified (D) v. Reproductive health clinic (P)

126 S. Ct. 961 (2006).

NATURE OF CASE: Appeal from invalidation of a New Hampshire statute on constitutional grounds.

FACT SUMMARY: New Hampshire enacted a statute requiring parental notification of a minor's pending abortion, but the statute did not include a health exception for the mother. Planned Parenthood (P) brought suit on constitutional grounds prior to the Act taking effect.

🏛 RULE OF LAW
Judicial remedies should be narrowly tailored to address the issue raised.

FACTS: New Hampshire enacted the Parental Notification Prior to the Abortion Act in 2003. It required notification of a minor's parents prior to that minor obtaining an abortion. Legislators wrote exceptions for parental notification into the statute including in case of impending death, if the parent had already been notified, or if the minor received a judicial bypass. Nothing in the statute permitted a physician to perform an abortion procedure on a minor absent parental notification if the minor's health was in danger. Planned Parenthood (P) filed suit before the act took effect, claiming the act was unconstitutional because the act lacked a health exception. The district court declared the act unconstitutional and permanently enjoined its enforcement. The First Circuit affirmed, and this court granted certiorari.

ISSUE: Should judicial remedies be narrowly tailored to address the issue raised?

HOLDING AND DECISION: (O'Connor, J.) Yes. Judicial remedies should be narrowly tailored to address the issue raised. This Court has previously upheld parental involvement statutes, but no abortion-related statute may restrict access when a mother's life or health is at issue. New Hampshire does not appear to dispute the fact that a small percentage of minors seeking abortions may need one immediately to preserve life or health. The judicial remedy with this statute, however, may have gone too far. The courts below struck down the statute in its entirety when the state had included a request for a more narrow remedy. It is preferred to invalidate a statute in part rather than in whole, so as to preserve the legislative work and to avoid the judiciary standing in place of the elected representative. It is not the place of the courts to write or rewrite state law. It is also not the place of the courts to substitute their judgment for that of the legislative intent. Perhaps the legislature would prefer a partial statute rather than none at all, or vice versa. Here, declaratory judgment and an injunction prohibiting an unconstitutional application of the statute could perhaps suffice to save the statute's constitutionality. The legislative intent must be divined, but there is at least one possibility to save the statute. Judgment vacated and remanded to determine legislative intent.

▶ ANALYSIS

Critics of this law feared that physicians could be criminally prosecuted for making a medically necessary decision to provide an immediate abortion to protect a mother's health. The statute put too much of the onus on the physician to set aside medical judgment and wait, perhaps for as long as two weeks, for the courts to grant permission for an emergency abortion absent parental notification. The parties agreed that the percentage of applicable cases would be small, but most physicians did not want to take the risk. Multiple physician organizations, including the American Medical Association, filed amicus briefs on behalf of the plaintiffs. This case was also the first abortion-related case to be argued before the Supreme Court under the purview of newly appointed Chief Justice Roberts.

Quicknotes

AMICUS BRIEF A brief submitted by a third party, not a party to the action, which contains information for the court's consideration in conformity with its position.

CERTIORARI A discretionary writ issued by a superior court to an inferior court in order to review the lower court's decisions; the Supreme Court's writ ordering such review.

DECLARATORY JUDGMENT A judgment of the court establishing the rights of the parties.

INJUNCTION A court order requiring a person to do, or prohibiting that person from doing, a specific act.

People v. Humphrey

State (P) v. Battered woman (D)

Cal. Sup. Ct., 13 Cal. 4th 1073, 921 P.2d 1 (1996).

NATURE OF CASE: Appeal from conviction for involuntary manslaughter.

FACT SUMMARY: Evelyn Humphrey (D) shot and killed her live-in boyfriend, Albert Hampton. She immediately confessed to the killing and made a claim of self-defense at trial. Trial counsel introduced evidence of Battered Woman Syndrome, which the judge instructed the jury to disregard when considering the objective reasonableness of her actions.

🏛 RULE OF LAW
Evidence of Battered Woman Syndrome is relevant to both the reasonableness and the subjective belief for the necessity of self-defense and a jury may consider the evidence for both prongs.

FACTS: Evelyn Humphrey (D) shot and killed her live-in boyfriend, Albert Hampton. She immediately confessed to police, stating she "couldn't take him beating on me no more." Humphrey (D) claimed that Hampton shot a gun at her the night before, barely missing her. At trial, Humphrey (D) claimed self-defense and put on expert and non-expert testimony of Battered Woman Syndrome. The court instructed the jury to consider the Battered Women's Syndrome evidence for purposes of determining whether defendant subjectively and honestly believed her life was in danger. The court further instructed that the jury could not consider Battered Woman Syndrome evidence to determine the reasonableness of defendant's behavior. The jury convicted Humphrey (D) of voluntary manslaughter and personal use of a firearm. The court sentenced Humphrey (D) to eight years. The court of appeal affirmed in part and remanded for resentencing on the use of the firearm. Humphrey (D) appeals.

ISSUE: Is evidence of Battered Woman Syndrome relevant to both the reasonableness and the subjective belief for the necessity of self-defense, and may a jury consider the evidence for both prongs?

HOLDING AND DECISION: (Chin, J.) Evidence of Battered Woman Syndrome is relevant to both the reasonableness and the subjective belief for the necessity of self-defense, and a jury may consider the evidence for both prongs. Battered Woman Syndrome is admissible evidence to support a claim of self-defense in a criminal action. Evidence of Battered Woman Syndrome is also relevant to dispel stereotypes and myths about battered women and why they may stay with their abusers. In California, self-defense requires the reasonable belief of imminent danger to life or great bodily injury. A finding of reasonable belief is "perfect" self-defense and results in an acquittal. "Imperfect" self-defense is the finding that the defendant had a subjective

and honest belief of imminent danger, but the action was objectively unreasonable. In this case, the trial court allowed the Battered Woman Syndrome evidence on the issue of the subjective belief, but instructed the jury to not consider it on the objective reasonableness. Two prior California cases held that Battered Woman Syndrome evidence is irrelevant to reasonableness; the jury, however, is to consider the situation from the defendant's perspective when considering objective reasonableness. The expert here testified that battered women are often excellent judges of the abuser's behavior and the potential escalation for violence. This information is relevant for the jury to consider the reasonableness of defendant's fear for her life. The evidence is relevant but determinative because the standard is still a reasonable person, not a reasonable battered woman. The prior California cases held in contrary are overruled to the extent that they are inconsistent with this opinion. Judgment reversed.

▶ ANALYSIS

The psychological effects of domestic violence show up in criminal cases and custody cases. Courts have historically tended to blame the victim for not leaving her abuser. Such attitudes resulted in murder convictions and lost custody. One California court actually awarded custody of two minor girls to the abusive father because of fear that the girls would incorporate the "learned helplessness" of the abused mother. See *In re Heather A*, 97 C.D.O.S. 568 (1997). Courts have since taken a more informed approach toward allowing evidence of Battered Woman Syndrome, which explains the strength and survivor attitude of battered women put into impossible circumstances. The remaining concern lies in the courts' ability to balance the evidence of Battered Woman Syndrome without excusing unnecessary violence couched as self-defense.

■═■

Quicknotes

REASONABLE BELIEF A reasonable basis for believing that a crime is being or has been committed.

REASONABLE PERSON STANDARD The standard of case exercised by one who possesses the intelligence, education, knowledge, attention, and judgment required by society of its members when governing behavior; the standard applies to a person's judgment when determining breach of a duty under the theory of negligence.

SUBJECTIVE STANDARD A standard that is based on the personal belief of an individual.

■═■

R. v. Malott

Parties not identified.

Canada Sup. Ct., 1998 WL 1714234 (1998).

NATURE OF CASE: [Nature of case not stated in casebook excerpt.]

FACT SUMMARY: [Facts not stated in casebook excerpt.]

🏛 **RULE OF LAW**
[Rule of law not stated in casebook excerpt.]

FACTS: [Facts not stated in casebook excerpt.]

HOLDING AND DECISION: [Holding and decision not stated in casebook excerpt.]

CONCURRENCE: (L'Heureux-Dube, J.) Judicial advances have been made in a willingness to consider a woman's entire experience as relevant and perhaps different from a man's entire experience. Battered Woman Syndrome evidence is admissible to instruct the jury on myths and stereotypes of battered women, but a new stereotype of a "battered woman" must be avoided. Battered women may have fought back, may be professionals, and may be women of color. The reasonableness standard is not that a battered woman must be reasonable "like a man" or "like a battered woman" when she is claiming self-defense. The evidence should be introduced for the purpose of explaining the reasonableness of her actions, not for the purpose of explaining why she stayed with her abuser. Stereotypes have no place in the courtroom and a judge and jury should be instructed on the relevance of the Battered Woman Syndrome evidence.

Quicknotes

REASONABLE PERSON STANDARD The standard of case exercised by one who possesses the intelligence, education, knowledge, attention, and judgment required by society of its members when governing behavior; the standard applies to a person's judgment when determining breach of a duty under the theory of negligence.

■══■

Giovine v. Giovine

Wife (P) v. Husband (D)

N.J. Super. Ct., 284 N.J. Super. 3, 663 A.2d 109 (1995).

NATURE OF CASE: Appeal from dismissal of tort claims and jury trial.

FACT SUMMARY: The wife (P) sought to include tort claims in her complaint for divorce from her husband (D), which was the second time the couple had separated. On husband's motion, the trial court dismissed the counts related to actions occurring prior to the applicable statute of limitations to the present case.

🏛 RULE OF LAW
Evidence of Battered Woman Syndrome may toll a statute of limitations for tortious claims if the tortious behavior was of a continuous nature such that the victim could not alter her circumstances.

FACTS: Mr. (D) and Mrs. (P) Giovine married in 1971 and separated in 1978. During the divorce action, they reconciled and dismissed their case with prejudice. In 1994, Mrs. Giovine (P) filed a new complaint for divorce and Mr. Giovine (D) counterclaimed based on extreme cruelty. Mrs. Giovine (P) included tort claims in her complaint based on Mr. Giovine's (D) alleged tortious acts occurring in part prior to 1992. She also demanded a jury trial. Mr. Giovine (D) moved to dismiss the tort claims occurring prior to 1992 based on the two-year statute of limitations for tort claims. The trial court granted Mr. Giovine's (D) motion and denied Mrs. Giovine's (P) request for a jury trial. Mrs. Giovine (P) appeals.

ISSUE: May evidence of Battered Woman Syndrome toll a statute of limitations for tortious claims if the tortious behavior was of a continuous nature such that the victim could not alter her circumstances?

HOLDING AND DECISION: (Kleiner, J.) Yes. Evidence of Battered Woman Syndrome may toll a statute of limitations for tortious claims if the tortious behavior was of a continuous nature such that the victim could not alter her circumstances. Mrs. Giovine (P) argues that the trial court should have followed *Cusseaux v. Pickett*, 279 N.J. Super. 335 (1994), which held that Battered Woman Syndrome was the result of ongoing abusive behavior and should be treated as a continuous tort. The *Cusseaux* court felt it would be unfair to limit battered women to the statute of limitations for assault and battery. The court then enunciated a four-part test for Battered Woman Syndrome, which included the inability of the victim to alter her situation after continuous abuse by her dominant spouse or significant other resulting in psychological or physical injury. This court agrees with the *Cusseaux* factors and now holds that a wife may include tort claims against

her spouse if she can provide expert testimony establishing the inability to alter her situation as a result of the ongoing abuse. Contrary to the *Cusseaux* court, however, this court does not agree that Battered Woman Syndrome is a continuous tort. Rather, it is the psychological result of abusive behavior which may be continuous. Prior case law allows for the abrogation of a statute of limitations when the ongoing abuse may render the victim unable to alter the situation, such as in cases of incest or insanity. Here, if the wife can demonstrate by expert testimony that the ongoing abuse rendered her unable to alter her situation, she may be able to sue her husband in tort. Mrs. Giovine (P) can include all of the marital behavior, including those incidents occurring prior to 1992. Reversed.

CONCURRENCE AND DISSENT: (Skillman, J.) The majority should not have created a new tort—battered women's tort. The judicial system offers remedies for persons in abusive situations, including existing tort remedies for assault and battery. Further, the plaintiff could establish the existence of a continuous tort or a state of insanity to toll the statute of limitations. The majority does not explain its inconsistency in disagreeing with the *Cusseaux* court's finding that Battered Woman Syndrome itself was a continuous tort but holding that the abusive behavior resulting in Battered Woman Syndrome is a continuous tort. In this case, the plaintiff does not allege insanity, a factual basis for finding a continuous tort, or any expert testimony that she suffers Battered Woman Syndrome. Her marital tort claims should not have been allowed.

▶ ANALYSIS

Courts increasingly accept Battered Woman Syndrome as the psychological explanation for women staying in abusive relationships rather than continuing with the historical pattern of blaming the victim. An additional sticking point in tort actions based on domestic violence is the fact that spouses traditionally had inter-spousal immunity from torts committed during the marital relationship. Strangers asserting tort claims had more protection than the spouse suffering from tortious behavior at the hands of his or her spouse. This case continued the trend of allowing Battered Woman Syndrome to be used as a cause of action rather than a defense.

■=■

Continued on next page.

Quicknotes

INTRAFAMILY TORT IMMUNITY The immunity of family members from tort liability in actions brought by another member of the family.

STATUTE OF LIMITATIONS A law prescribing the period in which a legal action may be commenced.

TOLL To bar, suspend, or stop, such as a statute of limitations period.

TORT A legal wrong resulting in a breach of duty by the wrongdoer, causing damages as a result of the breach.

TORTIOUS ACTS Acts that constitute legal wrongs, resulting in breach of a duty.

■≡■

Mitchell v. Mitchell

Parties not identified.

Mass. Ct. App., 62 Mass. App. 769, 821 N.E.2d 79 (2005).

NATURE OF CASE: Appeal from order vacating abuse prevention order.

FACT SUMMARY: Mary Mitchell obtained an abuse prevention order against James Mitchell, her husband, which was extended for an additional year. After Mary and James were in contact by telephone and spent time alone together attending James's mother's funeral, James moved to have the order reconsidered or vacated.

> **🏛 RULE OF LAW**
> A party requesting relief from an order affecting the safety and well-being of another party must make a more substantial showing warranting revision or being vacated.

FACTS: Mary Mitchell filed an abuse prevention order against her husband, James Mitchell, after ten years of abuse. An affidavit and three police reports supported her complaint. The judge issued the ex parte abuse prevention order on December 20, 2001. The order was to expire on January 3, 2002. The husband appeared pro se and the order was extended to January 3, 2003. On June 20, 2002, the husband moved to reconsider or vacate the order because of contact he claimed his wife had initiated. James stated that Mary telephoned him and "chit-chatted," including about their pets, and that she had voluntarily been alone with him, including attending a movie and his mother's funeral with him in California. Mary's affidavit stated that she only contacted James because their pets were ill and they needed to discuss medical care and she was not voluntarily alone with him in California, although she did attend his mother's funeral services. She made arrangements so that she would not be alone with him and the two occasions she was were not voluntary. The husband's sister filed an affidavit that Mary was still afraid of James and had requested that arrangements be made while both were in California to maintain her safety. The family had tried to abide by those requests, but Mary was involuntarily left alone with James on two occasions. The judge granted the motion vacating the abuse prevention order. Mary appealed.

ISSUE: Must a party requesting relief from an order affecting the safety and well-being of another party make a more substantial showing warranting revision or vacation?

HOLDING AND DECISION: (Duffly, J.) Yes. A party requesting relief from an order affecting the safety and well-being of another party must make a more substantial showing warranting revision or vacation. A party does not need to make a new showing of abuse to extend an abuse prevention order and a judge is not limited to a one-year

extension after the initial complaint. The absence of abuse during the time period of an abuse prevention order is not sufficient to vacate the order, although either party may move at any time for a revision or to vacate. The abuse prevention statute in this case, however, does not articulate a standard of review for motions to modify, vacate, or terminate the order. A judge's discretion in these cases is broad, but a standard does need to be articulated. Looking at similar areas of the law, a substantial showing is necessary for a change in a decree, or a second option is a more flexible standard that a significant change warrants revision of the decree. The First Circuit viewed decree revisions along a continuum with those having little to do with a party's safety and welfare on one end of the continuum and a decree affecting a party's safety at the other end of the continuum, requiring a more substantial showing of the need for relief. The basis for the initial abuse prevention order is not subject to attack or review and requires "the most extraordinary circumstances" to set aside. In this case, James did not meet the heavy burden of demonstrating that the abuse prevention order was no longer necessary to protect Mary. Mary should have had the opportunity on January 3, 2003 to extend the order had it not been vacated in July 2002. She must therefore be allowed to have that opportunity. Judgment reversed.

▶ ANALYSIS

Abuse prevention orders can usually be obtained ex parte, when courts are closed by contacting local law enforcement agencies, and free of charge. The relative ease of filing for such an order is to encourage victims of relationship violence to step forward and take action against the abuser. If the courts easily modify or vacate the order after a survivor of violence obtains one, then the purpose behind offering the orders is frustrated.

■═■

Quicknotes

AFFIDAVIT A declaration of facts written and affirmed before a witness.

EX PARTE A proceeding commenced by one party.

PRO SE An individual appearing on his own behalf.

■═■

C.O. v. M.M.

Mother of victim (P) v. Alleged abuser (D)

442 Mass. 648, 815 N.E.2d 582 (2004).

NATURE OF CASE: Review of extension for abuse prevention order.

FACT SUMMARY: M.M. (D) allegedly sexually assaulted C.O.'s (P) daughter. C.O. sought and obtained an abuse prevention order against M.M.

🏛 RULE OF LAW
The court must apply the express statutory factors in determining the appropriateness of an abuse prevention order.

FACTS: Seventeen-year-old M.M. (D) allegedly drove C.O.'s (P) fifteen-year-old daughter home from school. He then invited her inside and forcibly sexually assaulted her. M.M. (D) disputes the assault, but C.O. (P) obtained an ex parte emergency temporary abuse prevention order. The next day, M.M. (D) was arrested, arraigned, and released on bail. This resulted in his suspension from school. The district court judge extended the abuse prevention order for a period of one year. M.M. (D) appealed. This court transferred the case on its own motion.

ISSUE: Must the court apply the express statutory factors in determining the appropriateness of an abuse prevention order?

HOLDING AND DECISION: (Cowin, J) Yes. The court must apply the express statutory factors in determining the appropriateness of an abuse prevention order. The abuse prevention statute is not intended to cover stranger or acquaintance violence, but it is intended to be flexible so that it covers family violence and protects those in a "substantive dating relationship." M.M. (D) claims that C.O. (P) failed to prove the existence of a substantive dating relationship. The statute directs courts to consider (1) the length of time of the relationship; (2) the type of relationship; (3) the frequency of interaction between the parties; and (4) if the relationship has been terminated by either person, the length of time elapsed since the termination of the relationship. This is a case-by-case determination, and interpretation of the statute is not necessary. This court should not add further definition. C.O. (P) failed to meet her burden of proving by preponderance of the evidence the existence of a substantive dating relationship between the parties. The district court judge improperly ignored the four statutory factors and instead based his issuance of the order on the fact that a criminal case was pending and on the age of the victim. Order vacated.

▶ ANALYSIS

Abuse prevention orders are not meant to be obtained automatically or without sufficient support. Persons cannot obtain such orders against random members of the public, even if there is some form of acquaintance, criminal or otherwise, between the parties. The court sought to prevent harassment of third parties by the thoughtless extension of abuse prevention orders just as it seeks to protect survivors of abuse by the issuance of appropriate abuse prevention orders.

Quicknotes

EX PARTE A proceeding commenced by one party.

Turner v. Lewis

Parties not identified.

Mass. Sup. Jud. Ct., 434 Mass. 331, 749 N.E.2d 122 (2001).

NATURE OF CASE: Appeal from denial of extension of protective order.

FACT SUMMARY: Custodial paternal grandmother sought abuse protection order against non-resident biological mother after mother assaulted the grandmother.

RULE OF LAW
Paternal grandparent of a child whose parents were never married is related by blood to the child's mother for purposes of the abuse protection statute.

FACTS: The paternal grandmother has custody of the ten-year-old child. The biological mother has visitation rights, but does not live with the grandmother and child. One day, the mother entered the grandmother's home and assaulted the grandmother, threatened her, and appeared "obviously high." The grandmother obtained an emergency protective order and then sought to have it extended. The judge denied the extension on the basis that the parties were not related by blood, marriage, or household membership. Grandmother appealed and filed a motion for reconsideration, which was also denied. Grandmother appeals that denial.

ISSUE: Is a paternal grandparent of a child whose parents were never married related by blood to the child's mother for purposes of the abuse protection statute?

HOLDING AND DECISION: (Ireland, J) Yes. A paternal grandparent of a child whose parents were never married is related by blood to the child's mother for purposes of the abuse protection statute. The abuse prevention statute requires the abuse to be perpetrated by family or household member related by blood or marriage. The statute provides that persons with a child in common are considered family, regardless of whether they have ever married or even cohabitated. Grandmother claims that she is related by blood to the child as the mother is related by blood, thus mother and grandmother are related by blood. The statute is intended to have flexibility and broad application to protect those in familial relationships. Mother and grandmother in this case have such a relationship, because mother has visitation rights and will likely continue to come in contact with grandmother and the child. Grandmother is entitled to protection from violence in such a setting. Public policy supports such a determination as there is an increase in single parent households as well as grandparents raising grandchildren. Caregivers, such as the grandmother here, should be protected from domestic abuse from the child's parents. Mother and grandmother are thus related "by blood" and public policy

supports the determination that the grandmother is entitled to protection from domestic abuse. Denial of the extension is vacated and case remanded.

DISSENT: (Cowin, J.) The legislative history contradicts the majority's finding. Unmarried parents were considered members of the same household or family because of their status as parents, not because of blood relation to the child. The 1990 amendment to the statute again defined unmarried parents as family members because of their status, not because of blood relation. While the amendments of the statute have broadened the definition of family, the statute simply does not extend to custodial grandparents if not related by blood to the perpetrator of the violence. The court's duty is to construe the statute as it exists, not to incorporate social "trends."

▌ ANALYSIS

Abuse prevention orders are to protect survivors of abuse from further abuse by a family member or significant other. Courts struggle to define "family" in contexts other than the domestic violence context. One well-known example is the 1974 U.S. Supreme Court case of *Village of Belle Terre v. Borass.* That case considered the definition of "family" as related to who could reside in single-family residences for zoning purposes. Most courts resort to a flexible definition of "family" so that more people benefit from the protections of laws meant for them without suffering from exclusion of laws that should include them.

■▬■

Quicknotes

PUBLIC POLICY Policy administered by the state with respect to the health, safety and morals of its people in accordance with common notions of fairness and decency.

■▬■

Ba v. United States

Convicted abuser (D) v. Federal government (P)

D.C. Ct. App., 809 A.2d 1178 (2002).

NATURE OF CASE: Appeal from conviction for civil protection order violation.

FACT SUMMARY: Howard obtained a civil protection order (CPO) against her ex-boyfriend, Ba (D). The couple reconciled temporarily while the CPO was still in effect, but then Howard sought to have the CPO enforced. Ba (D) argued that Howard's temporary consent was a complete defense to any charge of violating the CPO.

🏛 RULE OF LAW
Temporary consent to contact while a civil protection order is in effect does not vitiate the order when consent is revoked.

FACTS: In December 1999, Lashance Howard sought a civil protection order against her ex-boyfriend, Ba (D). The court granted the CPO for a twelve-month period and ordered Ba (D) to stay at least one hundred feet away from Ms. Howard, her home, and her workplace. From late December 1999 until March 2000, Ba (D) and Lashance attempted to reconcile and even lived together at times. In March 2000, Lashance informed Ba (D) that the relationship was over and she sought to have the CPO enforced against him if he attempted to contact her. One evening, Lashance feared that Ba (D) was attempting to contact her, so she called the police. An officer responded and found Ba (D) at Ms. Howard's home and Ba (D) attempted to approach Ms. Howard. He was about ten to twelve feet from Ms. Howard when the officer arrested him. Ba (D) was charged with violating the CPO. The trial court found Ba (D) guilty and sentenced him to jail. Ba (D) appeals.

ISSUE: Does temporary consent to contact while a civil protection order is in effect vitiate the order when consent is revoked?

HOLDING AND DECISION: (Reid, J.) No. Temporary consent to contact while a civil protection order is in effect does not vitiate the order when consent is revoked. Ba (D) argues on appeal that Ms. Howard's consent to contact from December through March is a complete defense to his later contact with Ms. Howard. The government (P) argues that consent cannot be a defense because this was a criminal action and Ms. Howard's consent is not able to void the order. It would be too difficult for the court to determine whether consent had been freely given. Further, a defendant would have to make contact with any complainant in an attempt to gain consent and that contact would in itself be a violation of the order. The government (P) must simply prove that Ba (D) willfully disobeyed a protective court order. The court will not consider Ba's (D) proposed defense of consent because in any case the consent was temporary and revoked as of March 2000. As Ba's contact was in May 2000, he clearly violated the CPO. Judgment affirmed.

▶ ANALYSIS

Voluntariness is a key issue in requests to rescind abuse prevention orders. If a victim requests to vacate an order, the court must explore the reasons behind the request. Was contact truly voluntary or did the abuser re-assert pressure to force the victim into the desired behavior? Can the court ever count on the fact that a victim is truly voluntarily agreeing to contact? Applying a general rule that consent does not vitiate the court order seems to be the most commonsense compromise for a court to make.

Quicknotes

CIVIL PROTECTION ORDER A restraining order or injunction issued in a civil proceeding granted by the court upon a petition filed requesting such protection with notice to the opposing party, issued to protect a person from harassment.

Town of Castle Rock v. Gonzales

City (D) v. Domestic abuse survivor (P)

545 U.S. 78, 125 S. Ct. 2796 (2005).

NATURE OF CASE: Appeal from denial of motion to dismiss.

FACT SUMMARY: Gonzales (P) attempted to have the police enforce a restraining order against her ex-husband when the ex-husband took their three daughters on a day he did not have visitation. The police did not respond in a timely manner to Gonzales's (P) many requests for help and the ex-husband murdered the girls. Gonzales (P) filed a claim in federal district court that her constitutional rights had been violated because the police did not enforce the restraining order.

🏛 RULE OF LAW
An individual does not have a constitutionally protected property interest in police enforcement of a state-issued restraining order.

FACTS: Jessica Gonzales (P) obtained a restraining order against her husband as part of their divorce proceedings. The husband was to stay away from Gonzales (P) and their three daughters, except during court-approved visitation times. The preprinted restraining order had a notice on its reverse side to law enforcement officials that they should use every reasonable means to enforce the order, including arrest or to seek an arrest warrant if arrest was not viable. The enforcement was to occur anytime that police had probable cause that the restraining order was being violated or there was an attempt at violation. One evening, the ex-husband took the three daughters from Gonzales's (P) front yard on a day he did not have visitation. Gonzales (P) alerted the police at 7:00 p.m., but was told to wait until 10:00 p.m. to see if the girls were returned. At 8:30 p.m., the ex-husband spoke with Gonzales (P) on the phone and told her that he had the children with him at an amusement park. Gonzales (P) again called the police and asked for them to find her ex-husband or his vehicle, but the officer refused and again told her to wait until 10:00 pm. At 10:10 p.m., she called the police, but was told to wait until midnight. She called at midnight, while driving to her ex-husband's apartment, but found nobody there. She called again at 12:10 a.m. and was told to wait for an officer, but none arrived. At 12:50 a.m. she arrived at the police station and filed an incident report, but the reporting officer did not follow up and went to dinner. At 3:20 a.m., the ex-husband arrived at the police station with a semi-automatic handgun and began firing. The police shot back and killed him and later found the bodies of the three daughters in the ex-husband's pickup truck. Gonzales (P) filed a claim in federal district court claiming that the police had violated her Fourteenth Amendment rights when they refused to enforce the restraining order despite having probable cause that it was being violated. Gonzales (P) claimed that it was "the official policy or custom" to not respond and to tolerate such action. Castle Rock (D) filed a motion to dismiss, which the district court granted on the basis that the claim did not consist of a substantive or procedural due process claim. Gonzales (P) appealed and the Court of Appeals found that Gonzales (P) had a viable procedural due process claim. Castle Rock (D) filed a motion for rehearing and the appellate court en banc affirmed. Castle Rock (D) appealed to this court, which granted certiorari.

ISSUE: Does an individual with a state-issued restraining order have a constitutionally protected property interest in the enforcement of that restraining order when police have probable cause to believe it has been violated?

HOLDING AND DECISION: (Scalia, J.) No. An individual does not have a constitutionally protected property interest in police enforcement of a state-issued restraining order. Gonzales (P) claims that the Fourteenth Amendment provides her a property interest in having the police enforce the restraining order against her husband once they had probable cause. She fails, however, to delineate the exact entitlement claimed because she does not specify if the police are mandated by statute to arrest, or to seek an arrest warrant, or to just use reasonable means to enforce the restraining order. Colorado has not created a mandatory arrest requirement within the restraining order statute. It is public policy for the police to have discretion, even in mandatory arrest cases. The legislature would need to unambiguously indicate that enforcement of a restraining order required arrest of the violator. In this case, the preprinted form did not create such a mandate. Judgment reversed.

CONCURRENCE: (Souter, J.) Gonzales (P) has not shown a property interest in police enforcement. Police must have discretion in any given situation and individuals cannot instruct the police to arrest or to refrain from arresting. Gonzales (P) blends entitlement to a property interest as well as to a process to protect that entitlement. Such a claim is not protected under the Fourteenth Amendment and would turn federal due process on its head.

DISSENT: (Stevens, J.) The majority unnecessarily broadens the issue present: whether the Fourteenth Amendment protects the property interest created by a restraining order. The Constitution, federal statute, and Colorado statute in this matter did not provide Gonzales (P)

Continued on next page.

or her children with a guarantee of individual police protection. When Gonzales (P) sought a restraining order, however, she sought a government service which could result in a property interest being created. The majority seems to dismiss mandatory arrest in a context of domestic violence when most states created mandatory arrest in that context. The police are not meant to have that level of discretion. Colorado precedent does not speak to this issue, but other state courts have so stated. A mandatory arrest statute does not allow a government official to use discretion, which creates a protected entitlement. The majority also states that Gonzales (P) did not have a traditional property interest at issue here; however, procedural due process extends to cover a variety of property interests, including welfare benefits, for example. Finally, the state law here guaranteed protection to Gonzales (P) once she obtained the requisite order, and she was entitled to rely on that guarantee. State officials could not deprive Gonzales (P) of her property interest in the enforcement of her restraining order, therefore the police behavior clearly created a due process violation.

▶ *ANALYSIS*

Advocates for supporters of domestic victim survivors followed this case closely to determine the level of the court's support for domestic violence victims' protections. A victim should be able to rely on the existing judicial protections rather than have the protections be no more than words on a page. Here, the court determined that the mother was at least perhaps entitled to an explanation for the city's lack of response—whether policy or tragic mistake.

Quicknotes

CERTIORARI A discretionary writ issued by a superior court to an inferior court in order to review the lower court's decisions; the Supreme Court's writ ordering such review.

ENTITLEMENT A right or interest that may not be denied without due process.

FOURTEENTH AMENDMENT Declares that no state shall make or enforce any law that shall abridge the privileges and immunities of citizens of the United States. No state shall deny to any person within its jurisdiction the equal protection of the laws.

FOURTEENTH AMENDMENT DUE PROCESS CLAUSE Provides that protections mandated by the U.S. Constitution and observed by the federal government are equally applicable, and therefore must be observed by the states.

PROBABLE CAUSE A reasonable basis for believing that a crime has been committed.

PROPERTY INTEREST A legal right in specified personal or real property.

PUBLIC POLICY Policy administered by the state with respect to the health, safety and morals of its people in accordance with common notions of fairness and decency.

Cheshire Medical Center v. Holbrook

Medical provider (P) v. Husband of patient (D)

N.H. Sup. Ct., 140 N.H. 187, 663 A.2d 1344 (1995).

NATURE OF CASE: Motion for determination of the viability of the Doctrine of Necessaries under state law.

FACT SUMMARY: When Cheshire Medical Center (P) filed a petition to attach property owned by Mr. Holbrook (D) to pay for services provided to Mrs. Holbrook, Mr. Holbrook (P) questioned whether the Doctrine of Necessaries remained state law.

🏛 RULE OF LAW
A husband or wife is not liable for necessary medical expenses incurred by his or her spouse unless the resources of the spouse who received the services are insufficient to satisfy the debt.

FACTS: Mrs. Holbrook, who had been treated at Cheshire (P), was subsequently incarcerated and could pay only $10 each month on her bill of $7,080. Cheshire (P) sought to attach real property owned by Mr. Holbrook (D), who questioned the viability of the Doctrine of Necessaries in New Hampshire. The superior court approved a motion by both parties to transfer the issue without ruling to the state supreme court.

ISSUE: Is a husband or wife liable for necessary medical expenses incurred by his or her spouse if the resources of the spouse who received the services are sufficient to satisfy the debt?

HOLDING AND DECISION: (Johnson, J.) No. A husband or wife is not liable for necessary medical expenses incurred by his or her spouse unless the resources of the spouse who received the services are insufficient to satisfy the debt. As traditionally formulated, the Necessaries Doctrine is unconstitutional, and should be revised to impose reciprocal responsibilities upon husbands and wives. The Equal Protection clauses of both the state and federal constitutions forbid common law rules distributing benefits or burdens on the basis of gender, in the absence of a compelling state interest. There is no compelling justification for the gender bias embodied in the traditional Necessaries Doctrine, which made a husband legally liable for essential goods or services provided to his wife by third parties. Imposing a reciprocal obligation on both parties to the marital contract is consistent with the policy underlying the state gender-neutral support laws. Remanded.

▌ *ANALYSIS*

The court in this case held that the spouse who receives the necessary goods or services is primarily liable for payment. The other spouse is only secondarily liable. At common law, upon marriage a woman forfeited her legal existence and became the property of her husband. The husband was obligated to provide her with all necessaries, such as food, clothing, or medical needs.

■══■

Quicknotes

DOCTRINE OF NECESSARIES A party who sells items that are necessary for sustenance or support to a wife or child may charge the husband or father for the cost of those items.

EQUAL PROTECTION CLAUSE A constitutional provision that each person be guaranteed the same protection of the laws enjoyed by other persons in like circumstances.

■══■

Skylarsky v. New Hope Guild Center

Decedent's husband (P) v. Psychiatric center (D)

806 N.Y.S.2d 448 (2005).

NATURE OF CASE: Motion to add counterclaim for indemnity and contribution.

FACT SUMMARY: Skylarsky's (P) wife was under psychiatric care of a physician at New Hope (D). During a psychotic episode, where she was threatening suicide, Skylarsky (P) contacted a New Hope (D) physician requesting help and was told to take his wife to an emergency room. He agreed to do so, but instead waited until the next morning. The wife committed suicide during the night and Skylarsky (P) sued New Hope (D) alleging psychiatric malpractice.

🏛 RULE OF LAW
A spouse has a legal duty to seek medical care for a helpless or incapacitated adult spouse in need of medical service.

FACTS: Sophia Skylarsky sought psychiatric care in January 2000 after her second discharge from an inpatient treatment facility. Physicians at New Hope (D) treated Sophia for approximately six months and diagnosed her as having a psychotic disorder, but her condition continued to deteriorate. In June 2000, her condition deteriorated to the point that her husband called a physician at New Hope (D) seeking an appointment for his wife that evening. New Hope (D) did not have onsite medication or the ability to restrain a psychotic patient, so the physician recommended that Skylarsky (P) take his wife to a hospital emergency room. Skylarsky (P) agreed and the conversation ended. Sophia Skylarsky's social worker contacted Skylarsky (P) by telephone and again encouraged Skylarsky (P) to take his wife to a hospital emergency room. Skylarsky (P) agreed, but later decided to wait until morning to do so. During the night, Sophia Skylarsky fell from a fourth-story fire escape, apparently committing suicide. Skylarsky (P) filed suit against New Hope (D) claiming psychiatric malpractice. New Hope (D) moved to counterclaim against Skylarsky (P) for indemnity and contribution because of Skylarsky's (P) alleged intervening negligence contributing to his wife's death.

ISSUE: Does a spouse have a legal duty to seek medical care for a helpless or incapacitated adult spouse in need of medical service?

HOLDING AND DECISION: (Rosenberg, J.) Yes. A spouse has a legal duty to seek medical care for a helpless or incapacitated adult spouse in need of medical service. New Hope (D) claims that Skylarsky (P) had a duty to obtain medical care for his incapacitated wife and his refusal to do so was a direct and proximate cause leading to Sophia Skylarsky's death. His intervening negligence should therefore, according to New Hope (D), lessen any liability on the

part of New Hope (D). The question becomes whether Skylarsky (P) breached a legal duty to act in the face of his spouse's need for emergency medical services. An expert psychiatrist testified that Skylarsky (P) had the ability to understand that his wife had a medical emergency requiring care and to understand the instructions of the physicians and the social worker to take his wife to an emergency room. The expert also testified that it is custom practice in the psychiatric community to rely on a spouse's assurance to seek medical care in a medical emergency for the incapacitated spouse. However, New Hope (D) needs to demonstrate that more than a moral duty, but a legal duty exists. Competent adults may refuse medical care without fear of spouses being held criminally liable. Courts have long held that persons are under no legal duty to aid another adult person. Several state courts have held, however, that a spouse may have a legal duty to obtain medical care for the incompetent, helpless spouse in need. Such is the case here where Sophia Skylarsky was helpless and unable to make a rational decision regarding her medical care. Her spouse, Skylarsky (P), had a legal duty to obtain that medical care for her. He breached that duty when he failed to take Sophia to a hospital emergency room and therefore may have contributed to her death. Motion granted.

▶ ANALYSIS

This case creates a greater responsibility for caretaker spouses who must now ensure medical care for the incapacitated spouse. At the conclusion of the evidence, the jury found Mr. Skylarsky 30% responsible for his wife's death. No award was granted because the parties settled under a "high-low" arrangement where Mr. Skylarsky received approximately $325,000 and neither party could appeal. The resolution of the case, however, supports the court's initial instinct that spouses should be responsible for obtaining medical care if the ill spouse cannot. This is a rare exception to the rule that persons are not required to intervene for the medical care of another adult.

■━■

Quicknotes

CONTRIBUTION The right of a person or party who has compensated a victim for his injury to seek reimbursement from others who are equally responsible for the injury in proportional amounts.

Continued on next page.

INDEMNITY The duty of a party to compensate another for damages sustained.

LEGAL DUTY TO ACT The duty to take some action to assist another in danger; such a duty is only imposed under certain circumstances, such as in accordance with a statute, contract, or relationship between the parties; when the defendant voluntarily assumes responsibility for care of the victim; or if the defendant creates the circumstances placing the victim in danger.

MALPRACTICE A failure to perform one's professional duties during the course of a client relationship, either intentionally or negligently, or the poor or improper discharge of one's professional obligations.

PROXIMATE CAUSE The natural sequence of events without which an injury would not have been sustained.

■━■

Divorce

Quick Reference Rules of Law

Benscoter v. Benscoter

Husband (P) v. Wife (D)

Pa. Super. Ct., 200 Pa. Super. 251, 188 A.2d 859 (1963).

NATURE OF CASE: Appeal from dismissal of complaint for divorce.

FACT SUMMARY: Benscoter (P) contended he was entitled to divorce because his wife verbally abused him for their failure to have a female child.

🏛 **RULE OF LAW**
Cruelty as a ground for divorce is established through evidence of a course of conduct rather than sporadic episodes.

FACTS: Benscoter (P) sued his wife for divorce on the grounds of cruelty. He testified his wife verbally abused him for his failure to produce a female offspring. Such abuse occurred after the parties had been married for 15 years and had four sons. Mrs. Benscoter (D), who was suffering from multiple sclerosis, contended she was the innocent and injured spouse, and, therefore, no divorce should be granted. The master recommended a divorce be granted, yet the trial court, finding Mrs. Benscoter's (D) behavior sporadic rather than pursuant to a course of conduct, dismissed the complaint. Mr. Benscoter (P) appealed.

ISSUE: Must cruelty be established through a course of conduct to serve as a basis for divorce?

HOLDING AND DECISION: (Ervin, J.) Yes. Cruelty as a ground for divorce is established through evidence of a course of conduct rather than sporadic episodes. No complaints were alleged until three months before the hearing. Further, substantial evidence was presented, allowing for a finding that Mr. Benscoter (P) was seeing another woman and that the true reason for his complaint was Mrs. Benscoter's (D) multiple sclerosis. Thus, no cruelty was shown, and the complaint was properly dismissed. Affirmed.

▶ **ANALYSIS**

Until relatively recently, fault had to be found before a divorce was granted. This led to many collusive suits and many distasteful trials. Some jurisdictions only recognized adultery as a ground for divorce, leading to many couples living together in misery rather than being allowed to divorce. The current standard allows for no-fault divorce where a mere showing of either party of irreconcilable differences will allow for a divorce.

Quicknotes

ADULTERY Sexual intercourse between a married person and another, who is not that person's spouse, or between a person and another who is married.

NO-FAULT DIVORCE A basis for terminating a marriage without the need for demonstrating misconduct on the part of either spouse.

Hughes v. Hughes

Wife (P) v. Husband (D)

La. Ct. App., 326 So. 2d 877 (1976).

NATURE OF CASE: Appeal from order granting separation from bed and board.

FACT SUMMARY: Mrs. Hughes (P) contended she was entitled to divorce on the basis of mental cruelty due to her husband's abusive behavior toward her and their daughter.

RULE OF LAW
A divorce may be granted on the basis of mental cruelty.

FACTS: Mrs. Hughes (P) contended her husband abused alcohol and treated her indifferently and coldly before ordering her from their home in November 1971. She returned in November 1972, at which time her husband cursed her on many occasions and declared he did not love either her or their daughter. She sued for divorce on the basis of mental cruelty and was granted a separation. Mr. Hughes (D) appealed.

ISSUE: May a divorce be granted on the basis of mental cruelty?

HOLDING AND DECISION: (Price, J.) Yes. A divorce may be granted on the basis of mental cruelty. The course of conduct of Mr. Hughes (D) prior to the separation did not constitute cruelty. However, his statements and actions after the reconciliation destroyed any possibility of cohabitation on a loving basis. Affirmed.

ANALYSIS

Cruelty as a basis for divorce originally was recognized only through physical abuse. It had evolved to the point where it was the most used fault ground for divorce before the advent of no-fault systems. Courts now recognize psychological cruelty as well to support a finding of a breakdown of the marriage.

Quicknotes

NO-FAULT DIVORCE A basis for terminating a marriage without the need for demonstrating misconduct on the part of either spouse.

SEPARATION When a husband and wife cease to cohabitate.

Arnoult v. Arnoult

Wife (P) v. Husband (D)

La. Ct. App., 690 So. 2d 101 (1997).

NATURE OF CASE: Appeal from an order granting Elden Arnoult (D) a divorce from Patricia Arnoult (P) on grounds of adultery.

FACT SUMMARY: When Patricia (P) sued for divorce, Elden (D) also filed a petition for divorce, and later amended his petition to allege Patricia (P) was guilty of adultery.

🏛 RULE OF LAW
A prima facie case of adultery can be made where the only evidence presented is the testimony of hired investigators.

FACTS: After Patricia (P) petitioned the court for a divorce, Elden (D) also filed for divorce, alleging Patricia (P) had committed adultery after they had physically separated, but prior to a ruling on the divorce proceeding. Two private investigators hired by Elden (D) testified they had seen her kissing and hugging another man. Patricia (D) denied committing adultery. Circumstantial evidence presented was found to be sufficient by the trial court. The trial court found from the totality of the evidence presented that Patricia (P) had committed post-separation adultery, and granted Elden (D) a divorce on those grounds. Patricia (P) appealed.

ISSUE: May a prima facie case of adultery be made where the only evidence presented is the testimony of hired investigators?

HOLDING AND DECISION: (Daley, J.) Yes. A prima facie case of adultery can be made where the only evidence presented is the testimony of hired investigators. Although any testimony from an investigator hired by one spouse to watch the other spouse should be corroborated by other evidence or testimony, a prima facie case of adultery can be made out by showing facts or circumstances that lead fairly and necessarily to the conclusion that adultery has been committed. After observing the demeanor of the witnesses, the trial court found the testimony of the investigators more credible than that of the other witnesses. The trial court's factual findings were not manifestly erroneous. Affirmed.

▍ANALYSIS

The court in this case supported the trial court's factual findings because the trial court had the ability to evaluate the credibility of Patricia's (P) denials. The investigators testified that they had seen Patricia (P) with another man on two different occasions. Once, Patricia (D) was observed to have spent the night at the other man's home.

◼◼◼

Quicknotes

ADULTERY Sexual intercourse between a married person and another, who is not that person's spouse, or between a person and another who is married.

CIRCUMSTANTIAL EVIDENCE Evidence that, though not directly observed, supports the inference of principal facts.

PRIMA FACIE CASE An action where the plaintiff introduces sufficient evidence to submit the issue to the judge or jury for determination.

◼◼◼

Crosby v. Crosby

Wife (P) v. Husband (D)

La. Ct. App., 434 So. 2d 162 (1983).

NATURE OF CASE: Appeal from denial of alimony.

FACT SUMMARY: The trial court found Mrs. Crosby (P) was not free from fault in the breakup of her marriage and, thus, denied her an award of permanent alimony.

🏛 RULE OF LAW
A statute requiring a wife to abide by the domicile decisions of her husband is unconstitutional, and alimony cannot be denied based on its violation.

FACTS: Mrs. Crosby (P) was married to Mr. Crosby (D) for 18 years. She sued successfully for divorce yet was denied an award of permanent alimony based on her refusal to follow her husband's decision to change domiciles. This violated a Louisiana statute binding a wife to a husband's domicile decisions. On the basis of this resolution, the court found she was not completely without fault in the divorce and, thus, not entitled to permanent alimony. She appealed, contending the domicile statute violated equal protection.

ISSUE: Is a statute requiring a wife to abide by the domicile decision of her husband unconstitutional and any denial of alimony for its violation invalid?

HOLDING AND DECISION: (Gaudin, J.) Yes. A statute requiring a wife to abide by the domicile decisions of her husband is unconstitutional, and alimony cannot be denied for its violation. Such statute clearly discriminates on the basis of gender and is not substantially related to serving any important governmental interests. Thus, the case must be remanded for a determination whether Mrs. Crosby (P) was clear of fault in the absence of the statute.

▶ ANALYSIS

A slim majority of states recognize desertion as a valid ground for divorce. At common law, a woman lost her legal existence upon marriage and became her husband's chattel. This is the basis for the domicile requirement. As the chattel theory has been abrogated, so has the domicile concept.

Quicknotes

ALIMONY Allowances (usually monetary) which husband or wife by court order pays other spouse for maintenance while they are separated, or after they are divorced (permanent alimony), or temporarily, pending a suit for divorce (pendente lite).

CHATTEL An article of personal property, as distinguished from real property; a thing personal and movable.

EQUAL PROTECTION A constitutional guarantee that no person shall be denied the same protection of the laws enjoyed by other persons in life circumstances.

Rankin v. Rankin

Husband (P) v. Wife (D)

Pa. Super. Ct., 181 Pa. Super. 414, 124 A.2d 639 (1956).

NATURE OF CASE: Appeal from divorce decree.

FACT SUMMARY: Mrs. Rankin (D) contended the trial court erred in granting her husband a divorce because of his contributory fault in the breakup of the marriage.

🏛 RULE OF LAW
To obtain a divorce on the basis of indignities, it must appear from the evidence that the plaintiff was the injured and innocent spouse.

FACTS: Mr. Rankin (P) sued Mrs. Rankin (D) for divorce on the basis of indignities to the person. He presented evidence indicating his wife, among other things, spit in his face, swore at him, threw water on him, and threatened him with a butcher knife. In defense, Mrs. Rankin (D) presented evidence of Mr. Rankin's (P) use of profanity and his use of physical violence against her. The trial court granted Mr. Rankin (P) a divorce, and Mrs. Rankin (D) appealed, contending Mr. Rankin (P) could not be considered the injured and innocent spouse and thus could not obtain a divorce on the basis of indignities.

ISSUE: Must the plaintiff be found to be the innocent and injured spouse to obtain a divorce on the basis of indignities?

HOLDING AND DECISION: (Wright, J.) Yes. To obtain a divorce on the basis of indignities, it must appear from the evidence that the plaintiff was the injured and innocent spouse. In this case, the evidence indicated both spouses had visited physical and emotional abuse on the other. Thus, neither could be considered the innocent and injured party, and the divorce should not have been granted. Reversed.

▶ ANALYSIS

In a fault system of divorce, one available defense was recrimination, as illustrated by this case. Many defenses date back to the ecclesiastical courts, which fashioned them to protect women from suffering extreme economic hardship as a result of the divorce. Today, the use of recrimination does not enjoy the same rationale and thus is not widely recognized.

■=■

Quicknotes

RECRIMINATION An allegation by a defendant against a plaintiff in a divorce action of some misconduct on the part of the plaintiff, resulting in the barring of dissolution of the marriage.

■=■

Sargent v. Sargent

Husband (P) v. Wife (D)

N.J. Ch. Ct., 114 A. 428 (1920).

NATURE OF CASE: Petition for divorce for adultery.

FACT SUMMARY: Sargent (P) sued for divorce, contending his wife committed adultery with his chauffeur.

🏛 RULE OF LAW
A spouse providing the other spouse with the opportunity and inducement to commit adultery cannot obtain a divorce when such is committed.

FACTS: Sargent (P), suspecting his wife would commit adultery with his chauffeur, left her alone with him on several occasions and did nothing to prevent contact between them. He then petitioned for divorce on the basis of adultery.

ISSUE: Can a spouse providing the other spouse the opportunity and inducement to commit adultery obtain a divorce by showing the act was committed?

HOLDING AND DECISION: (Fielder, J.) No. A spouse providing the other spouse with the opportunity and inducement to commit adultery cannot obtain a divorce when such is committed. Mr. Sargent (P) clearly had reason to believe his wife was inclined toward adultery. Therefore, he should have terminated the chauffeur and kept him away from her. His failure to do so implies his consent to such actions, and he cannot rely thereon to obtain a divorce. Petition denied.

▶ ANALYSIS

The defense illustrated by this case is known as connivance. This is present where the petitioning spouse implicitly induces the other spouse to commit an actionable offense. This, like many defenses, dates back to the common law and is not codified.

Quicknotes

ACTIONABLE Unlawful activity from which a cause of action may arise.

ADULTERY Sexual intercourse between a married person and another, who is not that person's spouse, or between a person and another who is married.

CONNIVANCE In a suit for divorce, a defense that the plaintiff impliedly or expressly consented to or authorized an unlawful act committed by the defendant.

Willan v. Willan

Husband (P) v. Wife (D)

England and Wales Ct. App., 2 All E.R. 463 (1960).

NATURE OF CASE: Appeal from denial of divorce petition.

FACT SUMMARY: The trial court denied Mr. Willan's (P) petition for divorce on the ground he had condoned the cruelty he had charged.

🏛 RULE OF LAW
Condonation of cruelty eliminates it as a viable ground for divorce.

FACTS: Willan (P) contended his wife repeatedly assaulted him and used profanity toward him. She constantly pestered him to engage in sexual intercourse and physically abused him until he agreed. He continued to live and have sexual intercourse with his wife for many years. He finally left her and sued for divorce on the basis of cruelty. His petition was denied on the ground he had condoned any cruelty visited upon him. He appealed.

ISSUE: Does condonation of cruelty eliminate it as a viable ground for divorce?

HOLDING AND DECISION: (Willmer, L.J.) Yes. Condonation of cruelty eliminates it as a viable ground for divorce. The fact that Willan (P) engaged in sexual intercourse indicates some degree of voluntary behavior in the conduct of his marriage. While his wife's conduct could clearly constitute cruelty, his failure to leave the house constituted condonation of such, and he cannot now obtain the relief sought. Affirmed.

▶ ANALYSIS

The court rejected Willan's (P) argument that the cruelty was revived by his spouse's actions taken after a brief reconciliation. Had this argument been accepted, the defense of condonation would have been defeated. Some critics have argued that the defense of condonation is irreconcilable with society's interest in promoting reconciliation between spouses.

■=■

Fuchs v. Fuchs

Husband (P) v. Wife (D)

N.Y. Sup. Ct., 64 N.Y.S.2d 487 (1946).

NATURE OF CASE: Motions to set aside divorce decree entered by default.

FACT SUMMARY: Mrs. Fuchs (D) moved to set aside a default judgment of divorce which she voluntarily allowed to be entered against her pursuant to an agreement with Mr. Fuchs (P).

🏛 **RULE OF LAW**
A party who collusively allows a default judgment of divorce to be entered against him may set the judgment aside and litigate the case on its merits.

FACTS: The Fuchses agreed that in exchange for full custody of their child, Mrs. Fuchs (D) would allow a default judgment of divorce to be entered against her. The judgment was so entered, and Mr. Fuchs (P) remarried. Mrs. Fuchs (D) subsequently moved to set aside the default.

ISSUE: May a party who collusively allows a default judgment of divorce to be entered against him set the judgment aside and litigate the matter on its merits?

HOLDING AND DECISION: (Daly, J.) Yes. A party who collusively allows a default judgment of divorce to be entered against him may set the default aside and litigate the case on its merits. In other types of civil litigation, a party voluntarily submitting to a default would be barred from setting it aside. However, the state has an interest in the integrity of the marital relationship, and, thus, a collusively entered default is an attempt to abrogate the state's right to regulate the process of divorce. Thus, this default may be set aside.

▶ *ANALYSIS*

The court found no impediment to its decision to set aside the default in the fact the husband had remarried. It explained that the divorce decree would stand, pending a trial on the merits. If the defendant was successful, this divorce complaint would be dismissed and the decree set aside. If the defense was unsuccessful, the decree would stand to protect the second wife.

Quicknotes

COLLUSION An agreement between two or more parties to engage in unlawful conduct or in other activities with an unlawful goal, typically involving fraud.

DEFAULT JUDGMENT A judgment entered against a defendant due to his failure to appear in a court or defend himself against the allegations of the opposing party.

DIVORCE DECREE A decree terminating a marriage.

Anonymous v. Anonymous

Husband (P) v. Wife (D)

N.Y. Sup. Ct., 37 Misc. 2d 773, 236 N.Y.S.2d 288 (1962).

NATURE OF CASE: Action for divorce on grounds of adultery.

FACT SUMMARY: Wife (D) contended she was suffering from mental and emotional disorders so as to make her incompetent and not responsible for the charged act of adultery and therefore asserted Husband's (P) petition for divorce should be denied.

🏛 RULE OF LAW
Insanity, as a defense to a divorce action, must be proved by the defendant by a preponderance of the evidence, overcoming a presumption of sanity.

FACTS: Husband (P) sued Wife (D) for divorce. Wife (D) presented evidence through the testimony of her psychiatrist indicating she was mistreated by him and that she felt forced to commit adultery to get back at her father and her Husband (P). The psychiatrist testified that Wife (D) did not or could not determine the act was wrong; however, she did resist the act. Husband (P) presented psychiatric testimony indicating she was able to determine right from wrong and, therefore, was sane at the time of the act.

ISSUE: Must a defendant overcome a presumption of sanity in order to successfully assert insanity as a defense in a divorce action?

HOLDING AND DECISION: (Meyer, J.) Yes. A defendant must overcome a presumption of sanity in order to successfully assert insanity as a defense in a divorce action. In this case, Wife (D) indicated she resisted the act of adultery but felt compelled to carry through in order to get back at her father and Husband (P). This clearly indicates she perceived the act as wrong; otherwise, it would not have its desired effect. Thus, Wife (D) failed to meet her burden of proof. Divorce granted to Husband (P).

▌ANALYSIS

The rationale behind recognizing insanity as a defense in divorce actions is the common law notion of the husband's duty to support the wife, which includes the obligation to supply medical care. While the defense is recognized, it is not codified. Thus, courts have difficulty determining the applicable standard of sanity to use. Some courts borrow the test of sanity from criminal law. The court in this case felt it unnecessary to apply any particular standard as it felt Wife (D) failed to meet her burden under any standard.

Quicknotes

ADULTERY Sexual intercourse between a married person and another, who is not that person's spouse, or between a person and another who is married.

INSANITY DEFENSE An affirmative defense to a criminal prosecution that the defendant suffered from a mental illness, thereby relieving him of liability for his conduct.

In re Marriage of Dennis D. Kenik

Parties not identified.

Ill. Ct. App., 181 Ill. App. 3d 266, 536 N.E. 2d 982 (1989).

NATURE OF CASE: Appeal from entry of divorce order.

FACT SUMMARY: The judgment for dissolution of marriage was entered despite uncontradicted testimony that the parties had not lived in separate residences for the statutory two-year period.

⚖ RULE OF LAW
The requirement that parties seeking dissolution of marriage live "separate and apart" does not mean separate residences.

FACTS: Dennis and Irene Kenik ended marital relations one year prior to filing a divorce petition, lived in separate bedrooms, had separate finances, and engaged in limited communication. In February 1986, Irene received an order for temporary support maintenance with Dennis to pay one half of monthly household expenses and for their child, and each party was responsible for individual personal expenses. In August or September 1986, the two parties moved to separate residences. Their living arrangement was not contradicted at the hearing on January 21, 1988. The judge entered a judgment of dissolution of marriage. Dennis appealed, claiming that the parties did not live "separate and apart" for the statutory two-year period.

ISSUE: Does the requirement that parties seeking a dissolution of marriage live "separate and apart" mean separate residences?

HOLDING AND DECISION: (Hartman, J.) No. The requirement that parties seeking a dissolution of marriage live "separate and apart" does not mean separate residences. The Illinois Marriage and Dissolution of Marriage Act requires parties to live "separate and apart" for two years continuously. Legislative history reveals the intent for a broad reading of the phrase "separate and apart." Illinois case law has held that "separate and apart" means separate lives rather than separate residences. Dennis cites to Illinois case law interpreting "separate abode," rather than "separate and apart," as well as case law from other jurisdictions. Here, the parties clearly lived separate lives, thus satisfying the statutory requirement, despite not having lived in separate residences continuously for a full two years. Judgment affirmed.

▶ ANALYSIS

Illinois allows for attempts at reconciliation during the two-year period that does not count against the couple if the reconciliation fails. Critics decry any statutory waiting period because couples making the dissolution decision should not be subject to court attempts to force a family to stay together. On the other hand, it is clearly public policy to support intact families and reconciliation in cases of marriages in trouble. The existence of waiting periods is meant to avoid rash decisions to end a marriage.

■══■

Quicknotes

DISSOLUTION Annulment or termination of a formal or legal bond, tie or contract.

PUBLIC POLICY Policy administered by the state with respect to the health, safety and morals of its people in accordance with common notions of fairness and decency.

SPOUSAL SUPPORT Payments made by one spouse to another in discharge of the spouse's duty pursuant to law, or in accordance with a written divorce or separation decree, in order to provide maintenance for the other spouse.

■══■

Massar v. Massar

Wife (P) v. Husband (D)

N.J. Super. Ct., 279 N.J. Super. 89, 652 A.2d 219 (1995).

NATURE OF CASE: Appeal from an order enforcing an agreement limiting grounds for divorce.

FACT SUMMARY: After the parties had signed an agreement not to seek termination of the marriage for any reason other than eighteen months continuous separation, Mrs. Massar (P) filed a complaint for divorce on grounds of extreme cruelty.

🏛 **RULE OF LAW**
The enforceability of negotiated provisions in agreements between spouses is subject to review on a case-by-case basis to determine if the application of the provision is fair and just according to the circumstances of the particular case.

FACTS: Prior to their marriage, the second for both, the Massars signed a prenuptial agreement. When the marriage later deteriorated, they signed an agreement not to seek termination of the marriage for any reason other than eighteen months continuous separation. Pursuant to this agreement, Mr. Massar (D) moved out of the family home. Mrs. Massar (P) filed a complaint for divorce on the ground of extreme cruelty six months later. Mr. Massar (D) filed a motion to dismiss the complaint and enforce the prenuptial agreement. The court upheld the agreement and dismissed the complaint, finding that no fact issue concerning duress was established, and that the agreement was supported by consideration. Mrs. Massar (P) appealed from that portion of the order enforcing the agreement to seek a divorce solely on "no fault" grounds.

ISSUE: Is the enforceability of negotiated provisions in agreements between spouses subject to review on a case-by-case basis to determine if the application of the provision is fair and just according to the circumstances of the particular case?

HOLDING AND DECISION: (Cuff, J.) Yes. The enforceability of negotiated provisions in agreements between spouses is subject to review on a case-by-case basis to determine if the application of the provision is fair and just according to the circumstances of the particular case. There is insufficient evidence to suggest that Mrs. Massar's written (P) waiver of any cause of action other than no-fault divorce was not a knowing and voluntary act, and a plenary hearing was not warranted. The court declines to adopt a per se rule that agreements confining a spouse to a particular cause of action are against public policy and unenforceable. There is no suggestion in this record of any physical or mental abuse, and the record suggested that Mrs. Massar (P) filed the complaint for divorce only when her initial proposal for equitable distribution was not instantly embraced by Mr. Massar (D). Affirmed.

▶ **ANALYSIS**

The court in this case noted that marital agreements are essentially consensual and voluntary and, as a result, they are approached with a predisposition in favor of their validity and enforceability. The state does not promote divorce and has always had a strong public interest in promoting marriage. The court further noted that there was good reason to encourage a cooling-off period for spouses to assess their relationship.

■■■

Quicknotes

ANTENUPTIAL AGREEMENT An agreement entered into by two individuals, in contemplation of their impending marriage, in order to determine their rights and interests in property upon dissolution or death.

DURESS Unlawful threats or other coercive behavior by one person that causes another to commit acts that he would not otherwise do.

NO-FAULT DIVORCE A basis for terminating a marriage without the need for demonstrating misconduct on the part of either spouse.

PER SE By itself; not requiring additional evidence for proof.

PUBLIC POLICY Policy administered by the state with respect to the health, safety and morals of its people in accordance with common notions of fairness and decency.

■■■

Diosdado v. Diosdado

Abandoned wife (P) v. Unfaithful husband (D)

Cal. Ct. App., 97 Cal. App. 4th 470, 118 Cal. Rptr. 2d 494 (2002).

NATURE OF CASE: Appeal from grant of judgment on the pleadings.

FACT SUMMARY: Donna Diosdado (P) sued for breach of contract, seeking liquidated damages as specified in the "Marital Settlement Agreement" previously signed by both Manuel Diosdado (D) and Donna (P).

🏛 RULE OF LAW
A contract between a husband and wife providing for liquidated damages if one is sexually unfaithful is unenforceable.

FACTS: Manuel (D) had an affair resulting in Donna's (P) moving out of the marital home. Manuel (D) and Donna (P) agreed to preserve the marriage and entered into a "Marital Settlement Agreement," which included a liquidated damages clause if either spouse was shown in court to have been unfaithful. A few years after Manuel (D) and Donna (P) signed this agreement, Manuel (D) had another affair. The parties separated and later divorced. Donna (P) filed a breach of contract action, seeking liquidated damages as specified in the settlement. The trial court granted judgment on the pleadings on its own motion in favor of Manuel (D). Donna (P) appealed.

ISSUE: Is a contract between a husband and wife providing for liquidated damages in the event one is sexually unfaithful to the other enforceable?

HOLDING AND DECISION: (Epstein, Acting P.J.) No. A contract between a husband and a wife providing for liquidated damages in the event of sexual unfaithfulness is not enforceable. The trial court determined that the agreement was unenforceable because it ran contrary to the state's public policy of no-fault divorce. If the contract's purpose is to find a marital party at "fault," then the contract has no "lawful object" as required by state statute. Donna's (P) argument that the contract here is similar to premarital contracts upheld by courts fails because marital contracts are limited by statute and social policy. Affirmed.

▶ ANALYSIS

The majority of states have abolished the tort of alienation of affections, and contracts such as the one in *Diosdado* may appear to be an attempt to reestablish the tort. Courts must be wary of marital agreements which penalize partners because of fault when most divorces in today's society are "no-fault." Also, marital contracts must be limited by statute and social policy, or spouses could unwittingly contract away rights in alimony or custody.

■=■

Quicknotes

ALIENATION OF AFFECTIONS A cause of action arising from the willful and malicious interference with a marital relationship.

NO-FAULT DIVORCE A basis for terminating a marriage without the need for demonstrating misconduct on the part of either spouse.

PUBLIC POLICY Policy administered by the state with respect to the health, safety and morals of its people in accordance with common notions of fairness and decency.

■=■

Twyman v. Twyman

Wife (P) v. Husband (D)

Tex. Sup. Ct., 855 S.W.2d 619 (1993).

NATURE OF CASE: Appeal from an award of damages for negligent infliction of emotional distress in a divorce action.

FACT SUMMARY: Sheila Twyman (P) added an action for infliction of emotional distress to her divorce petition.

 RULE OF LAW
An action for intentional infliction of emotional distress may be joined with a divorce suit.

FACTS: Sheila (P) and William Twyman (D) married in 1969. In 1985, Sheila (P) filed for divorce and added a general claim for emotional harm, alleging that William attempted to engage her in deviant sexual acts. The trial court dissolved the marriage, divided the marital estate, and awarded Sheila (P) $15,000 for her emotional distress claim. William (D) appealed the emotional distress portion of the judgment, contending that interspousal tort immunity barred recovery for negligent infliction of emotional distress. The court of appeals affirmed, and William (D) appealed. While the case was still pending, the Texas Supreme Court refused to adopt the tort of negligent infliction of emotional distress. Consequently, the supreme court granted review of William's (D) appeal to determine whether the court of appeals' judgment could be affirmed on alternative grounds.

ISSUE: Can an action for intentional infliction of emotional distress be joined with a divorce suit?

HOLDING AND DECISION: (Cornyn, J.) Yes. An action for intentional infliction of emotional distress may be joined with a divorce suit. The Restatement (Second) of Torts provides a tort remedy for intentional infliction of emotional distress. The required elements are: (1) the defendant acted intentionally or recklessly; (2) the conduct was extreme and outrageous; and (3) the actions caused the plaintiff to suffer severe emotional distress. Forty-six states recognize this tort, and forty-three have adopted the Restatement formulation. Texas should recognize this tort because the rigorous legal standards of the Restatement strike a reasonable balance between the competing public interests. Interspousal tort immunity has been abolished for intentional torts for nearly twenty years. Thus, there is no impediment to prevent spouses from bringing such an action. The joinder of tort claims to the divorce action is encouraged because it avoids the need for two trials and can settle all of the matters existing between the parties in a single proceeding. However, trial courts must be careful not to allow double recovery of damages when the intentional infliction claim is joined with a divorce action. This case must be remanded to determine whether Sheila (P) can recover on a claim of intentional infliction of emotional distress. Reversed and remanded.

CONCURRENCE AND DISSENT: (Phillips, C.J.) When marriages break, it is inevitable that the parties will suffer emotional distress. Courts handling divorce actions already have discretion to divide community property taking into account one party's extreme conduct. The court should recognize the tort but disallow it between spouses, as most states have held.

CONCURRENCE AND DISSENT: (Hecht, J.) The tort of intentional infliction of emotional distress is too broad and subjective. It will result in erratic decisions since there is no clear standard.

DISSENT: (Spector, J.) The negligent infliction of emotional distress is a necessary tort action to protect women from men's outrageous conduct. The majority has done women a great disservice in abolishing an alternative way of righting a grievous wrong.

▶ ANALYSIS

Justice Hecht further described in greater detail the claims made by Sheila Twyman (P). Hecht made the valid point that sexual relations between spouses are so intimate that any perceived breach by one of the spouses will be the cause of great distress to the other party. Such an inquiry by the courts into marital sexual conduct is too great an intrusion.

■■■

Quicknotes

INTENTIONAL INFLICTION OF EMOTIONAL DISTRESS Intentional and extreme behavior on the part of the wrongdoer with the intent to cause the victim to suffer from severe emotional distress, or with reckless indifference, resulting in the victim's suffering from severe emotional distress.

INTERSPOUSAL IMMUNITY A common law doctrine precluding spouses from commencing actions against one another. Some states have abolished the doctrine.

JOINDER OF CLAIMS The joining of claims in a single suit by a party; the party seeking relief may join as many claims as he has against the opposing party.

■■■

Aflalo v. Aflalo

Wife (P) v. Husband (D)

N.J. Super. Ct., 295 N.J. Super. 527, 685 A.2d 523 (1996).

NATURE OF CASE: Motion to be relieved as counsel for defendant when ordered to consent to a Jewish divorce.

FACT SUMMARY: When Sondra Aflalo (P) sued for dissolution of marriage, and Henry Aflalo (D) answered that he did not want a divorce and had applied to Jewish authorities to have a hearing on his attempts at reconciliation, Henry's (D) attorney moved to be relieved as counsel.

> 🏛 **RULE OF LAW**
> Where resolution of the disputes cannot be made without extensive inquiry by civil courts into religious law and polity, the First and Fourteenth Amendments mandate that civil courts shall not disturb the decisions of the highest ecclesiastical tribunal within a church of hierarchical polity, but must accept such decisions as binding on them, in their application to the religious issues of doctrine or polity before them.

FACTS: The Aflalos were married in Israel and had one daughter. Sondra Aflalo (P) sued for divorce and Henry (D) refused to provide a "get," which is required by Jewish law in order for the divorce to be final. Henry (D) did not want a divorce and took action with the Union of Orthodox Rabbis of the United States (the Beth Din) to have a hearing on his attempts at reconciliation. Henry's (D) attorney claimed that, as a practicing Orthodox Jew, he would definitely have a religious problem representing a man who refused to give his wife a "get" at the conclusion of a divorce proceeding, and sought to be relieved as counsel. Sondra (P) also sought a court order requiring Henry (D) to cooperate with the obtaining of a Jewish divorce upon pain of having his visitation rights curtailed.

ISSUE: Where resolution of the disputes cannot be made without extensive inquiry by civil courts into religious law and polity, do the First and Fourteenth Amendments mandate that civil courts shall not disturb the decisions of the highest ecclesiastical tribunal within a church of hierarchical polity, but must accept such decisions as binding on them, in their application to the religious issues of doctrine or polity before them?

HOLDING AND DECISION: (Fisher, J.) Yes. Where resolution of the disputes cannot be made without extensive inquiry by civil courts into religious law and polity, the First and Fourteenth Amendments mandate that civil courts shall not disturb the decisions of the highest ecclesiastical tribunal within a church of hierarchical polity, but must accept such decisions as binding on them, in their

application to the religious issues of doctrine or polity before them. Civil courts cannot override a decision of a religious tribunal or interpret religious law or canons. The Free Exercise Clause prohibits governmental regulation of religious beliefs. To pass constitutional muster, a law must have both a secular purpose and a secular effect; it must not be based upon a disagreement with a religious tenet or practice. In attempting to coerce Henry (D), the civil court would be, in essence, overruling or superseding any judgment which the Beth Din can or will enter, contrary to First Amendment principles. Since Henry (D) stated under oath that he would follow the recommendations of the Beth Din, and would give the "get" if that was the end result of those proceedings, his counsel's stated concerns are eliminated. For these reasons, the court denies the motion to be relieved as counsel. Any relief sought by either party with respect to any proceedings either currently being maintained or contemplated in the Beth Din is denied. The parties are directed to engage in a four-way conference within seven days and to report back to the court. Henry's (D) consent, or refusal to consent, to the providing of a "get," and Sondra's (P) consent or refusal to appear before the Beth Din are matters which are not to be bargained for or against. Motions denied.

⬛ **ANALYSIS**

The court in this case disapproved of the holding of a prior case. In *Minkin v. Minkin*, 180 N.J. Super. 260, 434 A.2d 665 (Child. Diversity. 1981), the court, relying on expert testimony that the acquisition of a "get" was not a religious act, granted an order compelling the husband to secure a "get." The New York legislature has passed a law requiring a husband of the Jewish faith to provide his wife with a "get."

■═■

Quicknotes

FIRST AMENDMENT Prohibits Congress from enacting any law respecting an establishment of religion, prohibiting the free exercise of religion, abridging freedom of speech or the press, the right of peaceful assembly and the right to petition for a redress of grievances.

FREE EXERCISE OF RELIGION The right to practice one's religious beliefs free from governmental conduct or interference.

"GET" A bill of divorce in Jewish law which the husband gives to his wife to free her to marry again.

■═■

Boddie v. Connecticut

Married indigent (P) v. State (D)

401 U.S. 371 (1971).

NATURE OF CASE: Action for declaratory judgment on constitutionality of state statute.

FACT SUMMARY: Indigents claimed that a state law requiring court fees for the filing of a divorce action denied them access to the courts and that the law was a denial of due process as applied to them.

RULE OF LAW

Under the Due Process Clause, states may not require, as a condition for judicial dissolution of marriage, the payment of court fees from indigent persons who in good faith seek a divorce.

FACTS: Boddie (P) and other similarly situated welfare recipients brought an action for declaratory judgment in federal court challenging certain state requirements for the commencement of litigation as those rules were applied to them. Connecticut law required the payment of $45 when filing an action for divorce. An additional $15 was required for service of process by the sheriff. Potentially, fees could increase another $50 if notice by publication were required. Boddie (P) and other plaintiffs were unsuccessful in their attempt to bring their divorce actions in the state court only because they were indigent and unable to pay the court fees and costs. A three-judge federal court concluded that a state could require fees which effectively barred indigents from commencing actions for divorce.

ISSUE: Does the Due Process Clause prohibit a state from denying access to its courts to individuals who seek a judicial divorce solely on the ground of those individuals' inability to pay court fees?

HOLDING AND DECISION: (Harlan, J.) Yes. The state monopolizes the means of dissolving the marriage relationship, which involves interests which are of basic importance to society. Due process requires that, absent a countervailing state interest of overriding importance, persons forced to settle their claims through the judicial process must be given a meaningful opportunity to be heard. The state's interests in preventing frivolous litigation, in using court fees to allocate scarce judicial resources, and in balancing the defendant's rights to notice and the plaintiff's right to access to the court are not sufficient in overcoming the interests of indigents in having access to the only possible means of obtaining a divorce. This holding is limited to good faith litigation, and there are other alternatives open to provide notice and allocate the costs without denying indigents access to the courts. This law is constitutionally invalid as it is applied to indigents because it operates to deprive them of a protected right, although the law's validity as a measure enacted under the police power of the state is beyond question. A state may not preempt the right to dissolve marriage without affording all citizens access to the means for doing so.

▶ ANALYSIS

At early common law, absolute divorce was unknown because marriage was based on a religious sacrament and thus indissoluble. From that beginning, the marriage relationship, at least in its dissolution, was in the sole control of the state. This case simply extends other decisions concerning due process and indigents. Whenever the state extends a right to all people, that right cannot be denied because it cannot be afforded. One of the clearest examples of this arises in criminal law. Following conviction, appeal has become an almost matter-of-fact stage in the judicial process. Transcripts of the trial must be included with the appellate briefs. An indigent cannot be denied the right to appeal simply because he cannot afford to pay for a copy of the transcript. The state must provide a copy without charge to the indigent. Similarly, where the state extends the availability of divorce to everyone, some cannot be denied the right to such action because they cannot afford to pay filing fees.

Quicknotes

DECLARATORY JUDGMENT A judgment of the court establishing the rights of the parties.

DUE PROCESS CLAUSE Clauses found in the Fifth and Fourteenth Amendments to the United States Constitution providing that no person shall be deprived of "life, liberty, or property, without due process of law."

Sosna v. Iowa

Wife (P) v. State (D)

419 U.S. 393 (1975).

NATURE OF CASE: Appeal from dismissal of divorce petition.

FACT SUMMARY: Sosna (P) contended that Iowa's (D) durational residency requirement for divorce decrees was unconstitutional.

🏛 RULE OF LAW
States may constitutionally provide for durational residency requirements for divorce decrees.

FACTS: Sosna (P), after separating from her husband in New York, moved to Iowa. After residing in Iowa for one month, she filed for divorce. Her husband successfully attacked the Iowa court's jurisdiction on the basis of a state statute requiring a one-year residency in the state prior to entitlement to petition for divorce. Sosna (P) appealed the dismissal of her petition, contending the durational residency requirement was unconstitutional as in violation of equal protection and the right to travel. The court of appeal and Iowa Supreme Court affirmed, and Sosna (P) appealed to the U.S. Supreme Court.

ISSUE: May states impose durational residency requirements on petitioners for divorce?

HOLDING AND DECISION: (Rehnquist, J.) Yes. States may impose durational residency requirements on petitioners for divorce. Divorce has traditionally been an area left exclusively to state regulation. It is also an area in which both spouses are equally interested. Thus, allowing one spouse to obtain a decree in a foreign state would unreasonably infringe on the other spouse's right to contest the action. As a result, the residency requirement was valid. Affirmed.

DISSENT: (Marshall, J.) Delaying access to state courts forces parties to endure marriage for an arbitrary time period.

▶ ANALYSIS

The majority indicates that while durational residency requirements may be unconstitutional when applied to medical or welfare benefits, divorce is of a different nature. The harm done is less severe and completely reversible upon the lapse of the time period involved. Thus, the degree of harm is negligible on balance with the state interest involved.

■≡■

Quicknotes

EQUAL PROTECTION CLAUSE A constitutional provision that each person be guaranteed the same protection of the laws enjoyed by other persons in like circumstances.

RESIDENCY REQUIREMENTS Requirements imposed by the states in order to receive the privileges and benefits of residing therein.

■≡■

Custody of Children

Quick Reference Rules of Law

In re Marriage of Carney

Father (P) v. Mother (D)

Cal. Sup. Ct., 24 Cal. 3d 725, 598 P.2d 36 (1979).

NATURE OF CASE: Appeal from custody order.

FACT SUMMARY: William Carney (P) contended that the trial court unconstitutionally deprived him of custody of his children based upon his physical handicap.

🏛 RULE OF LAW
A physical handicap that affects a parent's ability to participate with his children in purely physical activities may not by itself be used to deny custody.

FACTS: The Carneys were married in 1968, and two sons were born of the marriage. In 1972, Mrs. Carney (D) left her husband and sons and relinquished custody of the children to Mr. Carney (P). In 1976, Mr. Carney (P) was paralyzed and rendered a quadriplegic in an automobile accident. Shortly thereafter, he filed for a divorce, and Mrs. Carney (D) petitioned for an order awarding her custody of the children. Mr. Carney (P) was physically unable to take care of himself as well as the two boys. He was living with a woman who took care of him both physically and emotionally. The trial court awarded custody to Mrs. Carney (D), and Mr. Carney (P) appealed.

ISSUE: May a physical handicap by itself be used to deny a parent custody of his children?

HOLDING AND DECISION: (Mosk, J.) No. "A physical handicap that affects a parent's ability to participate with his children in purely physical activities is not a changed circumstance of sufficient relevance and materiality to render it either essential or expedient for their welfare that they be taken from his custody." The overwhelming weight of the evidence presented at trial indicated that Mr. Carney (P) demonstrated a superior ability to act as parent to the boys. The sole reason for the trial court's decision to change custody was his physical disability. The physical disability was not proven to act so as to contravene the children's best interest, and the custody should not have been changed. Reversed.

▶ ANALYSIS

Because Mr. Carney (P) had exercised custody for approximately five years prior to the divorce, it was necessary for Mrs. Carney (D) to show a change in circumstances in order to change custody. The court in this case indicated that the physical handicap suffered by Mr. Carney (P) was not a sufficient change in circumstance to allow for a change in custody. Clearly, however, the issue to be resolved is what would be in the children's best interest. It is clear from the record that Mr. Carney's (P) exercise of custody

was clearly in the children's best interest, and, therefore, custody remained with him.

Quicknotes

BEST INTERESTS OF CHILD Standard used by courts when rendering decisions which involve a child or children.

CUSTODY The granting of care and control of a child or children to a parent pursuant to an action for dissolution or separation.

Hollon v. Hollon

Parties not identified.

Miss. Sup. Ct., 784 So. 2d 943 (2001).

NATURE OF CASE: Appeal of custody award.

FACT SUMMARY: Custody of the couple's minor son was awarded to the father after allegations of the mother's homosexual lifestyle arose and became a focal point of the custody determination. The mother argued that the custody determination was contrary to the evidence submitted.

🏛 RULE OF LAW
A custody ruling should consider factors related to the "best interest" of the child, and a finding should be made on each factor.

FACTS: Beth had a son from a prior marriage when she met and married Tim. Two years later, Beth and Tim had a son, Zach. The family lived in an apartment provided rent-free because Beth was property manager. Tim was a police officer for the city. The couple separated once, and Beth remained the primary caretaker for the two children. When Zach was just over two, the couple separated again and filed for divorce. Tim moved out of the marital home, and Beth remained the primary caretaker for the two minor children. To cover living expenses, Beth asked a friend, Beth Dukes (Dukes), and her minor son to move in with her and the two children. The five people shared a three-bedroom apartment with Beth's older son having his own bedroom, the two little boys having their own bedroom, and Beth and Dukes sharing a bedroom. At the custody hearing, Beth denied a sexual relationship with Dukes, but another witness testified that Beth had previously admitted the sexual relationship. Tim heard the rumors about Beth and Dukes and entered the apartment to take photographs of the living situation. Pictures of Dukes's clothing in the closet and beer bottles scattered about the apartment were entered into evidence over Beth's objection. During the trial, Beth and her two sons moved into her parents' five-bedroom home temporarily, until they could move into a renovated three-bedroom home provided as part of her new compensation package as property manager. Dukes and her son did not move with them and were not planning to join them in the new home. The court awarded custody of Zach to Tim with visitation rights to Beth. Beth appeals.

ISSUE: Should a custody ruling consider factors related to the "best interest" of the child and a finding be made on each factor?

HOLDING AND DECISION: (Diaz, J.) Yes. A custody ruling should consider factors related to the "best interest" of the child and a finding should be made on each

factor. The court in custody cases must consider the best interest and welfare of the child. The eleven factors are as follows: (1) age, health, and sex of the child; (2) primary caretaker before separation; (3) parent with the best parenting skills and the willingness to be the primary caretaker; (4) parents' employment; (5) parents' health and age; (6) relationship between parent and child; (7) parents' moral fitness; (8) the home, school, and community record of the child; (9) if age appropriate, the child's preference; (10) parents' stability of home and employment; and (11) other relevant factors. The presumption is to affirm the trial court's findings absent abuse of discretion. First, Beth is the preferred parent because the child is under the age of three, and although weakened, the Tender Years doctrine still presumes the mother is the better caretaker for a young child. Second, Tim did not express an interest in being the primary caretaker, nor was he the primary caretaker until allegations of homosexuality arose. Third, Tim did not remain current on child support payments, nor did he exercise his visitations rights with any regularity. Beth was the primary caretaker. Fourth, Tim's employment consists of a set schedule which includes weekends and holidays at times. He also alternates between day shift and night shift. Beth's schedule is thirty-five hours a week with no evenings, weekends, or holidays. Fifth, the factors balance equally between Beth and Tim for their physical and mental health and age. Sixth, the trial court did not find this factor in favor of one parent or the other because Zach is not of the age to express a preference, but the trial court failed to note that Zach had been primarily in Beth's care since the separation. Seventh, the court focused on the moral fitness of Beth. Despite noting that the mere existence of a homosexual lifestyle is not sufficient to award custody to the other parent, the court spent an inordinate amount of time focusing on Beth's alleged sexual behavior. The court also noted the beer bottles being photographed, but did not include findings on Tim's admitted drinking to the point of excess and his gambling habits. The moral factor should have been considered equally among the other factors and should not have been a focus of the finding. The court's finding that Tim's home situation is more favorable than Beth's has no basis in the evidence, given Tim's employment schedule, and the fact that Beth's move resulted from the judge's implication that she should leave the apartment with the Dukes. The court's determination cannot necessarily be said to be manifest error, but it lacked specific findings for the statutory factors. Beth clearly had more factors weighing in her favor and her

Continued on next page.

sexuality should not have been the defining factor. Judgment reversed and remanded to determine Tim's visitation rights.

▶ ANALYSIS

A court must begin with the concept that both parents have equal rights to the child in a custody case. Without enumerated factors to consider, the judiciary would be open to accusations of rampant favoritism depending on the personalities of each parent in each case. With the statutory requirement to find the "best interests" of the child as defined in the eleven steps, courts are more likely to arrive at the true best situation for any particular custody matter. While parents may be more likely to point fingers at bad behavior of the other parent, it is the court's job to rise above the emotion of the issues and determine what is truly in the child's best interests.

■■■

Quicknotes

ABUSE OF DISCRETION A determination by an appellate court that a lower court's decision was based on an error of law.

CHILD SUPPORT Payments made by one parent to another in satisfaction of the non-custodial parent's legal obligation to provide for the sustenance of the child.

CUSTODY The granting of care and control of a child or children to a parent pursuant to an action for dissolution or separation.

TENDER YEARS DOCTRINE Presumption traced back to 1830 that it would violate the laws of nature to remove an infant from the care of its mother; thus, children under the age of four should reside with their mother.

VISITATION Rights awarded by the court in a divorce or custody proceeding to a parent who does not have custody over the child or children, permitting that parent to visit with the child or children.

■■■

Palmore v. Sidoti

Mother (D) v. Father (P)

466 U.S. 429 (1984).

NATURE OF CASE: Appeal from a child custody decree.

FACT SUMMARY: The trial court terminated Palmore's (D) custody of her daughter because, after being awarded custody, Palmore (D) had remarried a man of a different race.

> ## 🏛 RULE OF LAW
> A natural mother cannot be divested of the custody of her child merely because of her remarriage to a person of a different race.

FACTS: Sidoti (P) petitioned for a modification of a prior judgment awarding custody of his daughter to his former wife, Palmore (D), due to Palmore's (D) remarriage to a man outside her race. The trial court found that Palmore (D) and her husband adequately cared for the child; however, the social pressure that would be imposed on the child due to the mixed marriage would be so great that it would be in her best interest to award Sidoti (P) custody. Palmore (D) appealed.

ISSUE: Can a natural mother be divested of custody of her child merely because of her remarriage to a person of a different race?

HOLDING AND DECISION: (Burger, C.J.) No. A natural mother cannot be divested of custody of her child merely because of her remarriage to a person of a different race. Private biases and their prejudicial impact cannot be made to determine judicial decisions. Racial discrimination is wholly contrary to public policy, and custody decisions cannot turn on racial considerations. The trial court held that, but for the mixed marriage, Palmore (D) was fit for custody. To deny custody would be to deny basic constitutional rights. Reversed.

▌ ANALYSIS

The recurring theme permeating child custody determinations is the best interest of the child. What is in the best interest must be decided after evaluating all relevant factors. As such, cases in which a court has based its determination on essentially a single factor are uniformly reversed. In *Moye v. Moye*, 627 P.2d 799 (1981), the Idaho Supreme Court reversed a lower court judgment denying custody to a mother because she was epileptic. Similarly, in *In re Marriage of G.B.S.*, 641 S.W.2d 776 (1982), a Missouri court held that adultery alone could not preclude

custody. The reason these are rejected is that these factors alone do not render a parent unfit for custody.

◼═◼

Quicknotes

BEST INTERESTS OF CHILD Standard used by courts when rendering decisions which involve a child or children.

CUSTODY The granting of care and control of a child or children to a parent pursuant to an action for dissolution or separation.

PUBLIC POLICY Policy administered by the state with respect to the health, safety and morals of its people in accordance with common notions of fairness and decency.

◼═◼

Jones v. Jones

Parties not identified.

542 N.W. 2d 119 (S.D. 1996).

NATURE OF CASE: Appeal of custody award to father.

FACT SUMMARY: Dawn Jones appealed the court's award of custody to her former husband, Kevin Jones, claiming race should not have been a factor in the determination.

> ## 🏛 RULE OF LAW
> The court may properly consider race in a custody determination as the issues relate to a child's ethnic heritage and the more appropriate parent to address that heritage.

FACTS: Dawn Jones, twenty-five, and Kevin Jones, thirty, have three children. Kevin, adopted at age seven, has an extremely close and supportive family. Kevin is an enrolled member of the Sisseton-Wahpeton Dakota Nation, and Dawn is a Caucasian. Kevin has an ownership interest in and works for his family's farm. Kevin and Dawn lived on the farm property with their children. Dawn is in the nursing program at the local community college. Kevin is a recovering alcoholic and has been sober since 1992, and Dawn suffers from depression. The marriage ended due to the alcoholism, depression, financial problems, and lack of communication. When he was drinking, Kevin could exhibit violence toward Dawn and indifference toward his children. The trial court awarded custody to Kevin and rehabilitative alimony to Dawn so that she could complete her nursing program. Dawn appeals.

ISSUE: May the court properly consider race in a custody determination as the issues relate to a child's ethnic heritage and the more appropriate parent to address that heritage?

HOLDING AND DECISION: (Johns, J.) Yes. The court may properly consider race in a custody determination as the issues relate to a child's ethnic heritage and the more appropriate parent to address that heritage. Dawn argues that the trial court impermissibly considered race when awarding custody to Kevin because the children have Native American features and the trial court felt that Kevin could better address their ethnic heritage. Dawn cites *Palmore v. Sidoti*, 466 U.S. 429 (1984), for support for her argument because *Palmore* held that potential prejudice exhibited to a biracial child does not justify removal of that child from an appropriate custodial parent of a race typically not discriminated against. The trial court here noted that it had to make a determination on racially neutral grounds although it also noted Kevin's desire to raise the children in the tribal traditions and his concern that they would be discriminated against outside the family farm. *Palmore* does not require that racial heritage be completely ignored and the better parent to expose a child to that racial heritage is an appropriate consideration. The trial court here stated in its record that it made its decision on racially neutral grounds and this court will not second guess it. Judgment affirmed.

▶ ANALYSIS

Evaluators well-versed in the cultural mores of both the non-dominant and the dominant culture should become familiar with the particular family undergoing a custody evaluation. Children may or may not be highly involved with specific ethnic or cultural traditions and that can affect the custody determination. Evaluators and the courts should also consider the specific parent's understanding of the heritage. While courts cannot make a decision on racial grounds, the factor of race and ethnic heritage certainly has a place in an overall determination of custody and the "best interests" of the child.

■═■

Quicknotes

CUSTODY The granting of care and control of a child or children to a parent pursuant to an action for dissolution or separation.

REHABILITATIVE ALIMONY Payments made by one spouse to another in order to aid that spouse to become self-supporting in the future.

■═■

Kendall v. Kendall

Wife (P) v. Husband (D)

Mass. Sup. Jud. Ct., 426 Mass. 238, 687 N.E.2d 1228 (1997).

NATURE OF CASE: Appeal from provisions of a divorce judgment.

FACT SUMMARY: When Mr. Kendall (D) became a member of a fundamentalist Christian church, his marriage deteriorated, and Mrs. Kendall (P), an Orthodox Jew, filed for divorce and sought to limit the children's exposure to their father's religion.

🏛 RULE OF LAW
When demonstrable evidence of substantial harm to the children has been found, a divorce judgment limiting the children's exposure to religious indoctrination does not burden the parent's right to practice religion under the Free Exercise clauses of the state and federal Constitution.

FACTS: Although the Kendalls had agreed to raise their children in the Jewish religion, Mr. Kendall (D) later became a fundamentalist Christian and wanted to convert his children as well. After filing for divorce, Mrs. Kendall's (P) request for the appointment of a guardian ad litem (GAL) was granted in order to address the inter-religious conflict between the parties. The judge found it substantially damaging to the children to leave each parent free to expose the children to his or her religion and included in the divorce decree certain restrictions upon religious exposure, decreeing that the GAL was to explain the terms of the agreement to the children. Mr. Kendall (D) appealed, arguing that the judge's findings did not demonstrate substantial harm to the children so as to warrant the limitations imposed on his liberty interest in educating his children in the tenets of his religion.

ISSUE: When demonstrable evidence of substantial harm to the children has been found, does a divorce judgment limiting the children's exposure to religious indoctrination burden the parent's right to practice religion under the Free Exercise clauses of the state and federal Constitution?

HOLDING AND DECISION: (Lynch, J.) No. When demonstrable evidence of substantial harm to the children has been found, a divorce judgment limiting the children's exposure to religious indoctrination does not burden the parent's right to practice religion under the Free Exercise clauses of the state and federal Constitution. A diversity of religious experiences may, in particular circumstances, disturb a child to its substantial injury, physical or emotional, and will have a like harmful tendency for the future. The children may experience choosing a religion as choosing between parents, a task that is likely to cause significant emotional distress. Clear evidence of substantial harm has been found in this case. Affirmed.

▶ ANALYSIS

The court in this case afforded substantial weight to the GAL's report. The report indicated that the children considered themselves to be Jewish. The court felt that exposure to their father's belief that those who did not accept his religion were damned to go to hell would cause the children significant emotional distress.

Quicknotes

FIRST AMENDMENT Prohibits Congress from enacting any law respecting an establishment of religion, prohibiting the free exercise of religion, abridging freedom of speech or the press, the right of peaceful assembly and the right to petition for a redress of grievances.

FREE EXERCISE OF RELIGION The right to practice one's religious beliefs free from governmental conduct or interference.

GUARDIAN AD LITEM Person designated by the court to represent an infant or ward in a particular legal proceeding.

LIBERTY INTEREST A right conferred by the Due Process Clauses of the state and federal constitutions.

McMillen v. McMillen

Father (P) v. Mother (D)

Pa. Sup. Ct., 602 A.2d 845, 529 Pa. 198 (1992).

NATURE OF CASE: Appeal from the reversal of an order granting child custody to the father.

FACT SUMMARY: When his son told him that he would rather live with him, Mr. McMillen (P) successfully sought to modify the custody order, but was later reversed on appeal.

🏛 RULE OF LAW
Although the express wishes of a child are not controlling in custody decisions, such wishes do constitute an important factor that must be carefully considered in determining the child's best interests.

FACTS: When the McMillens were divorced, the mother was awarded primary custody. The father (P) repeatedly sought to modify the custody order and finally was awarded custody when the child testified that he preferred to live with his father. On appeal, the court vacated the order and reinstated the previous order based on its determination that the record failed to present any circumstances warranting a change in custody and the child's best interests would not be served by changing custody merely because the child wished it. McMillen (P) appealed.

ISSUE: Although the express wishes of a child are not controlling in custody decisions, do such wishes constitute an important factor that must be carefully considered in determining the child's best interests?

HOLDING AND DECISION: (Larsen, J.) Yes. Although the express wishes of a child are not controlling in custody decisions, such wishes do constitute an important factor that must be carefully considered in determining the child's best interests. The child's steadfast wish to live with his father was properly considered, and there was no abuse of discretion in the amount of weight afforded that preference. Reversed.

▌ ANALYSIS

The scope of review of an appellate court reviewing a child custody order is of the broadest type. The appellate court is not bound by the deductions or inferences made by the trial court from its findings of fact. An appellate court may not interfere with the factual conclusions unless they are unreasonable in view of the trial court's factual findings, and thus represent a gross abuse of discretion.

Quicknotes

ABUSE OF DISCRETION A determination by an appellate court that a lower court's decision was based on an error of law.

BEST INTERESTS OF CHILD Standard used by courts when rendering decisions which involve a child or children.

CUSTODY The granting of care and control of a child or children to a parent pursuant to an action for dissolution or separation.

K.J.B. v. C.M.B.

Parties not identified.

Miss. Ct. App., 779 S.W.2d 36 (1989).

NATURE OF CASE: Appeal from termination of father's visitation and temporary custody.

FACT SUMMARY: Mother sought modification of custody order based on allegations of abuse by the father and paternal grandparents. The father claims he did not have the same discovery opportunities as the mother and seeks review of the termination of his visitation rights.

🏛 RULE OF LAW
The court must consider all factors in custody determination and may not conclusively base a decision on mental health experts' opinions.

FACTS: In October 1987, the mother moved to modify the custody order based on allegations of physical, psychological, and sexual abuse of her two minor children by their father and paternal grandparents. The hearing was continued to January 1988 and psychological counseling was ordered in the meantime. Father and mother agreed upon a counselor, and father was ordered to meet individually with the counselor prior to joint counseling with the two children. Determining that the father was not willing to work on any issues and was simply complying with the court order, the therapist ended counseling with the father after two sessions. The court awarded full custody to the mother and terminated father's visitation rights.

ISSUE: Must the court consider all factors in custody determination and not conclusively base a decision on mental health experts' opinions?

HOLDING AND DECISION: (Karohl, J.) Yes. The court must consider all factors in a custody determination and may not conclusively base a decision on mental health experts' opinions. Father appealed the custody order on several grounds, including that he was denied access to the children for discovery purposes and that the court improperly found that he was unwilling to comply with court orders and the psychological evaluations. Mother and father each retained multiple experts in this case who testified at trial. The father had a psychologist meet with the children, father and mother agreed on a psychologist who met with children, and the children met with two other psychologists pending the hearing. All of the mental health experts opined that the relationship between the children and their father and maternal grandparents was "abnormal." Father's claim that he did not have the same discovery opportunities as the mother to develop expert testimony fails because the children saw multiple experts and the father had at least three opportunities for mental health experts to meet with the children. Father's visitation rights, however, should not have been unilaterally terminated. The therapist met with the father twice and determined that he was not fully cooperating with the psychological process. To the contrary, father complied with every court order and indicated an intention to continue compliance. The therapist's concern seems to be that the father did not admit to the abuse of his children nor did he admit that his parents had abused his children. Such abuse was the subject matter of the hearing and the therapist should not have required such admissions prior to making a determination that it was safe for the children to visit with the father. The therapist also testified that he was not sure what his opinion would be if the abuse allegations were found to be untrue. At trial, many of the allegations were unproven. Counseling in this case was likely premature, given that the issues at trial had to be determined before the therapist felt comfortable with father's compliance with the therapy process. Judgment affirmed in part, reversed in part, and remanded to determine visitation for father.

▶ *ANALYSIS*

A court should not rely conclusively on a mental health expert's opinion because no set standards exist for what constitutes a "good parent." While the opinions are certainly relevant and may be ultimately persuasive, the court should still consider the other factors in the custody determination. Critics also worry that so-called "experts" may have excellent courtroom presentation but are actually incompetent custody evaluators. A court must take all of this into account when including the expert evaluations as part of the custody determination.

Quicknotes

CUSTODY The granting of care and control of a child or children to a parent pursuant to an action for dissolution or separation.

CHILD ABUSE Conduct harmful to a child's physical or mental health.

DISCOVERY Pretrial procedure during which one party makes certain information available to the other.

VISITATION Rights awarded by the court in a divorce or custody proceeding to a parent who does not have custody over the child or children, permitting that parent to visit with the child or children.

Schult v. Schult

Mother (P) v. Father (D)

Conn. Sup. Ct., 241 Conn. 767, 699 A.2d 134 (1997).

NATURE OF CASE: Appeal from an order granting child custody.

FACT SUMMARY: When the child's maternal grandmother intervened in the Schults' dissolution of marriage action and was granted sole custody, the child's guardian ad litem appealed.

> ## RULE OF LAW
> It is within the trial court's discretion to determine, on a case-by-case basis, whether to allow the child's attorney to advocate a position that is different from that recommended by the guardian ad litem.

FACTS: Cheryl Schult (P) brought a dissolution of marriage action against Jeffrey Schult (D) and sought custody of their only child. The child's maternal grandmother intervened and the trial court appointed both an attorney and a guardian ad litem for the child. Jeffrey (D) filed a cross-complaint in which he, too, sought custody of the child. The trial court granted sole custody to the intervenor, at the request of the child's attorney. Cheryl (P) and the guardian ad litem objected, but the trial court overruled their objections. Cheryl (P) appealed, alleging that the trial court abused its discretion by allowing the child's attorney to argue against the recommendation of the child's guardian ad litem.

ISSUE: Is it within the trial court's discretion to determine, on a case-by-case basis, whether to allow the child's attorney to advocate a position that is different from that recommended by the guardian ad litem?

HOLDING AND DECISION: (Borden, J.) Yes. It is within the trial court's discretion to determine, on a case-by-case basis, whether to allow the child's attorney to advocate a position that is different from that recommended by the guardian ad litem. We reject a rule that would unduly restrict the trial court's ability to receive information that might aid it in determining where the best interests of a child lie. In light of the trial court's findings that Cheryl's (P) boyfriend had abused the child, and that Cheryl (P) had sided with the boyfriend against the safety of the child, we cannot conclude that the attorney for the child should have been prevented from advocating that custody not be awarded to the plaintiff. Affirmed.

ANALYSIS

The court in this case decided that the Connecticut Rules of Professional Conduct were not violated in this case. Normally, an attorney representing a client under a disability, which includes minority, is under an obligation to maintain a lawyer-client relationship that is as normal as possible and is required to advocate for the position of the guardian ad litem. In this case, the guardian ad litem was appointed by the court at the request of the plaintiff, not the child's attorney.

Quicknotes

CUSTODY The granting of care and control of a child or children to a parent pursuant to an action for dissolution or separation.

GUARDIAN AD LITEM Person designated by the court to represent an infant or ward in a particular legal proceeding.

Pusey v. Pusey

Mother (P) v. Father (D)

Utah Sup. Ct., 728 P.2d 117 (1986).

NATURE OF CASE: Appeal of custody award of older child to father.

FACT SUMMARY: Older minor child expressed preference to live with father, and other factors being equal, the trial court awarded custody of the older son to father and the younger son to mother.

🏛 RULE OF LAW
The custody order should no longer be based on an arbitrary maternal preference.

FACTS: The older minor child stated a preference to live with his father. A social worker and the mother's brother, who had provided professional family counseling, recommended joint custody. The court considered all of the factors and awarded custody of the older son to the father and the younger son to the mother. Mother appealed the custody order as to the older child.

ISSUE: Should the custody order no longer be based on an arbitrary maternal preference?

HOLDING AND DECISION: (Durham, J.) Yes. The custody order should no longer be based on an arbitrary maternal preference. The mother appeals the custody award of her older son to his father on the basis of the "tender years doctrine." Case law supports her argument that there is a maternal preference in custody decisions. The "tender years doctrine," however, has been found to be unconstitutional by several other courts and promotes outdated stereotypes. It was perhaps useful when fathers primarily worked outside of the home and mothers were the primary caretakers, but that is no longer the case, especially in post-separation, single-parent households. Factors for the custody of children should include the children's primary caretaker, the person better able to care for the children because of flexible employment, and the relationship between the parent and child. Cases that support an arbitrary maternal preference are now disapproved. Here, the trial court considered the factors appropriately, and despite not following the opinions of the social worker or the plaintiff's brother, found that custody of the older son was appropriate for the father. Judgment affirmed.

▶ ANALYSIS

Judges have historically considered a mother to be "naturally superior" in caring for a young child, thus the development of the "tender years doctrine." As more women entered the workforce in 1970s, the doctrine became a focus of attack on the judicial and legislative fronts because fathers became more involved in child-rearing. In today's society, the mother as the primary care-taker of a minor child may be a reality, but is certainly not a presumption.

■═■

Quicknotes

CUSTODY The granting of care and control of a child or children to a parent pursuant to an action for dissolution or separation.

TENDER YEARS DOCTRINE Presumption traced back to 1830 that it would violate the laws of nature to remove an infant from the care of its mother; thus, children under the age of four should reside with their mother.

■═■

Garska v. McCoy

Father (P) v. Mother (D)

W. Va. Sup. Ct. App., 167 W. Va. 59, 278 S.E.2d 357 (1981).

NATURE OF CASE: Appeal from a custody decree.

FACT SUMMARY: McCoy (D) contended the trial court erred in failing to favor her as the mother in awarding custody of her child to Garska (P), the father.

🏛 RULE OF LAW
A child's best interest is served by awarding custody to the primary caretaker parent regardless of sex.

FACTS: McCoy (D) gave birth to a boy out of wedlock and lived with and cared for the infant during his first year without any support from Garska (P), the father. The child developed a respiratory problem, and McCoy's (D) grandparents petitioned the court to adopt the baby so that their medical insurance would cover him. Garska (P) then began to send small amounts for the child's support and filed a petition for habeas corpus to gain custody of the child. At all times, McCoy (D) lived with and cared for the child. The trial court awarded Garska (P) custody, finding him to be better educated, more economically stable, and having a better demeanor than McCoy (D). McCoy (D) appealed, contending she should have been favored to receive custody as the mother of the child.

ISSUE: Should a court disregard the sex of the parents and award custody to the primary caretaker?

HOLDING AND DECISION: (Neely, J.) Yes. A child's best interest is served by disregarding the sex of the parents in determining custody and awarding custody to the parent who is found to be the primary caretaker. The primary caretaker most likely will have developed the more stable relationship with the child through their day-to-day interaction. To award custody to the noncaretaker parent would be unduly disruptive to the child. Therefore, if the court determines that the primary caretaker parent achieves the minimum objective standard of parental fitness, it must award him or her custody. In this case, McCoy (D) was shown to be a fit parent, and, therefore, she should have received custody as the primary caretaker. Reversed.

▌ ANALYSIS

The standard articulated in this case requires the trial court to make a preliminary determination concerning which parent was the primary caretaker. Some factors identified by the court to aid in this determination were: which parent takes care of day-to-day needs and which parent is primarily responsible for education and discipline.

Quicknotes

BEST INTERESTS OF CHILD Standard used by courts when rendering decisions which involve a child or children.

CHILD CUSTODY DECREE A court order awarding responsibility for the care and control over a child or children in a dissolution or separation proceeding.

■=■

Squires v. Squires

Parties not identified.

Ky. Sup. Ct., 854 S.W.2d 765 (1993).

NATURE OF CASE: Appeal from order of joint custody and discretionary statutory review.

FACT SUMMARY: The court awarded joint custody to the parents of the minor child but the mother did believe that cooperation was possible due to the hostility during the divorce proceedings.

🏛 RULE OF LAW
Parental cooperation is not a precedent to a joint custody order if such an order is in the child's best interest.

FACTS: Mother and father were married for four months and had a child. Upon dissolution of their marriage, they had a custody dispute and the court assigned the case to a Domestic Relations Commissioner. The commissioner did not recommend joint custody because of the hostility between the parties, although he found them good candidates for joint custody. The court determined that hostility did not preclude a joint custody award and therefore entered an order for joint custody. On appeal, the majority affirmed noting that joint custody has many positive aspects and subsequent litigation is available if it proves unworkable. The appellate court dissent argued that the parties must be found sufficiently mature for joint custody to work. Mother appeals to this court.

ISSUE: Is parental cooperation a precedent to a joint custody order if such an order is in the child's best interest.

HOLDING AND DECISION: (Lambert, J.) No. Parental cooperation is not a precedent to a joint custody order if such an order is in the child's best interest. Mother claims that the trial courts have no direction for the application of the joint custody award and argues that such an order should only be made upon agreement by the parties. The best interest of the child, she argues, is clearly not met when the parties are completely incapable of cooperation as is alleged here. Father relies on the statute, which allows a court to grant joint custody if it is in the best interest of the child, to support his argument that the trial court acted within its discretion. A party's unwillingness to cooperate could block any court's attempt to grant joint custody. The ideal situation in American society is a child being raised in a two-parent household. However, the courts obviously cannot count on that in a divorce situation and must therefore attempt to replicate the setting as closely as possible. A mandatory award of sole custody to one parent or the other is not recommended because the non-custodial parent may become insignificant if an atmosphere of joint decision-making and support is not encouraged. The trial

court may make the determination that the positive aspects of joint custody outweigh the negative with respect to the child's best interests. In any case, a court must consider the statutory factors set out to determine what is in the child's best interest and then consider the potential for future parental cooperation. Present hostility during the dissolution of a marriage does not necessarily indicate future hostility. The emotional maturity of the parents should be taken into consideration. An award of joint custody does not necessarily place all of the decisions in both parents' hands because the court may make such orders as necessary to effectuate joint custody that is in the best interest of the child. For example, prior case law allows court to designate a child's usual residence. While here the trial court noted a "policy" of granting joint custody, the court did not avoid an application of the best-interest factors in blind reliance on such a "policy." Judgment affirmed.

DISSENT: (Leibsom, J.) Joint custody requires exceptionally mature adults capable of setting aside the emotional hostility for their children's benefit. The mother cited significant social science data supporting her position, but the majority disregards it. The trial found a "national trend" for joint custody, yet this is not sufficient for an award. A determination that the parents are emotionally mature and capable of cooperating in a joint custody situation should be made prior to awarding joint custody. The legislature should take such steps to require proof of such maturity and therefore guide the trial court in its determination of an appropriate custody award.

▶ ANALYSIS

The courts are forced to focus on the emotional maturity of the divorcing parents when the emotional stability of the children should be the focus. Absent an abusive situation, children thrive with the presence of both parents and joint custody is a goal to work toward. When two parents are equally capable of providing appropriate parenting, joint custody should at least be a consideration if not the first choice.

Quicknotes

BEST INTERESTS OF CHILD Standard used by courts when rendering decisions which involve a child or children.

Continued on next page.

CUSTODY The granting of care and control of a child or children to a parent pursuant to an action for dissolution or separation.

NONCUSTODIAL PARENT A parent who is not awarded the primary care and control of a child by the court in a dissolution or separation proceeding.

Young v. Hector

Husband/father (D) v. Wife/mother (P)

Fla. Ct. App., 740 So. 2d 1153 (1989).

NATURE OF CASE: Appeal from final determination of dissolution of marriage.

FACT SUMMARY: Both mother (P) and father (D) were working professionals and had hired in-home childcare for their two minor children when they lived in New Mexico. After a move to Florida, mother (P) continued her professional career and cared for the children with the help of an au pair or housekeeper. Father (D) neglected to obtain new employment and was absent for significant periods of time. The marriage ended and, after trial, the court awarded sole custody to the mother (P).

RULE OF LAW

A custody decision must be based on substantial competent evidence and may not take into account legally impermissible factors such as gender bias.

FACTS: Alice Hector (P) and Robert Young (D) married in New Mexico. Young (D) was an architectural designer with his own firm and had a publishing company. Hector (P) was an attorney in private practice at her own firm. Both had been married before, and Hector (P) had two grown children from the prior marriage. Hector (P) and Young (D) had two children and retained a live-in nanny to help with childcare while they maintained their professional careers outside of the home. After some time, the parties agreed to relocate to Miami, Florida with the intention that both parties would obtain professional employment once relocated. Hector (P) and the two children moved to Florida. Hector (P) took the bar exam and obtained employment with a mid-sized law firm. Young (D) stayed behind in New Mexico to finish renovations on two homes. Young (D) moved to Miami a few months later, and he passed the Florida contractor's examination. Young (D) proceeded to renovate two homes in Miami, in which the family resided, while Hector (P) continued her law career. From 1989 to 1993, the children were either in school or cared for by their live-in housekeeper until Hector (P) arrived home in the evenings when she became their primary caretaker. Hector (P) and Young (D) began arguing over finances, and Hector (P) expected Young (D) to gain outside employment. Neither party had ever agreed that Young (D) would be a stay-at-home parent and Young (D), in fact, was not a stay-at-home parent, but was involved with construction on the marital residences. The family continued to suffer financially, and Young (D) continued to refuse to obtain outside employment. Instead, he began traveling back to New Mexico, spending time with family, taking care of his deceased brother's affairs and going on a fourteen-month treasure hunt. During

Young's (D) absence, Hector (P) continued practicing law and caring for the children with the help of a housekeeper, who arrived at three and left at eight p.m. every weekday. When Young (D) returned to Miami in 1993, Hector (P) asked for a divorce based on his continued unemployment and his extramarital affair. Young (D) then began spending more time with the girls, primarily from three p.m. to six thirty p.m. on weekdays. At trial, Young (D) contended that he was the primary caretaker for the children, which the trial court viewed with skepticism. Young (D) testified that either he or the housekeeper would pick the children up from school, the housekeeper would prepare dinner for the children and himself, and then she would clean up after them. She would then draw a bath for one of the daughters and leave at eight o'clock in the evening. Upon the court's inquiry, Young (D) explained that he could not find employment in his architectural field because he was computer illiterate. Young (D) also testified that people with incomes over three hundred thousand dollars could usually afford outside help. At this time, Hector (P) was making such an income. The court awarded sole custody to the mother and Young (D) appealed.

ISSUE: May a court consider gender in a custody award?

HOLDING AND DECISION: (Green, J.) No. A custody decision must be based on substantial competent evidence and may not take into account legally impermissible factors such as gender bias. The court's questioning was not evidence of a gender bias, but would have been appropriate had the mother similarly refused to obtain outside employment in the face of the family's continued financial crises. Additionally, the court relied on a guardian ad litem report which recommended primary custody be granted to the mother. The report focused on the fact that Hector (P) had been economically stable throughout the children's lives and had continually remained employed, albeit at a variety of salaries. Young (D) voluntarily withdrew from the work world for various reasons. Second, Hector (P) had constantly been in the children's lives, while Young (D) often disappeared for months at a time and only visited upon Hector's (P) insistence. Young (D) was presently available on a more consistent basis, but had not been historically present throughout the children's lives. Finally, Hector (P) had a much better control of her anger around the children, while Young (D) had a tirade in front of the guardian ad litem and the children at one point. Order affirmed and remanded for determination of liberal visitation for father.

Continued on next page.

DISSENT: (Schwartz, C.J.) The parents had clearly agreed that Young (D) would be the primary caretaker. The children are equally devoted to both parents and are well-adjusted, well-behaved children. The children benefited from the arrangement that existed prior to the judgment and that arrangement should have been considered prior to making a change in custody. Trial court clearly considered gender in making its custody award. Had the situations been reversed, the stay-at-home mother architect would never have lost custody of her children. A custody decision is within the trial court's discretion, but that decision must be based on legally permissible factors. Judicial dislike for the character or choices of one of the parents should not be a factor.

DISSENT: (Goderich, J.) One parent did not work outside of the home for three years prior to the dissolution action, and one parent worked significantly long hours as a senior partner in a large Miami law firm. Parties may not have expressly agreed that the father would be the primary caretaker and stay-at-home parent, but this arrangement existed for three years and the mother did nothing to change it. The children had a father who was active in their school and after-school activities, and the mother could work her long hours, benefiting her career. The majority felt that the trial court's questioning related to the financial status of the family rather than gender bias. However, if the roles were reversed, a judge would likely not question a mother's choices to remain at home and be the primary caretaker for her children nor would the existence of a nanny be questioned. In this case, the mother was making a significant income to provide for the children's basic necessities, and the father would not have added significantly had he obtained outside employment. Furthermore, the guardian ad litem report also demonstrated gender bias, because had the situation been reversed, economic stability would not have been a "determinative" factor. The father's absences were due to improving the marital residence in New Mexico for its resale value, to care for his ill brother and then to handle his brother's estate, and finally, to direct a treasure hunt project. The majority applies that that is a "crazy or weird notion," but the mother's parents and trial counsel invested similarly in the hunt. Finally, Young (D) had returned to the family to become the primary caretaker for the three years prior to the dissolution of the marriage. Young's (D) anger may also have been justified, because he was angry about the alimony award and distribution of marital assets and liabilities.

▶ *ANALYSIS*

More states have fathers' rights groups starting to protect the rights of fathers against maternal presumptions in custody determinations. It can be true that a father's work schedule can be used against him when faced with a stay-at-home mother's ability to care for the children.

As in this case, however, the reverse situation does not necessarily result in the custody to the father. The courts simply cannot just consider the parents' employment situation, but all the factors that make up the "best interests" standard. Courts must always be on the guard against gender bias.

■=■

Quicknotes

BEST INTERESTS OF CHILD Standard used by courts when rendering decisions which involve a child or children.

GUARDIAN AD LITEM Person designated by the court to represent an infant or ward in a particular legal proceeding.

SOLE CUSTODY Arrangement whereby the care and control of the child or children is awarded to one parent exclusively.

■=■

Hassenstab v. Hassenstab

Ex-husband (P) v. Ex-wife (D)

Neb. Ct. App., 6 Neb. App. 13, 570 N.W.2d 368 (1997).

NATURE OF CASE: Appeal from an order denying an application to modify child custody arrangements.

FACT SUMMARY: When Thomas Hassenstab (P) requested that the court modify the prior custody determination by awarding him custody of his daughter, the district court dismissed his application and ordered an increase in child support.

RULE OF LAW
The party seeking modification of child custody bears the burden of showing that a material change in circumstances has occurred.

FACTS: The Hassenstabs were divorced and custody of their young daughter had been awarded to Carol (D), the mother. Thomas (P), the father, applied for a modification awarding him custody, and Carol (D) cross-filed a petition for increased child support. The district court found that no substantial and material change in circumstances had occurred that showed that Carol (D) was unfit to retain custody or that the child's best interests required a modification of her custody. Thomas (P) appealed, alleging that Carol's (D) homosexual relationships made her an unfit mother.

ISSUE: Does the party seeking modification of child custody bear the burden of showing that a material change in circumstances has occurred?

HOLDING AND DECISION: (Body, J.) Yes. The party seeking modification of child custody bears the burden of showing that a material change in circumstances has occurred. Sexual activity by a parent is governed by a rule which mandates that the establishment of a material change in circumstances justifying a change in custody requires showing that the minor child was exposed to such activity or was adversely affected or damaged by reason of such activity and that a change of custody is in the child's best interests. Because the evidence did not establish any harmful effect on the child because of Carol's (D) homosexual relationship, there has been no showing of a material change of circumstances. Affirmed.

ANALYSIS

The court in this case found that there was no evidence that the daughter was directly exposed to her mother's homosexual activities or that she was in any way harmed. Since the child was found to be happy and healthy, it was not in her best interests to have custody changed. Evidence of the custodial parent's behavior during the year or so before the hearing on the motion to modify is of more significance than the behavior prior to that time.

Quicknotes

BEST INTERESTS OF CHILD Standard used by courts when rendering decisions which involve a child or children.

CUSTODY The granting of care and control of a child or children to a parent pursuant to an action for dissolution or separation.

Wetch v. Wetch

Parties not identified.

N.D. Sup. Ct., 539 N.W.2d 309 (1995).

NATURE OF CASE: Appeal of custody award to the father.

FACT SUMMARY: Mother and father stipulated that mother would have sole custody and father would have liberal visitation rights. Mother later sought to move to another state, and father objected, seeking a change in custody.

🏛 **RULE OF LAW**
A trial court must consider pre-divorce conduct on a change of custody motion if the original custody order was by stipulation of the parties.

FACTS: Cheryl and Kirk Wetch married and had two daughters. The parties were divorced in March 1993 and agreed by stipulation that Cheryl would retain custody of the two daughters and Kirk would receive liberal visitation rights. Approximately one year later, Cheryl and the girls sought to move to Tennessee, and Kirk objected and sought physical custody of the girls. In April 1994, the parties agreed by stipulation that Cheryl would retain custody, but had to stay within sixty miles of Fargo-Moorhead. Cheryl moved the two girls to Tennessee in the summer of 1994, and Kirk moved for a change of custody. In September 1994, the court held a hearing on the motion, but refused to consider the parties' conduct and activities prior to April 1994. The court awarded Kirk physical custody of the two girls, and Cheryl appealed.

ISSUE: Must a trial court consider pre-divorce conduct on a change of custody motion if the original custody order was by stipulation of the parties?

HOLDING AND DECISION: (Sandstrom, J.) Yes. A trial court must consider pre-divorce conduct on a change of custody motion if the original custody order was by stipulation of the parties. Cheryl claims the trial court should have considered pre-April 1994 conduct and activities. In modifying a custody award, a trial court must determine whether there is a significant change of circumstance requiring a modification of the child custody for that child's best interest. Cheryl conceded that moving to Tennessee was a significant change of circumstance. She claims, however, that the modification is not necessary because it is not in the best interest of the children considering the pre-divorce conduct and activities of Kirk. Kirk argues that res judicata applies so that the parties' pre-divorce conduct and activities cannot be considered. The res judicata doctrine, however, should to be flexible to avoid injustice, especially in custody issues. Authority exists from other courts for the premise that pre-divorce conduct should be considered by the trial court when the previous

custody order was by stipulation or default. This is true because the trial court had no prior opportunity to examine the pre-divorce conduct and apply the statutory best-interest factors to the custody award. Such is the case here and all relevant evidence should be considered. Judgment reversed.

▷ **ANALYSIS**

The court was correct in noting today's mobile society, especially for employment purposes. A custodial parent may be unable to find employment locally and has an absolute need to move to another state. So long as the custodial parent is not attempting to thwart the rightful visitation rights of the non-custodial parent, the court should seriously consider the need for the parent to move. Parents should engage in reasonably necessary behavior to encourage a continuing relationship between the children and the non-custodial parent.

■■■

Quicknotes

CUSTODIAL PARENT A parent who is awarded the care and control of a child by the court in a dissolution or separation proceeding.

CUSTODY The granting of care and control of a child or children to a parent pursuant to an action for dissolution or separation.

NONCUSTODIAL PARENT A parent who is not awarded the primary care and control of a child by the court in a dissolution or separation proceeding.

RES JUDICATA The rule of law that a final judgment by a court precludes subsequent litigation between the parties regarding the same cause of action.

SOLE CUSTODY Arrangement whereby the care and control of the child or children is awarded to one parent exclusively.

VISITATION Rights awarded by the court in a divorce or custody proceeding to a parent who does not have custody over the child or children, permitting that parent to visit with the child or children.

■■■

Baures v. Lewis

Mother (P) v. Father (D)

N.J. Sup. Ct., 167 N.J. 91, 770 A.2d 214 (2001).

NATURE OF CASE: Appeal from denial of mother's removal request.

FACT SUMMARY: Carita Baures (P) filed a complaint for divorce from her husband, Steven Lewis (D), which included a request to remove their minor child from their home state of New Jersey to Wisconsin. Lewis (D) opposed the removal request.

🏛 RULE OF LAW
In a removal action, the custodial parent must establish the prima facie case with a good faith reason for the move and demonstrating that the move will be in the child's best interests.

FACTS: Carita Baures (P) and Steven Lewis (D) married in Wisconsin in 1985. Lewis was a naval officer, and the couple moved to various locations pursuant to navy orders. In 1990, their son, Jeremy, was born. In 1994, the family was stationed in New Jersey. It soon became apparent that Jeremy had special needs, and he was diagnosed with a form of autism. Jeremy received particular care from school and a local outreach program. The couple's finances suffered, and they began to discuss moving to Wisconsin to be near Baures's (P) parents after Lewis (D) was discharged from the Navy in 1998. In reliance on that plan, Baures's parents relocated within Wisconsin to be closer to an appropriate program for autistic children. In 1996, the marriage began to deteriorate, and the couple scheduled a court hearing on custody matters because Lewis (D) feared Baures (P) planned to take Jeremy to Wisconsin. Baures (P) denied the claim and filed for divorce the day before the hearing. At the hearing, the couple entered into a consent order regarding custody, which prohibited either party from leaving New Jersey. In April 1997, Baures (P) filed an amended divorce complaint, which included a request to remove Jeremy to Wisconsin. The trial court denied the removal after a three-day hearing on the basis that the move was not in Jeremy's best interests despite Baures (P) having a good faith reason for the move. The trial court found that Lewis (D) simply did not have the ability to visit as often as desired nor could he move to Wisconsin with them because of his duty to the navy. The trial court affirmed its decision on rehearing, and the Appellate Division also affirmed. Baures (P) appeals.

ISSUE: In a removal action, must a parent establish a prima facie case with a good faith reason for the move and demonstrating that the move will be in the child's best interests?

HOLDING AND DECISION: (Long, J.) Yes. In a removal action, the custodial parent must establish the prima facie case with a good faith reason for the move

and demonstrating that the move will be in the child's best interests. Confusion apparently reigns among the Bar, the bench, and litigants over the applicable legal standards in a removal action. Courts historically disapproved of post-divorce removal of minor children because of the perceived damage to the relationship between the noncustodial parent and the child. In today's increasingly mobile society, however, removal is common and may even be a necessity for the custodial parent. Technology allows multiple forms of easy communication across great distances, so removal may not be as damaging as once thought. Further evidence demonstrates that the happiness of the custodial parent greatly affects the minor children and a custodial parent may need to move for his or her own well-being. As a result of these changing factors, courts are now trending toward granting more custodial parent removal requests. The custodial parent can meet the relatively light burden of proving his or her prima facie case and then the noncustodial parent has the opportunity to contradict the presented evidence. If the noncustodial parent can demonstrate in good faith that, for example, the educational opportunities in the proposed location are not the equivalent of those in the present location, that the child's extended family is nearer the present location, or that the change in visitation will adversely affect the child, then the noncustodial parent may very well have overcome the custodial parent's prima facie case. The custodial parent can refute the offered evidence, but the court must rest its decision on what is in the child's best interests. The court may also take into account a noncustodial parent's "lackadaisical" attitude in exercising his or her visitation rights. Here, facts may have changed because of the passage of time, so the parties should have a second chance to present their evidence. Reversed and remanded.

▶ ANALYSIS

On remand, Lewis and Baures settled and all three moved to Wisconsin. The New Jersey courts had not had their final say, however. The Appellate Division in *O'Connor v. O'Connor*, 349 N.J. Super. 381 (2002), articulated a different standard for removal actions that involved parents with shared physical custody who spent a nearly equal amount of time with the children. This is not a radical departure from the *Baures* court because that court pointed out that a parent's visitation behavior should play a part in the decision. If parents spend equal time with the children, then one parent's lifestyle choices should not automatically

Continued on next page.

weigh more than the other's. It is ideal if all parties and the court consider first the child's best interests.

Quicknotes

CUSTODIAL PARENT A parent who is awarded the care and control of a child by the court in a dissolution or separation proceeding.

GOOD FAITH An honest intention to abstain from taking advantage of another.

NONCUSTODIAL PARENT A parent who is not awarded the primary care and control of a child by the court in a dissolution or separation proceeding.

PRIMA FACIE CASE An action where the plaintiff introduces sufficient evidence to submit the issue to the judge or jury for determination.

VISITATION Rights awarded by the court in a divorce or custody proceeding to a parent who does not have custody over the child or children, permitting that parent to visit with the child or children.

Eldridge v. Eldridge

Parties not identified.

Tenn. Sup. Ct., 42 S.W.3d 82 (2001).

NATURE OF CASE: Appeal of visitation order granting unrestricted overnight visitation to mother.

FACT SUMMARY: Julia and Anthony Eldridge divorced and agreed to shared custody of their two minor daughters. Julia entered into a cohabitating homosexual relationship with Lisa Franklin. Anthony was awarded sole custody with visitation rights granted to Julia. Anthony then objected to his older daughter's overnight visits with her mother if Lisa was present and sought to have Lisa's presence restricted during the visits.

RULE OF LAW
A trial court may properly restrict noncustodial parental visitation rights in the presence of a non-spouse if the restrictions are in the child's best interests and the appellate court should affirm the trial court absent a finding of error.

FACTS: Anthony and Julia Eldridge had two daughters, Andrea, 8, and Taylor, 9. After the Eldridges divorced, they agreed to joint custody of the girls. Julia then entered into a homosexual relationship with Lisa Franklin, and Julia moved into the house that Lisa owned. A custody dispute arose, and Julia sought a court-ordered visitation schedule. Anthony countered for sole custody of the girls, which the trial court granted. Court-ordered counseling to establish a visitation schedule failed, and the court appointed a guardian ad litem (GAL) on Anthony's motion. The GAL recommended overnight visitations with Julia, which the court ordered. Julia later sought extended overnight visitation, which Anthony opposed. After further recommendations from a mutually agreed upon Special Master, the trial court granted Julia unrestricted overnight visitations with Taylor. The Court of Appeals reversed for abuse of discretion in failing to restrict Lisa's presence during Taylor's overnight visits. This court granted review.

ISSUE: May a trial court properly restrict noncustodial parental visitation rights in the presence of a non-spouse if the restrictions are in the child's best interests, and should the appellate court then affirm the trial court absent a finding of error?

HOLDING AND DECISION: (Holder, J.) Yes. A trial court may properly restrict noncustodial parental visitation rights in the presence of a non-spouse if the restrictions are in the child's best interests and the appellate court should affirm the trial court absent a finding of error. The Court of Appeals here modified the trial court's order, but failed to state a basis for doing so. The appellate court specifically noted that it did not alter the order based on Julia's homosexuality, but did not specifically note the error

it was correcting. The case law cited is inapposite as the facts of that case dealt with a homosexual partner's inappropriate behavior resulting in jeopardy to the child in "either a physical or moral sense." Such is not the case here. The appellate court itself noted that Lisa's behavior was not jeopardizing Taylor. In fact, the trial record shows substantial testimony from Julia and Lisa that they do not sleep in the same room, are not physically affectionate around Taylor, and that Lisa and Taylor have a good relationship. Anthony and his wife, Chantal, argued that Taylor did not agree with a homosexual lifestyle and that Anthony was uncomfortable with the cohabitation example set by Julia and Lisa. The testimony about Taylor's emotions related to the visits, however, demonstrated that Taylor exhibited behavior consistent with many children of divorce. Taylor wanted to please both parents so would deny enjoying her visits with Julia and Lisa when talking to Chantal and Anthony. Taylor would also become withdrawn and uncommunicative during her visits with Julia when it neared time for her return to her father. No testimony by the parties or the experts suggested that Taylor was suffering because of Lisa's presence. The Court of Appeals cannot "tweak" a trial court opinion because it came up with a "better" result. As the record demonstrates that the trial court's order is not unreasonable and the Court of Appeals failed to note any error, the order should have stood. Reversed.

▶ ANALYSIS

Gay rights advocates hailed this case as a major victory in the fight for equality in custody decisions for gay parents. Many cited the seeming absurdity of the appellate court's order that the homeowner could not be allowed in the house during her lover's children's overnight visits. The children's well-being was not particularly at issue because the trial court and the reviewing courts all found that the lesbian couple was doing nothing untoward in the children's presence, and the child was not suffering moral corruption from the unrestricted visits. Amici in the case argued that children benefited from unrestricted access to their parents absent harm from the contact.

Quicknotes

ABUSE OF DISCRETION A determination by an appellate court that a lower court's decision was based on an error of law.

Continued on next page.

AMICUS BRIEF A brief submitted by a third party, not a party to the action, that contains information for the court's consideration in conformity with its position.

CUSTODY The granting of care and control of a child or children to a parent pursuant to an action for dissolution or separation.

GUARDIAN AD LITEM Person designated by the court to represent an infant or ward in a particular legal proceeding.

NONCUSTODIAL PARENT A parent who is not awarded the primary care and control of a child by the court in a dissolution or separation proceeding.

SOLE CUSTODY Arrangement whereby the care and control of the child or children is awarded to one parent exclusively.

VISITATION Rights awarded by the court in a divorce or custody proceeding to a parent who does not have custody over the child or children, permitting that parent to visit with the child or children.

Zummo v. Zummo

Noncustodial parent (D) v. Custodial parent (P)

Pa. Sup. Ct., 394 Pa. Super. 30, 574 A.2d 1130 (1990).

NATURE OF CASE: Appeal from grant of order restricting religious worship attendance.

FACT SUMMARY: After their divorce, Mrs. Zummo (P), the custodial parent and a Jew, obtained a court order prohibiting Mr. Zummo (D), a Roman Catholic, from taking their Jewish children to Catholic religious services.

RULE OF LAW
A court may not restrict a parent from exposing his children to his religious practices unless the activity substantially threatens to harm the children, and the restriction is by the least intrusive means possible.

FACTS: Before they were married, Mrs. Zummo (P), a Jew, and Mr. Zummo (D), a Roman Catholic, had agreed to raise any children they might have in the Jewish faith. After the divorce, when Mr. Zummo (D), the noncustodial parent, insisted on taking their children to Catholic services periodically, Mrs. Zummo (P) sought a court order restraining Mr. Zummo (D) from doing so. The trial court prohibited him from taking the children to any religious services "contrary to the Jewish faith" and ordered him to arrange for the children to attend synagogue during his weekend visitations. Mr. Zummo (D) appealed, arguing that the order violated his and his children's constitutional right of freedom of religion.

ISSUE: May a noncustodial parent expose his children to his religious practices so long as the activity does not substantially threaten to harm the children?

HOLDING AND DECISION: (Kelly, J.) Yes. Although the desire to provide stability in a child's life plays a key role in custody decisions, courts constitutionally cannot attempt to maintain the stability of a child's religious beliefs. The First Amendment does not allow the court to prefer one religion over another, or to consider whether Judaism and Christianity are reconcilable. Unless the child is suffering from severe conflict and distress, a court should not intervene in a religious upbringing dispute between parents. If intervention is warranted, however, the restriction must be by the least intrusive means adequate to prevent the harm. In this case, Mrs. Zummo (P) could not show that exposure to contradictory religions presented a substantial threat of harm to her children, so the restriction must be vacated. But since both parents do have the right to instill religious beliefs in their children, the court may require Mr. Zummo (D) to cut short his visitation time and present the children at synagogue for Sunday school. Vacated in part; affirmed in part.

ANALYSIS

Most courts, like the one above, draw a distinction between actual restrictions on visitation rights, which are generally struck down, and more benign "accommodations," which are allowed to interfere with visitations. In this way, courts protect the noncustodian's First Amendment right to practice his religion, while at the same time recognizing the custodian's fundamental right to determine and control her children's education and religious training.

Quicknotes

FIRST AMENDMENT RIGHTS Rights conferred by the First Amendment to the United States Constitution prohibiting Congress from enacting any law respecting an establishment of religion, prohibiting the free exercise of religion, abridging freedom of speech or the press, the right of peaceful assembly and the right to petition for a redress of grievances.

NONCUSTODIAL PARENT A parent who is not awarded the primary care and control of a child by the court in a dissolution or separation proceeding.

VISITATION Rights awarded by the court in a divorce or custody proceeding to a parent who does not have custody over the child or children, permitting that parent to visit with the child or children.

Troxel v. Granville

Paternal grandparents (P) v. Mother of children (D)

530 U.S. 57 (2000).

NATURE OF CASE: Petition seeking visitation rights.

FACT SUMMARY: The Troxels (P) petitioned a Washington Superior Court for the right to visit their grandchildren more often than permitted by the children's mother (D).

RULE OF LAW

A parent has a fundamental right in the care, custody, and control of his or her child.

FACTS: Tommie Granville (D) and Brad Troxel had two daughters together but never married. The couple separated and Brad later committed suicide. Granville (D) notified the Troxels (P) that she wished to limit their visitation to one short visit per month, and they brought suit seeking to obtain visitation rights. Their petition was based on Wash. Rev. Code § 26.10.160(3) (1994), which provides that, "Any person may petition the court for visitation rights at any time including, but not limited to, custody proceedings." The superior court entered a visitation decree ordering visitation for one weekend per month, one week during the summer, and four hours on each of the grandparents' (P) birthdays. Granville (D) appealed, and the case was remanded, during which time she married. Her husband later adopted the children. The court of appeals reversed the lower court's decision and dismissed the petition, holding that nonparents lack standing to seek visitation unless a custody action is pending. The Washington Supreme Court found that the Troxels (P) had standing to seek visitation under the statute but concluded that they could not obtain visitation because § 26.10.160(3) unconstitutionally infringes on the fundamental rights of parents to rear their children. This Court granted certiorari.

ISSUE: Does a parent have a fundamental right in the care, custody, and control of his or her child?

HOLDING AND DECISION: (O'Connor, J.) Yes. A parent has a fundamental right in the care, custody, and control of his or her child. The Fourteenth Amendment prohibits states from "depriv[ing] any person of life, liberty, or property, without due process of law." The clause also provides heightened protection against government interference with certain fundamental rights and liberty interests. The liberty interest at issue here is that of parents in the care, custody, and control of their children. Section 26.10.160(3) here unconstitutionally infringes on Granville's (D) fundamental parental right. The statute is extremely broad, permitting any third party to subject any

decision by a parent concerning visitation of the parent's children to state-court review placing the best interests determination exclusively in the hands of the judge. Several factors compel the conclusion that the section as applied violates due process. First, the Troxels (P) did not allege, nor did the court find, that Granville (D) was an unfit parent. There is a presumption that fit parents act in the best interests of their children and there is usually no reason for the state to interject itself into the private realm of the family. The superior court's decision directly contravened this presumption and failed to provide any protection for Granville's fundamental constitutional right to make decisions regarding the rearing of her own daughters. Affirmed.

CONCURRENCE: (Souter, J.) The state court's facial invalidation of the statute was appropriate as the provision allowed a court to award visitation whenever it thought it could make a better decision than the parent.

CONCURRENCE: (Thomas, J.) The plurality does not address, nor do the parties argue, that the Due Process Clause precludes judicial enforcement of its unenumerated rights. Similarly, no one suggests that courts have wrongly decided prior substantive due process cases. Therefore, these issues are left for another day.

DISSENT: (Stevens, J.) The Court should identify the two flaws in the Washington Supreme Court's ruling and remand for further deposition. That court's holding that the Federal Constitution requires a showing of actual or potential "harm" to the child before a court may order visitation over a parent's objections has no support in case law. This Court has never held that a parent's liberty interest is so inflexible as to establish a shield protecting every parental decision from challenge absent a showing of harm. The Due Process Clause should allow the states to consider the impact on a child of potentially arbitrary decisions that neither serve nor are motivated by the child's best interests.

DISSENT: (Scalia, J.) Legislators are the proper parties to argue that the state may not interfere with parental authority over their children's upbringing. That is not a constitutionally enumerated right, however, and judges do not have the power to deny effect to laws that may so interfere. The diversity in precedence on this issue precludes a reliance on stare decisis. Family law will become judicially prescribed if the judiciary must craft constitutionally

Continued on next page.

protected parental rights when the Constitution does not actually address such rights. State legislatures, not judges, are the appropriate crafters of family law.

DISSENT: (Kennedy, J.) The state Supreme Court erred in implying that courts cannot apply the best interests standard in third-party visitation cases and must apply a harm to the child standard. Remand is appropriate to correct this error and allow the court an opportunity to determine if the statute would allow visitation to anyone at any time or if the best interests standard provides sufficient protection. The harm to the child standard is distinct from the best interests standard, and one does not necessarily take precedence over the other. Parties seeking visitation should not have to prove harm to the child if denied visitation if the grant of visitation is clearly within the child's best interests. Family courts are in ideal positions to sift through the facts of each case to determine which standard is appropriate. For example, the best interests standard could apply in a *de facto* parent visitation case while harm to the child standard may be more appropriate in a stranger seeking visitation case. The constitutionality of applying one standard or another is not supported in historical review or case law, so the state Supreme Court should be reversed.

▶ *ANALYSIS*

It is surprising that, after *Troxel*, a number of lower courts have ruled various state provisions facially unconstitutional, reasoning that a fit parent has a liberty interest in the care, custody, and control of the child.

■━■

Quicknotes

BEST INTERESTS OF CHILD Standard used by courts when rendering decisions which involve a child or children.

DE FACTO STATUS In fact; something which is recognized by virtue of its existence in reality, but is illegal for failure to comply with statutory requirements.

DUE PROCESS CLAUSE Clauses found in the Fifth and Fourteenth Amendments to the United States Constitution providing that no person shall be deprived of "life, liberty, or property, without due process of law."

STARE DECISIS Doctrine whereby courts follow legal precedent unless there is good cause for departure.

■━■

Kinnard v. Kinnard

Father (P) v. Stepmother (D)

Alaska Sup. Ct., 43 P.3d 150 (2002).

NATURE OF CASE: Appeal from shared custody award to stepmother.

FACT SUMMARY: Bernard Kinnard (P) and Debra Kinnard (D) divorced and the court awarded shared custody of Bernard's biological daughter from a previous relationship to both parties. Bernard (P) claimed that Debra (D) had not proved harm to the daughter absent visitation with Debra (D) sufficient to justify a custody award.

🏛 RULE OF LAW
Courts should evaluate custody disputes between a third party and a biological parent with the "detriment to the child" standard.

FACTS: Bernard Kinnard (P) had two young children, Brandon and Kristine, from prior relationships when he married Debra Kinnard (D) in 1993. Debra (D) quickly bonded with the two children and became their psychological parent. Bernard (P) filed for divorce in 1999 and Debra (D) sought primary physical custody of Brandon and joint physical custody of Kristine. The trial court ordered a custody evaluation. The evaluator determined that Brandon would be 18 prior to the custody determination, so his custody would not be a factor. The evaluator then concluded that Debra (D) was indeed the psychological parent to Kristine and recommended joint custody with alternating weeks between parents. Bernard (P) claimed Debra (D) should not even have visitation rights to Kristine and that he should have sole custody. The trial court awarded joint custody based on "overwhelming" evidence that Debra (D) stood *in loco parentis* to Kristine. Bernard (P) appealed.

ISSUE: Should courts evaluate custody disputes between a third party and a biological parent with the "detriment to the child" standard?

HOLDING AND DECISION: (Fabe, C.J.) Courts should evaluate custody disputes between a third party and a biological parent with the "detriment to the child" standard. Bernard (P) claimed that the trial court applied the "best interests of the child" standard, but that was clearly not the case. The evidence was "uncontroverted" and "overwhelming" that Kristine would suffer psychological damage if Debra (D) was removed from her life. Debra (D) certainly stood in the place of mother to Kristine. Had the court applied the "best interests" standard as between two biological parents of Kristine, Bernard (P) would have completely lost custody. Thus, the court had to have applied the "detriment" to the child standard. The order does not conflict with *Troxel v. Granville* because the court found

that Kristine's loss of Debra (D) would have a devastating impact on Kristine's life. Such a finding of detriment absent visitation/custody complies with *Troxel*. Judgment affirmed.

▶ ANALYSIS

The presumption of course is that the biological parent will have custody of the child. Courts have a responsibility, however, to look beyond the biological tie to consider what is in the child's best interests, even if not applying the statutory "best interests" factors. Here, Kristine would obviously have suffered serious psychological harm if she could not be with Debra, so the court had to take that into consideration. Complying with *Troxel*, courts could also award visitation as opposed to custody if that was better for the child.

■━■

Quicknotes

BEST INTERESTS OF CHILD Standard used by courts when rendering decisions which involve a child or children.

CUSTODY The granting of care and control of a child or children to a parent pursuant to an action for dissolution or separation.

IN LOCO PARENTIS A situation in which a person has assumed the responsibilities and obligations of a lawful parent without undergoing the legal adoption process.

SOLE CUSTODY Arrangement whereby the care and control of the child or children is awarded to one parent exclusively.

■━■

Simons By & Through Simons v. Gisvold

Psychological mother (P) v. Biological mother (D)

N.D. Sup. Ct., 519 N.W.2d 585 (1994).

NATURE OF CASE: Appeal from custody order.

FACT SUMMARY: Debra Simons (P) sought custody of her nine-year-old stepdaughter after her husband died. The daughter's biological mother, Joelle Gisvold (D), also sought custody.

🏛 RULE OF LAW
A biological parent's custodial rights trump a psychological parent's custodial rights absent a finding of detriment to the child if the psychological parent is denied custody.

FACTS: Bruce Simons and Joelle Gisvold (D) had a daughter, Jessica. Soon after Jessica's birth, Bruce and Gisvold (D) divorced and the court awarded custody to Bruce. Gisvold (D) received liberal visitation rights and maintained a close, loving relationship with Jessica. Bruce and Debra Simons (P) soon married and Debra (P) stayed home with Jessica while Bruce worked outside of the home. When Jessica was nine, Bruce died of cancer. Both Debra (P) and Gisvold (D) sought custody of Jessica. The trial court awarded custody to Gisvold (D), and Debra (P) appealed.

ISSUE: Does a biological parent's custodial rights trump a psychological parent's custodial rights absent a finding of detriment to the child if the psychological parent is denied custody?

HOLDING AND DECISION: (Sandstrom, J.) Yes. A biological parent's custodial rights trump a psychological parent's custodial rights absent a finding of detriment to the child if the psychological parent is denied custody. The trial court here found that both Debra (P) and Gisvold (D) could provide a stable, loving, supportive home. Both women had loving, attached relationships with Jessica. Further, Jessica had not been asked for nor expressed a preference between the women. Debra (P) argued that the court should apply the "best interests" standard because she was a psychological parent to Jessica and not just a third party seeking custody. The court correctly applied the "detriment to the child" standard, however, and found that Jessica would suffer no detriment if custody was awarded to Gisvold (D). An appropriate biological parent should receive paramount consideration over a third party, even if that party is a psychological parent to the child. Judgment affirmed.

▶ ANALYSIS

While courts tend to take a broad view of "family," a third party simply cannot automatically receive greater rights to

a child than that child's biological parent. In cases such as this one, with all things being equal, the biological parent receives custody merely by the biological bond. That bond cannot trump the child's best interests or a finding of detriment to the child, but it cannot be discounted either. Liberal visitation for the psychological parent can be the best compromise because it still recognizes the importance of the relationship without overriding that of the biological family.

Quicknotes

BEST INTERESTS OF CHILD Standard used by courts when rendering decisions which involve a child or children.

CUSTODY The granting of care and control of a child or children to a parent pursuant to an action for dissolution or separation.

VISITATION Rights awarded by the court in a divorce or custody proceeding to a parent who does not have custody over the child or children, permitting that parent to visit with the child or children.

Quinn v. Mouw-Quinn

Father/stepfather (P) v. Mother (D)

S.D. Sup. Ct., 552 N.W.2d 843 (1996).

NATURE OF CASE: Appeal from visitation and child support order.

FACT SUMMARY: The court awarded visitation with the three minor children to Patrick Quinn (P). The daughter, however, was not Patrick's (P) biological child. The daughter had never known another father and was not aware of the circumstances of her birth. Her mother, Tamara Quinn (D), argued against Patrick's (P) visitation with her daughter.

🏛 RULE OF LAW
Courts may grant stepparent visitation when such visitation is in the child's best interests and under extraordinary circumstances.

FACTS: Tamara Quinn (D) and Patrick Quinn (P) married in 1984 and divorced in 1986. Tamara (D) gave birth to a daughter, Samantha, who is not Patrick's (P) biological child. Patrick (P) helped Tamara (D) throughout her pregnancy, including attending birth classes with her. The couple then reconciled and remarried in 1989. Tamara (D) and Patrick (P) had two sons, Jacob and Connor. Patrick (P) always treated Samantha as his own child, supported her financially, and she remains unaware of the circumstances of her birth. Samantha refers to Patrick (P) as "Daddy" and has known no other father. In 1993, Patrick (P) filed for divorce from Tamara (D) and sought sole custody of the three children. Tamara (D) countersued for custody and the trial court awarded custody to Tamara (D). The court also awarded visitation rights for all three children to Patrick (P). The court further ordered Patrick (P) to pay child support for all three children. Tamara (D) appeals the visitation order and support order as they apply to Samantha.

ISSUE: May courts grant stepparent visitation when such visitation is in the child's best interests and under extraordinary circumstances?

HOLDING AND DECISION: (Gilbertson, J.) Yes. Courts may grant stepparent visitation when such visitation is in the child's best interests and under extraordinary circumstances. Patrick (P) and Samantha clearly have established a parent-child relationship. Patrick (P) argued that he had a statutory right to visitation with Samantha because the courts may award custody or visitation of "children of the marriage" when in the children's best interests. That argument fails, however, because Samantha is not a "child of the marriage." Patrick (P), despite being the only father Samantha has known, is legally only Samantha's stepfather. Tamara (D) argues that Patrick (P), as Samantha's stepfather, has no legal right to visitation. The case law she cites as precedent addresses custody determinations where one parent is unfit. Here, Tamara (D) will retain custody regardless of the outcome of this matter and no one has alleged parental unfitness. The trial court found that it was in all three children's best interests that they be able to exercise visitation with Patrick (P) at the same time. It would be highly detrimental to Samantha to deny her access to Patrick (P) when her two half-siblings are allowed to visit with him. Such restrictions would also be detrimental to the sibling relationship. Courts may regulate the self-destructive behavior of warring parties pursuant to their *parens patriae* power. Here, the trial court found that awarding visitation with Patrick (P) was in Samantha's best interests, the children's best interests, and refusal would be detrimental to Samantha. Judgment affirmed.

DISSENT: (Amundson, J.) Patrick (P) is not Samantha's biological or adoptive parent. Direct precedent speaks to the issue of non-parental visitation rights. A non-parent seeking custody must definitely demonstrate the unfitness of the biological parent before proceeding. When the biological parent disputes visitation of a non-parent with a child, the same showing should be made. No such allegation of Tamara's (D) parental unfitness has been made.

▶ *ANALYSIS*

The biological parent had the historical right to determine the communication between a third party and the child, even when that third party was a stepparent or former cohabitant. Courts are becoming more open to the concept that it is potentially detrimental to a child to support the complete removal of a party from a child's life when that party may have played an intimate role. The biological parent's wishes are not discounted or overruled, but the court has a duty to consider the best interests of the child rather than solely the wishes of the parent. Some critics fear that a continued lessening of the authority of the biological parent's wishes could open the door to stranger visitation for children. Obviously, the courts are already equipped to address such a situation because the visitation must be in the child's best interests and/or a result of preventing a detriment to the child.

Continued on next page.

Quicknotes

CHILD SUPPORT Payments made by one parent to another in satisfaction of the non-custodial parent's legal obligation to provide for the sustenance of the child.

PARENS PATRIAE Maxim that the government as sovereign is conferred with the duty to act as guardian on behalf of those citizens under legal disability.

VISITATION Rights awarded by the court in a divorce or custody proceeding to a parent who does not have custody over the child or children, permitting that parent to visit with the child or children.

Stanley v. Illinois

Unwed father (P) v. State (D)

405 U.S. 645 (1972).

NATURE OF CASE: Appeal by an unwed father from denial of custody of his children.

FACT SUMMARY: Peter Stanley (P) lived with Joan Stanley intermittently for 18 years, but they were never married, so when Joan died the statute declared their three illegitimate children to be wards of the state.

🏛 RULE OF LAW
All parents are constitutionally entitled to a hearing on their fitness before their children are removed from their custody, and denying such a hearing to a particular classification of parents is violative of the Equal Protection Clause.

FACTS: Peter Stanley (P) lived with Joan Stanley inter-mittently for 18 years but never married. They had three children. When Joan died, Illinois (D) declared the three children to be wards of the state even though Stanley (P) was never shown to be an unfit father. The Illinois Supreme Court held that there was no equal protection claim and that Stanley (P) could lose custody of his children on the fact that he and the deceased mother were not married regardless of his fitness as a father.

ISSUE: Is it a violation of equal protection under the Fourteenth Amendment to deny a classification of parents of custody of their children without a hearing regarding the parents' fitness?

HOLDING AND DECISION: (White, J.) Yes. As a matter of due process of law, Stanley (P) was entitled to a hearing on his fitness as a parent before his children were taken from him. By denying him a hearing but extending one to all other parents whose custody was challenged by the state, it was a denial of equal protection under the Fourteenth Amendment. The interest of a parent in the many facets of raising a child "comes to this court with a momentum for respect lacking when appeal is made to liberties which derive merely from shifting economic arrangements." The law has not refused to recognize family relationships unlegitimized by marriage. Neglectful parents may certainly be separated from their children, but it first must be determined that they are neglectful. The state gets no benefit in taking children from an unwed father, particularly if he is fit to care for them. The separation would be needless. The procedure failed to examine fitness, needlessly risking "running roughshod" over the important interests of parent and child.

▶ ANALYSIS

The hearings to be provided unwed fathers require the usual procedural guarantees such as notice, service of process, etc. This has had a great effect on adoption practices where the unwed father must be found and heard before the child can be put up for adoption, but unwed fathers who do not promptly respond lose their right to later complain.

■ ═ ■

Quicknotes

CUSTODY The granting of care and control of a child or children to a parent pursuant to an action for dissolution or separation.

EQUAL PROTECTION CLAUSE A constitutional provision that each person be guaranteed the same protection of the laws enjoyed by other persons in like circumstances.

FOURTEENTH AMENDMENT DUE PROCESS CLAUSE Provides that protections mandated by the U.S. Constitution and observed by the federal government are equally applicable, and therefore must be observed by the states.

■ ═ ■

Lehr v. Robertson

Unwed father (P) v. Husband of married mother (D)

463 U.S. 248 (1983).

NATURE OF CASE: Appeal of an adoption order.

FACT SUMMARY: Lehr (P) contended that a New York statute which allowed his biological child to be adopted without his receiving notice was unconstitutional.

🏛 RULE OF LAW
Due process does not require that notice be given in all cases to a biological father of the pendency of an adoption proceeding concerning the child.

FACTS: Lehr (P) petitioned the court to declare him the father of Jessica M., a child born to Lorraine Robertson. After the birth, Robertson married Mr. Robertson, and Lehr (P) never supported the child and rarely saw her. Lehr (P) failed to place his name with the New York State putative father registry, which would have entitled him to notice of any adoption proceeding concerning the child. Before the court ruled on his petition, another court issued an order of adoption in favor of Mr. Robertson (D). Lehr (P) challenged the order, claiming because he was not notified of the adoption, even though the court was aware of his paternity action, he was denied due process. The New York Court of Appeals upheld the order as constitutional, and Lehr (P) appealed to the U.S. Supreme Court.

ISSUE: Does due process require that in all cases notice be given to a biological father of the pendency of an adoption proceeding?

HOLDING AND DECISION: (Stevens, J.) No. Due process does not require in all cases that notice be given to a biological father of the pendency of an adoption proceeding concerning the child. Only where an unwed father demonstrates a commitment to the responsibilities of parenting by participating in the rearing of the child does his relationship deserve substantial protection under the Due Process Clause. Mere biological relationships do not command the same constitutional protection because standing alone they lack the emotional connection which is the basis of the concept of family. In this case, the only claim to parenthood asserted by Lehr (P) was biological. His right to notice, therefore, is significantly less than it would have been had he established a relationship with the child. His right to due process was adequately protected by the availability of the putative father registry. His failure to register relieved any duty of notice owed him. Therefore, the adoption order was valid. Affirmed.

DISSENT: (White, J.) Any parental relationship, whether solely biological or solely emotional, is constitutionally recognized and protected. The adoption order deprived Lehr (P) of a constitutionally protected interest, and, therefore, he must be afforded notice and an opportunity to be heard before the order can be granted finality. Further, no legitimate state interest is served by denying him notice and hearing. Therefore, entry of the order denied him due process.

▶ ANALYSIS

It has been argued that the holding in this case disregards probably the most important consideration, that of the child's right or interest in having a relationship with a biological father. It is further argued that the emotional relationship identified as necessary to establish a strong parental relationship cannot be accomplished if the biological parent is shut off from the child by the custodial parent.

■■■

Quicknotes

DUE PROCESS The constitutional mandate requiring the courts to protect and enforce individuals' rights and liberties consistent with prevailing principles of fairness and justice and prohibiting the federal and state governments from such activities that deprive its citizens of a life, liberty or property interest.

PUTATIVE FATHER REGISTRY Registry where unwed father may file to demonstrate intent to claim paternity of child born out of wedlock, and to protect right to notice of any adoption proceeding.

■■■

V.C. v. M.J.B.

Psychological mother (P) v. Biological mother (D)

N.J. Sup. Ct., 163 N.J. 200, 748 A.2d 539 (2000).

NATURE OF CASE: Appeal from denial of custody and visitation application.

FACT SUMMARY: V.C. (P) acted as the psychological parent of the two minor children and sought joint legal custody and visitation when she and her lesbian partner, M.J.B. (D), the biological mother of the two children, ended their relationship.

🏛 RULE OF LAW
When the legal parent willingly encourages any third party not related by blood or adoption to develop a psychological parent relationship with the child, visitation will be awarded to that psychological parent, unless visitation is shown to cause physical or emotional harm to the child.

FACTS: V.C. (P) and M.J.B. (D), a lesbian couple, discussed having children early in their relationship. M.J.B. (D), without V.C.'s (P) knowledge, underwent artificial insemination and became pregnant with twins. M.J.B. (D) and V.C. (P) prepared for the twins' births together and the four of them proceeded to live together as a family. Approximately one year after the women participated in a commitment ceremony symbolizing marriage, they consulted an attorney regarding V.C.'s (P) potentially adopting the twins, but no further action was ever taken. Soon after, M.J.B. (D) ended the relationship. She permitted V.C. (P) to visit with the children on a regular basis and V.C. (P) continued to contribute financially to the household, but eventually M.J.B. (D) stopped allowing the visitation and no longer accepted the financial help. V.C. (P) sought joint legal custody and visitation and the trial court denied her applications. V.C. (P) appealed.

ISSUE: Should a third party not related by blood or adoption to a child be awarded visitation and custody rights when the legal parent willingly encouraged the third party to develop a psychological parent relationship, and visitation would not cause physical or emotional harm to the child?

HOLDING AND DECISION: (Long, J.) Yes. When the legal parent willingly encourages any third party not related by blood or adoption to develop a psychological parent relationship with the child, visitation will be awarded to that psychological parent, unless visitation is shown to cause physical or emotional harm to the child. V.C. (P) developed her relationship with the twins with M.B.J.'s (D) encouragement and approval, and she acted as a co-parent for much of the twins' early lives. V.C. (P) contributed to the household emotionally and financially,

and M.B.J. (D) gave V.C. (P) significant co-parenting responsibility. A legal parent's rights and responsibilities do not dissolve by the mere regular presence of a third party in the child's life. However, those rights are constrained when the legal parent encourages a parent-like relationship between the third party and the child, and a bond develops that should be protected by the courts. Just as with custody determinations involving legal parents, the best interests of the children should be considered with psychological parent relationships, and visitation should not be awarded when it would cause physical or emotional harm. V.C. (P) is entitled to visitation with the twins because of her psychological parent relationship with them and because it is in their best interest. Reversed.

▶ ANALYSIS

In the majority of courts, a non-parent must prove that the parent is unfit before the court will allow a third party non-parent to engage in a custody or visitation dispute. Modern legal scholars are questioning this traditional approach as more children are involved in parent-child relationships with third parties not related by blood or adoption, with the increase in gay and lesbian parenting. Perhaps the best interests standard is the most appropriate standard to apply regardless of the status of the complainant because it fully addresses the needs of the children involved rather than the wishes of the adults.

■══■

Quicknotes

BEST INTERESTS OF CHILD Standard used by courts when rendering decisions which involve a child or children.

CUSTODY The granting of care and control of a child or children to a parent pursuant to an action for dissolution or separation.

VISITATION Rights awarded by the court in a divorce or custody proceeding to a parent who does not have custody over the child or children, permitting that parent to visit with the child or children.

■══■

Titchenal v. Dexter

Lesbian partner (P) v. Adoptive mother (D)

Vt. Sup. Ct., 166 Vt. 373, 693 A.2d 682 (1997).

NATURE OF CASE: Appeal from grant of defendant's motion to dismiss.

FACT SUMMARY: Diane Dexter (D) adopted Sarah during Diane's same-sex relationship with Chris Titchenal (P). Dexter (D) and Titchenal (P) intended to raise Sarah together, but Titchenal (P) never adopted Sarah. The relationship ended and Titchenal (P) sought visitation rights with Sarah.

> ## RULE OF LAW
> A court may not consider a claim for visitation pursuant to its *parens patriae* equitable powers absent statutory authority.

FACTS: Chris Titchenal (P) and Diane Dexter (D) were same-sex partners sharing a home, joint banking accounts, and vehicles titled in both their names. They intended to remain life-partners and wished to raise a child together. After insemination with a sperm donor was unsuccessful, Dexter (D) adopted Sarah. Titchenal (P) and Dexter (D) did not believe that Vermont law allowed Titchenal (P) to adopt Sarah as a second parent, so she never sought to adopt her. The relationship ended and Dexter (D) moved out with Sarah. Initially, Titchenal (P) and Sarah enjoyed liberal visitation Wednesdays through Fridays, but then Dexter (D) curtailed the visits and refused Titchenal's (P) offers of financial support. Titchenal (P) filed a count for visitation in the superior court and Dexter (D) filed a motion to dismiss based on lack of jurisdiction. The court granted Dexter's (D) motion and Titchenal (P) appealed.

ISSUE: May a court consider a claim for visitation pursuant to its *parens patriae* equitable powers absent statutory authority?

HOLDING AND DECISION: (Allen, C.J.) No. A court may not consider a claim for visitation pursuant to its *parens patriae* equitable powers absent statutory authority. Titchenal (P) argues that nontraditional parent-figures should be able to seek parent-child visitation rights pursuant to the superior court's equitable jurisdiction. The family court could continue to ascertain the legal rights of family members pursuant to statutory authority. The argument must fail, however, because a court cannot exercise equitable powers without first establishing jurisdiction over the matter. Equitable powers are appropriate pursuant to common-law, statute, constitutional rights, or currently unrecognized legal rights that should be recognized pursuant to public policy. Titchenal (P) meets none of these bases. Titchenal (P) concedes that she does not meet most of the bases but argues that public policy supports the recognition of third-party rights to visitation and custody for de facto parents. To the contrary, de facto parents already have legal remedies to protect their custody and visitation rights. Titchenal (P) could have attempted to adopt Sarah, but elected not to do so. The court understands that the couple believed it to be a legal impossibility, but the facts are that the laws had changed and adoption was possible. It must also be noted that allowing superior court jurisdiction absent statutory authority could result in limitless third-party challenges to parental decisions against visitation. The Legislature is more appropriate than the judiciary to address providing superior court equitable jurisdiction to such claims. Judgment affirmed.

▶ ANALYSIS

The courts simply cannot exercise jurisdiction over a case involving parties with no legal relationship. Here, Dexter and Titchenal had no legal relationship and neither did Titchenal and Sarah. Allowing Titchenal's case to go forward could have resulted in any number of unrelated third persons petitioning for visitation rights against parental wishes, as unlikely as that scenario may seem. Some states, such as Kentucky, address de facto parenting through statute while other states, such as West Virginia, reject the notion entirely. As the nuclear family continues to erode and the definition of family changes, more states will be faced with de facto parenting and will need to find a way of uniformly addressing such issues.

◼▬◼

Quicknotes

DE FACTO STATUS In fact; something which is recognized by virtue of its existence in reality, but is illegal for failure to comply with statutory requirements.

PARENS PATRIAE Maxim that the government as sovereign is conferred with the duty to act as guardian on behalf of those citizens under legal disability.

PUBLIC POLICY Policy administered by the state with respect to the health, safety and morals of its people in accordance with common notions of fairness and decency.

VISITATION Rights awarded by the court in a divorce or custody proceeding to a parent who does not have custody over the child or children, permitting that parent to visit with the child or children.

◼▬◼

Chaddick v. Monopoli

Mother (P) v. Father (D)

Fla. Sup. Ct., 714 So. 2d 1007 (1998).

NATURE OF CASE: Appeal from dismissal of motion to enforce a divorce decree from another state.

FACT SUMMARY: A Florida court dismissed Chaddick's (P) motion to enforce her divorce decree because it determined that another state was the appropriate forum under the Uniform Child Custody Jurisdiction and Enforcement Act (UCCJA).

🏛 RULE OF LAW
Determination of whether an evidentiary hearing must be conducted regarding the issue of another state's appropriate exercise of jurisdiction is within the discretion of the trial judge.

FACTS: Chaddick (P) and Monopoli (D) were divorced in Massachusetts and custody of their two minor children was awarded to Chaddick (P). Chaddick (P) later moved to Florida and sent the children to visit Monopoli (D), their father, who was then living in Virginia. When Monopoli (D) was unable to ascertain Chaddick's (P) address in Florida so he could return custody of the children, he filed a custody petition in Virginia, alleging that Chaddick (P) was pregnant and living with a man to whom she was not married. An order was entered in Virginia awarding custody to Monopoli (D). Chaddick (P) retained a Virginia attorney to contest the Virginia court's jurisdiction but the court ruled against her there. Chaddick (P) then filed a petition in Florida seeking enforcement of the Massachusetts decree. The Florida trial judge called the Virginia court and ruled that he did not have jurisdiction of the case under the UCCJA and dismissed. On appeal, a divided Fifth District Court of Appeal affirmed. Chaddick (P) appealed, claiming the trial court erred in conducting the telephone call to the Virginia court out of her presence and off the record, and in failing to conduct a full evidentiary hearing as to whether the Virginia court exercised its jurisdiction substantially in conformity with the UCCJA, as required by Florida case precedent.

ISSUE: Is determination of whether an evidentiary hearing must be conducted regarding the issue of another state's appropriate exercise of jurisdiction within the discretion of the trial judge?

HOLDING AND DECISION: (Overton, J.) Yes. Determination of whether an evidentiary hearing must be conducted regarding the issue of another state's appropriate exercise of jurisdiction is within the discretion of the trial judge. Chaddick (P) was clearly seeking to have the Florida court overrule the Virginia court's determination of jurisdiction and to reconsider the Virginia court's determination of custody. Under the UCCJA, a Florida court must defer to a court in another state if a similar case is pending or decline to exercise its jurisdiction under the circumstances of the case if a court of another state is a more appropriate forum. Since Chaddick (P) had already voluntarily appeared in Virginia and lost, it was too late for her to file in Florida. The trial judge appropriately dismissed Chaddick's (P) petition under the circumstances of this case. To ensure future cases are not jeopardized by an inadequate record on this issue, the parties must be given the opportunity to be present during a Florida judge's conversation with a judge of a sister court but the parties may not participate in that conversation, and the Florida judge must explicitly set forth in the record the reasons for the judge's finding that the sister state was or was not exercising its jurisdiction in substantial conformity with UCCJA. Affirmed.

▶ ANALYSIS

The holding regarding proper procedures to be followed in Florida was prospective only. Under the circumstances of this case, the court found that Chaddick (P) was not entitled to enforce her decree in Florida after appearing in Virginia on the same matter. She was not entitled to "two bites at the apple."

■■■

Quicknotes

FORUM NON CONVENIENS An equitable doctrine permitting a court to refrain from hearing and determining a case when the matter may be more properly and fairly heard in another forum.

UCCJA 9 U.L.A. 123 (1988) - First promulgated by the National Commissioners on Uniform State Laws in 1968, all states have since adopted it. Its purpose is to bring order to interstate custody disputes and sets out procedures to be followed when a court of another state is exercising jurisdiction over the same matter.

VENUE The specific geographic location over which a court has jurisdiction to hear a suit.

■■■

Thompson v. Thompson

Father (P) v. Mother (D)

484 U.S. 174 (1988).

NATURE OF CASE: Appeal from custody order.

FACT SUMMARY: Mr. Thompson (P) contended that the federal court had jurisdiction to determine a jurisdictional dispute between states over a custody determination.

🏛 RULE OF LAW
There is no federal cause of action under the Parental Kidnapping Prevention Act (PKPA) to determine the validity of conflicting state custody orders.

FACTS: The Thompsons divorced, and joint custody of their child was ordered. Mrs. Thompson (D) obtained a California court order that she was to have sole custody when she left for Louisiana, subject to the results of an investigator's report on custody. She left and obtained a Louisiana order granting her sole custody. The California court thereafter reviewed the investigator's report and granted sole custody to Mr. Thompson (P). He then sued in federal court to have the validity of the competing orders determined under the Parental Kidnapping Prevention Act. The district court held that it had no jurisdiction as the Act did not establish a private cause of action. The court of appeals affirmed, and the Supreme Court granted certiorari.

ISSUE: Is there a federal cause of action under the PKPA to determine the validity of competing state custody orders?

HOLDING AND DECISION: (Marshall, J.) No. There is no federal cause of action under the PKPA to determine the validity of competing state custody orders. The history and purpose of the Act was to provide authority for sister states to give full faith and credit to their respective custody orders. The Act does not envision the determination of competition in the federal court. Enforcement was meant to be accomplished in the state court. Thus, the suit was properly dismissed. Affirmed.

▶ ANALYSIS

It is recognized that custody, as in most family law matters, is handled in state courts. This has resulted in such courts developing an expertise in these areas. Congress was not induced to place these issues in federal court, where an entire educational process would have to be undertaken. Thus, it left enforcement in the state courts.

■═■

Ohlander v. Larson

Mother (P) v. Father (D)

114 F.3d 1531 (10th Cir. 1997).

NATURE OF CASE: Appeal from a judgment denying a mother's motion to dismiss a petition.

FACT SUMMARY: When Ohlander (P) returned to Sweden with her child and the jurisdiction of the Swedish court over custody had been established, she sought to have her earlier petition in a Utah court dismissed.

RULE OF LAW
Once a defendant files an answer, a plaintiff may voluntarily dismiss an action only upon order of the court, and a district court normally should grant such a petition, absent legal prejudice to the defendant.

FACTS: Ohlander (P), a Swedish citizen and Larson (D), a United States citizen, were married in Utah and their daughter was born in Utah. While visiting Sweden, Ohlander (P) went into hiding and severed contact with Larson (D), who later returned to the U.S. alone. Ohlander (P) later rejoined Larson (D) in Utah but then returned to Sweden with their daughter. Two years later, Larson (D) was visiting Sweden when he took the child back to Utah without Ohlander's (P) consent. Ohlander (P) filed a petition seeking her daughter's return pursuant to the Hague Convention in the United States District Court in Utah and she secured an order from the district court directing peace officers to take the child into protective custody and to release her to Ohlander (P), but prohibiting Ohlander (P) from removing the child from Utah. Ohlander (P) disobeyed the court order and returned to Sweden with the child. The district court issued an order finding Ohlander (P) in contempt and Larson (D) filed a Convention application for the child's return, which was forwarded to Swedish authorities. Ohlander (P) then filed a motion to dismiss her district court petition based on the Convention's Art. 12 which authorizes a judicial authority to stay or dismiss the application or judicial proceedings seeking a child's return, which was denied. Larson (D) petitioned the Swedish court for the child's return and both parents were present during Swedish court proceedings which ruled that the child's habitual residence had changed from Utah to Sweden. Ohlander (P) filed a motion to stay enforcement of the Utah district court's order and to set aside the United States judgment, which were both denied. Ohlander (P) appealed.

ISSUE: Once a defendant files an answer, may a plaintiff voluntarily dismiss an action only upon order of the court, and should a district court normally grant such a petition, absent legal prejudice to the defendant?

HOLDING AND DECISION: (Brorby, J.) Yes. Once a defendant files an answer, a plaintiff may voluntarily dismiss an action only upon order of the court, and a district court normally should grant such a petition, absent legal prejudice to the defendant. The district court did not consider the merits of Ohlander's (P) motion, due exclusively to her contumacious conduct. The district court's decision to deny Ohlander's (P) motion solely on the grounds of her contempt amounted to a failure to exercise discretion, and is consequently an abuse of discretion. By failing to dismiss the United States action, we would allow two conflicting decisions regarding the child's state of habitual residence to stand, which could very well require a Hague convention decision to determine which one is valid. This would be absurd. Reversed and remanded.

ANALYSIS

The court in this case noted that the parameters of what constituted legal prejudice were unclear. Relevant factors the district court should consider were listed. Among them were the opposing party's effort and expense in preparing for trial, excessive delay and lack of diligence on the part of the movant, insufficient explanation of the need for a dismissal, and the present stage of litigation.

Quicknotes

CONTEMPT An act of omission that interferes with a court's proper administration of justice.

HAGUE SERVICE CONVENTION Multilateral treaty governing service of process in foreign jurisdictions.

Silverman v. Silverman

Parties not identified.

338 F.3d 886 (8th Cir. 2003).

NATURE OF CASE: Appeal from district court ruling on Hague Convention claim.

FACT SUMMARY: Julie and Robert Silverman moved with their two minor sons to Israel from Minnesota. The Silvermans' marriage was failing, but Robert refused to allow Julie to remove the children from Israel. When Julie and the boys ostensibly returned to the United States for a vacation, Julie filed for legal separation from Robert and sole custody of their sons. Robert filed a claim under the Hague Convention for a determination that the boys' habitual residence was Israel.

🏛 RULE OF LAW
The Hague Convention requires custody determinations to be made by the country of the children's habitual residence with the children's presence to be in that country absent a risk of grave physical danger to the children.

FACTS: Julie and Robert Silverman married and had two sons, Jacob and Sam. The family resided in Minneapolis until they determined to move to Israel. Julie initially pushed for the move, but then became hesitant because the marriage was in trouble. The family went ahead with the move, however. They sold their home in Minnesota, applied for and received immigration status to Israel, moved their family pets with them to Israel, and signed a one-year lease on an Israeli residence. The boys enrolled in school, learned Hebrew, and Sam participated in extracurricular activities. Julie returned to Minnesota to declare bankruptcy and arrived back in Israel to find that Robert had taken out a restraining order prohibiting her from removing the children from Israel. He confronted Julie about her affair with a Massachusetts man. The couple attempted to reconcile and Robert lifted the restraining order, but Robert remained adamant that Julie could not leave Israel with the children. Robert and Julie returned to Minnesota to finalize bankruptcy proceedings and listed their permanent residence as Plymouth, Minnesota. The two also filed joint Income Tax Returns with Plymouth, Minnesota, listed as their address. After returning to Israel, Julie consulted with an attorney and learned that she would likely not receive custody if she separated from Robert in Israel. Julie then ostensibly took the boys to the United States on a summer vacation with Robert's permission. He threatened Julie at the airport that she must return to Israel with the boys. Once back in the United States, Julie filed for legal separation from Robert and sought sole custody of Jacob and Sam. Robert received summons in Israel and immediately moved to dismiss the action for lack of jurisdiction because

no determination had been made as to the children's habitual residence under the Hague Convention. Robert filed a "Request for Return of Abducted Children" pursuant to the Hague Convention and then filed a Hague petition in both Israel and federal district court in Minnesota for the return of the boys. Despite notice of the pending Hague petitions, Julie received an interlocutory order granting her temporary custody. She moved with the boys to Massachusetts to be with her boyfriend. In the meantime, the Israeli courts determined the boys' habitual residence to be Israel and found that Julie wrongfully retained the boys in violation of the Hague Convention. Regardless of this finding, the Minnesota court issued a final order granting sole custody to Julie and finding that Minnesota was the home state. The court did not issue a ruling on the habitual residence of the boys nor their wrongful removal and retention. The next year, the federal court ruled that Minnesota was the boys' habitual residence, and in the alternative, that returning the boys to Israel would place them in grave physical danger. Robert appeals this ruling.

ISSUE: Does the Hague Convention require custody determinations to be made by the country of the children's habitual residence with the children's presence to be in that country absent a risk of grave physical danger to the children?

HOLDING AND DECISION: (Beam, J.) Yes. The Hague Convention requires custody determinations to be made by the country of the children's habitual residence with the children's presence to be in that country absent a risk of grave physical danger to the children. Both issues involve mixed issues of facts and law so the court must review "grave risk of harm" and "habitual residence" de novo. Parents must be able to rely on articulated standards rather than face losing children if each case of habitual residence is determined by an uncertain status of the law. The district court should have considered the status of the family at the time of the separation. The boys were involved with school in Israel, the family had sold their Minnesota residence, the family pets were in Israel, and the intent at the time of the relocation was that it was a permanent move. The only appropriate conclusion is that Sam and Jacob's habitual residence was Israel. The district court erred in ruling otherwise. As for "grave risk of harm," no case has determined that Israel is a "zone of war" which would place the children at physical risk. The children's school is a significant distance from fighting, schools and businesses are open, and Julie travel freely to and from

Continued on next page.

Israel. Nothing indicates that the children could not safely return to Israel. Israel is the appropriate court to make the custody determinations. Reversed.

DISSENT: (Heaney, J.) The majority determined that the children would not suffer risk of physical harm if returned to Israel. The Convention, however, protects against the risk of physical *or* psychological harm. The majority neglected to consider the potential psychological harm to the children in being removed from their mother and the United States after spending the majority of their lives here.

▶ *ANALYSIS*

The Hague Convention was enacted to ensure that children wrongfully removed from their country of habitual residence would be promptly returned. Unfortunately, the Convention does not define "habitual residence." The court appropriately noted that parents must have articulated standards upon which to rely or they could never allow their children to leave their present country of residence. The Convention requires judicial enforcement to add teeth to its regulations. Courts are encouraged to read the undefined terms of the Convention broadly.

■━━■

Quicknotes

DE NOVO The review of a lower court decision by an appellate court, which is hearing the case as if it had not been previously heard and as if no judgment had been rendered.

HABITUAL RESIDENCE Location where a person lives with the intent to remain for an unspecified time.

HAGUE SERVICE CONVENTION Multilateral treaty governing service of process in foreign jurisdictions.

INTERLOCUTORY ORDER An order entered by the court determining an issue that does not resolve the disposition of the case, but is essential to a proper adjudication of the action.

RESTRAINING ORDER An order, similar to an injunction, prohibiting a defendant from certain activities until a hearing regarding an injunction on such activities may be conducted.

SOLE CUSTODY Arrangement whereby the care and control of the child or children is awarded to one parent exclusively.

■━━■

Wolf v. Wolf

Father (P) v. Mother (D)

Iowa Sup. Ct., 690 N.W.2d 887 (2005).

NATURE OF CASE: Appeal from award of punitive damages to ex-husband for custodial interference.

FACT SUMMARY: Timothy Wolf (P) was awarded primary custody of the minor daughter, but his ex-wife Joan Wolf (D) continued to fight the award and keep the daughter with her in contravention of court orders. Timothy (P) eventually filed to recover damages for custodial interference.

RULE OF LAW

Punitive damages are available to custodial parents in tortious custodial interference actions.

FACTS: Timothy (P) and Joan (D) Wolf divorced in 1990, and the Iowa court awarded Joan (D) sole physical custody of their minor daughter, Ashley. In 1993, the court modified the order to give Timothy (P) primary physical custody. In 1998, the court modified the order to give Joan (D) primary physical custody. Timothy (P) appealed and the court of appeals reaffirmed physical custody with Timothy (P). Ashley and Joan (D) had moved to Arizona in the meantime, but the Arizona court declined to award custody to Joan (D). Eleven months after the Iowa court of appeals order, Joan (D) still had not returned Ashley to Timothy (P) in Iowa. Timothy (P) sought and obtained a writ of habeas corpus in Iowa and flew to Arizona to retrieve Ashley. Ashley stayed with Timothy (P) for just over one month and then flew back to Arizona to live with Joan (D). Joan (D) again petitioned the Arizona court for custody, but the Arizona court again ruled that Iowa retained jurisdiction. In November 2000, both Ashley and Joan (D) returned to Iowa to testify in a modification hearing. The court ordered all parties to remain in Iowa for the duration of the proceedings, and Joan promised to do so. Despite the court order, Joan (D) and Ashley immediately returned to Arizona. In December, the court affirmed Timothy's (P) custody award. In 2002, Timothy (P) filed suit against Joan (D) for damages based on tortious intentional interference with custody. Joan (D) moved to dismiss, which the court denied. The court awarded $25,000 to Timothy (P) in punitive damages, which Joan (D) appealed.

ISSUE: Are punitive damages available to custodial parents in tortious custodial interference actions?

HOLDING AND DECISION: (Larson, J.) Yes. Punitive damages are available to custodial parents in tortious custodial interference actions. Case law, legislation, and public policy support the award of punitive damages in tortious-interference cases. Punitive damages are recoverable if the tort was committed maliciously. Objectionable conduct is insufficient and a showing of legal or actual malice must be made.

Here, Joan (D) argued that she was simply being a good mother. The facts demonstrate otherwise. She deliberately kept Ashley from Timothy (P), enabled Ashley to leave Timothy's (P) custody, and deliberately disobeyed direct court orders. Joan's (D) willful and wanton conduct warrants the imposition of punitive damages. Joan (D) also argues that the amount of the award was excessive. The U.S. Supreme Court has provided three guideposts for reviewing the appropriateness of a punitive award: (1) degree of reprehensibility of defendant's misconduct; (2) disparity of actual harm and punitive award; and (3) difference in punitive award and civil penalties imposed in comparable cases. The $25,000 award here was not excessive. Finally, Joan (D) argues that the difference between the actual damages of $1 and punitive damages is excessive. Timothy (P) only claimed $1 in actual damages because he wanted Ashley to know that he was not pursuing the issue for money reasons. The actual damage award simply does not reflect the true damage that occurred in the lost father-daughter relationship and the money spent in the legal actions. Judgment affirmed.

ANALYSIS

Punitive damages are meant to discourage similar behavior in the present party and in persons contemplating similar actions in the future. Although intended to also punish the offending party, nothing can truly repair the damage done in a custodial interference case. The parent-child relationship can be permanently lost and actual damages difficult to quantify. Courts are restrained from awarding punitive damages simply because the conduct was distasteful. The conduct must be intentionally malicious and harmful, as was the conduct here. Similar damages are not available to noncustodial parents because of the fear of constant litigation that could arise.

Quicknotes

CUSTODIAL PARENT A parent who is awarded the care and control of a child by the court in a dissolution or separation proceeding.

SOLE CUSTODY Arrangement whereby the care and control of the child or children is awarded to one parent exclusively.

PUBLIC POLICY Policy administered by the state with respect to the health, safety and morals of its people in accordance with common notions of fairness and decency.

WRIT OF HABEAS CORPUS A proceeding in which a defendant brings a writ to compel a judicial determination of whether he is lawfully being held in custody.

United States v. Amer

Federal government (P) v. Father (D)

110 F.3d 873 (2nd Cir. 1997).

NATURE OF CASE: Appeal from a criminal conviction.

FACT SUMMARY: When Amer (D) was convicted for violation of the International Parental Kidnapping Crime Act (IPKCA), he alleged that the statute was unconstitutionally overbroad and vague.

🏛 RULE OF LAW
A challenger who engages in some conduct that is clearly proscribed by the challenged statute cannot complain of the vagueness of the law as applied to the conduct of others.

FACTS: When Amer (D) took his children secretly to Egypt and then returned to the United States alone, he was convicted for violating the IPKCA. Amer (D) appealed, alleging that the IPKCA was vague because it did not specify the length of time a child must have been in the United States before the IPKCA will be triggered by the child's removal or retention. Amer (D) also alleged that the IPKCA must be invalidated because it punishes parents for engaging in the constitutionally protected act of returning their children to the land of their parents' birth for religious reasons and is therefore overbroad.

ISSUE: May a challenger who engages in some conduct that is clearly proscribed by the challenged statute complain of the vagueness of the law as applied to the conduct of others?

HOLDING AND DECISION: (Newman, C.J.) No. A challenger who engages in some conduct that is clearly proscribed by the challenged statute cannot complain of the vagueness of the law as applied to the conduct of others. To succeed, a proponent of the void for vagueness argument must demonstrate that the law is impermissibly vague in all of its applications. The conduct for which Amer (D) was convicted falls squarely within the core of the IPKCA. Amer's (D) act of removing long-term residents of the United States and retaining them for more than six months in Egypt in order to frustrate their mother's lawful exercise of her right to physical custody under New York law falls squarely within the coverage of the IPKCA. Therefore, Amer's argument for vagueness cannot succeed. The overbreadth argument, based on Amer's (D) assertion of his right to freely exercise his religion, was not raised until this appeal and was hence forfeited. Affirmed.

▌ *ANALYSIS*

Two of the three children in this case were born in the United States and had resided in the United States their entire lives. Both parents had emigrated from Egypt, where

their first child was born. The mother was awarded custody of the children in a N.Y. court after they had been abducted by their father. An Egyptian court granted the father full legal custody when the mother failed to appear.

■═■

Quicknotes

IPKCA 18 U.S.C. § 1204 - Enacted in 1993, this statute provides that whoever removes a child from the United States with intent to obstruct the lawful exercise of parental rights shall be fined or imprisoned or both.

FREE EXERCISE OF RELIGION The right to practice one's religious beliefs free from governmental conduct or interference.

VAGUENESS AND OVERBREADTH Characteristics of a statute that make it difficult to identify the limits of the conduct being regulated.

■═■

Hendrickson v. Hendrickson

Parties not identified.

N.D. Sup. Ct., 603 N.W.2d 896 (2000).

NATURE OF CASE: Appeal from order denying visitation to mother.

FACT SUMMARY: Diane and Mark Hendrickson divorced after fifteen years of marriage and the court awarded custody to Diane. She continually thwarted Mark's visitation efforts, and Mark claims that she alienated the children from him.

🏛 RULE OF LAW
A change of custody may be appropriate in response to frustration of visitation where circumstances have significantly changed since the first custody order and the change is in the children's best interests.

FACTS: Diane and Mark Hendrickson married in 1980 and lived in Jamestown. Mark worked in another town during the week, while Diane stayed in Jamestown with their four minor children. In 1995, the couple divorced, and the court awarded custody to Diane. The court found that the children had a closer relationship with their mother and ties established in Jamestown. Mark was awarded visitation of two weekends a month and Christmas. Diane repeatedly thwarted Mark's visitation attempts, however. In 1997, Mark moved for a modification of the custody order based on a claim of alienation of affection. A guardian ad litem had been appointed and her report disclosed that Diane believed herself to be completely blameless in the breakup and unaware of Mark's parenting skills. Diane admitted to hanging up on Mark when he telephoned and threatened to continue to do so unless he paid her $20,000. The guardian ad litem concluded that Diane's behavior and Mark's early absence from the home had resulted in an alienation of affection between the children and Mark. The court ordered the children in the county's custody and the family into counseling. The county refused to take custody, however. In a subsequent order, the trial court expressed its outrage and disgust at Diane's behavior, but did not modify the custody order because of the alienation between the father and the children. The court ordered continued reasonable visitation for Mark and ordered Mark's child support payments held in escrow. Both parties appealed. On appeal, the court held it was error to hold the support payments in escrow because Diane could have been jailed for contempt rather than punished by withholding the child support. The court further held that alternative remedies should be considered prior to ordering a change of custody. Mark filed an additional motion to change custody prior to the appellate court decision on the prior appeal. On that motion, the court found a significant change in circumstance and ordered a change in custody. It further ordered that Diane not have visitation for one year and ordered her into counseling with a therapist selected by Mark. Diane appeals these orders.

ISSUE: Is a change of custody appropriate in response to frustration of visitation where circumstances have significantly changed since the first custody order and the change is in the children's best interests?

HOLDING AND DECISION: (Maring, J.) Yes. A change of custody may be appropriate in response to frustration of visitation where circumstances have significantly changed since the first custody order and the change is in the children's best interests. The trial court expressly found that circumstances had changed so as to support a modification of the original custody order. The court further found that Diane repeatedly and consistently thwarted the visitation orders, and was in fact an unhealthy parent figure. Diane steadfastly refused to change her behavior, so alternatives to a change in custody had been exhausted. The legislature also allows for modification of custody beyond the standard two-year time limit when a willful interference with visitation persists. Such is the case here. The court implied that it was in the children's best interests to change the custody order. Judgment affirmed.

▶ ANALYSIS

Courts are placed in a nearly impossible position when one parent alienates a child from the other parent. Courts are bound to consider the best interests of the children, which may not be transferring custody to the parent from the children are now alienated. It is also difficult to prohibit the continued alienating behavior without further punishing the children. As in the *Hendrickson* case, courts do not want to jail offending parents because the children suffer the most. When all else fails, courts are left with transferring custody as the only real impediment to further alienation.

■■■

Quicknotes

CHILD SUPPORT Payments made by one parent to another in satisfaction of the non-custodial parent's legal obligation to provide for the sustenance of the child.

Continued on next page.

CUSTODY The granting of care and control of a child or children to a parent pursuant to an action for dissolution or separation.

GUARDIAN AD LITEM Person designated by the court to represent an infant or ward in a particular legal proceeding.

VISITATION Rights awarded by the court in a divorce or custody proceeding to a parent who does not have custody over the child or children, permitting that parent to visit with the child or children.

Farmer v. Farmer

Parties not identified.

Ind. Ct. App., 735 N.E.2d 285 (2000).

NATURE OF CASE: Appeal from contempt citation and visitation order.

FACT SUMMARY: Farmer was not paying child support for his minor child with ex-wife Susan Feliciano (formerly Susan Farmer). Farmer sought a modification of the visitation order. The trial court conditioned its visitation orders on Farmer's continued child support payments.

🏛 RULE OF LAW
Courts may not condition or commingle visitation rights and child support obligations.

FACTS: Farmer and Susan Feliciano (formerly Susan Farmer) were married and had a minor daughter together. The court awarded custody to Susan and Farmer received visitation. Farmer was not meeting his child support obligations. Farmer filed for modification of the visitation orders, and Susan filed for a Show Cause for failure to pay child support. The trial court ordered Farmer to pay his child support or face restricted visitation rights. Further, the court ordered Farmer to maintain his visitation schedule or face the revocation of his suspended sentence originally imposed for failure to pay child support. Farmer appeals the orders.

ISSUE: May courts condition or commingle visitation rights and child support obligations?

HOLDING AND DECISION: (Barnes, J.) No. Courts may not condition or commingle visitation rights and child support obligations. Courts are in similar positions with custodial parents in that they may not interfere with visitation rights because the noncustodial parent fails to pay child support. A trial court may modify a visitation order if there is a finding of child endangerment or impairment to the child's emotional development. The court made no such finding here except for the failure to pay child support affecting the child. The trial court erred in threatening to restrict Farmer's visitation rights if he did not meet his child support obligations. Next, the trial court attempted to force Farmer to abide by his visitation schedule. Visitation is an entitlement, not an obligation. The courts cannot force a relationship between parent and child. Threatening Farmer with the revocation of his suspended sentence was improper. It is disturbing that a parent would prefer not to visit his child, but Farmer is correct in arguing that a court cannot force visitation. Judgment reversed in part. [The court affirmed in part on other grounds not stated in the casebook.]

▶ ANALYSIS

Courts seek to enforce orders issued in the best interests of the children. Courts cannot, however, force a relationship between the parent and child if it is not desired. As distasteful as the *Farmer* court found it, it recognized that forced visitation is not judicially acceptable. Courts are limited in their remedies for forcing a parent to "behave" and are significantly limited in their abilities to force a parent to do the morally right thing.

Quicknotes

CHILD SUPPORT Payments made by one parent to another in satisfaction of the noncustodial parent's legal obligation to provide for the sustenance of the child.

CIVIL CONTEMPT CITATION One party's failure to comply with a court order requiring that party to undertake an action for the benefit of another party to the action.

CUSTODY The granting of care and control of a child or children to a parent pursuant to an action for dissolution or separation.

NONCUSTODIAL PARENT A parent who is not awarded the primary care and control of a child by the court in a dissolution or separation proceeding.

SHOW CAUSE Generally referred to as an order to show cause or a show cause order. The order is directed to the opposing party to appear and show cause why a certain order should not be enforced or confirmed, or give reason why a court should take or not take a proposed action.

VISITATION Rights awarded by the court in a divorce or custody proceeding to a parent who does not have custody over the child or children, permitting that parent to visit with the child or children.

Property, Alimony, and Child Support Awards

Quick Reference Rules of Law

Innerbichler v. Innerbichler

Ex-husband (P) v. Ex-wife (D)

132 Md. App. 207, 752 A.2d 291 (2000).

NATURE OF CASE: Appeal from marital property division in dissolution of marriage.

FACT SUMMARY: Husband (P) began a business just prior to his marriage to Wife (D). When making the property award, the court found the increase to the value of the business was marital property subject to equitable division.

🏛 RULE OF LAW
In a dissolution, all property is found to be marital unless traced to a non-marital source, then assigned a value, and all marital property must be equitably divided.

FACTS: Nicholas R. Innerbichler (P) and Carole Jean Innerbichler (D) married on January 21, 1984. Just over one year prior to the parties' marriage, Mr. Innerbichler (P) co-founded TAMSCO with a partner. Mr. Innerbichler (P) owned 51% and the partner owned 49%. Approximately six months prior to the parties' marriage, Mr. Innerbichler (P), an Hispanic-American, applied to obtain 8(a) certification through the U.S. Small Business Administration. The "8(a) program" was meant to "assist small businesses owned and controlled by socially and economically disadvantaged persons." Less than three months after the parties' marriage, the 8(a) certification came though, which enabled TAMSCO to obtain government contracts. Profits rapidly increased due to the 8(a) contracts, and Mr. Innerbichler (P) was doing very well financially. The couple were married for 11 years before Mr. Innerbichler (P) moved out of the marital home and filed a complaint for Limited Divorce. Mrs. Innerbichler (D) counterclaimed for an Absolute Divorce based on adultery and later amended her claim to include a two-year separation. At trial, Mr. Innerbichler (P), now 55, was living with his mistress in a $600,000 home. Mr. Innerbichler (P) was able to obtain a mortgage and loan from his business to finance his home. Mrs. Innerbichler (D), now 47, was a high-school graduate with one semester of college. The trial court granted the divorce and began determining the equitable division of marital property. By the time of trial, TAMSCO was no longer participating in the 8(a) program, but was still receiving residual 8(a) business. Mrs. Innerbichler (D) claimed TAMSCO's value as marital property while Mr. Innerbichler (P) claimed that any TAMSCO success was directly related to a pre-marriage contract award, thus removing TAMSCO's increase in value from the marital estate. The trial court heard testimony on TAMSCO's value and found the increase as well as Mr. Innerbichler's (P) 51% TAMSCO stock to be marital. The trial court subsequently awarded $2,880,000 plus

alimony to Mrs. Innerbichler (D). After post-trial motions, the court reevaluated the property order and revised the award to Mrs. Innerbichler (D) to $2,581,864.75, payable over five years without interest. Mr. Innerbichler (P) appealed.

ISSUE: In a dissolution, is all property found to be marital unless traced to a non-marital source, then assigned a value, and all marital property must be equitably divided?

HOLDING AND DECISION: (Hollander, J.) Yes. In a dissolution, all property is found to be marital unless traced to a non-marital source, then assigned a value, and all marital property must be equitably divided. The court must also consider the 11 statutory factors to determine if an equitable division will result if marital property is divided according to title. If an equitable division will not result, then a monetary award may be made to the party experiencing the shortfall. Mr. Innerbichler (P) claims that TAMSCO was not a marital asset because it was existing and successful prior to the marriage. He disputes the trial court's determination that his efforts alone grew TAMSCO. Mr. Innerbichler (P) further claims that marital property should include only his precise work efforts that contributed to the increase in TAMSCO's value and also that his 51% stock is not automatically marital property merely because he owned that much. During the marriage, TAMSCO grew from being a home-based business with two employees to one of the top ten firms nationwide in the 8(a) program. The trial court concluded that the increase constituted marital property largely due to Mr. Innerbichler's (P) efforts to grow TAMSCO during the marriage. The court recognizes Mr. Innerbichler's (P) argument that one person alone does not make a successful company, but the trial court did not err in finding the increase in value is largely attributable to him. Prior cases have distinguished between mere ownership of a business and an owner's active efforts resulting in the business's success, thus creating marital property. The trial court did not have to accept Mr. Innerbichler's (P) offered evidence that TAMSCO's success was due to others. The trial court also properly determined that it was just 51% of the increase in value of TAMSCO which constituted marital property because Mr. Innerbichler (P) only owned 51% of TAMSCO stock. Half of that 51% increase in value became Mrs. Innerbichler's (D) monetary award. The trial court did consider the 11 statutory factors, including Mr. Innerbichler's (P) adultery and desertion when making

Continued on next page.

the award. The trial court committed neither error nor abuse of discretion. Affirmed.

▶ *ANALYSIS*

Nicholas Innerbichler was the recipient of a *Forbes* Magazine Award for his contributions to the business world through his companies such as TAMSCO. In 1992, he was recognized as a Regional Entrepreneur of the Year by *Inc.*com. Clearly he did not build his successful business solely on his own, but he also could not claim that TAMSCO succeeded in a vacuum separate from his participation. He was and is a visionary business developer. The sole contract promised to TAMSCO prior to the marriage could not support Mr. Innerbichler's contention that the court could trace TAMSCO's success to a non-marital source. It can be difficult to demonstrate the existence of a non-marital source for property absent unambiguous title documents, and the court does not have to accept a party's proffered evidence of non-marital sources.

■■■■

Quicknotes

DISSOLUTION Annulment or termination of a formal or legal bond, tie or contract.

MARITAL PROPERTY Property accumulated by a married couple during the term of their marriage.

PETITION FOR LIMITED DIVORCE Requests a dissolution of the marriage with the decree or order of dissolution containing no provision for support.

■■■■

Thomas v. Thomas

Parties not identified.

Ga. Sup. Ct., 259 Ga. 73, 377 S.E.2d 666 (1989).

NATURE OF CASE: Appeal from property division in marital dissolution case.

FACT SUMMARY: Husband and wife each brought separate property into marriage and then increased the value of that separate property through marital contributions. The court's attempt to make an equitable distribution of property resulted in distributing some admittedly non-marital property between the parties.

> 🏛 **RULE OF LAW**
> In making an equitable distribution of property, the court must first determine which property is marital and then equitably distribute only that property while protecting the spouse's non-marital contribution pursuant to the source of funds rule.

FACTS: Wife, a Florida resident, met future Husband, a Georgia resident, through work and then married. Husband soon left his family and Wife gave him $38,967.00 to help with his increased expenses due to his separation. Wife then moved to Atlanta and purchased a home titled in her name with $75,000.00 down and obtained a mortgage. Wife made the first seven months of mortgage payments. Once the parties married, the mortgage payments were made through a combination of marital and Wife's contributions. Prior to the marriage, Husband earned stock options, which he exercised during the marriage through a combination of marital and his separate funds. At the divorce trial, the court attempted to protect Wife's pre-marital contribution to Husband by removing $38,967.00 of assets from Husband's property award. The court elected to remove the $30,000.00 profit from the stock sale to be considered marital property subject to equal distribution despite court's concession that the stock was primarily a non-marital asset because it was paid for through non-marital loans. The court also determined the home sale proceeds should go primarily to Wife. Husband appealed.

ISSUE: In making an equitable distribution of property, must the court first determine which property is marital and then equitably distribute only that property while protecting the spouse's non-marital contribution pursuant to the source of funds rule?

HOLDING AND DECISION: (Hunt, J.) Yes. In making an equitable distribution of property, the court must first determine which property is marital and then equitably distribute only that property while protecting the spouse's non-marital contribution pursuant to the source of funds rule. Husband argues that non-marital assets, such as the stock proceeds here, are not subject to equitable

distribution. This is true because the court must first classify property as marital or non-marital and then make an equitable distribution solely of the marital property. The court cannot attempt to protect a party's non-marital contribution by distributing other non-marital property. If part of the stock profits may properly be considered marital property, then the court may use the standard criteria to determine an equitable distribution of that property. The house's appreciation was $90,905.00. During the marriage, the parties reduced the mortgage debt by $6,393.00 and Wife reduced the debt by $1,117.00. The court looked at the ratio of the marital reduction in debt to the equity of $82,623.00 and determined that 7% of the appreciation was subject to marital distribution. This is the "source of funds" rule set out fully in *Harper v. Harper*, 448 A.2d 916 (Md. 1982). That case looked at sister states to determine the appropriate equitable division of the marital home as separate property paid for by marital funds. The Maryland court and this court have adopted the "source of funds" rule, which holds that the court must consider the "ratio of the non-marital investment to the total non-marital and marital investment in the property" when determining each spouse's interest in the property. The balance is then considered marital property subject to equitable distribution. This protects any spouse's non-marital contribution. Husband's claim that the appreciation value occurred because of joint efforts is not supported by the evidence and the trial court did not err in its award of the home profits to Wife. Affirmed in part; reversed and remanded to determine the marital property value of the stock profits and to make an equitable distribution of that value.

▶ **ANALYSIS**

The source of funds rule ideally protects all non-marital investments in what could be determined to be a marital asset. For example, the spouse who uses a non-marital family loan or inheritance to improve the marital home does not necessarily lose that investment when it comes time for equitable property distribution. This rule also protects the spouse who purchased the home and improved upon it years prior to the marriage. As more people wait until they are older to get married and thus likely bring greater home equity into the marriage, this rule protects those early investments. It can be exhausting, however, to trace the property investments back to their original source when property was commingled years ago. The initial

Continued on next page.

determination of what constitutes marital and non-marital property is meant to avoid courts making an "equal" distribution rather than "equitable" distribution of all property.

■━━■

Quicknotes

MARITAL PROPERTY Property accumulated by a married couple during the term of their marriage.

■━━■

Ferguson v. Ferguson

Wife (P) v. Husband (D)

Miss. Sup. Ct., 639 So. 2d 921 (1994).

NATURE OF CASE: Appeal from a grant of divorce and award of marital property.

FACT SUMMARY: After the chancery court awarded Linda Ferguson (P) a divorce, custody of a minor son, debt-free ownership of the marital home and four surrounding acres, along with an interest in other marital assets accumulated during the couple's twenty-four-year marriage, Billy Ferguson (D) appealed.

RULE OF LAW
A spouse who has made a material contribution toward the acquisition of property which is titled in the name of the other may claim an equitable interest in such jointly accumulated property incident to a divorce proceeding.

FACTS: Linda Ferguson (P) filed for divorce from Billy Ferguson (D) after twenty-four years of marriage and two children, one of whom still resided with his parents. During the marriage, Linda (P) had worked both as a homemaker and as a beautician. The chancellor granted Linda's (P) request for divorce, awarding her custody of their son, child support, periodic alimony, the marital home and its contents, together with four acres of land, debt-free title to be vested in Linda (P), a lump-sum alimony payment, along with a one-half interest in Billy's (D) pension plan, stock ownership plan, and savings and security plan. Billy (D) appealed.

ISSUE: May a spouse who has made a material contribution toward the acquisition of property which is titled in the name of the other claim an equitable interest in such jointly accumulated property incident to a divorce proceeding?

HOLDING AND DECISION: (Prather, J.) Yes. A spouse who has made a material contribution toward the acquisition of property which is titled in the name of the other may claim an equitable interest in such jointly accumulated property incident to a divorce proceeding. In this case, the property was not titled solely in Billy's (D) name but titled to both Billy (D) and Linda (P). Moreover, both parties requested an equitable division of their jointly accumulated property. Through an evolution of case law, the chancellor was within his authority and power to order an equitable division. However, Linda (P) was divested of her undivided one-half interest in the adjoining thirty-three acres of jointly owned and accumulated real property, which was awarded to Billy (D), along with other property. Thus, the issue of property division is reversed and remanded for consideration in light of the factors determining substantial contribution to the accumulation of that property.

ANALYSIS

The separate property system, the equitable distribution system, and a system of fixed rules (community property) are all reflected in American jurisprudence. The court determined that the state's use of the separate property system resulted in an unfair division of property because it did not take account of a spouse's non-financial contributions, which, in the case of many traditional housewives, are often considerable. Examining its prior holdings and acknowledging that its decisions had evolved into an equitable distribution system, the court set guidelines to apply when attempting an equitable division of marital property.

Quicknotes

EQUITABLE DISTRIBUTION SYSTEM Marriage viewed as a partnership with both spouses contributing to the marital estate in the manner which they have chosen.

MARITAL PROPERTY Property accumulated by a married couple during the term of their marriage.

Postema v. Postema

Wife (P) v. Husband (D)

Mich. Ct. App., 189 Mich. App. 89, 471 N.W.2d 912 (1991).

NATURE OF CASE: Appeal of property distribution pursuant to dissolution of marriage.

FACT SUMMARY: Mrs. Postema (P) contended that Mr. Postema's (D) professional degree should be taken into account in valuing the marital estate.

RULE OF LAW
In a divorce, one spouse's advanced degree should be taken into account in the property distribution.

FACTS: The Postemas were married in 1984, just as Mr. Postema (D) entered law school. He graduated in 1987, the same year the parties separated. They later filed for divorce. In splitting the marital estate, the court valued Mr. Postema's (D) degree at $80,000, and awarded Mrs. Postema (P) $32,000 as her "share" of the degree. The parties cross-appealed.

ISSUE: In a divorce, should one spouse's advanced degree be taken into account in the property distribution?

HOLDING AND DECISION: (Maher, J.) Yes. In a divorce, one spouse's advanced degree should be taken into account in the property distribution. The basic goal of property division in a divorce is to promote fairness. A professional degree is what might be called a "concerted family effort"; both spouses sacrifice with the expectation that the degree will benefit both members. To allow the receiving spouse to walk away without the non-receiving spouse being compensated would be unfair. Some courts take degrees into account in awarding alimony. This is conceptually wrong, as alimony is a form of support, and the non-receiving spouse should be entitled to compensation without regard for whether she needs support. The better view is to award the non-receiving spouse the value of her sacrifice toward the degree, less what she has already obtained. Here, the case must be returned to the trial court because it incorrectly looked to the "value" of the degree, not the value of Mrs. Postema's (P) investment in assisting Mr. Postema (D) in earning the degree. Remanded.

ANALYSIS

Some have argued that an advanced degree is "property" subject to division. The court here did not feel it necessary to rule on this issue. It is difficult to call a degree "property" without stretching the concept. Property normally has the attributes of transferability, divisibility, and pledgability. A degree has none of these characteristics.

Quicknotes

MARITAL PROPERTY Property accumulated by a married couple during the term of their marriage.

Elkus v. Elkus

Opera star wife (P) v. Husband (D)

N.Y. Sup. Ct., 169 A.D.2d 134, 572 N.Y.S.2d 901 (1991).

NATURE OF CASE: Appeal from order of marital property determination.

FACT SUMMARY: Frederica von Stade Elkus (P), a world-renowned opera star, moved for an order determining that her career value was not a marital asset subject to equitable distribution in dissolution proceedings with her husband. Husband (D) claimed that his emotional and career support contributed to Stade Elkus's (P) success, thus increasing the value of her celebrity and making her career a divisible marital asset.

🏛 RULE OF LAW
Marital property is determined by the nature of the contribution to its value and not by its status as a licensed or otherwise tangible existence.

FACTS: Frederica von Stade Elkus (P) was a minor player with the Metropolitan Opera Company at the start of her marriage to Mr. Elkus (D). Throughout their seventeen-year marriage, Mr. Elkus (D) traveled extensively with Stade Elkus (P), critiqued her performances, photographed her for marketing purposes, and served as her voice coach for ten years during the marriage. Stade Elkus's (P) career subsequently flourished, and she eventually became a very successful, world-renowned operatic star. Stade Elkus (P) and Mr. Elkus (D) stipulated to a divorce judgment and to custody arrangements for their two minor children after Stade Elkus (P) filed for divorce. Stade Elkus (P) then moved for a pre-trial determination that her career and celebrity status were not marital assets subject to equitable distribution. The trial court granted her motion and Mr. Elkus (D) appealed. The remaining dissolution determinations have been stayed pending appeal.

ISSUE: Is marital property determined by the nature of the contribution to its value rather than its status as a licensed or otherwise tangible existence?

HOLDING AND DECISION: [Judge not stated in casebook excerpt.] Yes. Marital property is determined by the nature of the contribution to its value and not by its status as a licensed or otherwise tangible existence. Stade Elkus (P) argues that her career is not licensed, trademarked, or owned as a separate business entity and therefore does not constitute divisible marital property. Domestic Relations Law defines "marital property" broadly without regard to title. Nothing in the law requires marital property to be tangible, transferable property but merely something of value acquired during the marriage. Examples of intangible marital property subject to distribution per prior case law include professional licenses, degrees, and fellowships. The purpose is to compensate the spouse who supported the obtaining of those licenses and degrees and the case law does not limit the "property" to licenses. Anything requiring joint effort of the spouses can be considered marital property. When the property cannot be physically distributed, statutory law provides for monetary compensation to the deserving spouse. Stade Elkus's (P) inherent talent cannot discount Mr. Elkus's (D) concrete contributions to her success. The appreciation in value of her career is a direct result of his efforts in child-rearing, coaching, and support. Reversed.

▶ ANALYSIS

The economic partnership of a marriage is what determines the status of marital property within that marriage. The joint efforts of the couple to increase the value of any asset results in the effects of that effort becoming subject to equitable distribution. Here, Elkus contributed more than homemaker services and was entitled to compensation for his investment in Stade Elkus's career. Subsequent New York jurisdiction cases held that the courts must, however, consider whether the non-celebrity spouse's efforts actually contributed to the celebrity spouse's increased stature and value. The celebrity spouse should have benefited in some tangible way by the aid and support of the other.

Quicknotes

MARITAL PROPERTY Property accumulated by a married couple during the term of their marriage.

Siegel v. Siegel

Wife (P) v. Husband (D)

N.J. Super. Ct., Chan. Div., 241 N.J. Super. 12, 574 A.2d 54 (1990).

NATURE OF CASE: Appeal from a divorce order.

FACT SUMMARY: When Mr. Siegel (D) alleged that his gambling losses should be equally distributed at dissolution, Mrs. Siegel (P) alleged that they were really a dissipation of funds and were to be borne solely by Mr. Siegel (D).

🏛 RULE OF LAW
The contribution of each party to the acquisition or dissipation of the marital property is to be considered in determining the equitable distribution.

FACTS: After Mrs. Siegel (P) filed for divorce, Mr. Siegel (D) executed a note for alleged gambling debts to a closely held corporation of which he was an equal one-third shareholder. When the court denied his application to compel Mrs. Siegel (P) to execute joint income tax returns for the 1998 calendar year, Mr. Siegel (D) forged her signature to the return. Mrs. Siegel (P) claimed that the gambling debts should be borne by Mr. Siegel (D) alone, and appealed.

ISSUE: Is the contribution of each party to the acquisition or dissipation of the marital property to be considered in determining the equitable distribution?

HOLDING AND DECISION: (Berman, J.) Yes. The contribution of each party to the acquisition or dissipation of the marital property is to be considered in determining the equitable distribution. The debt belongs to the gambler, with no offset or credit. The court is unconvinced of the actuality of the alleged losses, or Mrs. Siegel's (P) knowledge of them. Reversed.

▶ ANALYSIS

The court in this case found that financial dishonesty or unfairness between the spouses can be material. Admitted dissipation of marital funds, as in gambling, has been found by other courts to be presumptively fraudulent. The gambling losses were thus excluded from the matrimonial pot.

■═■

Quicknotes

DISSIPATION OF FUNDS The improvident spending of money.

EQUITABLE DISTRIBUTION The means by which a court distributes all assets acquired during a marriage by the spouses equitably upon dissolution.

FRAUD A false representation of facts with the intent that another will rely on the misrepresentation to his detriment.

■═■

Laing v. Laing

Parties not identified.

Alaska Sup. Ct., 741 P.2d 649 (1987).

NATURE OF CASE: Appeal as to disposition of a nonvested pension.

FACT SUMMARY: When their twenty-year marriage ended, Kenneth Laing challenged the trial court's characterization of his nonvested pension rights as marital property.

RULE OF LAW
A spouse's nonvested pension rights are properly characterized as marital property.

FACTS: When the Laings' twenty-year marriage ended, the trial court awarded Kenneth his nonvested pension, set its present value at $27,000, and awarded Marla offsetting marital assets. Kenneth challenged the award on the grounds that there was insufficient evidence to support the $27,000 figure, and that Marla's share should not have been awarded in a lump sum.

ISSUE: Are a spouse's nonvested pension rights properly characterized as marital property?

HOLDING AND DECISION: (Compton, J.) Yes. A spouse's nonvested pension rights are properly characterized as marital property. The trend is to consider pensions as marital property regardless of whether they have vested. The contingencies that may prevent the employee spouse from ever collecting his or her nonvested pension should not bar the nonemployee spouse from recovering a share if the pension is in fact paid out. However, the present value approach used by the trial court was inherently unfair, therefore, the reserved jurisdiction approach is preferable. The nonvested pension should not have been considered when the trial court made the initial property division at the time of the divorce. Once the pension has vested, the trial court can determine which approach is appropriate in a given case and adapt that approach to the specific circumstances presented. On remand, the trial court was directed to investigate the applicability of the Retirement Equity Act of 1984 (REACT), which applied to retirement benefit plans covered by the Employee Retirement Income Security Act of 1974 (ERISA). If Kenneth's plan was not covered by ERISA, the trial court was directed to retain jurisdiction so that an appropriate division could be made if and when Kenneth's pension vested. Reversed and remanded with directions.

▶ ANALYSIS

The court declares that the reserved jurisdiction approach more fairly allocates the risk of forfeiture between the parties. In addition, under REACT, a qualified domestic relations order (QDRO) can be filed with the administrator of the employee spouse's pension plan. If and when the employee spouse's pension vests and matures, payments are made directly to the nonemployee former spouse. This solves the problem of continuing financial entanglement between former spouses, and ensures that the nonemployee spouse receives the payments to which he or she is entitled.

Quicknotes

MARITAL PROPERTY Property accumulated by a married couple during the term of their marriage.

VESTED INTEREST A present right to property, although the right to the possession of such property may not be enjoyed until a future date.

Niroo v. Niroo

Parties not identified.

Md. Ct. App., 545 A.2d 35 (1988).

NATURE OF CASE: Appeal from property disposition in dissolution proceedings.

FACT SUMMARY: David Niroo, an insurance salesman and branch manager, was entitled to renewal commissions on policies sold during his marriage to Mrs. Niroo. The divorce trial court agreed with Mrs. Niroo that such commissions, even if paid post-dissolution, constitute marital property subject to equitable distribution.

🏛 RULE OF LAW
Anticipated post-dissolution commissions earned during the marriage constitute divisible marital property.

FACTS: David Niroo and Mrs. Niroo married in 1977. One year later, David Niroo began a career as an insurance salesman. He was later promoted to branch manager and became entitled to share in profits earned from insurance renewal commissions. His interest in the profits vested and was payable to his heirs and assigns in the case of his death. The Niroos filed for divorce, and each presented expert testimony at trial on the present-day valuation of the anticipated renewal commissions. The trial court found the anticipated commissions to be marital property and accepted David Niroo's expert valuation. David Niroo also presented evidence that he had taken advances from the company against the renewal commissions, but the court found those advances to be an "economic circumstance" separate from marital property. The court then made a monetary award of $200,000 to Mrs. Niroo. David Niroo appealed.

ISSUE: Do anticipated post-dissolution commissions earned during the marriage constitute divisible marital property?

HOLDING AND DECISION: (Murphy, C.J.) Yes. Anticipated post-dissolution commissions earned during the marriage constitute divisible marital property. David Niroo's claim focuses on the fact that the renewal commissions are speculative because they might not actually occur. David Niroo also asserts that he will have to perform additional post-marriage work on the accounts thus removing them from any joint marital efforts but still providing his ex-wife with the benefits of his separate endeavors. Contractually vested rights are a marital asset subject to division. David Niroo's anticipated post-dissolution work on the renewals does not remove them from the status of marital property because his primary effort was expended during the marriage in establishing the accounts in the first place. The court recognizes that David Niroo will have to continue to abide by his contractual terms to obtain payment of the renewal commissions, but those requirements are not so unbearable that they unfairly burden him. Nor is the speculative nature of the renewals so high that it is more likely than not that they will not be paid. Finding vested commission rights to be a marital asset supports the policy of compensating a spouse for the joint efforts in obtaining those commissions initially and for the loss of the ability to depend on those renewals in full.

▶ ANALYSIS

Maryland's common law title system was replaced by an equitable distribution system in 1974. Under Maryland law, the court may not transfer title to property but may only make a monetary judgment. The general rule is that income earned during the marriage is classified as marital property even though its receipt is deferred until after the divorce.

■=■

Quicknotes

MARITAL PROPERTY Property accumulated by a married couple during the term of their marriage.

■=■

In re Marriage of Wilson

Parties not identified.

Cal. Sup. Ct., 201 Cal. App. 3d 913 (1988).

NATURE OF CASE: Appeal from order terminating spousal support.

FACT SUMMARY: Elma appealed the court termination of her spousal support after 58 months, despite her request for continuation of such payments and her former husband's ability to continue making payments.

> ## 🏛 RULE OF LAW
> In a dissolution judgment, the court may order a party to pay any amount for the support of the other party for any period of time as the court may deem just and reasonable considering all the statutorily stipulated circumstances of the respective parties.

FACTS: Tom and Elma Wilson were separated after being married for 70 months. At the time of their marriage, Elma was a middle-aged bartender with adult children. Her lifestyle was already established. Two years before their separation, Elma had been injured in a fall. Either as a result of her injuries or an infection following dental work, she could no longer work as a bartender. In the opinion of a clinical psychologist, Elma suffered brain damage, which left her "lacking in social judgment, common sense, and social intelligence." The psychologist felt Elma would probably not succeed where she had to make decisions using common sense. In a stipulated interlocutory judgment, Tom received his navy pension and a Volkswagen, while Elma took the house, a Jaguar automobile, and spousal support of $500 per month for two years plus medical insurance coverage for the same period. Elma was later granted an extension of her spousal support for another year. Elma again sought continuing spousal support, claiming she was still unemployed and neither rehabilitated nor capable of rehabilitation. Tom argued that Elma should not be entitled to lifetime support from him based on a 70-month marriage. Although the court found that Tom had the earning capacity to continue to make support payments—his monthly income was in excess of $3,200—and Elma had a need for such payments, because she was both disabled and could not regain her previous income earning status, the court terminated her spousal support after 58 months. Elma contended it was an abuse of discretion to terminate spousal support where there was no present evidence of her ability to be self-supporting. Weighing the length and nature of the marriage, the fact that there were no children of the marriage, and the duration of the spousal support payment, the court ruled that Tom no longer had the legal obligation to support his former spouse. Elma appealed.

ISSUE: In a dissolution judgment, may the court order a party to pay any amount for the support of the other party for any period of time as the court may deem just and reasonable considering all the statutorily stipulated circumstances of the respective parties?

HOLDING AND DECISION: (Haden, J.) Yes. In a dissolution judgment, the court may order a party to pay any amount for the support of the other party for any period of time as the court may deem just and reasonable considering all the statutorily stipulated circumstances of the respective parties. The record reflects that the trial court weighed each of the eight factors listed in the statute before exercising discretion to terminate support. Finally, the court balanced the equities and decided, under these circumstances, the obligation to assist Elma should shift from Tom to society. The court recognized both the grievous and permanent nature of Elma's disability but noted it was beyond the court's power to render her self-supporting. "In short-term marriages spousal support will most usually be ordered where the needs of minor children or the employment circumstances of the supported spouse require spousal support until the supported spouse can readjust to single status." Neither minor children nor any reasonable likelihood of employment readjustment was present here. Under the facts of this case, there was no abuse of discretion by the lower court. Affirmed.

▶ ANALYSIS

Under § 4801 of the Cal. Civ. Code, a court must consider the extent to which the supported spouse contributed to the attainment of an education, training, a career position, or a license by the other spouse. In addition, the needs of each party; the obligations and assets, including the separate property of each; the duration of the marriage; the ability of the supported spouse to engage in gainful employment without interfering with the interests of dependent children in the custody of the spouse; the age or health of the parties; the standard of living of the parties; and any other factors which it deems just and equitable must be considered by the court. The court distinguished *In re Marriage of Morrison*, 20 Cal. 3d 437, 573 P.2d 41 (1978), as involving a "long-term" marriage of 28 years and, thus, not applicable here.

Continued on next page.

Quicknotes

ABUSE OF DISCRETION A determination by an appellate court that a lower court's decision was based on an error of law.

INTERLOCUTORY JUDGMENT An order entered by the court determining an issue that does not resolve the disposition of the case, but is essential to a proper adjudication of the action.

SPOUSAL SUPPORT Payments made by one spouse to another in discharge of the spouse's duty pursuant to law, or in accordance with a written divorce or separation decree, in order to provide maintenance for the other spouse.

Clapp v. Clapp

Ex-wife (P) v. Ex-husband (D)

Vt. Sup. Ct., 163 Vt. 15, 653 A.2d 72 (1994).

NATURE OF CASE: Appeal from property and maintenance orders issued following a divorce decree.

FACT SUMMARY: When Mr. Clapp (D) was ordered to pay maintenance to his former spouse using an income equalization approach, he challenged the award as excessive.

> 🏛 **RULE OF LAW**
> The family court has broad discretion in determining the amount of maintenance and will be reversed only if there is no reasonable basis to support the award.

FACTS: The trial court ordered Mr. Clapp (D) to pay monthly maintenance to Mrs. Clapp (P), following their divorce. Mr. Clapp (D) appealed the amount awarded, claiming that it exceeded the amount necessary for Mrs. Clapp (P) to meet her reasonable needs. The court had recognized her significant non-monetary contribution to the marriage as a homemaker in determining the award. Mr. Clapp (D) claimed that the terms of the state statute limited a maintenance award to the amount necessary to meet only the former spouse's "reasonable needs."

ISSUE: Does the family court have broad discretion in determining the amount of maintenance?

HOLDING AND DECISION: (Dooley, J.) Yes. The family court has broad discretion in determining the amount of maintenance and will be reversed only if there is no reasonable basis to support the award. The statute is based on a concept of relative, not absolute, need. Reasonable need is not to be judged in relation to subsistence, but in light of the standard of living established during the marriage. One purpose of maintenance under the statute is to compensate a homemaker for contributions to the family's well-being not otherwise recognized in the property distribution. The family court acted within its discretion in awarding permanent maintenance, and the amount is also within its discretion. Affirmed.

▶ ANALYSIS

Restitution for past homemaker contributions had been explicitly recognized by the Vermont Supreme Court in an earlier case, *Klein v. Klein*, 555 A.2d at 387. Since such contributions are, by their nature, non-monetary, the court noted that they cannot be easily quantified. The main objective of the award was to maintain the wife's standard of living at the level established during the marriage.

Quicknotes

MAINTENANCE AWARD An order entered by the court requiring one spouse to make payments to the other for sustenance.

Graham v. Graham

Ex-wife (P) v. Ex-husband (D)

597 A.2d 355 (D.C. 1991).

NATURE OF CASE: Appeal from order modifying award of alimony and child support.

FACT SUMMARY: When Mr. Graham's (D) salary increased dramatically at about the time their divorce decree was to become final, this action ensued after negotiations between the parties for increased support payments broke down.

> 🏛 **RULE OF LAW**
> An increase in the noncustodial parent's ability to pay can, by itself, constitute a material change in circumstances sufficient to justify an increase in support.

FACTS: Under a 1982 divorce decree, Mr. Graham (D) was ordered to make alimony and child support payments, along with mortgage and private school tuition payments. Mr. Graham's (D) salary was raised from $100,000 in 1981 to $185,000 in 1982, and was to increase every year until 1985, when he would be earning $255,000. The parties could not agree about increasing support payments in light of these salary increases, and Mrs. Graham (P) filed a motion to enforce agreement or in the alternative for increased alimony and child support. The trial court held that an increase in the non-custodial parent's income, no matter how great, was, by itself, an insufficient basis upon which to modify a support order. But finding that the needs of Mrs. Graham (P) and the children had increased, the court raised both the amount of child support and alimony awarded.

ISSUE: Can an increase in the noncustodial parent's ability to pay, by itself, constitute a material change in circumstances sufficient to justify an increase in support?

HOLDING AND DECISION: (Per curiam) Yes. An increase in the noncustodial parent's ability to pay, by itself, can constitute a material change in circumstances sufficient to justify an increase in support. A material change in either the parent's income or in the needs of the children and the other spouse may be the basis for modification of the support order. By insisting that there could be no increase in support without a commensurate increase in the needs of Mrs. Graham (P) and the children, the trial court effectively nullified the first prong of this standard. The basic standard for a modification applies to both alimony and child support orders. Reversed and remanded.

CONCURRENCE AND DISSENT: (Terry, J.) I am willing to remand the child support matter for reconsideration but cannot go along with sending the alimony claim back to the trial court.

▶ **ANALYSIS**

The disjunctive standard which the court applied was developed in its prior decision, *Hamilton v. Hamilton*, 247 A.2d 421, 423 (D.C. 1968). The court expressed its concern that noncustodial parents did not increase their own standard of living without also ensuring that their children live as well as they do. Stated differently, although spouses may divorce, the children's legal relationship with both parents continues, and the children's station in life should not therefore be fixed forever to their parents' station in life at the time of the divorce.

■══■

Quicknotes

ALIMONY Allowances (usually monetary) which husband or wife by court order pays to the other spouse for maintenance while they are separated, or after they are divorced (permanent alimony), or temporarily, pending a suit for divorce (pendente lite).

CHILD SUPPORT MODIFICATION The alteration of the payment structure pursuant to which one parent provides payments to another in satisfaction of the non-custodial parent's legal obligation to provide for the sustenance of the child.

NONCUSTODIAL PARENT A parent who is not awarded the primary care and control of a child by the court in a dissolution or separation proceeding.

■══■

D'Ascanio v. D'Ascanio

Husband (P) v. Wife (D)

Conn. Sup. Ct., 237 Conn. 481, 678 A.2d 469 (1996).

NATURE OF CASE: Appeal from an order modifying an alimony award.

FACT SUMMARY: When the trial court failed to apply the provisions of a modification agreement entered into by the parties, the husband (P) appealed.

> ## 🏛 RULE OF LAW
> Once the initial issue of cohabitation is established, a court must enforce the terms of a modification agreement entered into by the parties and approved by the court.

FACTS: Following the dissolution of their marriage, Mr. D'Ascanio (P) was to pay $900 per week as alimony to Mrs. D'Ascanio (D). A modification agreement was later reached which stated that alimony would be reduced by one-half in the event the wife (D) remarried or cohabitated. When the husband (P) later alleged that the wife (D) was cohabitating, the court reduced the alimony by only $100 per week. The husband (P) appealed, seeking enforcement of the agreement to decrease the alimony payment by one-half.

ISSUE: Once the initial issue of cohabitation is established, must a court enforce the terms of a modification agreement entered into by the parties and approved by the court?

HOLDING AND DECISION: (Berdon, J.) Yes. Once the initial issue of cohabitation is established, a court must enforce the terms of a modification agreement entered into by the parties and approved by the court. A deviation from the terms of the modification agreement by the trial court was improper. Reversed and remanded.

▶ ANALYSIS

The trial court in this case thought that the parties' agreement should not limit the court's discretion. The court sua sponte decided that reducing the alimony further would be inequitable and would amount to a penalty. But, on appeal, it was held that the modification agreement was controlling, and the court had only to make the initial determination of cohabitation to trigger the agreement's provisions.

∎▬∎

Quicknotes

SUA SPONTE An action taken by the court by its own motion and without the suggestion of one of the parties.

∎▬∎

Marvin v. Marvin

Female cohabiter (P) v. Male cohabiter (D)

Cal. Sup. Ct., 18 Cal. 3d 660, 557 P.2d 106 (1976).

NATURE OF CASE: Appeal of dismissal of action to recover property accumulated during an unmarried domestic relationship.

FACT SUMMARY: Following the termination of seven years of cohabitation, Michelle Marvin (P) brought an action against Lee Marvin (D) to recover property accumulated during that time.

🏛 RULE OF LAW
Where cohabitation is expressly or impliedly founded on a sharing-of-property basis, the nonacquiring partner has an interest in property acquired during cohabitation.

FACTS: Michelle (P) and Lee (D) Marvin allegedly entered a cohabitation arrangement whereby Michelle (P) agreed not to pursue her career and to live with Lee (D), performing domestic services in exchange for equal sharing of the household income. This arrangement lasted seven years, with the pair eventually separating. Michelle (P) subsequently filed an action seeking to recover one-half of all the property acquired by Lee (D) during the arrangement. The trial court granted judgment on the pleadings, and the appellate court affirmed.

ISSUE: Where cohabitation is expressly or impliedly founded on a sharing-of-property basis, does the nonacquiring partner have an interest in property acquired during the cohabitation?

HOLDING AND DECISION: (Tobriner, J.) Yes. Where cohabitation is expressly or impliedly founded on a sharing-of-property basis, the nonacquiring partner has an interest in property acquired during the cohabitation. The law states that contracts based solely on sexual consideration are invalid, but cohabitation arrangements go far beyond sexual services. When the nonsexual aspects of a living arrangement are expressly based on a sharing of income, basic contract law compels the conclusion that the nonacquiring partner has an interest in income and property acquired during the arrangement. Even if no express contract exists, an implied contract may be found if the circumstances so indicate. Where the nonacquiring partner has a contractual right to property acquired during the cohabitation, the fact that a sexual relationship may have been involved does not defeat that right. Reversed.

▶ ANALYSIS

This action was the one that popularized the phrase "palimony." The term was and is a misnomer, as property division, not support, was at issue. In fact, the court, at footnote 26, expressly reserved the question of whether the nonacquiring partner would have a right to support.

━━■

Norton v. Hoyt

Mistress (P) v. Adulterous husband (D)

278 F. Supp. 2d 214 (R.I. 2003).

NATURE OF CASE: Motion for summary judgment.

FACT SUMMARY: The parties had a twenty-three year adulterous relationship during which Hoyt (D) repeatedly promised to divorce his wife and to provide for Norton's (P) economic well-being. When Hoyt (D) failed to live up to his promises, Norton (P) sued him based on promissory estoppel.

RULE OF LAW
A broken promise to marry and to initiate divorce proceedings cannot support a claim for promissory estoppel, because it is against public policy.

FACTS: Gail M. Norton (P) met Russell L. Hoyt (D) through mutual acquaintances, and the pair began a romantic relationship. Norton (P) soon learned that Hoyt (D) was married despite his promises to the contrary, but she continued her relationship with him. Hoyt (D) made repeated promises to divorce his wife, marry Norton (P), and provide for her economically for the rest of her life. The couple traveled extensively, entertained lavishly, and shared two residences. Norton (P) was a schoolteacher when they met but she resigned, ostensibly to travel with Hoyt (D). Hoyt (D) paid for the majority of their lifestyle accoutrements. After twenty-three years of adulterous bliss, Hoyt (D) ended the relationship, but continued to contribute financially to Norton (P) for two years. Norton (P) claimed that the breakup resulted in several medical and psychological maladies. Norton (P) also claimed that Hoyt (D) stated that he had written a letter to his attorney outlining instructions for $100,000 to be placed into an account for Norton (P) and for a trust to be established for her financial care the rest of her life. After the break-up, Norton (P) learned that the letter did not exist. Norton (P) proceeded to file suit against Hoyt (D) based in part on promissory estoppel. Hoyt (D) moved for summary judgment.

ISSUE: Can a broken promise to marry and to initiate divorce proceedings support a claim for promissory estoppel?

HOLDING AND DECISION: (Lagueu, J.) No. A broken promise to marry and to initiate divorce proceedings cannot support a claim for promissory estoppel because it is against public policy. Promissory estoppel requires: "(1) A clear and unambiguous promise; (2) Reasonable and justifiable reliance upon the promise; and (3) Detriment to the promise, caused by his or her reliance on the promise." Norton (P) frames her claim as one based upon Hoyt's (D) alleged promise to "care for her for life" which she interprets to mean financial provisions for her. Norton (P), however, responded in interrogatories that she

remained in the relationship based upon Hoyt's (D) promise to divorce his wife, which is a promise outside of financial care. The promise is certainly ambiguous as it could mean financial or emotional care for Norton's (P) lifetime. Norton (P) also did not reasonably rely upon Hoyt's (D) statements because she was well aware that he remained married and continued to spend time with his wife and children. She was relying on an unreliable man, who was making little to no attempt to fulfill his promises to her. Finally, Norton's (P) claim that she relied on Hoyt's (D) promises to her detriment cannot be supported. She remained in an adulterous relationship for twenty-three years and it should have become clear to her that he was not going to leave his wife. Norton (P) is seeking to enforce a promise that would result in the initiation of divorce proceedings, which is against public policy supporting the institution of marriage. Further, the claim is too similar to a claim for breach of promise to marry, which is already dismissed. Finally, Rhode Island does not recognize palimony claims, which is essentially what this suit sets forth despite being labeled otherwise. Defendant's motion for summary judgment is granted.

ANALYSIS

The court's tenor was one of contempt for both parties, which makes this case one of the more entertaining reads but also provides insight into the public policy reasons for denying Norton's claim. The public does not want to support interference in the institution of marriage even if it benefits a cad to allow him to get out of his promises. The public also discourages parties from turning a blind eye to the realities of a situation. Norton should not be rewarded for pretending for twenty-three years that her relationship was something other than it was. In 2005, after Hoyt's death, the First Circuit affirmed this court's decision on Norton's appeal.

Quicknotes

PALIMONY Support payments made from one person to another following the termination of a non-marital relationship.

PROMISSORY ESTOPPEL A promise that is enforceable if the promisor should reasonably expect that it will induce action or forbearance on the part of the promisee, and does in fact cause such action or forbearance, and it is the only means of avoiding injustice.

Schmidt v. Schmidt

Mother (P) v. Father (D)

S.D. Sup. Ct., 444 N.W.2d 367 (1989).

NATURE OF CASE: Appeal of changes ordered in custody and child support.

FACT SUMMARY: Some time after the trial court awarded custody of their three sons to Mrs. Schmidt, Mr. Schmidt moved to modify the child custody and support provisions of the divorce decree.

🏛 RULE OF LAW
Child support obligation shall be established in accordance with the obligor's net income and number of children affected, unless specific findings permit deviation from these guidelines.

FACTS: When the Schmidts divorced, they agreed by stipulation that Mrs. Schmidt would have custody of their three sons. Mr. Schmidt later made a motion to modify the child custody and support provisions, requesting custody of the oldest boy, and that all three boys be permitted to reside with him on his farm during the summer months, with suitable modification of his child support obligations. The trial court granted Mr. Schmidt's custody requests, and his child support was reduced accordingly. Mrs. Schmidt appealed the custody changes, and Mr. Schmidt appealed the amount of child support. [The casebook excerpt did not identify plaintiff and defendant.]

ISSUE: Shall child support obligation be established in accordance with the obligor's net income and number of children affected, unless specific findings permit deviation from these guidelines?

HOLDING AND DECISION: (Sabers, J.) Yes. Child support obligation shall be established in accordance with the obligor's net income and number of children affected, unless specific findings permit deviation from these guidelines. The trial court determined Mr. Schmidt's child support under the guidelines in SDCL 25-7-7. Following the change of custody, Mr. Schmidt was obligated to pay support for two children based on his net monthly income, and Mrs. Schmidt was obligated to pay support for one child based on her net monthly income. Since her net monthly income exceeded his, her child support obligation for one nearly canceled out his child support obligation for two under the guidelines. However, SDCL 25-7-7 does not permit deviation from the guidelines absent specific findings. On remand, the trial court may make additional specific findings which may support deviations from the child support guidelines. The custody changes are affirmed. Affirmed in part, reversed and remanded in part.

CONCURRENCE AND DISSENT: (Henderson, J.) The result in the change of custody is appropriate. But under the rules of equity, the trial court's award of child support should be affirmed since there was no abuse of discretion.

▶ ANALYSIS

Both Congress and the state legislature have now revised the guidelines, allowing for deviation where their application would end in an unjust or inequitable application. In the notes following the instant case, the author reports that until well into this century, most courts held that only fathers were legally obligated to support children. However, while it now seems appropriate to hold both parents responsible for supporting children, it is not easy to determine what share each should pay, since taking care of a child is surely a form of support.

■══■

Quicknotes

CHILD SUPPORT MODIFICATION The alteration of the payment structure pursuant to which one parent provides payments to another in satisfaction of the non-custodial parent's legal obligation to provide for the sustenance of the child.

CUSTODY The granting of care and control of a child or children to a parent pursuant to an action for dissolution or separation.

■══■

In re Marriage of Bush

Mother (P) v. Father (D)

Ill. Ct. App., 191 Ill. App. 3d 249, 547 N.E.2d 590 (1989).

NATURE OF CASE: Appeal from child support award.

FACT SUMMARY: Both parties in this dissolution action appealed, challenging the amount awarded in child support to Bush (P) on a variety of grounds.

RULE OF LAW
Even though specific guidelines exist for determining child support awards, the trial court may vary from these guidelines by setting a figure for child support below the guideline amount when dictated by the income of both parents and taking into account the life-style the child would have enjoyed absent the dissolution.

FACTS: Bush (P) and Turner (D), both doctors, were married in 1982. They had one child from that marriage, but they were separated eight days after the child's birth, and they were never effectively reconciled. Bush filed for dissolution two months later, in December 1984, and received the decree of dissolution of marriage in January 1985, on the grounds of mental cruelty. As doctors, the salaries of Bush (P) and Turner (D) were quite substantial, with Turner's (D) salary in the range of approximately $25,000 per month. In September 1988, the court entered its final order with respect to child support. Turner (D) was ordered to pay directly to Bush (P) $800 a month for child support. In addition, the court required Turner (D) to establish a trust fund for his child, which consisted in part of temporary child support arrearages, and he was further required to contribute 20% of his income (net) to the trust. Turner (D) challenged the court's order, contending that the award of child support was excessive, and Bush (P) challenged the court order, contending the trial court abused its discretion by ordering Turner (D) to pay the child support arrearages into the trust and further that the award of $800 per month was insufficient.

ISSUE: May a trial court vary from existing specific guidelines for determining child support awards?

HOLDING AND DECISION: (Lund, J.) Yes. Where justified by the income of the divorcing parents and the lifestyle the child would have enjoyed absent the dissolution, a trial court may set a figure of child support which is below the amount dictated by existing specific guidelines for determining child support. [The court first determined that the trial court abused its discretion by requiring Turner (D) to pay child support arrearages into the trust fund.] The trial court's award requiring Turner (D) to pay 20% of his net income, amounting to

approximately $30,000, was excessive and constituted an abuse of discretion. That amount is more than the average income of most Americans. Reasons for not adhering to guideline amounts must be specified but exist where, as in the present case, both parents have more than enough income to provide for the child. The child in the present case has no unmet needs which require such an excessive award. A large income will not necessarily trigger an extravagant lifestyle or a personal trust fund and, in the present case, constitutes a windfall. The court must accommodate the reasonable needs of the child with the available means of the parents. Remanded.

ANALYSIS

On remand, Bush (P) lost her appeal, as Turner (D) was required to pay child support in the amount of $800 a month. In the present case, the child was blessed with abundant financial resources. The rule in the present case should also allow for a modification of child support awards in the event that, due to changed circumstances, the financial resources available to the child increase. Some cases hold that, unlike requests for spousal support, a request for an increase in child support need not be related to the family's standard of living during the marriage, considering the child an innocent victim. See *In re Marriage of Catalano*, 251 Cal. Rptr. 370 (1988).

Quicknotes

CHILD SUPPORT Payments made by one parent to another in satisfaction of the non-custodial parent's legal obligation to provide for the sustenance of the child.

Solomon v. Findley

Ex-wife (P) v. Ex-husband (D)

Ariz. Sup. Ct., 167 Ariz. 409, 808 P.2d 294 (1991).

NATURE OF CASE: Petition for review of court of appeals' opinion.

FACT SUMMARY: When Findley (D) failed to provide post-majority educational funds for their daughter's college education, as he agreed to do in the dissolution decree, Solomon (P) attempted to enforce the agreement.

🏛 RULE OF LAW
A provision for post-majority educational support does not merge into the dissolution decree, but remains independent and enforceable as a contract claim.

FACTS: When Solomon (P) and Findley (D) dissolved their marriage, Findley (D) agreed to provide educational funds for their daughter through college or until she reached the age of 25, whichever came first. The divorce court approved the agreement, and the decree was entered by default because Findley (D) was absent. Solomon (P) first tried to enforce the decree by filing an order to show cause, alleging failure to provide the educational funds. Because their daughter was beyond the age of minority, the divorce court denied the relief requested on the ground that it lacked jurisdiction. Solomon (P) then filed a breach of contract action, but the trial court granted Findley's (D) motion to dismiss, finding that the doctrine of merger applied in the judgment and that Solomon's (P) claim stemmed from the judgment. The court of appeals allowed Solomon (P) to pursue the claim for post-majority educational support in contract, rather than by enforcement of the dissolution decree.

ISSUE: Does a provision for post-majority educational support merge into the dissolution decree, rather than remain independent and enforceable as a contract claim?

HOLDING AND DECISION: (Cameron, J.) No. A provision for post-majority educational support does not merge into the dissolution decree but remains independent and enforceable as a contract claim. While the states that have addressed this issue have reached different solutions, they have uniformly upheld such agreements for post-majority educational support. Of the different approaches used for enforcement, the better approach is that the contract for post-majority support should be enforced in a separate contract action. This is so because the divorce court only has jurisdiction to enforce child support provisions until the child reaches majority. The court of appeals' decision is approved, and the case is remanded for proceedings consistent with this opinion.

▶ **ANALYSIS**

A few courts have enforced such post-majority support provisions by contempt, an approach the court in the instant case declined to follow. In the notes following the case, the author recognizes that the trend toward lowering the age of majority from twenty-one to eighteen has highlighted the issue of parental responsibility for financing higher education. Further, very few statutes require such support.

■■■

Curtis v. Kline

Father (P) v. State (D)

Pa. Sup. Ct., 542 Pa. 249, 666 A.2d 265 (1995).

NATURE OF CASE: Review of constitutionality of state statute.

FACT SUMMARY: Father (P) contested the constitutionality of Act 62, authorizing a court to order divorced, separated or unmarried parents to provide equitably for the educational costs of their children, even after they reach 18 years of age.

> ## 🏛 RULE OF LAW
> A state law which distinguishes between children of married and divorced, separated or unmarried parents for the purpose of authorizing a court to order the parents to provide equitably for the post-secondary educational costs of the child is unconstitutional under the Equal Protection Clause of the Fourteenth Amendment.

FACTS: In July 1991 a court order for support was entered on behalf of the father's (P) children. The father (P) petitioned to terminate his support obligation as to his children Amber and Jason, both college students. After Act 62 was promulgated, the father (P) was granted leave to include a constitutional challenge to the Act as a basis for seeking relief from his obligation to pay the children's educational support.

ISSUE: Is a state law, which distinguishes between children of married and divorced, separated or unmarried parents for the purpose of authorizing a court to order the parents to provide equitably for the post-secondary educational costs of the child unconstitutional under the Equal Protection Clause of the Fourteenth Amendment?

HOLDING AND DECISION: (Zappala, J.) Yes. A state law, which distinguishes between children of married and divorced, separated or unmarried parents for the purpose of authorizing a court to order the parents to provide equitably for the post-secondary educational costs of the child is unconstitutional under the Equal Protection Clause of the Fourteenth Amendment. Act 62 does not implicate a suspect class or infringe upon a fundamental right. The Act authorizes a court to order separated, divorced or unmarried parents to provide equitably for a child's educational costs, including those incurred after the child has reached 18 years of age. There is no state or federal right to a college education. The Act must be reviewed under a rational basis analysis, and will be upheld if there is any rational basis for the prescribed classification. The overall category of young people in need of financial assistance for post-graduate education is subdivided according to the marital status of the parents. An argument that children of non-intact families have a greater need for financial assistance is not sufficient justification because it assumes that the need does in fact exist merely because of the family's "non-intact" status. A student's financial need could arise from married parents simply being unwilling to help. The statute has the effect of treating similarly situated children, those in need of financial aid for college education, differently. No rational basis for the unequal treatment exists. The Act is unconstitutional.

DISSENT: (Montemuro, J.) The majority of courts that have addressed this issue have held that the Equal Protection Clause is not violated by statutes seeking to remedy the disparate treatment of children of divorced, separated or unmarried parents. Courts have noted that divorce has a particularly negative impact on children's opportunities for higher education, and typically the custodial parent bears the burden of the child's educational expenses.

▶ ANALYSIS

The court expressly rejects the holding of the New Hampshire Supreme Court in *LeClair v. LeClair,* 624 A.2d 1350 (1993). In that case the court upheld a similar statute on the basis that, due to the unique problems of divorced families, the legislature could rationally conclude that those families needed greater assistance in providing for financial assistance for their college education.

Quicknotes

CUSTODIAL PARENT A parent who is awarded the care and control of a child by the court in a dissolution or separation proceeding.

EQUAL PROTECTION A constitutional guarantee that no person shall be denied the same protection of the laws enjoyed by other persons in life circumstances.

RATIONAL BASIS TEST A test employed by the court to determine the validity of a statute in equal protection actions, whereby the court determines whether the challenged statute is rationally related to the achievement of a legitimate state interest.

Ainsworth v. Ainsworth

Ex-wife (P) v. Ex-husband (D)

Vt. Sup. Ct., 154 Vt. 103, 574 A.2d 772 (1990).

NATURE OF CASE: Appeal of decision as to modification of child support.

FACT SUMMARY: After the Ainsworths divorced and Reginald (D) remarried, Julie (P) sought an increase of the awarded child support, but the trial court reduced the amount based on Reginald's (D) second family expenses.

RULE OF LAW
Expenses for a second family may enter into the determination of child support for the preexisting family, even where the second family consists of a spouse and stepchild.

FACTS: When the Ainsworths divorced in 1986, they stipulated that Reginald (D) would pay child support of $70 per week to Julie (P), $35 for each of their two children. He remarried in August of 1987, establishing a new home with his wife and her son. Then, Julie (P) filed a motion for modification pursuant to 15 V.S.A. § 660, seeking increased support in an amount to be determined under the guidelines mandated by the statute which became effective on April 1, 1987. Although the trial court decided that Reginald (D) did not have a duty to support his stepson under the statute, it held that a child support order based on the guidelines sought by Julie (P) would be inequitable under § 659 and ordered him to pay less than what would be required under the guidelines.

ISSUE: May expenses for a second family enter into the determination of child support for the preexisting family, even where the second family consists of a spouse and stepchild?

HOLDING AND DECISION: (Dooley, J.) Yes. Expenses for a second family may enter into the determination of child support for the preexisting family, even where the second family consists of a spouse and stepchild. Under the guideline regulations, a basic support amount for the children is derived from tables based solely on the total gross income of the parents and the number of children. If the court finds that a child support order based on the guidelines would be inequitable under § 659, it may establish support after considering the relevant factors listed in the statute. Contrary to the finding of the trial court, the statute does create a general obligation of support for stepchildren, but the financial resources of the stepchild's mother are also relevant. The findings and conclusions of the trial court are too incomplete and do not specify the reasons for the amount of support awarded or show consideration of the statutory factors. Reversed and remanded.

DISSENT: (Morse, J.) The legislature clearly intended for children's lifestyles to remain as they were during the marriage insofar as possible. The court should not be able to deviate from the child support guidelines based on the facts of this case because the father should be able to place the expenses of his home and furnishings before his child support obligations. The child support statute is meant to be construed narrowly and should only allow for discretion when the court is presented with extraordinary expenses. While the father obviously has a duty to provide for his stepson, the legislature has previously determined that children from a first marriage are simply entitled to a greater benefit than children of a second marriage. It was the father's decision to assume the added costs of a second family, and that decision should not affect the children of the first family. The court still has discretion to ensure support for the second-family children, but that discretion does not require broadening. The majority decision today allows too much room for individual determination when the guidelines are intended to provide stability and predictability. A judge's opinion of fairness should not be taken into account.

ANALYSIS

The court stated that it is particularly important to emphasize that consideration of a case under the inequitable language of § 659 does not necessarily mean a lower support amount in second-family cases. The legislature intended to give trial courts discretion to ensure that support awards are just. However, the escape valve of § 659 must not be allowed to eat up the rule and destroy the predictability of amounts and the maintenance of the standard of living of the children that are the desired results of a guideline system.

Quicknotes

15 V.S.A. § 659 Permits deviations from child support guidelines if the court finds a child support order based on the support guidelines would be inequitable.

CHILD SUPPORT Payments made by one parent to another in satisfaction of the non-custodial parent's legal obligation to provide for the sustenance of the child.

Little v. Little

Parties not identified.

Ariz. Sup. Ct., 193 Ariz. 518, 975 P.2d 108 (1999).

NATURE OF CASE: Appeal from child support award.

FACT SUMMARY: Father resigned from full-time employment to become a full-time college student. He then sought a reduction in his child support obligation, claiming his student status constituted a sufficient change in circumstances to justify the modification.

> ## 🏛 RULE OF LAW
> A court should not apply a good faith standard in determining a downward modification in a child support obligation based upon an obligor's voluntary decision to leave full-time employment.

FACTS: Billy Little and Lisa Little divorced in 1995 when Billy was an Air Force lieutenant earning $48,000 annually. The trial court ordered Billy to pay child support for the couple's two minor children in the monthly amount of $1,186. One year later, Billy resigned his commission and enrolled as a full-time law student. He petitioned the court to modify his child support obligation to $239 monthly but the trial court found an insufficient change in circumstances. The trial court specifically found that Billy voluntarily left full-time employment, did not consider the financial effect on his children, and that his children would financially suffer from the reduced award. The court did modify the award to $972 monthly because Lisa obtained a higher-paying job. Billy appealed, and the court of appeals applied a good faith test to determine that Billy's enrollment in law school was reasonable and justified a modification down in his support obligation. Lisa appealed.

ISSUE: Should a court apply a good faith standard in determining a downward modification in a child support obligation based upon an obligor's voluntary decision to leave full-time employment?

HOLDING AND DECISION: (McGregor, J.) No. A court should not apply a good faith standard in determining a downward modification in a child support obligation based upon an obligor's voluntary decision to leave full-time employment. A trial court has the discretion to impute income to a parent voluntarily and unreasonably working below his or her full-capacity employment. In considering the reasonableness of the voluntary action and in fashioning the actual support order, the court could apply one of the three tests. The good faith test looks at the intent of the party in leaving employment and whether it was to avoid the support obligation and then considers only the actual income. The strict rule test

considers only the earning capacity of the party rather than the actual income. The intermediate test considers both the earning capacity and the actual income. The good faith test presupposes that the obligor is making his decision with his family's best interests at heart. The parent's freedom to choose takes priority over his legal duty to support his children so long as he is not intentionally avoiding the support obligation. The court is not able to determine effectively a party's subjective intention in leaving full-time employment. The parent's motivation cannot be the determining factor for the court, so the good faith test cannot apply here. The strict rule test is too inflexible and does not take into account any benefit that could result from a parent seeking additional education. This court, therefore, adopts the intermediate test with the primary consideration being the financial impact of the parent's decision upon the supported children. If the children would not suffer unreasonably, the court may consider other questions to determine the reasonableness of the parent's action. Questions may involve whether the party will see a significant increase in earning capacity or whether other financial resources exist to aid the parent in meeting his or her support obligations. Finally, the court should consider whether the decision was made to avoid the support obligation or if it was made in good faith. In the instant case, the trial court did consider these questions when overruling Billy's motion. The trial court found that Billy's decision would have left his children suffering a significant financial impact because of the small income Lisa makes. Further, Billy already holds two advanced degrees and made no attempt to obtain outside employment or even a part-time job to supplement his school loans and meet his support obligations. Billy did not act in his children's best interests when he enrolled in school full-time, and his children must take priority over even his personal dreams. The court of appeals decision is vacated and the trial court decision is affirmed.

▶ ANALYSIS

States have addressed this situation quite differently. Wisconsin allowed a physician mother to quit her full-time employment to stay at home with her three school-aged children, thus significantly increasing the father's support obligation. The father unsuccessfully argued that the mother had an equal duty to support her children and should not be allowed to stay at home. See *Chen v. Warner.*

Continued on next page.

Perhaps the court would consider the overall benefit to the children of having a stay-at-home mother rather than additional financial benefits, but the court certainly did not consider the father's wishes in place of his ability to pay. The legislatures and the courts have attempted to force parents to place the support and well-being of their children above all else, but human nature does not automatically comply. Courts can only do so much in determining the underlying motivations for individual decisions thus the reason for the child support guidelines.

■═■

Quicknotes

CHILD SUPPORT MODIFICATION The alteration of the payment structure pursuant to which one parent provides payments to another in satisfaction of the non-custodial parent's legal obligation to provide for the sustenance of the child.

GOOD FAITH An honest intention to abstain from taking advantage of another.

■═■

Bender v. Bender

Parties not identified.

Pa. Super. Ct., 297 Pa. Super. 461, 444 A.2d 124 (1982).

NATURE OF CASE: Appeal from suspension of child support obligation.

FACT SUMMARY: Mother elected to stay at home with Nicole rather than return to work. Father had sole custody of Heather and was not the biological father of Nicole. Mother successfully suspended her support obligation for Heather so that she could remain with Nicole.

> ## 🏛 RULE OF LAW
> A parent's decision to remain at home with a young child, the nurturing parent doctrine, is not an automatic exception to the support obligation.

FACTS: Mother and Father initiated divorce proceedings and Father obtained sole custody of Heather. Mother, eight-months pregnant with another man's child, was ordered to pay $25 weekly support for Heather until her child's birth. She was given a six-week suspension at which time her support obligation would begin again at $16 weekly with $4 weekly paid for arrears. Mother made no payments before or after the birth of her second daughter, Nicole. She then elected to stay at home with Nicole rather than return to work to meet her obligation for Heather's support. She moved the court for a permanent suspension of her support obligation, which the court granted pursuant to the "nurturing parent doctrine" which encourages a parent of a young child to be a stay-at-home parent. Father appealed.

ISSUE: Is a parent's decision to remain at home with a young child, the nurturing parent doctrine, an automatic exception to the support obligation?

HOLDING AND DECISION: [Judge not stated in casebook excerpt.] No. A parent's decision to remain at home with a young child, the nurturing parent doctrine, is not an automatic exception to the support obligation. This court did not set forth a strict rule in *Wasiolek* that a parent cannot have income imputed to her simply because she chooses to become a stay-at-home parent. While it is an important consideration that a child may significantly benefit from the presence of a stay-at-home parent, the court must consider all relevant factors. The other parent's earning capacity, the age of the child to be nurtured, child-care options, and the fact that other children require support are just some of the factors to be considered. Here, the court did not allow questions about Father's ability to support Heather solely. The court could also consider the fact that Heather is not the child to benefit from Mother's decision to stay at home, but she is the child

intended to benefit from the support order. Mother is not entitled to her decision as of right. Reversed.

▶ ANALYSIS

A determination under the Nurturing Parent Doctrine is rather fact-specific and the courts cannot rely on any bright-line rules. Pennsylvania attempted to codify the doctrine in 1997, but child advocates balked because of the potential detriment to children in need of the child support. A strict rule excusing parental support obligations because of a decision to remain at home does not consider that parent's ability to produce income despite not working outside of the home. The courts must be able to consider the individual circumstances of each case, including potential passive income that could provide for the children despite a parent's election not to work full-time.

■══■

Quicknotes

CHILD SUPPORT Payments made by one parent to another in satisfaction of the non-custodial parent's legal obligation to provide for the sustenance of the child.

■══■

Miller v. Miller

Mother (P) v. Stepfather (D)

N.J. Sup. Ct., 97 N.J. 154, 478 A.2d 351 (1984).

NATURE OF CASE: Appeal from denial of child support award.

FACT SUMMARY: Gladys Miller (P) had two minor children from a previous marriage when she married Jay Miller (D). After the Millers divorced, Gladys (P) sought child support from Jay (D).

> 🏛 **RULE OF LAW**
> A divorced stepparent may be liable for child support to former stepchildren based on equitable estoppel.

FACTS: Gladys Miller (P) had two minor children, Michelle and Suzette, from her previous marriage to Ralph Febre when she married Jay Miller (D) in 1972. Ralph supported his daughters financially despite the lack of a court-ordered obligation until he went to prison on a drug conviction. Prior to serving his sentence, he gave Gladys (P) $5,000 for the girls' support, and he continued to communicate with Gladys (P) about the girls after his release. Gladys (P) and Jay (D) married while Ralph was in prison and Jay (D) provided financially for the girls. Jay (D) strenuously objected to Ralph's involvement in the girls' lives, including them receiving financial support from Ralph. Gladys (P) filed for divorce in 1980 and sought child support from Jay (D). She claimed that he stood *in loco parentis* to her children and should be equitably estopped from denying a legal duty to provide child support for them. Jay (D) claimed that his legal relationship with and legal duties to the children terminated with the divorce. The trial court ordered Jay (D) to pay $75 weekly per child based on Jay's (D) emotional bond with the children. The Appellate Division affirmed based on a determination that Jay (D) detrimentally interfered with the relationship between the children and their biological father. Jay (D) appealed.

ISSUE: May a divorced stepparent be liable for child support to former stepchildren based on equitable estoppel?

HOLDING AND DECISION: (Garibaldi, J.) Yes. A divorced stepparent may be liable for child support to former stepchildren based on equitable estoppel. A stepparent has no statutory duty of support once the legal relationship with the children is terminated by divorce from their natural parent. A stepparent's support obligation is voluntary and arises from the stepparent's standing *in loco parentis*. Equitable estoppel claims require that intentional actions occur resulting in anticipated reliance to the relying party's detriment. *Pendente lite* support awards are appropriate where the moving parent demonstrates no

financial assistance from the other biological parent and the stepparent's active interference in the relationship between the child and the other biological parent. Children are entitled to support and may obtain it from a former stepparent temporarily if they cannot obtain it from a biological parent. The moving parent then must demonstrate each element of equitable estoppel to obtain a permanent support order from the former stepparent. The parent does not have to demonstrate that the children believed the former stepparent to be their biological parent, but the parent does have to show that the former stepparent made a representation of a responsibility of support to the children or to the parent. Gladys (P) does state that Jay (D) developed an emotional bond with the girls, but this court cannot enforce a support order merely because of the existence of a family unit during the marriage. Gladys (P) must also demonstrate that the girls will suffer financially absent a support order to Jay (D) because of the lack of available support from Ralph. Gladys (P) first has a duty to attempt to obtain support from Ralph before she can seek support from Jay (D). A stepparent does not displace a biological parent for support obligation. A stepparent's support obligation is provisional until the biological parent's support obligation is determined. Reversed and remanded.

CONCURRENCE AND DISSENT: (Handler, J.) Equitable estoppel is intended to address unique factual situations such as the one at issue here. The concept should be broadened in matrimonial cases where one party's actions result in certain reliance. The necessary detriment element can be found when that party repudiates his prior actions. Here, Jay deliberately interfered with Ralph's relationship with the girls and set about to become their parent. The girls are undoubtedly now at a financial disadvantage because they do not have the financial support of Jay or Ralph. The emotional relationship among Jay and the girls is not the issue. Rather, the issue is that Jay was their sole financial support and terminated their financial support from their biological father. His deliberate conduct results in an ongoing obligation. Until Ralph can be located and ordered to comply with a support obligation, Jay should continue his financial support.

▍ *ANALYSIS*

Adoption is the best way to ensure a legal duty to support biologically unrelated children, but that entails the termination of biological parents' rights. Some courts have also

Continued on next page.

determined that a stepparent who once provided financially may have to continue a financial contribution even if a biological parent is still contributing but a shortfall exists. The best protection is a written marital agreement or a voluntary contribution on the part of the stepparent. Once again, courts are attempting to force all parties involved to place children's needs before all else, but that can be difficult to enforce. The courts are left to sort out the obligations of the adults to best ensure adequate support for the children. That may entail support orders for biological parents at the same time as stepparents.

■═■

Quicknotes

CHILD SUPPORT Payments made by one parent to another in satisfaction of the non-custodial parent's legal obligation to provide for the sustenance of the child.

ESTOPPEL An equitable doctrine precluding a party from asserting a right to the detriment of another who justifiably relied on the conduct.

IN LOCO PARENTIS A situation in which a person has assumed the responsibilities and obligations of a lawful parent without undergoing the legal adoption process.

PENDENTE LITE A matter that is contingent on the disposition of a pending suit.

■═■

Johnson v. Louis

Mother (P) v. Father (D)

Iowa Sup. Ct., 654 N.W.2d 886 (2002).

NATURE OF CASE: Appeal from child support modification order.

FACT SUMMARY: Louis (D) provided financial support for his son, Jared, with his girlfriend, Johnson (P). Johnson (P) sought to have the support order modified to include post-secondary educational support after Jared turned 18.

🏛 RULE OF LAW
Children of unmarried parents are not discriminated against by having court-ordered support pursuant to a different statute than that support ordered after dissolution of a marriage.

FACTS: Debbie Johnson (P) and Michael Louis (D) never married, but had a son, Jared, together in 1982. After Jared's birth, the child support recovery unit obtained a paternity order and support order against Louis (D). In 2000, Johnson (P) sought a modification of the order to provide for a post-secondary educational subsidy for their son. The trial court denied the order, and Johnson (P) appealed. The court of appeals reversed on the basis that support orders under the statute governing marital dissolutions provided for post-secondary educational subsidies thus support orders under the statute affecting children of unmarried parents discriminated against those children. Louis (D) appealed.

ISSUE: Are children of unmarried parents discriminated against by having court-ordered support pursuant to a different statute than that support ordered after dissolution of a marriage?

HOLDING AND DECISION: (Carter, J.) No. Children of unmarried parents are not discriminated against by having court-ordered support pursuant to a different statute than support ordered after dissolution of a marriage. Support orders after the dissolution of marriage are pursuant to chapter 598. Support orders for children of unmarried parents are pursuant to chapter 252A. The court of appeals decided the issue on an Equal Protection analysis, so the court must now determine if a rational basis exists for the statutory classifications here. Contrary to the court of appeals' decision, no discrimination exists between children of married and children of unmarried parents. Jared is in the same situation as other children whose support orders are determined pursuant to chapter 252A and as children whose parents remain married. Only children whose parents are divorced have support determined pursuant to the other statute. The educational benefits provided to the children of divorced parents are in exchange for the loss of their intact family. Jared similarly does not have an intact family, but that was a voluntary choice made by his parents. A rational basis exists for the classification. The court of appeals' decision is vacated and the trial court decision is affirmed.

▶ ANALYSIS

The court mentioned the parents' decision to previously avoid state involvement in their relationship. The legislatures and courts always seek to protect children's interests and to encourage involved adults to place the children's interests before all else. Parents electing to remain unmarried, however, cannot expect to receive the same benefits and burdens of married parents even for their children.

∎═∎

Quicknotes

CHILD SUPPORT MODIFICATION The alteration of the payment structure pursuant to which one parent provides payments to another in satisfaction of the non-custodial parent's legal obligation to provide for the sustenance of the child.

EQUAL PROTECTION CLAUSE A constitutional provision that each person be guaranteed the same protection of the laws enjoyed by other persons in like circumstances.

RATIONAL BASIS REVIEW A test employed by the court to determine the validity of a statute in equal protection actions, whereby the court determines whether the challenged statute is rationally related to the achievement of a legitimate state interest.

∎═∎

Vanderbilt v. Vanderbilt

Ex-wife (P) v. Ex-husband (D)

354 U.S. 416 (1957).

NATURE OF CASE: Appeal from support order.

FACT SUMMARY: Mr. Vanderbilt (D) contended that a New York support order was invalid as it unconstitutionally conflicted with a Nevada divorce order previously entered in his favor.

> 🏛 **RULE OF LAW**
> A state is obligated to give full faith and credit to a sister state judgment only where the sister state judgment was entered pursuant to that state's exercise of valid personal jurisdiction over both parties.

FACTS: The Vanderbilts separated while living in California. Mrs. Vanderbilt (P) moved to New York, and Mr. Vanderbilt (D) moved to Nevada, where he successfully petitioned for divorce. Mrs. Vanderbilt (P) was never served with process in Nevada and did not appear before the Nevada court. Subsequently, Mrs. Vanderbilt (P) petitioned the New York court for an order of divorce, even though it had no personal jurisdiction over Mr. Vanderbilt (D). The New York court entered a decree of divorce in favor of Mrs. Vanderbilt (P) and attached Mr. Vanderbilt's (D) property located within that state. Mr. Vanderbilt (D) had appeared specially in the New York action and contended that the full faith and credit clause of the United States Constitution required the New York court to give full faith and credit to the Nevada state divorce court order which terminated Mrs. Vanderbilt's (P) right to support. The New York court found that the Nevada court lacked personal jurisdiction over Mrs. Vanderbilt (P), and, therefore, its divorce order had no force and effect to terminate her right to support. Mr. Vanderbilt (D) appealed.

ISSUE: Must a state give full faith and credit to a sister state judgment even though the sister state lacked personal jurisdiction over the parties?

HOLDING AND DECISION: (Black, J.) No. A court need not give full faith and credit to a sister state judgment entered in the absence of personal jurisdiction over the parties. The Full Faith and Credit Clause is limited to the enforcement of valid sister state decrees. A court which lacks jurisdiction over the parties lacks jurisdiction to enter any binding orders. As a result, because Nevada had no personal jurisdiction over Mrs. Vanderbilt (P), its order had no force and effect and could not terminate her right to support. Affirmed.

▶ **ANALYSIS**

Divorce cases, as any other civil litigation, require that each court have jurisdiction over the parties to the action.

Any action taken by a court without jurisdiction has no force or effect. While the New York court clearly did not have personal jurisdiction over Mr. Vanderbilt (D), it clearly had jurisdiction over his property located within the state's boundaries.

■━■

Quicknotes

FULL FAITH AND CREDIT ACT As provided in the U.S. Constitution, Article IV, any state judicial proceedings shall have such faith and credit given them in every court in the United States as they would in their own state.

■━■

Kulko v. Superior Court of California

Father (P) v. State court (D)

436 U.S. 84 (1978).

NATURE OF CASE: Appeal from denial of motion to quash service of summons in action for child custody and support.

FACT SUMMARY: Kulko (P) argued that he had insufficient contacts with California to give its courts jurisdiction over him in his wife's suit for an increase in child support.

🏛 RULE OF LAW
A state court may not exercise in personam jurisdiction over a nonresident, nondomiciliary person unless that nonresident has certain "minimum contacts" with the forum state such that the maintenance of the suit does not offend "traditional notions of fair play and substantial justice."

FACTS: Kulko (P) and his wife, residents of New York throughout their marriage, stopped in California only to get married while Kulko (P) was en route to a tour of duty in Korea. Upon their separation several years later, Kulko's (P) wife moved to San Francisco, but she flew to New York to sign a separation agreement drawn up there. It provided that their children, a boy and a girl, would live with Kulko (P) in New York but would stay with their mother in California during Christmas, Easter, and summer vacations. Child support was set at $3,000 per year. After procuring a Haitian divorce, Kulko's (P) ex-wife returned to California and remarried, taking the name "Horn." When Kulko's (P) daughter expressed her desire to stay on with her mother after Christmas vacation, Kulko (P) consented and bought her a one-way ticket to California. When the son told his mother he also desired to live with her, she sent him a ticket, without telling Kulko (P). After both children were living with her, Horn sought to establish the Haitian divorce decree as a California judgment and to modify the judgment (1) to give her full custody of the children and (2) to increase Kulko's (P) child support obligations. Kulko (P), appearing specially, moved to quash service of summons on the ground that he was not a resident of California and lacked sufficient "minimum contacts" with California, under the *International Shoe* decision, to warrant the state's assertion of personal jurisdiction over him. The trial court (D) summarily denied the motion to quash, and the appellate court affirmed, holding that his consent to his children's living in California "caused an effect in the state" warranting the exercise of jurisdiction. The California Supreme Court affirmed, holding the "purposeful act" warranting the exercise of personal jurisdiction to have been Kulko's (P) action in actively and

fully consenting to his daughter's living in California for the school year and sending her there. Kulko (P) appealed.

ISSUE: When a state court seeks to exercise in personam jurisdiction over a nonresident, nondomiciliary person, must the nonresident have certain "minimum contacts" with the forum state such that its exercising jurisdiction does not offend "traditional notions of fair play and substantial justice"?

HOLDING AND DECISION: (Marshall, J.) Yes. *International Shoe* sets the prerequisite for a state court's exercising in personam jurisdiction over a nonresident, nondomiciliary person: the nonresident must have certain "minimum contacts" with the forum state such that maintenance of the suit does not offend "traditional notions of fair play and substantial justice." In this case, the alleged "minimum contact" was Kulko's (P) allowing his daughter to live in California during the school year. However, that was not sufficient contact by itself to confer jurisdiction. Allowing a child to spend more time elsewhere than required by a custody decree can hardly be said to be "purposefully availing oneself" of the "benefits and protection" of California's laws. Additionally, the court cannot consider the financial benefit to the father by the child's absence for nine months of the year because the mother should have sought an increase in father's support obligation. The question of his liability for increased amounts cannot be confused with the forum to adjudicate that liability. Basic considerations of fairness point decisively in favor of Kulko's (P) state of domicile as the proper forum for adjudication of this case. He resided there at all times during the marriage and continues to do so. He did no more than acquiesce to his child's wish to live with her mother, a single act a reasonable parent would not expect to result in the substantial burden of litigating a child-support suit 3,000 miles away. To make jurisdiction turn on whether Kulko (P) bought his daughter her ticket or unsuccessfully sought to prevent her departure would impose on family relations an unreasonable burden wholly unjustified by the "quality and nature" of his California-related activities. Reversed.

▶ ANALYSIS

The decision in this case did not leave Horn without remedy or force her to undergo great expense and personal strain in litigating her case 3,000 miles away in New York.

Continued on next page.

The Uniform Reciprocal Enforcement and Support Act, a version of which has been passed in California, would allow one in Horn's position to file a petition, for example, in California and have its merits adjudicated in New York without either party having to leave his/her respective state. A similar action to collect any support payments found owing is also possible under this legislation.

■═■

Quicknotes

CHILD SUPPORT Payments made by one parent to another in satisfaction of the non-custodial parent's legal obligation to provide for the sustenance of the child.

CUSTODY The granting of care and control of a child or children to a parent pursuant to an action for dissolution or separation.

IN PERSONAM JURISDICTION The power of a court over a person, as opposed to a court's power over a person's interest in property.

QUASH To vacate, annul, void.

■═■

Child Support Enforcement v. Brenckle

State agency (P) v. Father (D)

Mass. Sup. Jud. Ct., 424 Mass. 214, 675 N.E.2d 390 (1997).

NATURE OF CASE: Appeal from a judgment enforcing child support orders.

FACT SUMMARY: When the child support enforcement division of Alaska brought an action on behalf of a mother to collect past child support payments from Brenckle (D), he alleged that no finding had been made that he owed any duty of support or, alternatively, that the claim was barred by laches.

🏛 RULE OF LAW
Once registered, an Alaska child support order is enforceable in the same manner as an order issued by a Massachusetts court.

FACTS: Following his divorce in Alaska in 1978, Brenckle (D) moved to Massachusetts and stopped sending the $500 monthly child support payments he had agreed to pay for his son's upkeep. When the son turned seventeen and began to make plans for college, the mother filed an action in Alaska to recover the child support arrearages owed to her. A judgment was entered against Brenckle (D) by default and transmitted to the child support enforcement division in Massachusetts. In Massachusetts, Brenckle (D) filed a motion to dismiss or for summary judgment, which was denied. The district court conducted a hearing and found the father (D) liable for $107,365. Brenckle (D) appealed, alleging that before it could enforce the Alaska judgment the district court was required to make an independent finding that he owed a duty of support to his son, and that the mother had slept on her rights for thirteen years and her claim was barred by laches.

ISSUE: Once registered, is an Alaska child support order enforceable in the same manner as an order issued by a Massachusetts court?

HOLDING AND DECISION: (Marshall, J.) Yes. Once registered, an Alaska child support order is enforceable in the same manner as an order issued by a Massachusetts court. Under the Uniform Interstate Family Support Act (UIFSA), which is the statute applicable to these proceedings, once one court enters a support order, no other court may modify that order for so long as the party for whose benefit the order is entered continues to reside in the jurisdiction of that court. In this case, the son is a resident of Alaska. UIFSA requires no de novo or independent review by a Massachusetts court as to whether Brenckle (D) owes a duty of support to his son. Because Brenckle's (D) failure to make child support payments became vested as judgments by operation of law, the defense of laches is not available to him. Affirmed and remanded for enforcement.

▶ ANALYSIS

The court in this case applied UIFSA retroactively, since the earlier law, the Uniform Reciprocal Enforcement of Support Act (URESA), was repealed the day the judgment was entered in the Massachusetts district court. UIFSA was approved by the National Conference of Commissioners on Uniform State Laws in 1992, and has since been adopted in twenty-six states. The judgment was affirmed and the matter remanded to Probate and Family Court for such other proceedings as may be necessary to enforce the judgment.

■═■

Quicknotes

CHILD SUPPORT Payments made by one parent to another in satisfaction of the non-custodial parent's legal obligation to provide for the sustenance of the child.

LACHES An equitable defense against the enforcement of rights that have been neglected for a long period of time.

RETROACTIVE Having an effect on something that occurred in the past.

UIFSA Enacted to create a uniform basis for jurisdiction so that only one support order is in effect at any one time.

■═■

Eunique v. Powell

Non-paying obligor (P) v. Party not identified (D)

302 F.3d 971 (9th Cir. 2002).

NATURE OF CASE: Appeal from grant of summary judgment.

FACT SUMMARY: Eunique (P) applied for and was denied a passport because she was in significant arrears on child support payments. She claimed this was an unconstitutional denial.

🏛 RULE OF LAW
A person in arrears on child support payments may be constitutionally restricted from international travel.

FACTS: Eudene Eunique (P) wished to travel internationally and to see her sister in Mexico, so she applied for a passport. At the time, she was well over $20,000 in arrears on child support payments owed to her former husband for the benefit of their children in his sole custody. Eunique (P) never made a single support payment. California certified to the Secretary of Health and Human Services that she owed arrears over $5,000 and the Secretary then had the statutory authority to deny the issuance of a passport to Eunique (P). After receiving notification of the passport denial, Eunique (P) claimed the denial was a violation of her constitutional rights because of the lack of connection between child support obligations and the right to international travel. The district court ruled against Eunique (P) and she appealed.

ISSUE: May a person in arrears on child support payments be constitutionally restricted from international travel?

HOLDING AND DECISION: (Fernandez, J.) Yes. A person in arrears on child support payments may be constitutionally restricted from international travel. Eunique (P) asserts that the constitutional right to international travel may only be curtailed under specific and narrow circumstances, which do not include a failure to meet a child support obligation. The right, however, may be regulated as any other due process right under the Fifth Amendment and such regulations are subject to a rational basis test. Only when First Amendment concerns are implicated will strict scrutiny be applied. In applying the rational basis review, it is clear that an obligor's failure to meet her child support obligations is a serious offense within our society. It is certainly rational to restrain non-paying obligors within the country so that they are reachable. Furthermore, a parent's duty is to her child, and she should focus on that child's support rather than the joys of international travel. Congress requires Eunique (P) to place her children's welfare above her personal pleasures. Affirmed.

DISSENT: (Kleinfeld, J.) Rational basis review is too loose a standard to judge curtailment of the right to international travel. The government here has failed to tailor a narrow restriction and instead offers a punishment for past behavior. The purpose for Eunique's (P) travel is to explore potential job opportunities as a lawyer because her present legal practice pays a mere pittance. In other travel restriction cases, the courts have applied a compelling governmental interest test but restrictions of specific individuals should be subject to greater scrutiny. This statute is a restriction on travel from this country and limited to a specific class of persons. Eunique (P) has not been found to be in contempt and does not appear to be escaping her duties by leaving the country, so she is unreasonably and unconstitutionally restricted. The right to international travel is too important to be used as a punishment and restrictions should be limited to matters implicating national security or something equally important.

▶ ANALYSIS

Courts have come to different conclusions on this issue but it appears to depend on whether First Amendment rights are implicated. All jurisdictions agree that interstate travel is subject to strict scrutiny while international travel is at times subject to a lesser test. As the right to a passport is subject to the Fifth Amendment due process evaluations, the state absolutely must provide notice and an opportunity to be heard prior to denying or revoking a passport based on overdue child support obligations.

■═■

Quicknotes

DUE PROCESS CLAUSE Clauses found in the Fifth and Fourteenth Amendments to the United States Constitution providing that no person shall be deprived of "life, liberty, or property, without due process of law."

FIRST AMENDMENT RIGHTS Rights conferred by the First Amendment to the United States Constitution prohibiting Congress from enacting any law respecting an establishment of religion, prohibiting the free exercise of religion, abridging freedom of speech or the press, the right of peaceful assembly and the right to petition for a redress of grievances.

RATIONAL BASIS REVIEW A test employed by the court to determine the validity of a statute in equal protection actions, whereby the court determines whether the

Continued on next page.

challenged statute is rationally related to the achievement of a legitimate state interest.

SUMMARY JUDGMENT Judgment rendered by a court in response to a motion made by one of the parties, claiming that the lack of a question of material fact in respect to an issue warrants disposition of the issue without consideration by the jury.

■═■

Wisconsin v. Oakley

State (P) v. Convicted non-paying obligor (D)

Wis. Sup. Ct., 245 Wis. 2d 447, 629 N.W.2d 200 (2001).

NATURE OF CASE: Appeal from denial of post-conviction petition for relief from probation condition.

FACT SUMMARY: Oakley (D) was convicted for not paying his child support obligations for his nine children. He was sentenced to prison but allowed to remain free on probation so that he might obtain meaningful employment and begin to meet his support obligations. A condition of his probation was a prohibition against fathering additional children for the period of probation.

RULE OF LAW
A prohibition on procreation as a condition of probation is constitutional if it is narrowly tailored to meet the state's compelling interest and reasonably related to rehabilitation.

FACTS: David Oakley (D) fathered nine children with four women. He intentionally refused to pay child support for any of the children, and he intimidated two witnesses, including his own child, in a child abuse case against him. The State (P) charged him and he entered into a plea agreement. He was in arrears of $25,000 when he was sentenced. The State (P) requested six years imprisonment, and Oakley (D) requested that he be permitted to remain out of prison so that he might obtain meaningful employment and make payments toward his arrearage. The court determined that Oakley (D) would not be able to make support payments if in prison, so instead imposed three years imprisonment on one count, eight years stayed on the next two counts, and five years' probation consecutive to the prison term. A term of the probation was the prohibition against fathering more children unless Oakley (D) could demonstrate an ability to financially provide for the child while supporting his existing children. Oakley (D) filed for post-conviction relief from this condition. The court of appeals affirmed and Oakley (D) appealed to this court.

ISSUE: Is a prohibition on procreation as a condition of probation constitutional if it is narrowly tailored to meet the state's compelling interest and reasonably related to rehabilitation?

HOLDING AND DECISION: (Wilcox, J.) Yes. A prohibition on procreation as a condition of probation is constitutional if it is narrowly tailored to meet the state's compelling interest and reasonably related to rehabilitation. Refusal to pay child support is a felony in Wisconsin because of the gravity of the offense. A judge has discretion to avoid imposition of a jail sentence by imposing other punishments with conditions. The goal is to protect against future wrongdoing and to rehabilitate the wrongdoer. Here, the trial judge imposed a prison sentence to protect the children from future victimization and the probation to encourage Oakley (D) to do the right thing and support his existing children. The judge also sought to protect the existing children from harm by prohibiting Oakley (D) from adding to his support obligations without the ability to meet them. Oakley (D) argues that eliminating his right to procreate is a constitutional violation subject to strict scrutiny. The court did not eliminate Oakley's (D) right to procreate but merely restricted it unless he can support the new child. Oakley (D) argues, perhaps compellingly, that he will never be able to support additional children so his right is eliminated. The court, however, has the ability to impose additional burdens on convicted felons. Oakley (D) would also be in the same position if he was sentenced to the prison term where he would be physically restrained from additional procreation. Probation conditions may be imposed so long as they are not overly broad and are reasonably related to the issue being addressed. The condition certainly meets these standards. Oakley (D) can meet his condition by voluntarily supporting his existing nine children and developing a means of support for all future children. The condition is narrowly tailored to serve Wisconsin's (P) compelling interest in having support for all children. Oakley (D) is enjoying greater liberty with this current probation condition than he would had the prison sentence been imposed. Further, the restriction is reasonably related to the issue to be addressed because it will encourage Oakley (D) to support his children. This determination is highly fact-specific but this court does affirm.

DISSENT: (Sykes, J.) Even given the facts of this case, court-ordered prohibition of procreation is overly broad. *Zablocki v. Redhail* is not factually similar but the analysis is analogous. Procreation is a fundamental human right that cannot be lightly encumbered, even when it involves a convicted felon. Other, less restrictive means exist to achieve the State's (P) goal of obtaining support for Oakley's (D) children, including wage assignment, employment requirements, contempt.

ANALYSIS

An interesting fact about this decision is that the male members of the court were in the majority and the female members of the court dissented. The majority basically focuses on the fact that Oakley would not be able to

Continued on next page.

procreate anyway if his jail sentence had been imposed, which would have been an equally proper punishment. The dissents focused on the immutable, fundamental right to procreate and the fear that this was an inroad into regulations of that right. Wisconsin is the first state to impose such probation conditions. The courts are trying creative ways to get around the "deadbeat dads" problem in this country, but critics fear that the creativity may result in greater harm.

■══■

Quicknotes

COMPELLING STATE INTEREST Defense to an alleged Equal Protection Clause violation that a state action was necessary in order to protect an interest the government is under a duty to protect.

FELONY A criminal offense of greater seriousness than a misdemeanor; felonies are generally defined pursuant to statute as any crime that is punishable by death or by a term of imprisonment exceeding one year.

FUNDAMENTAL RIGHT A liberty that is either expressly or impliedly provided for in the United States Constitution, the deprivation or burdening of which is subject to a heightened standard of review.

■══■

Hicks v. Feiock

State (P) v. Father (D)

485 U.S. 624 (1988).

NATURE OF CASE: Appeal from decision upholding constitutional challenge to contempt conviction.

FACT SUMMARY: The State (P) appealed from a decision denying review of a decision of the court of appeals, which upheld Feiock's (D) challenge to the constitutionality of a state statute which required him to carry the burden of proving his inability to pay child support in order to avoid a contempt conviction for failure to pay child support.

RULE OF LAW

Where, in connection with contempt proceedings for failure to pay child support, a determinate sentence of imprisonment is imposed, it will be deemed to be civil in nature if the sentence imposed contains a purge clause.

FACTS: Feiock (D) fell behind in child support payments, and his wife instituted proceedings against him to obtain a court order enforcing payments. This was done, but he still failed to make the required payments. At his hearing on an order to show cause as to why he should not be held in contempt for failing to make child support payments, Feiock (D) defended himself, contending that he was unable to make the child support payments in question. He objected to the application of a state statute which required him to bear the burden of proving his inability to pay on constitutional grounds. The objection was rejected, and Feiock (D) was convicted of five counts of contempt. He was sentenced to five days of imprisonment on each of the counts. The sentence was suspended, and he was placed on probation for three years. As a condition of probation, he was required to continue to make child support payments, as well as to make payments to correct the accumulated arrearages. On appeal, Feiock's (D) challenge was upheld, and the contempt order was annulled. The state supreme court denied review, and from that decision, the State (P) appealed.

ISSUE: Where, in connection with contempt proceedings for failure to pay child support, a determinate sentence of imprisonment is imposed, will it be deemed to be civil in nature if the sentence imposed contains a purge clause?

HOLDING AND DECISION: (White, J.) Yes. Where, in connection with contempt proceedings for failure to pay child support, a sentence of imprisonment is imposed determinate, it will be deemed to be civil in nature if the sentence imposed contains a purge clause. The proper classification of the punishment imposed on Feiock (D) in the present case is dispositive. Ordinarily, when a sentence is imposed to obtain compliance with court order, the relief imposed will usually be classified as civil. Where it is imposed to vindicate the court's authority, the relief is punitive and, therefore, criminal in nature. In the present case, the imprisonment was suspended and probation imposed. What is unclear is whether Feiock (D) could purge this sentence by paying off his past-due child support. If the sentence can be purged in this manner, the punishment imposed would be considered civil in nature. This case must be remanded since the lower courts have yet to pass on this issue. Remanded.

ANALYSIS

On remand, the court determined that the contempt proceedings brought against Feiock (D) were criminal in nature. Thus, it appears clear that although the court in the present case found the motives underlying the contempt proceeding somewhat ambiguous, the state court had no trouble supporting its earlier determination that the contempt proceedings were criminal in nature and upholding Feiock's (D) constitutional challenge. See *In re Feiock*, 215 Cal. App. 3d 141 (1989).

United States v. Bongiorno

Federal government (P) v. Father (D)

106 F.3d 1027 (1st Cir. 1997).

NATURE OF CASE: Appeal from a criminal conviction and resulting civil restitutionary order.

FACT SUMMARY: When Bongiorno (D) failed to make child support payments, he was charged with violating the Child Support Recovery Act (CSRA) and the Federal Debt Collection Procedure Act (FDCPA).

RULE OF LAW

The CSRA is a valid exercise of Congressional power under the Commerce clause.

FACTS: Bongiorno (D), a successful surgeon and physician, was ordered by a Georgia state court to pay $5,000 monthly child support after a divorce decree was entered there. His daughter moved to Massachusetts with her mother. A Georgia order holding Bongiorno (D) in contempt was issued two years later because he had failed to make support payments, but he was living in Michigan at the time and the contempt order did not operate extraterritorially. Bongiorno (D) made only sporadic payments, and the Michigan court domesticated the Georgia order, and authorized garnishment of his salary. Bongiorno (D) quit and paid only $500 a month for child support for several months. He later failed to make payments of $300 a month ordered by a Michigan court. The United States (P) charged Bongiorno (D) with violating the CSRA, he was found guilty, ordered to pay restitution, and sentenced to five years probation. The Government (P) also commenced a civil proceeding under the FDCPA as a means of enforcing the restitutionary order. Bongiorno (D) appealed, challenging the constitutionality of the CSRA, and the applicability of the FDCPA.

ISSUE: Is CSRA a valid exercise of Congressional power under the Commerce clause?

HOLDING AND DECISION: (Selya, J.) Yes. The CSRA is a valid exercise of Congressional power under the Commerce clause. Activities that implicate the instrumentalities of interstate commerce (including persons or things in interstate commerce) can be regulated under the second prong of the Commerce Clause. Because child support orders that require a parent in one state to make payments to a person in another state are functionally equivalent to interstate contracts, such obligations are "things" in interstate commerce. Thus, it is appropriate for Congress to enact legislation that will prevent their nonfulfillment. The statute makes willful failure to pay a past due support obligation with respect to a child who resides in another state a federal crime. Because Congress drafted the CSRA to strengthen, and not to supplant, state enforcement

efforts, the law withstands Tenth Amendment scrutiny. A restitution order issued pursuant to the CSRA is not a debt within the meaning of the FDCPA. The conviction and sentence in the criminal case are affirmed, but the judgment in the civil case is reversed.

ANALYSIS

The court in this case dealt with two issues. It resolved the application of the CSRA, a criminal statute, in the government's favor. The civil suit under the FDCPA was settled in favor of the debtor.

Quicknotes

COMMERCE CLAUSE Article 1, section 8, clause 3 of the United States Constitution, granting Congress the power to regulate commerce with foreign countries and between the states.

CSRA 18 U.S.C. § 228 - Made failure to pay past due sup-port obligations a federal crime.

FDCPA 104 Stat. 4933 - Created a framework under which the United States might more efficiently collect debts owed to it.

INTERSTATE COMMERCE ACT § 1 (14) - Allows the Commission to prescribe per diem charges for the use of one railroad cars owned by another.

RESTITUTION The return or restoration of what the defendant has gained in a transaction to prevent the unjust enrichment of the defendant.

TENTH AMENDMENT The Tenth Amendment to the United States Constitution reserving those powers therein, not expressly delegated to the federal government or prohibited to the states, to the states or to the people.

WRIT OF GARNISHMENT Satisfaction of a debt by deducting payments directly from the debtor's wages before they are paid to him by his employer; due process requires that the debtor be first given notice and an opportunity to be heard.

Duffy v. Duffy

Parties not identified.

D.C. Ct. App., 881 A.2d 630 (2005).

NATURE OF CASE: Appeal from enforcement of separation agreement.

FACT SUMMARY: The Duffys set out the terms of their marital dissolution agreement, including child support obligations, in a letter, which Mrs. Duffy's attorney used to draft a Draft Separation Agreement. Mr. Duffy signed the letter but not the agreement, but nevertheless abided by its terms for one year. Mrs. Duffy then sought to enforce the agreement terms when Mr. Duffy arbitrarily lowered his child support payments.

> 🏛 **RULE OF LAW**
> Parties must abide by the terms of a negotiated and accepted settlement agreement despite later second thoughts.

FACTS: Mr. and Mrs. Duffy legally separated and began the process of selling the marital home, dividing assets, and determining child custody and support. In an effort to save attorneys' fees, they set out their desired terms in a letter. Both parties reviewed and signed the letter prior to Mrs. Duffy sending it to her attorney. Mrs. Duffy's attorney prepared a Draft Settlement Agreement based upon the letter's terms. Mr. Duffy did not execute the Agreement but abided by its terms for one year, including making monthly child support payments of $5,000. After one year, Mr. Duffy arbitrarily lowered his monthly support payments to $2,000. Mrs. Duffy sought to enforce the Agreement as part of the final divorce judgment. The trial court enforced the Agreement and Mr. Duffy appealed.

ISSUE: Must parties abide by the terms of a negotiated and accepted settlement agreement if experiencing later second thoughts?

HOLDING AND DECISION: (Ruiz, J.) Yes. Parties must abide by the terms of a negotiated and accepted settlement agreement despite later second thoughts. Divorcing parties are encouraged to develop separation agreements so that the court does not have to determine what is fair and reasonable for each individual. Mr. Duffy claimed that the agreement did not contain certain terms, such as a contingency for change in child support if he lost his job. The agreement does however contain the necessary terms so that the parties are reasonably certain of performance expectations, which is all that is required for a contract to be definite and enforceable. Whether Mr. Duffy may turn to the courts for a support modification order depends on whether the Agreement was incorporated by reference or merged into the divorce judgment. An incorporated agreement on support may be changed only upon a showing of an unforeseen circumstance resulting in a substantial and material change to the welfare of the children. Even then, the support amount cannot be lessened absent a showing of a contract theory relieving the parent of the duty to perform under the Agreement. It is only when the Agreement is merged that the court's order rather than the contractual agreement between the parties is at issue. The facts here place incorporation versus merger at issue because the court references the letter but adds additional terms in its own judgment. Further, Mrs. Duffy concedes that the merger standard would apply if Mr. Duffy sought a modification based on change in employment. Determination of incorporation or merger is not necessary here, however, because Mr. Duffy is not seeking a modification based on change of circumstance and he has repeatedly demonstrated an intent to abide by the terms of the agreement despite his later regrets. Affirmed.

▶ **ANALYSIS**

Parties to a separation agreement have two choices: incorporation or merger. If the agreement "merges" into the court's final judgment, it is always modifiable to the extent that a judge may modify any of its own judgments. If the agreement "survives" the final judgment, it is a separate contract subject only to contract theories of modification or breach. Typically, parties continue to involve the court in child custody and support issues so those merge into the judgments. Here, however, the parties were reasonable, informed adults attempting to draft a reasonable, comprehensive agreement and may not have desired future court involvement. A court cannot allow one party to back out of a negotiated contract merely because the party changes his mind. The parties seem to have intended though that pieces of the agreement merged into the final judgment and could someday be subject to court modification. The best defense to later confusion is to be explicit in the agreement as to the merger or incorporation intentions.

■━■

Quicknotes

BREACH OF CONTRACT Unlawful failure by a party to perform its obligations pursuant to contract.

CHILD SUPPORT Payments made by one parent to another in satisfaction of the non-custodial parent's legal obligation to provide for the sustenance of the child.

Continued on next page.

INCORPORATED BY REFERENCE The reference to another document in a writing, stating that the secondary writing should be considered as part of the principal document.

CONTRACT MODIFICATION A change to the terms of a contract without altering its general purpose.

SEPARATION AGREEMENT A written agreement between spouses who are separated and/or seeking a divorce, setting forth terms of support, custody and property division.

Toni v. Toni

Ex-wife (P) v. Ex-husband (D)

N.D. Sup. Ct., 2001 N.D. 193, 636 N.W.2d 396 (2001).

NATURE OF CASE: Appeal from denial of spousal support order modification.

FACT SUMMARY: Sheila Toni (P) moved the court to modify the amount of spousal support Conrad Toni (D) paid to her pursuant to an incorporated spousal support agreement. Conrad (D) argued that the court lacked jurisdiction to modify the amount.

🏛 RULE OF LAW
Courts have no jurisdiction over incorporated terms of settlement agreements.

FACTS: Sheila Toni (P) and Conrad Toni (D) married in 1971 and divorced in 1999. Conrad (D) was a urologist, and Sheila (P) was a bookstore clerk. Prior to the final divorce, the parties entered into a "Custody and Property Settlement Agreement," which divided their assets and handled custody and support terms. Sheila (P) was to receive $5,000.00 in monthly spousal support from Conrad (D) for three years or until death or her remarriage. Conrad (D) had counsel while Sheila (P) did not, but she asserted that she entered into the agreement voluntarily and knowingly. The support amount was incorporated into the final judgment so that the court had no jurisdiction to change the amount, but Conrad's (D) obligation to pay was merged into the final judgment so that the court could enforce it. Over one year later, Sheila (P) moved for a modification of the support amount based on several factors. She claimed that her investments did not do well that year, that an anticipated marriage did not take place, and that her income was not meeting her expenses. She sought additional funds from Conrad (D). Conrad (D) argued that the court lacked jurisdiction to modify the amount because the amount term was incorporated into rather than merged into the final divorce judgment. The trial court dismissed Sheila's (P) motion and Sheila (P) appealed.

ISSUE: Do courts have jurisdiction over incorporated terms of settlement agreements?

HOLDING AND DECISION: (VandeWalle, C.J.) No. Courts have no jurisdiction over incorporated terms of settlement agreements. Statutory law provides courts jurisdiction to modify spousal support upon a showing of changed circumstance unless the trial court fails to explicitly reserve that right and provides no initial support award. Sheila (P) asserted that the parties' intentions cannot divest the court of jurisdiction because the statute provides it regardless. While child support cannot be taken from the courts, because that right belongs to the child and not to the parents, the parties may certainly make an

individual determination regarding spousal support. Some jurisdictions do not recognize contractual divestments of court jurisdiction. The trend is to follow the contracting parties' intentions. The agreement here was found to be "fair and equitable" and Sheila (P) willingly and knowingly executed it. The legislature and public policy do not forbid such contractual terms. Furthermore, allowing contracting parties to set the modifiability of spousal support encourages predictability and future planning. The American Academy of Matrimonial Lawyers supports non-modification clauses for public policy reasons. If the court nullified such waivers, divorce settlement agreements would become more uncertain and less attractive to the parties. The clause here is unambiguous and Sheila (P) contracted for it. Affirmed.

DISSENT: (Maring, J.) Spousal support should remain within the court's jurisdiction to account for changes in circumstances that could render a spouse destitute and a burden on society.

▶ ANALYSIS

Courts and society benefit by parties amicably agreeing to certain terms of divorce. When two adults negotiate, agree to, and contract for spousal support, they can also negotiate, agree to, and contract for the court to no longer have jurisdiction over that agreement. There is a presumption that the contract terms are valid and enforceable, because the interested parties had every opportunity to change them. It's only when the terms affect children that the parties cannot bargain away rights because those rights belong to the children rather than the parties themselves. The majority of states allow for the parties to contract for the non-modification of spousal support amounts because of a preference for finality, predictability, and enforcement of agreed-upon contract terms.

Quicknotes

SPOUSAL SUPPORT Payments made by one spouse to another in discharge of the spouse's duty pursuant to law, or in accordance with a written divorce or separation decree, in order to provide maintenance for the other spouse.

Sidden v. Mailman

Ex-wife (P) v. Ex-husband (D)

N.C. Ct. App., 137 N.C. App. 669, 529 S.E.2d 266 (2000).

NATURE OF CASE: Appeal from order upholding validity of separation agreement.

FACT SUMMARY: The parties executed a separation agreement setting out the terms of their divorce and each complied fully with those terms. During the divorce trial, Sidden (P) asserted that she had suffered from a psychiatric condition during the execution of the agreement, and she therefore lacked the mental capacity to agree to its terms.

🏛 RULE OF LAW
Parties to a separation agreement owe a fiduciary duty to one another absent formal adversarial negotiations of the agreement terms.

FACTS: Judy Ann Sidden (P) and Richard Bernard Mailman (D) separated and began negotiating the terms of their divorce by drafting a separation agreement. The parties agreed to the terms and executed an informal draft document. Mailman (D) retained counsel to prepare a formal separation agreement based on the terms of the informal draft document. The parties then executed the formal Agreement before a notary. Sidden (P) had business attorneys but elected not to retain counsel to review the Agreement on her behalf. Sidden (P) immediately demanded the money due her from Mailman (D) under the agreement, so he drove her to a bank and gave her the money that day. Several months later, Mailman (D) realized they had omitted his State Retirement Account from the Agreement, so he contacted Sidden (P) about it. She informed him that she would get more than that from him and hung up on him. At trial, Sidden (P) testified that she had been psychotic during the time period of executing the Agreement because of a manic reaction to Zoloft. Her treating psychiatrist testified that he saw her during that time period and that she had previously been manic, but then seemed to have impaired judgment rather than mania. Sidden's (P) additional expert testified that she could have appreciated that she was signing the Agreement, but could not understand the consequences because of her mania disorder. Mailman (D), who has a Master's degree in Social Work, testified that he, did not notice any incapacity of Sidden (P) during the signing period. The trial court upheld the validity of the Agreement and Sidden (P) appealed.

ISSUE: Do parties to a separation agreement owe a fiduciary duty to one another absent formal adversarial negotiations of the agreement terms?

HOLDING AND DECISION: (Greene, J.) Yes. Parties to a separation agreement owe a fiduciary duty to one another absent formal adversarial negotiations of the agreement terms. Sidden (P) asserted that she lacked the mental capacity to execute the Agreement. The trial court disagreed based on the conflicting testimony and the fact that Sidden (P) directed Mailman (D) to take her immediately to the bank to perform the contract conditions. The trial court did not err in its findings. Sidden (P) also asserted that Mailman (D) exerted undue influence over her to obtain her signature. Contrary to her assertion, the evidence showed that Mailman's (D) counsel advised her to obtain independent counsel to review the Agreement, that the Agreement was executed two weeks after the informal document was executed, and that Sidden (P) had time to review the Agreement prior to signing it. Finally, Sidden (P) asserted fraud based upon a breach of the fiduciary duty Mailman (D) owed to her. The trial court found she presented no evidence of such breach, but this is error. Evidence showed that Mailman (D) failed to disclose a State Retirement Account, which may constitute a breach of his fiduciary duty to Sidden (P). A husband and wife are fiduciaries unless they have separated and become adversaries over negotiating the terms of the agreement. That was not the case here and Sidden (P) may base her fraud claim upon the husband's failure to meet his duty to disclose as her fiduciary. Even if the failure to disclose fails to rise to the level of fraud, it may constitute procedural unconscionability. Sidden (P) would have to prove a bargaining disparity between the parties if she attempted to set aside the agreement based on substantive unconscionability. The trial court must consider these claims. Affirmed in part, reversed and remanded in part.

▶ ANALYSIS

Courts encourage the use of separation agreements in dissolution cases because it allows the parties to negotiate the terms that will work the best of each of them in their individual cases. It also gets cases through the system much faster. The agreements are often similar to contracts, however, in that the court then will not interfere in the agreement terms once executed. Parties tend to rely on one attorney to draft the document and do not find it important to have independent counsel review the terms.

Continued on next page.

Perhaps if more people viewed the separation agreement as an objective business deal, fewer courts would be asked to revamp the negotiated terms.

■══■

Quicknotes

FIDUCIARY DUTY A legal obligation to act for the benefit of another, including subordinating one's personal interests to that of the other person.

■══■

Kelley v. Kelley

Ex-husband (P) v. Ex-wife (D)

Va. Sup. Ct., 248 Va. 295, 449 S.E.2d 55 (1994).

NATURE OF CASE: Appeal from determination that court had jurisdiction to modify separation agreement.

FACT SUMMARY: The Kelleys executed a separation agreement which was ratified and incorporated into the final divorce judgment. David Allen Kelley (P) petitioned the court for visitation and Marilyn Gibson Kelley (D) petitioned for child support.

🏛 RULE OF LAW
A ratified and incorporated by reference clause of a settlement agreement may be declared void and thus render the final judgment open to attack and vacation.

FACTS: David Allen Kelley (P) and Marilyn Gibson Kelley (D) negotiated and executed a separation agreement. One clause stated that David (P) agreed to give all of his equity in their marital home to Marilyn (D) in exchange for her foregoing any request for child support for their minor children. If David (P) was ordered to pay child support for any reason, Marilyn (D) agreed to indemnify and reimburse him. The trial court ratified and incorporated the Agreement by reference. The parties abided by the Agreement terms for six years until David (P) petitioned the court for definite visitation times. Marilyn (D) then petitioned the court for child support from David (P). David (P) countered for enforcement of the indemnification and reimbursement clause. The trial court declared that clause null and void, and David (P) appealed. The court of appeals reversed on the basis that the trial court had no jurisdiction to modify the Agreement terms. Marilyn (D) appealed.

ISSUE: May a ratified and incorporated by reference clause of a settlement agreement be declared void and thus render the final judgment open to attack and vacation?

HOLDING AND DECISION: (Stephenson, J.) Yes. A ratified and incorporated by reference clause of a settlement agreement may be declared void and thus render the final judgment open to attack and vacation. Parents cannot contract away the children's rights to child support from either parent. The court retains ongoing jurisdiction over child support and maintenance for minor children. The parties here clearly contracted away David's (P) support duty owed to the minor children. The Agreement is therefore null and void because it violates established law. This case differs from prior case law that divests the trial court of jurisdiction after twenty-one days post-judgment because this case involves the support of minor children.

Insofar as the final judgment relates to a void agreement, that judgment is void. A void judgment may be collaterally or directly attacked, so the trial court had jurisdiction in this matter. Reversed.

▶ ANALYSIS

Parties cannot affect the rights of their children when negotiating the terms of a marriage dissolution. Courts will always retain jurisdiction over the support and maintenance of minor children because adults cannot be counted on to put their children's interests first.

Quicknotes

CHILD SUPPORT Payments made by one parent to another in satisfaction of the non-custodial parent's legal obligation to provide for the sustenance of the child.

COLLATERAL ATTACK A proceeding initiated in order to challenge the integrity of a previous judgment.

INCORPORATED BY REFERENCE The reference to another document in a writing, stating that the secondary writing should be considered as part of the principal document.

INDEMNIFY Securing against potential injury; compensation for injury suffered.

REIMBURSEMENT The tendering of payment to a party for expenditures made on his behalf.

SEPARATION AGREEMENT A written agreement between spouses who are separated and/or seeking a divorce, setting forth terms of support, custody and property division.

VISITATION Rights awarded by the court in a divorce or custody proceeding to a parent who does not have custody over the child or children, permitting that parent to visit with the child or children.

Kelm v. Kelm

Husband (P) v. Wife (D)

Ohio Sup. Ct., 92 Ohio St. 3d 223, 749 N.E.2d 299 (2001).

NATURE OF CASE: Appeal of judgment of divorce allowing for arbitration of child custody and visitation disputes.

FACT SUMMARY: Wife (D) agreed with husband (P) in their judgment of divorce to submit any disputes between the parties regarding child custody or visitation to an arbitrator.

> ## 🏛 RULE OF LAW
> In a domestic relations case, matters of child custody and parental visitation are not subject to arbitration. Only the courts are empowered to resolve disputes relating to child custody and visitation. Any agreement to the contrary is void and unenforceable.

FACTS: The parties' judgment of divorce incorporated their shared parenting plan, which provided that any future disputes between the parties regarding child custody or visitation would be submitted to arbitration. In a prior judgment between the parties regarding their divorce, this court ruled that an arbitration clause in the parties' ante-nuptial agreement was enforceable as to matters relating to spousal and child support. Husband (P) asked the court to extend its prior judgment to allow matters regarding child custody and visitation to be resolved through arbitration. Wife (D) challenged the plan.

ISSUE: In a domestic relations case, can matters relating to child custody and visitation be resolved through arbitration?

HOLDING AND DECISION: (Sweeney, J.) No. Matters relating to child custody and visitation in a domestic relations case cannot be resolved through arbitration. Only the courts are empowered to resolve disputes relating to child custody and visitation. Custody and visitation have a much greater impact upon the child than child support does, in terms of both the child's daily life and his or her long-term development. The process of arbitration is not so useful when the delicate balancing of the factors composing the best interests of a child is at issue. While other jurisdictions allow custody issues to be resolved via arbitration, subject to *de novo* court review, such a process does not advance the child's best interest or the basic goals underlying arbitration because it wastes time and expense, and results in a duplication of effort. Furthermore, because the wife agreed to arbitrate custody and visitation matters, and that agreement was encompassed in the divorce decree, does not mean she has waived her rights to challenge the agreement. To permit arbitration of such issues would prevent the court from fulfilling its role as *parens patriae,*

and this is contrary to public policy. Moreover, in matters of child custody and visitation, the focus is the best interest of the child, and not the rights of the parent. The existing agreement is void and unenforceable.

CONCURRENCE: (Moyer, C.J.) The majority's opinion does not apply to post-mediation agreements but only to post-arbitration agreements.

▶ *ANALYSIS*

Contrary to the present Ohio opinion, in *Dick,* 534 N.W.2d 185 (1995), which took place in Michigan, the court upheld an arbitrator's decision on child custody issues because it found arbitration an acceptable and appropriate method of dispute resolution in cases where parties agree to participate.

■══■

Quicknotes

ARBITRATION   An agreement to have a dispute heard and decided by a neutral third party, rather than through legal proceedings.

DE NOVO   The review of a lower court decision by an appellate court, which is hearing the case as if it had not been previously heard and as if no judgment had been rendered.

PARENS PATRIAE   Maxim that the government as sovereign is conferred with the duty to act as guardian on behalf of those citizens under legal disability.

■══■

Crupi v. Crupi

Parties not identified.

Fla. Ct. App., 784 So. 2d 611 (2001).

NATURE OF CASE: Appeal from denial of motion to set aside Mediated Settlement Agreement.

FACT SUMMARY: Desmond moved to set aside the Mediated Settlement Agreement based on fraud and unfairness claims.

🏛 RULE OF LAW
A post-mediation agreement may only be set aside on grounds of fraud, misrepresentation in discovery, or coercion.

FACTS: Mary Margaret Desmond and her husband participated in court-ordered mediation and negotiated a settlement agreement before a trained mediator while each was represented by counsel. After executing the Mediated Settlement Agreement, Desmond sought to set the Agreement aside based on claims of fraud and unfairness. The trial court denied her motion and incorporated the Agreement into the final divorce judgment. Desmond appealed.

ISSUE: May a post-mediation agreement only be set aside on grounds of fraud, misrepresentation in discovery, or coercion?

HOLDING AND DECISION: (Pleus, J.) Yes. A post-mediation agreement may only be set aside on grounds of fraud, misrepresentation in discovery, or coercion. The trial court was correct, but used incorrect reasoning. The trial court relied on *Castro v. Castro*, 508 So. 2d 330 (Fla. 1987), to find a presumed lack of knowledge, which was overcome by evidence that Desmond had sufficient knowledge of the marital assets. *Castro* dealt with a post-nuptial agreement while this case involves a mediated agreement. The inquiry must be limited as it is with stipulated settlement agreements. Desmond had access to typical discovery procedures and review of the agreement prior to execution, so she cannot demonstrate lack of knowledge. Desmond testified at trial that she was under pressure to come to an agreement that day and that she had taken three Xanax. This is insufficient evidence of coercion to set the Agreement aside. As to fraud in discovery, the trial court did find inconsistencies in her husband's financial affidavit but also found that Desmond was aware of those inconsistencies and signed the Agreement anyway. The evidence of fraud was insufficient to set the Agreement aside. Affirmed.

CONCURRENCE AND DISSENT: (Sharp, J.) The court properly found insufficient evidence of fraud or misrepresentation. The court also properly found that Desmond had sufficient knowledge of the marital assets. The inquiry should not be limited, however, to evidence of fraud, misrepresentation, or coercion

▶ ANALYSIS

The courts may be more flexible with settlement agreements when the parties alone have negotiated its terms. Here, a certified mediator sat down with the parties and their attorneys, so Desmond had every opportunity to negotiate and review the terms. As the court noted, pressure to execute an agreement is insufficient to demonstrate coercion because pressure is inherently part of a dissolution proceeding. Desmond may have had a stronger argument for lack of knowledge had she not had access to typical discovery procedures and a chance to have her attorney explain the financial affidavits to her.

■=■

Quicknotes

AFFIDAVIT A declaration of facts written and affirmed before a witness.

COERCION The overcoming of a person's free will as a result of threats, promises, or undue influence.

DISCOVERY Pretrial procedure during which one party makes certain information available to the other.

FRAUD A false representation of facts with the intent that another will rely on the misrepresentation to his detriment.

SETTLEMENT AGREEMENT An agreement entered into by the parties to a civil lawsuit agreeing upon the determination of rights and issues between them, thus disposing of the need for judicial determination.

Procreation

Quick Reference Rules of Law

Carey v. Population Services International

State agency (D) v. Reproductive service agency (P)

431 U.S. 678 (1977).

NATURE OF CASE: Appeal of invalidation of state regulations concerning contraceptives.

FACT SUMMARY: New York (D) prohibited the sale of contraceptives to minors and by nonpharmacists.

RULE OF LAW
(1) A state may not limit the sale of non-medical contraceptives to pharmacists.
(2) A state may not prohibit the sale of contraceptives to minors.

FACTS: New York (D) had enacted statutes prohibiting the sale of contraceptives to minors and the sale of contraceptives to adults by nonpharmacists. These statutes were challenged by Population Services Int'l (P). A district court invalidated the statutes, and the appellate court affirmed.

ISSUE:
(1) May a state limit the sale of nonmedical contraceptives to pharmacists?
(2) May a state prohibit the sale of contraceptives to minors?

HOLDING AND DECISION: (Brennan, J.) (1) No. A state may not limit the sale of nonmedical contraceptives to pharmacists. (2) No. A state may not prohibit the sale of contraceptives to minors. This Court has stated that matters of procreation are a fundamental right and that therefore any regulations interfering with the exercise of that right must serve a compelling state interest. No such interest has been demonstrated in limiting the sale of nonmedical contraceptives to pharmacists. It cannot be said that ordinary citizens require the advice of a pharmacist in deciding when and how to use contraceptives. With respect to the ban on sales of contraceptives to minors, while it is true a state may regulate minors to a greater extent than adults, a compelling interest still must be shown for a burden to be placed on the minor's choice. The argument that availability of contraceptives encourages promiscuity has never been validated statistically and has, in fact, been contradicted. Affirmed.

CONCURRENCE: (White, J.) The Court's decision should not be read to mean that a minor has a constitutional right to put contraceptives to their intended use over the objections of both the state and the parents.

CONCURRENCE: (Powell, J.) Such heightened scrutiny should not be applied when dealing with regulation, as opposed to outright proscription, of access to contraceptives by minors.

CONCURRENCE: (Stevens, J.) A state's interest in protecting minors from their own indiscretions gives it greater rights to control a minor's choices in this area than the Court allows it.

DISSENT: (Rehnquist, J.) The power of a state to regulate the conduct of minors gives it the power to ban sales of contraceptives to them, if it so chooses. This is a decision best left to legislatures, not courts.

ANALYSIS

The opinion of the Court with respect to the sale of contraceptives to minors was a plurality opinion. It is difficult to determine exactly what precedent has been set in this area. It would seem that a majority of the justices, made up of those who dissented in part or in toto (Justices White, Rehnquist, Powell, and Stevens and C.J. Burger), would allow greater regulation in this area than the opinion would indicate. A clear majority, however (all justices but Rehnquist and Burger), would not allow an outright ban.

Quicknotes

COMPELLING STATE INTEREST Defense to an alleged Equal Protection Clause violation that a state action was necessary in order to protect an interest the government is under a duty to protect.

Rust v. Sullivan

Challenger to government regulations (P) v. Secretary of Department of
Health and Human Services (D)

500 U.S. 173 (1991).

NATURE OF CASE: Appeal from ruling upholding agency regulations.

FACT SUMMARY: When Sullivan (D) promulgated new regulations to implement Title X, Rust (P) alleged the regulations exceeded the Secretary's (D) authority, and violated the First and Fifth Amendments to the Constitution.

🏛 RULE OF LAW
The regulations adopted by the Department of Health and Human Services are a permissible construction of Title X and violate neither the First nor Fifth Amendments to the Constitution.

FACTS: Section 1008 of the Public Health Service Act provided that none of the funds appropriated for family-planning services shall be used in programs where abortion was a method of family planning. Sullivan (D) promulgated new regulations to provide guidance to grantees about how to preserve the distinction between Title X programs and abortion as a method of family planning. Rust (P) challenged the facial validity of the regulations, contending that they exceeded the Secretary's (D) authority under Title X, that they violated the First Amendment, and that they violated a woman's Fifth Amendment right to choose whether to terminate her pregnancy. The court of appeals upheld the regulations.

ISSUE: Are the regulations adopted by the Department of Health and Human Services a permissible construction of Title X and do they violate either the First or Fifth Amendments to the Constitution?

HOLDING AND DECISION: (Rehnquist, C.J.) Yes. The Regulations adopted by the Department of Health and Human Services are a permissible construction of Title X and violate neither the First nor Fifth Amendments to the Constitution. First, the broad language of Title X plainly allows the Secretary's (D) construction of the statute. Second, the Title X grantee is simply required to conduct its abortion-related activities through programs that are separate and independent from the project that receives Title X funds, not to refrain from them entirely. Third, the difficulty that a woman encounters when a Title X project does not provide abortion counseling or referral leaves her in no different position than she would have been if the government had not enacted Title X. Under the challenged regulations, a doctor's ability to provide, and a woman's right to receive, information concerning abortion and abortion-related services outside the context of the Title X project remains unfettered. Affirmed.

DISSENT: (Blackmun, J.) It cannot seriously be disputed that the counseling and referral provisions at issue here constitute content-based regulation of speech. The regulations are also clearly viewpoint-based, since they suppress speech favorable to abortion with one hand, and compel anti-abortion speech with the other.

DISSENT: (O'Connor, J.) The judgment should be reversed on the basis that the Secretary's interpretations are not reasonable and raise First Amendment concerns. This Court oversteps its bounds when it directs Congressional action before such action has occurred.

▶ ANALYSIS

The challenged regulations attach three principal conditions on the grant of federal funds for Title X projects. First, a Title X project may not provide counseling concerning the use of abortion as a method of family planning or provide referral for abortion as a method of family planning, even upon specific request. Second, the regulations broadly prohibit a Title X project from engaging in activities that encourage, promote, or advocate abortion as a method of family planning. Third, they require that Title X projects be organized so that they are physically and financially separate from prohibited abortion activities.

■━■

Quicknotes

FIFTH AMENDMENT Provides that no person shall be compelled to serve as a witness against himself, or be subject to trial for the same offense twice, or be deprived of life, liberty, or property without due process of law.

FIRST AMENDMENT Prohibits Congress from enacting any law respecting an establishment of religion, prohibiting the free exercise of religion, abridging freedom of speech or the press, the right of peaceful assembly and the right to petition for a redress of grievances.

■━■

Kassama v. Magat

Child (P) v. Physician (D)

Md. Ct. Special App., 136 Md. App. 637, 767 A.2d 348 (2001).

NATURE OF CASE: Appeal from jury finding of plaintiff's contributory negligence in wrongful life action.

FACT SUMMARY: Kassama (P) filed a claim for damages against Magat (D) based on "wrongful life." She was born with Down's Syndrome, and her mother claimed she would have aborted but for Magat's (D) negligence.

🏛 RULE OF LAW
Maryland does not recognize a "wrongful life" cause of action based upon the birth of a genetically defective child allegedly caused by physician negligence.

FACTS: Ibrion Fatuo Kassama (P) was born with Down's Syndrome. Her mother filed a "wrongful life" cause of action on behalf of Kassama (P) against the physician, Aaron Magat, M.D. (D) who cared for Mrs. Kassama during her pregnancy. Kassama (P) sought money damages for her extraordinary expenses owed to life with Down's Syndrome. The jury found Magat (D)'s negligence breached his standard of care and his duty of care owed to Kassama (P). The jury also found Mrs. Kassama contributorily negligent. The trial judge denied Kassama's (P) motions for judgment notwithstanding the verdict and new trial. Kassama (P) appealed and Magat (D) conditionally cross-appealed.

ISSUE: Does Maryland recognize a "wrongful life" cause of action based upon the birth of a genetically defective child allegedly caused by physician negligence?

HOLDING AND DECISION: (Salmon, J.) No. Maryland does not recognize a "wrongful life" cause of action based upon the birth of a genetically defective child allegedly caused by physician negligence. Maryland does recognize a "wrongful birth" cause of action. The difference between the two actions is that a "wrongful life" action seeks a determination of damages for the fact of a life versus nonexistence. The majority of states do not recognize a "wrongful life" tort. The injury is life itself and courts are not in the position to determine the value of human existence. Pennsylvania rejected the action on the basis of a lack of "legal injury." New York rejected the action on the basis of impossibility of determining damages. West Virginia held that the physician's negligence did not cause the injury. South Carolina based its rejection of the claim on the "preciousness of human life." The legislatures of eight states prohibit wrongful life claims. The few states that recognize such claims leap from the injury of life itself to damages. *Turpin v. Sortini* is the seminal case for wrongful life claims. The California court refused to allow general damages for wrongful life, but granted special damages for the expenses related to the child's total deafness. The court also affirmed that the child can bring the action because it should not depend on parental willingness or ability. New Jersey held similarly to allow a child to recover for extraordinary medical expenses throughout childhood and into majority. The dissent in that case argued that it was unfair to force physicians to pay for such claims. This court agrees with the twenty-three states which do not recognize wrongful life claims. The basis for this holding is the impossibility of calculating damages for the alleged injury of existence versus no life at all. Affirmed.

▶ ANALYSIS

The excerpt does not go into the factual history of the case to the extent of Mrs. Kassama's medical care. Mrs. Kassama took a test at her twenty-second week to determine the likelihood of her fetus having Down's Syndrome. She claimed that Dr. Magat failed to inform her of the test results showing increased chances that her child would have the genetic abnormality. Dr. Magat also allegedly told her that she would have to go out of state if she wanted to abort the fetus because Maryland prohibits abortion past the twenty-fourth week. This is the basis for the daughter's wrongful life claim that her mother would have aborted her if not for Dr. Magat's negligence. Most states have determined that this claim is repugnant to the sanctity placed on human life. It forces a child to make a claim that nonexistence would be preferable to existence with abnormalities or challenges. As the *Kassama* court notes, calculating damages to return that child to the position she would be in but for the injury would result in a determination of the value of nonexistence. Life cannot be recognized as an injury.

Quicknotes

CONTRIBUTORY NEGLIGENCE Behavior on the part of an injured plaintiff that combines with the defendant's negligence, resulting in injury to the plaintiff.

DUTY OF CARE A principle of negligence requiring an individual to act in such a manner as to avoid injury to a person to whom he or she owes a duty.

PROFESSIONAL STANDARD OF CARE That degree of care as reasonable persons in the particular profession would exercise.

Continued on next page.

WRONGFUL LIFE A medical malpractice action brought by the parents of a child born with severe birth defects against a doctor, claiming that but for the doctor's negligent treatment or advice they would not have given birth to the child.

■≡■

Stenberg v. Carhart

State (D) v. Physician (P)

530 U.S. 914 (2000).

NATURE OF CASE: Constitutional challenge to a Nebraska statute that banned partial birth abortions.

FACT SUMMARY: A Nebraska physician (P) who performed abortions brought a lawsuit seeking both a declaration that the Nebraska statute violated the United States Constitution, and an injunction forbidding its enforcement.

RULE OF LAW
Nebraska's law banning partial birth abortions was unconstitutional because it placed an undue burden on a woman's decision to obtain a previability abortion.

FACTS: Dr. Carhart (P) was a Nebraska physician who performed abortions. He brought a lawsuit in federal district court asking for both a declaration that the state law was unconstitutional and an injunction that would forbid its enforcement. The district court, after trial, held that the law was unconstitutional, and the court of appeals affirmed. The Nebraska law banned partial birth abortions.

ISSUE: Does a Nebraska statute that bans partial birth abortions, one method of performing abortions, violate the United States Constitution?

HOLDING AND DECISION: (Breyer, J.) Yes. The Nebraska statute violates the United States Constitution for two reasons. First, the statute fails to provide any exception for the preservation of the mother's health. It provides an exception only if the mother's life is in danger. The law does not directly advance an interest in protecting the potentiality of human life because it regulates only the *method* of abortion. And its stated goals of showing "concern for the unborn," preventing "cruelty," and preserving "the integrity of the medical profession" have no bearing on the crucial issue of the health exception. It is well established that a state may promote, but not endanger, a woman's health when it regulates the methods of abortion. Here, evidence indicates that the proscribed method is safer than other procedures in some cases. Nebraska's contention that it needs no health exception because the banned procedure is infrequently used is unconvincing. The state cannot prohibit a person from obtaining treatment simply by pointing out that most people do not need it. Second, the law is unconstitutional because it clearly could be interpreted to apply to a more commonly used abortion procedure prevalent in previability circumstances in which the state has even less legitimate regulatory interests. The threat of prosecution and punishment for performing this more common procedure would discourage providers and

result in an undue burden upon a woman's right to make an abortion decision. Affirmed.

CONCURRENCE: (O'Connor, J.) Women could still obtain abortions even if the D&X procedure was prohibited, so prohibition alone is not the obstacle. To be constitutional, this statute should include protections for the mother's health and life.

CONCURRENCE: (Ginsburg, J.) The Nebraska statute does not prohibit all abortions, protect women's health or lives, and does not address the most common abortion procedure. The most common abortion procedure can be described in as gruesome a fashion as "partial birth abortion."

DISSENT: (Thomas, J.) The Nebraska statute does not prohibit the D&E procedure, so the question becomes whether a state may prohibit partial birth abortion without a health exception for the mother. First is whether Nebraska has a legitimate state interest. *Casey* allows for states to "express profound respect" for life, which would allow Nebraska's statute. In this particular procedure, the fetus is terminated outside of the womb, which grants the fetus a certain autonomy from the mother's different from other abortion procedures. Nebraska therefore has a legitimate interest in prohibiting this procedure. The "answer is too obvious, and the contrary arguments too offensive . . . ." The next step is to consider the requirement of a health exception. The majority claims to be using a straightforward application of *Roe* and *Casey*. To the contrary, those cases mandate health exceptions when an abortion is "necessary." The majority here hold that "necessary" means whenever the physician and woman determine that this type of abortion is preferable. This creates unlawful abortion-on-demand. Omitting a health exception in this statute does not create an unlawful obstacle to abortion, so it is not required here. State regulations of abortion should be upheld absent a finding of an increased health risk. No such risk exists here for the statistically few women seeking partial birth abortion. The majority fails to pinpoint the "substantial medical evidence" supporting the preference for this method of abortion despite relying on the "substantial" body of work for its opinion. When a question of evidence exists, the court should err in the state's favor. This regulation is constitutional under *Casey*.

Continued on next page.

▶ *ANALYSIS*

Despite the Court's opinion that what occurs during a partial birth abortion is abhorrent, the Court was able to set aside personal beliefs and focus on the legality of the issue. The Court once again chose to protect a woman's right to choose and in this case that took the form of protecting the actual method a woman could select. Nevertheless, the case reveals the difficulties in applying the "undue burden" analysis. As Justice Scalia points out, it is inherently subjective.

■═■

Hathaway v. Worcester City Hospital
Mother (P) v. Hospital (D)
475 F.2d 701 (1st Cir. 1973).

NATURE OF CASE: Appeal from denial of injunction and damages for hospital's refusal to perform voluntary sterilization.

FACT SUMMARY: Pursuant to established policy, Worcester City Hospital (D) refused to sterilize Hathaway (P).

🏛 RULE OF LAW
A governmentally operated hospital may not refuse to perform sterilizations when it routinely performs surgical procedures of similar complexity.

FACTS: Hathaway (P), a mother of eight living below the poverty level, requested a tubal ligation prior to her eighth birth. Worcester City Hospital (D), which had a policy of not performing voluntary sterilizations, although it routinely performed surgical procedures of similar complexity, refused. Hathaway (P) brought an action against the Hospital (D), seeking injunctive relief and damages. The district court granted judgment in favor of the Hospital (D).

ISSUE: May a governmentally operated hospital refuse to perform sterilizations when it routinely performs surgical procedures of similar complexity?

HOLDING AND DECISION: (Coffin, C.J.) No. A governmentally operated hospital may not refuse to perform sterilizations when it routinely performs surgical procedures of similar complexity. *Roe v. Wade* established that the right to terminate a pregnancy is a fundamental right, and it is not much of a step in logic to conclude that the right to sterilization is also fundamental. Therefore, a state actor must show a compelling reason to allow it to deny a person this right, and the Hospital (D) has shown nothing of the sort. Reversed.

▶ ANALYSIS

The rationale of the instant case was borrowed directly from *Roe v. Wade*. The question then arises of the extent to which an individual's rights with respect to sterilization are coextensive with the right to an abortion. The Supreme Court has not decided nearly as many cases involving sterilization as it has abortions, so the question remains open.

Quicknotes
INJUNCTIVE RELIEF A court order issued as a remedy, requiring a person to do, or prohibiting that person from doing, a specific act.

In re Baby Boy Doe

Pregnant woman (D) v. State (P)

Ill. App. Ct., 260 Ill. App. 3d 392, 632 N.E.2d 326 (1994).

NATURE OF CASE: Appeal from denial of a state's petition to appoint a temporary custodian for a fetus.

FACT SUMMARY: After Doe (D) refused to have the cesarean section recommended by her physician, who had warned her that her viable, thirty-five-week-old fetus was not receiving enough oxygen, the state (P) petitioned the court to appoint the hospital as a temporary custodian to consent to the cesarean section.

RULE OF LAW

A woman's competent choice in refusing medical treatment as invasive as a cesarean section during her pregnancy must be honored, even in circumstances where the choice may be harmful to her fetus.

FACTS: Because Doe's (D) viable, thirty-five-week-old fetus apparently was not receiving enough oxygen, her physician, Dr. Meserow, recommended immediate delivery by cesarean section. Doe (D) and her husband refused because of personal religious beliefs. The state (P) then petitioned to have the hospital appointed custodian of the fetus. The court denied the petition, and the court of appeals affirmed, reserving the right to issue a future opinion. The ACLU then petitioned for a written opinion.

ISSUE: Must a woman's competent choice in refusing medical treatment as invasive as a cesarean section during her pregnancy be honored, even in circumstances where the choice may be harmful to her fetus?

HOLDING AND DECISION: (DiVito, J.) Yes. A woman's competent choice in refusing medical treatment as invasive as a cesarean section during her pregnancy must be honored, even in circumstances where the choice may be harmful to her fetus. A woman's right to refuse invasive medical treatment is not diminished during pregnancy since a woman is under no duty to guarantee the mental and physical health of her child at birth. Federal constitutional principles prohibiting the balancing of fetal rights against maternal health further bolster a woman's right to refuse a cesarean section. Moreover, the medical profession strongly supports upholding a pregnant woman's autonomy in medical decision-making. This court cannot issue an order that could be carried out only through the use of physical force or its equivalent. Affirmed.

ANALYSIS

Doe (D) ultimately delivered an apparently normal and healthy baby boy. In *Cruzan v. Director, Missouri Department of Health*, 497 U.S. 261 (1990), the Supreme Court held that the Due Process Clause of the Fourteenth Amendment conferred a significant liberty interest in avoiding unwanted medical procedures. Concurring, Justice O'Connor stated that the liberty guaranteed by the Due Process Clause must protect an individual's deeply personal decision to reject medical treatment.

Quicknotes

DUE PROCESS CLAUSE Clauses found in the Fifth and Fourteenth Amendments to the United States Constitution providing that no person shall be deprived of "life, liberty, or property, without due process of law."

State v. McKnight

State (P) v. Convicted murderer (D)

S.C. Sup. Ct., 52 S.C. 635, 576 S.E.2d 168 (2003).

NATURE OF CASE: Appeal from conviction for homicide by child abuse.

FACT SUMMARY: Regina McKnight (D) was convicted of homicide by child abuse because her cocaine use resulted in the death of her 35-37-week fetus. She appealed based on lack of criminal intent.

🏛 RULE OF LAW
Homicide by child abuse includes deliberate acts resulting in the death of a viable fetus.

FACTS: Regina McKnight (D) used cocaine during her final trimester of pregnancy and then delivered a stillborn daughter with benzoylecgonine in her system, which is metabolized by cocaine. McKnight (D) was arrested for homicide by child abuse because the pathologist determined the child had died 1-3 days prior to delivery due to the cocaine in her system. The jury convicted McKnight (D), and she was sentenced to twenty years suspended after twelve. McKnight (D) appealed on the basis that the trial court should have directed a verdict because she had no criminal intent.

ISSUE: Does homicide by child abuse include deliberate acts resulting in the death of a viable fetus?

HOLDING AND DECISION: (Waller, J.) Yes. Homicide by child abuse includes deliberate acts resulting in the death of a viable fetus. McKnight (D) argues that she did not exhibit the statutory requisite of "extreme indifference to human life" while ingesting cocaine in her third trimester. The Court of Appeals has defined "extreme indifference" in the homicide by child abuse statute to include deliberate acts resulting in a death. Reckless disregard for a person's safety also suffices. McKnight (D) had sufficient notice that late-term cocaine use placed her fetus at significant risk, and her cocaine use resulted in her daughter's death. McKnight's (D) claim for a directed verdict was rightly denied. McKnight's (D) second argument is that the statute does not apply here and that the legislature did not intend for the statute to apply to fetuses. Both arguments fail. First, the statute applies to a "child" and the term "child" expressly includes a viable fetus. Second, the legislature had opportunity to amend the statute to expressly exclude fetuses and it did not. Affirmed.

DISSENT: (Moore, J.) The abortion statute criminalizes feticide and provides for two years imprisonment or a $1,000 fine. The legislature could not have intended the homicide by child abuse statute to apply to a pregnant mother's drug use resulting in the death of her fetus because this particular statute has such a greater punishment.

Penal statutes must be strictly construed in the defendant's favor.

▶ ANALYSIS

McKnight's attorneys argued that South Carolina now supports the prosecution of women who suffer stillbirths. The statute has not yet been used to prosecute women who smoke or drink during pregnancy, but that slippery-slope argument was at the forefront. The U.S. Supreme Court forbids hospitals from testing mothers for drugs without their consent and turning those results over to police. Advocates for the women argue that the child can be tested for drugs in his system and those results could be used against the drug-using mother. This case set the stage for a pregnant woman's autonomy versus fetal rights outside of the abortion setting.

Quicknotes

CHILD ABUSE Conduct harmful to a child's physical or mental health.

HOMICIDE The killing of another individual.

Buck v. Bell

Feeble-minded woman (D) v. State agency (P)

274 U.S. 200 (1927).

NATURE OF CASE: Writ of error to review a judgment ordering sterilization.

FACT SUMMARY: Bell (P), the superintendent of the State Colony for Epileptics and Feeble Minded, was ordered by the court to have Carrie Buck (D), a feeble-minded inmate at said institution, sterilized pursuant to a statute authorizing such.

🏛 RULE OF LAW
The Constitution does not preclude a state from passing legislation authorizing the sterilization of institutionalized persons who are afflicted with hereditary forms of insanity, imbecility, etc., upon compliance with provisions designed to protect such persons from possible abuse.

FACTS: Carrie Buck (D), a feeble-minded daughter of a feeble-minded mother, was institutionalized in the State Colony for Epileptics and Feeble Minded. So was her mother. Carrie Buck (D) was 18 and already had an illegitimate, feeble-minded child when an action was brought that resulted in the court ordering Bell (P), as the superintendent of the State Colony, to have her sterilized. The Supreme Court of Appeals of the State of Virginia affirmed the judgment. A writ of error was brought to review the judgment, the argument being that the statute permitting such sterilization of institutionalized patients upon the superintendent's determination that such would be in the best interest of the patients and of society was unconstitutional.

ISSUE: Does the Constitution forbid state laws permitting the sterilization of those afflicted with hereditary forms of insanity, imbecility, etc., upon compliance with provisions therein designed to protect such persons from possible harm?

HOLDING AND DECISION: (Holmes, J.) No. There is nothing unconstitutional about a state law that permits the sterilization of an institutionalized person afflicted with hereditary forms of insanity, imbecility, etc., upon compliance with provisions therein designed to protect such persons from possible harm. The public welfare may call upon the best citizens for their lives and should be able to call upon those who already sap the strength of the state for these lesser sacrifices. It is better to take this kind of preventative action than to wait and execute degenerate offspring for crime or let them starve for their imbecility. It is better for the entire world if society can prevent those who are manifestly unfit from continuing their kind. Affirmed.

▶ ANALYSIS

Needless to say, the continued validity of the broad statements made in this decision is in grave doubt. The statute which it held constitutional was repealed in 1974. Modern case laws requires "clear and convincing" evidence to authorize sterilization under current statutes.

Quicknotes

WRIT OF ERROR A writ issued by an appellate court, ordering a lower court to deliver the record of the case so that it may be reviewed for alleged errors.

Conservatorship of Angela D.

Parent conservators (P) v. Mentally challenged daughter (D)

Cal Ct. App., 70 Cal. App. 4th 1410, 83 Cal. Rptr. 2d 411 (1999).

NATURE OF CASE: Conservatee's appeal from order granting conservators' motion for sterilization.

FACT SUMMARY: Angela D.'s (D) parents (P) had conservatorship over her because of her developmental disabilities. Her parents (P) sought to sterilize Angela (D) for medical reasons and the court granted their petition. Angela (D) appealed.

🏛 RULE OF LAW
Each of the statutory elements for sterilization of a developmentally disabled person must be proven beyond a reasonable doubt for the order to issue.

FACTS: Angela D. (D), 20, was developmentally disabled, suffered from diabetes, and had epileptic seizures. Her parents (P) had conservatorship over her person and estate. Doctors informed the conservators (P) that a pregnancy could result in Angela suffering fatal seizures that would also kill the fetus. The parents (P) subsequently sought a court order to grant medical consent for Angela's (D) sterilization. Angela's (D) court-appointed attorney recognized his duty to presumptively assume Angela's (D) opposition to the sterilization, but also reported that the conservators (P) could meet each requisite element for the petition to be granted. He thus did not oppose the petition. Angela (D) was not present at the hearing because of flu, and the court noted the requirement that she be present absent "medical inability." The hearing proceeded despite the temporary nature of Angela's (D) illness. The physicians testified via telephone. The only element that was questionable was the likelihood that Angela (D) might engage in sexual activity. Her parents (P) put forth evidence that they were not with her 24 hours a day, that she would graduate school at age 22 and would be interacting with the general public, and that her mental capacity could result in her going along with sexual pressure. The court found the elements proven beyond a reasonable doubt and issued the order with a stay pending this automatic appeal on Angela's (D) behalf.

ISSUE: Must each of the statutory elements for sterilization of a developmentally disabled person be proven beyond a reasonable doubt for the order to issue?

HOLDING AND DECISION: (Ramirez, P.J.) Yes. Each of the statutory elements for sterilization of a developmentally disabled person must be proven beyond a reasonable doubt for the order to issue. Angela (D) appeals on the basis that the likelihood of sexual activity was not proven beyond a reasonable doubt and that her due process rights were violated when her trial counsel did not oppose the petition and the trial was conducted without her present. The California legislature prohibited the sterilization of developmentally disabled persons until the state Supreme Court urged in a related holding for the legislature to reconsider and issue procedural safeguards. The resulting statutes allow for sterilization of the developmentally disabled upon a showing of the statutory factors beyond a reasonable doubt. The conservators (P) thus had to show beyond a reasonable doubt the likelihood of Angela's (D) engagement in sexual activity. The testimony revealed that Angela (D) would be placed in a day program after her graduation from high school at age 22. She would interact with male patients and other males in this new environment. Additionally, Angela (D) had a history of wandering off from supervised programs, and her father (P) was concerned for her safety outside of supervision. Angela (D) is legally unable to give her consent to sexual activity because of her disability. The statute at issue prohibits the court from considering the conservatee's vulnerability to unlawful sexual activity. Angela's (D) inability to give legal consent results in all sexual activity with her being unlawful. To the extent that the court cannot then consider Angela's (D) vulnerability to any sexual conduct, the statute cannot stand. Angela (D) must be granted the same rights, however, as a person able to grant legal consent to sterilization, so the statute cannot be struck down in its entirety. Facts may exist where the language of the statute does not undermine the purpose behind it, so the holding is limited to Angela's (D) case. Under the facts presented here, a real possibility exists that Angela (D) would be vulnerable to sexual activity. Angela (D) could present little evidence in opposition to the petition. Affirmed.

▶ ANALYSIS

The court noted the importance of granting equal rights to the developmentally disabled despite an inability to legally consent to medical procedures. Under the law, the disabled should have the ability to consent to what is in their best interests. In the *Angela D.* case, the facts were overwhelming that sterilization was in Angela's best health interests and the testimony supported the parents' medical consent.

■═■

In re Jane A.

Developmentally disabled pregnant ward (D) v.
Department of Mental Retardation (P)

Mass. Ct. App., 36 Mass. App. Ct. 236, 629 N.E.2d 1337 (1994).

NATURE OF CASE: Appeal from denial of petition to grant medical consent to terminate ward's pregnancy.

FACT SUMMARY: Jane A. (D) is a developmentally disabled woman in her first trimester of pregnancy. The Department of Mental Retardation (P) sought to have a guardian appointed for her to grant medical consent to terminate the pregnancy for Jane's (D) best interests.

RULE OF LAW
A temporary guardian may consent to the ward's pregnancy termination if the court determines that the ward would so choose if competent.

FACTS: Jane A. (D), 30, was severely developmentally disabled and suffered from seizures. The Department of Mental Retardation (P) sought to have a temporary guardian appointed for Jane (D) to grant consent to terminate Jane's (D) 18-week pregnancy. Jane (D) functions mentally at the level of a challenged 4–5-year-old and has violent outbursts if her routine is disrupted in the slightest manner. After hearing significant testimony in support of terminating the pregnancy as being in Jane's (D) best interests, the judge determined that the court could not presuppose Jane's (D) disinterest in her fetus. This appeal followed.

ISSUE: May a temporary guardian consent to the ward's pregnancy termination if the court determines that the ward would so choose if competent?

HOLDING AND DECISION: (Kass, J.) Yes. A temporary guardian may consent to the ward's pregnancy termination if the court determines that the ward would so choose if competent. Jane (D) was incapable of expressing a clear preference to keep her child or to terminate her pregnancy. Jane (D) does not particularly understand the facts of her pregnancy. The judge then had to rely on other factors and the doctrine of substitution of judgment. Jane's (D) family subscribes to no particular faith nor could they offer guidance on Jane's (D) possible preference. The judge relied primarily on the testimony of one of Jane's (D) treating physicians who stated that Jane (D) could suffer irreversible psychological damage if the pregnancy continued. Jane (D) could not be adequately prepared for the physical changes of a pregnancy or the pain of childbirth. It was likely that she would become violent at the forced prenatal dietary changes and the changes to her body. The doctor also testified that an abortion was an invasive procedure that could also cause psychological damage, which led in part to the trial judge's decision.

The findings that either path would cause psychological damage cannot be held to be equal, however. The pregnancy would be significantly more harmful to Jane's (D) psychological health. The termination, in contrast, would be one medical procedure and cause minimal discomfort. Reversed.

ANALYSIS

The doctrine of substitution of judgment entered American jurisprudence in the nineteenth century in the context of making financial decisions for "lunatics." Courts eventually expanded the doctrine to include medical decisions for minors and incompetent persons. Some courts began to over-expand the doctrine and employ a family member's or guardian's substituted judgment instead of making the difficult determination of the true wishes of the incompetent person had he been competent. It is an easier determination when the person was once competent, as in most right-to-die cases. The difficult factual scenario involves something similar to Jane where she has never been legally competent and the court must attempt to ascertain her wishes. Courts must tread very lightly when addressing issues involving the bodily integrity and privacy rights of incompetents.

Quicknotes

SUBSTITUTION OF JUDGMENT DOCTRINE Doctrine prevailing in certain jurisdictions authorizing the court to sanction an estate plan that decreases tax payments upon the petition of the guardian of an incompetent.

People v. Pointer

Government (P) v. Unfit mother (D)

Cal. Ct. App., 1st Dist., 151 Cal. App. 3d 1128 (1984).

NATURE OF CASE: Appeal of probation condition imposed upon conviction for child endangerment.

FACT SUMMARY: Pointer (D), convicted of child endangerment by forcing an unhealthy diet upon her children, was ordered not to procreate during the term of her probation.

RULE OF LAW
A court may not order a probationer not to procreate when less burdensome alternatives exist.

FACTS: Pointer (D) strictly adhered to a macrobiotic diet, which lacked in certain important nutrients. She imposed this diet upon her two children, despite serious concern expressed by doctors. Her two children eventually became so ill that they were removed from her custody. Pointer (D) was convicted of child endangerment. As a term of probation, the court ordered her not to bear a child, as the court found that the type of diet she followed would damage an unborn child. Pointer (D) appealed.

ISSUE: May a court order a probationer not to procreate when less burdensome alternatives exist?

HOLDING AND DECISION: (Kline, J.) No. A court may not order a probationer not to procreate when less burdensome alternatives exist. The right to procreate is a fundamental right, and interference with a fundamental right will be condoned only when absolutely necessary. While it does appear that the condition in question reasonably advances the cause of prevention of future child endangerment, such a condition will be validated only if less intrusive alternatives do not exist. Here, Pointer (D) could submit herself to pregnancy tests on a periodic basis and then have a prenatal regimen imposed on her. This is a less restrictive alternative than the one imposed. Reversed.

ANALYSIS

The court here applied a two-step test. The threshold question when dealing with a fundamental right was the reasonableness of the order interfering with it. The court found the order reasonable. However, the court held that even when reasonable the order had to pass an over-breadth test, which the order here failed.

International Union, UAW v. Johnson Controls

Labor union (P) v. Battery manufacturer (D)

499 U.S. 187 (1991).

NATURE OF CASE: Appeal from summary judgment for defendant.

FACT SUMMARY: When Johnson Controls (D) excluded women from certain jobs, International Union (P) sued, alleging sex discrimination in violation of Title VII.

🏛 RULE OF LAW
Women affected by pregnancy, childbirth, or related medical conditions shall be treated the same for all employment-related purposes as other persons not so affected, but similar in their ability or inability to work.

FACTS: Johnson Controls (D) manufactures batteries. Occupational exposure to lead, a primary ingredient of the manufacturing process, entails health risks, including the risk of harm to any fetus carried by a female employee. Johnson (D) did not employ women in any battery-manufacturing job before the Civil Rights Act of 1964, but began hiring them in 1977, after informing them of potential dangers. In 1982, Johnson (D) shifted from a policy of warning to a policy of exclusion. International Union (P) filed a class action challenging Johnson's (D) fetal-protection policy as sex discrimination that violated Title VII of the Civil Rights Act of 1964. Johnson (D) argued that its fetal-protection policy fell within the so-called safety exception to the bona fide occupational qualification (BFOQ) exception. The district court granted summary judgment for Johnson (D), the court of appeals affirmed. The Supreme Court granted certiorari.

ISSUE: Shall women affected by pregnancy, childbirth, or related medical conditions be treated the same for all employment-related purposes as other persons not so affected, but similar in their ability or inability to work?

HOLDING AND DECISION: (Blackmun, J.) Yes. Women affected by pregnancy, childbirth, or related medical conditions shall be treated the same for all employment-related purposes as other persons not so affected, but similar in their ability or inability to work. The safety exception is limited to instances in which sex or pregnancy actually interferes with the employee's ability to perform the job. We decline to expand the exception to allow fetal-protection policies that mandate particular standards for pregnant or fertile women. Concern for a woman's existing or potential offspring historically has been the excuse for denying women equal employment opportunities. The Pregnancy Discrimination Act (PDA)

prohibits discrimination on the basis of a woman's ability to become pregnant. Reversed and remanded.

▶ ANALYSIS

The court in this case applied the PDA. In fact, the court at one point stated, "we do no more than hold that the PDA means what it says." Courts are no better qualified than employers in deciding whether a woman's reproductive role is more important to herself and her family than her economic role.

Quicknotes

BFOQ § 703(e)(1) of Title VII - Narrow exception or defense to the Title VII prohibition of discrimination based on sex.

PDA 42 U.S.C. § 2000 Amended Title VII - Mandates that pregnant women be treated the same as other employees for all employment-related purposes.

PREGNANCY DISCRIMINATION ACT Provides that discrimination "on the basis of sex" includes discrimination "because of or on the basis of pregnancy, childbirth or related conditions."

TITLE VII Eliminated discrimination on the basis of sex.

In re Marriage of Witbeck-Wildhagen

Ex-wife (P) v. Ex-husband (D)

Ill Ct. App., 281 Ill. App. 3d 502, 667 N.E.2d 122 (1996).

NATURE OF CASE: Appeal from legal paternity determination.

FACT SUMMARY: Marcia Witbeck-Wildhagen (P) alleged that Eric Wildhagen (D), her husband, was the legal father of the child born during their marriage as a result of artificial insemination to which Wildhagen (D) did not consent. Wildhagen (D) objected to any determination of fatherhood.

🏛 RULE OF LAW
A father-child relationship and support obligation is precluded absent written consent to artificial insemination during a marriage.

FACTS: Marcia Witbeck-Wildhagen (P) married Eric Wildhagen (D) in 1990. In April 1992, the couple had a consultation regarding artificial insemination, but Wildhagen (D) made it clear to all involved that he did not support Witbeck-Wildhagen's (P) attempts to become pregnant. Wildhagen (D) always used protection when engaging in intercourse with Witbeck-Wildhagen (P). Witbeck-Wildhagen (P) claimed that Wildhagen (D) told her to go ahead with the reproductive techniques, and Witbeck-Wildhagen (P) underwent seven attempts at artificial insemination. Neither she nor the clinic informed Wildhagen (D). She became pregnant in 1993 and filed for dissolution of the marriage in 1994 while pregnant. Witbeck-Wildhagen (P) sought custody of the unborn child but claimed that she was unable to support herself and the child. She had a son in July 1994 and her attorney notified Wildhagen (D) of the seven artificial insemination attempts. Subsequent testing determined that Wildhagen (D) was not the biological father. Witbeck-Wildhagen (P) moved for summary judgment based on the Illinois Parentage Act. She requested the court find Wildhagen (D) was the legal father despite her concession that he had not granted permission for the insemination as the Act requires and he was not the biological father. The trial court entered the marital separation agreement and held that Wildhagen (D) was not the legal father of the son. Witbeck-Wildhagen (P) appeals.

ISSUE: Is a father-child relationship and support obligation precluded absent written consent to artificial insemination during a marriage?

HOLDING AND DECISION: (Knecht, J.) Yes. A father-child relationship and support obligation is precluded absent written consent to artificial insemination during a marriage. The Act requires written consent from the husband when the wife undergoes artificial insemination. One case has found a father-child relationship absent written

consent, but the husband had otherwise manifested his consent to the pregnancy attempts. Here, Wildhagen (D) did not support the pregnancy at all. Witbeck-Wildhagen (P) claims that the language allowing for father-child relationship absent physician certification of the signatures should be interpreted to include the possibility of a father-child relationship in spite of a physician's failure to obtain the written consent at all. The plain language does not support this interpretation nor does the legislature appear to have intended such an interpretation. The husband's written consent is a statutory prerequisite, and it is required each time the wife undergoes the procedure. Witbeck-Wildhagen (P) also argues that a support obligation should be ordered in spite of no finding of a legal father-son relationship because of public policy. Wildhagen (D), however, has the constitutional right to choose not to be a parent. Further, a nonparent cannot be forced to support a child especially where the parent can provide support. Wildhagen (D) is not the boy's parent. Affirmed.

▶ ANALYSIS

This case was significant for artificial reproductive technology cases and for inheritance issues. When the couple does not comply with the statutory requirements, the sperm donor remains the legal father. Many sperm donors, however, are anonymous and the child has no opportunity to claim inheritance from a father. When one donor's sperm is provided to several women, the claims on the father's estate could be significant. To date, most statutes require paternity to be adjudicated or acknowledged, and sperm donors can remain anonymous. Witbeck-Wildhagen may have intended to use her ex-husband's financial resources to raise her child, but she can now only turn to her (likely) anonymous sperm donor.

■═■

Quicknotes

PUBLIC POLICY Policy administered by the state with respect to the health, safety and morals of its people in accordance with common notions of fairness and decency.

SUMMARY JUDGMENT Judgment rendered by a court in response to a motion made by one of the parties, claiming that the lack of a question of material fact in respect to an issue warrants disposition of the issue without consideration by the jury.

■═■

Elisa B. v. Superior Court

Lesbian partner (D) v. County district attorney (P)

Cal. Sup. Ct., 37 Cal. 4th 108, 117 P.3d 660 (2005).

NATURE OF CASE: Appeal from award of child support.

FACT SUMMARY: The county district attorney (P) filed an action seeking child support from Elisa B. (D) for the support of the two biological children of Elisa's (D) lesbian partner, Emily. Elisa (D) claimed that she could not be determined to be a legal parent subject to a support order because the Uniform Parentage Act does not recognize such a parent-child relationship.

> ⚖ **RULE OF LAW**
> A lesbian partner can be determined to be the legal parent of her partner's biological children and subject to a support order if she accepted the children into her home and held them out as her natural children.

FACTS: Elisa (D) and Emily began a committed relationship in 1993 and held themselves out as partners. They discussed having children and both wished to bear children. Emily claimed that Elisa (D) agreed that Emily would be a stay-at-home mother while Elisa (D) would be the breadwinner. Both women underwent artificial insemination from the same anonymous sperm donor so that the children would be biologically related. Elisa (D) gave birth to Chance and a few months later Emily gave birth to twins Ry and Kaia. Ry was born with Down's Syndrome and required special care. Emily stayed home while Elisa (D) stayed at home with the three children. Both women breast-fed all three children, Elisa (D) informed a potential employer that she had triplets, Elisa (D) took out a life insurance policy naming Emily as the beneficiary to care for all three children in the event of Elisa's (D) death, and Elisa's (D) parents referred to the twins as their grandchildren. The women considered adoption of the other's children, but did not go forward with it. The women separated in 1999, and Emily remained in their house with the twins. Elisa (D) continued to pay the mortgage and other expenses. When they sold the house, Elisa (D) paid $1000 monthly to Emily and the twins. Elisa (D) then claimed that she lost her job and could no longer support them although she was earning $95,000 annually. Emily and the twins had to seek county support. In 2002, the trial court found that the women intended to create a family and that Elisa (D) was the de facto parent of the twins. The court further held that Emily would not have become pregnant but for Elisa's (D) promise of financial support. Elisa (D) was ordered to pay support of $1815 monthly. On Elisa's (D) petition for writ of mandate, the Court of Appeal ordered the trial court to vacate its order

because Elisa (D) was not a parent under the Uniform Parentage Act. This court granted review.

ISSUE: Can a lesbian partner be determined the legal parent of her partner's biological children and subject to a support order if she accepted the children into her home and held them out as her natural children?

HOLDING AND DECISION: (Moreno, J.) Yes. A lesbian partner can be determined to be the legal parent of her partner's biological children and subject to a support order if she accepted the children into her home and held them out as her natural children. The Uniform Parentage Act ("UPA") separately defines "mother" and "father" as well as defining the parent-child relationship. Emily is the twins' biological and legal mother pursuant to the UPA because she gave birth to them. The Court of Appeals relied on this court's holding in *Johnson v. Calvert* to determine that the twins could not have two legal mothers. To the contrary, however, *Johnson* did not hold that a child could not have two female parents but that only one of the parents can be the "natural mother." As in *Johnson*, which involved a surrogate birth mother and the genetic mother, two women can have a parental relationship to a child despite only one woman giving birth and have a mother-child relationship. Therefore, the legal parents of a child can certainly be two women. The question then becomes whether Elisa (D) is the twins' parent. The UPA presumes a parent-child relationship if the parent welcomes the child into the home and holds the child out as his/her natural child. The statutory provisions apply the father-child relationship to the mother-child relationship insofar as is practical. Prior case law finds a parent-child relationship between two persons not genetically related. The trial court has the discretion to allow the presumption of parenthood to be rebutted with proof of no biological relationship. That rebuttal is allowed in "appropriate actions." This is not an appropriate action. This case involves a special needs child and reliance on county support absent the finding of a parent-child relationship. The Legislature supports findings of paternity and the value of two parents in children's lives. Elisa (D) voluntarily set about to have a family with Emily and accepted the twins as her own for the first years of their lives. Elisa (D) accepted the children into her home with Emily and held themselves out as her natural children. Emily became pregnant during their relationship. Parenthood is not presumed when a person takes on financial responsibility for a

Continued on next page.

pregnant woman when he did not consent to the pregnancy, but that is not the case here. Elisa (D) is the presumptive parent of the twins and a support order is appropriate. Reversed.

▶ *ANALYSIS*

The court did not consider the gender, marital status, or sexual orientation of the parents in this case, but only whether a parent-child relationship legally existed. The focus here was on the fact that Elisa encouraged Emily's artificial insemination and that all five people existed as a family unit for a number of years. Same-sex partners cannot escape financial responsibility for the children of their families. Adoption and biology are not the only determining factors for a parent.

Quicknotes

CHILD SUPPORT Payments made by one parent to another in satisfaction of the non-custodial parent's legal obligation to provide for the sustenance of the child.

DE FACTO STATUS In fact; something which is recognized by virtue of its existence in reality, but is illegal for failure to comply with statutory requirements.

WRIT OF MANDATE The written order of a court directing a particular action.

In re Baby M.

Determination of surrogate motherhood contract

N.J. Sup. Ct., 109 N.J. 396, 537 A.2d 1227 (1988).

NATURE OF CASE: Appeal from judgment validating surrogacy contract.

FACT SUMMARY: Stern (P) sought to enforce a surrogate motherhood contract to gain custody of his natural child.

🏛 RULE OF LAW
Surrogate motherhood contracts are void as against public policy.

FACTS: Stern (P) and Whitehead (D) entered into a contract whereby Whitehead (D) would be artificially inseminated with Stern's (P) sperm and would carry the fetus to term. Thereafter, Stern (P) and his wife would retain custody of the child. Whitehead (D) would receive $10,000. The child, Baby M., was born and given to the Sterns (P). Thereafter, Whitehead (D) changed her mind and sought custody of the child, seizing it and fleeing out of state. Stern (P) sued to enforce the surrogacy contract, and Whitehead (D) defended, contending it was contrary to public policy. The trial court upheld the contract and granted custody to Stern (P). Whitehead (D) appealed.

ISSUE: Are surrogate motherhood contracts valid?

HOLDING AND DECISION: (Wilentz, C.J.) No. Surrogate motherhood contracts are void as they are violative of public policy. The statutes in New Jersey prohibit the payment of money for placing a child for adoption. It is clear that this contract does just that. Public policy requires that the court, wherever possible, maintain the relationship between the child and its natural parents. This contract violates this public policy. Further, the contract cannot serve as the basis of a termination of parental rights. Such must be accomplished through statutory design. Because the contract is void, it cannot be used as a basis for the determination of custody. The best interest of the child must be the primary consideration. Affirmed in part; reversed in part; and remanded for further proceedings.

▶ ANALYSIS

This case represents the first state supreme court ruling on the validity of surrogate motherhood contracts. Whether the contract would be upheld in another jurisdiction is unclear. The basis for its invalidity is the payment of money and the termination of parental rights by contract. The state must retain final authority over such decisions.

Quicknotes

PUBLIC POLICY Policy administered by the state with respect to the health, safety and morals of its people in accordance with common notions of fairness and decency.

In re C.K.G.

Gestational mother (P) v. Biological father (D)

Tenn. Sup. Ct., 173 S.W.3d 714 (2005).

NATURE OF CASE: Appeal from maternity determination and custody and support order.

FACT SUMMARY: Cindy C. (P) gave birth to triplets who were conceived with anonymously donated eggs and Charles K.G.'s (D) sperm. The two intended to raise the children as their own. When the relationship deteriorated, Charles (D) disputed Cindy's (P) right to custody based on her lack of biological relationship to the triplets.

> 🏛 **RULE OF LAW**
> A gestational mother is the legal mother when she is the intended mother, carried the children to term and gave birth, and no custody dispute exists between her and the genetic mother.

FACTS: Cindy C. (P), 45, and Charles K.G. (D), mid-forties, had an unsteady relationship but determined to have a child together. Cindy (P), a nurse, was concerned about her eggs' viability, so the couple elected to have artificial insemination using donated eggs and Charles's (D) sperm. The couple executed all necessary artificial insemination clinic documents and did not correct the documents' standard language identifying them as "husband and wife." Cindy (P) was implanted with two fertilized eggs and one divided. Cindy (P) gave birth to triplets. Cindy (P) spent the latter portion of her pregnancy on bedrest, so she moved in with Charles (D), an emergency room physician, and he cared for her and the household. After Cindy's (P) maternity leave, Charles (D) took a one-year leave of absence to care for the children while Cindy (P) returned to work four days a week. The family bought a house, and Cindy (P) and Charles (D) agreed to be equally responsible for the financial obligations. In 2001, the unmarried couple began to have serious problems, and Charles (D) admitted to having at least one affair. He stopped spending time with the children and stopped providing for them financially. The utilities were shut off in 2002, so Cindy (P) filed a petition to establish parentage, and she sought custody of the children and a support order. Charles (D) countered that Cindy (P) had no biological relationship to the children and therefore had no standing to request custody or support. Cindy (P) conceded that Charles (D) spent more time with the children after she filed her petition. Charles (D) paid Cindy (P) $3000 monthly pursuant to a pendente lite order and they continued to live together. At trial, the parties stipulated that Cindy (P) had no genetic relationship to the children. The trial court ruled that Cindy (P) was the "mother" of the children because she intended to birth the children for her and Charles (D) to raise together. The court awarded joint custody with primary physical custody to Cindy (P). Charles (D) was awarded visitation rights and ordered to pay $3000 support monthly. The Court of Appeals affirmed, and this court granted review.

ISSUE: Is a gestational mother the legal mother when she is the intended mother, carried the children to term and gave birth, and no custody dispute exists between her and the genetic mother?

HOLDING AND DECISION: (Drowota III, C.J.) Yes. A gestational mother is the legal mother when she is the intended mother, carried the children to term and gave birth, and no custody dispute exists between her and the genetic mother. Technology has resulted in five potential parents of a child and sixteen methods of conception. A child's parents may comprise the gestational mother, the two genetic parents, and two unrelated persons intending to raise the child. The Tennessee parentage statutes do not address the technological advancements and are not applicable here. The legislature specifically did not intend to cover sperm and egg donation when it defined "mother" and "father." In the absence of legislative guidance, the appellate court turned to other jurisdictions. Two tests have developed: the intent test and the genetic test. California courts primarily developed the intent test. The *Johnson v. Calvert* case involved a surrogate mother, the genetic mother, and the genetic father litigating maternity and custody. The court set forth the intent test to break the dispute, holding that whichever woman intended to procreate is the natural mother. Ohio set forth the genetic test in *Belsito* in a similar fact pattern. The court did not recognize two legal mothers so it required the intended parents to be declared the legal parents if the genetic parents did not waive parental rights. If the genetic mother waives her parental rights, the gestational mother is the natural mother. This court disagrees with both tests, however. The intent test is too broad and the genetic test could result in the invalidation of surrogacy agreements or force a gestational mother to have to adopt her own children. The lower courts adoption of the intent test is thus invalidated. The case at issue must be resolved on narrow grounds specific to its facts. Cindy (P) intended to carry the children to term, birth them, and raise them with Charles (D). Both Charles (D) and Cindy (P) intended for her to be the children's mother notwithstanding their need for a genetic egg donor. Finally, the genetic donor is not disputing

Continued on next page.

custody. Cindy (P) is the children's legal mother with all attendant rights and obligations. Affirmed.

DISSENT: (Birch Jr., J.) The legislature should act to address the disconnect between existing statutes and technological advancements. This holding is just a stop-gap measure. The majority claims to discount the intent test and then relies heavily on it to develop its holding. Proof of intent is difficult to surmise, it is not supported in socially basic public policy areas, and it fails to fully recognize genetic providers' rights. The children's mother in this case is simply anonymous; this is not a case of a "motherless child." Cindy (P) is a nonparent and should not be placed on equal footing with the biological father. The statutes sufficiently address the facts here. Cindy (P) could always adopt the children. The court should interpret the existing law rather than make new law.

▶ *ANALYSIS*

The court aptly points out that the legislature needs to stay abreast of technological advancements to avoid the court having to make decisions more appropriately left to the legislative process. Alternative reproductive techniques have enabled otherwise childless persons to become parents, and procreation is a basic societal plus. The same techniques, however, have resulted in multiple potential parents for one child and outdated definitions of what constitutes a legal parent. Courts have addressed the parentage of non-biologically related families for years because of stepparenting, adoption, and surrogacy. The best situation would be if the individuals involved addressed these issues prior to the child's birth, but the legislature should promulgate guidelines for the court.

■=■

Quicknotes

CUSTODY The granting of care and control of a child or children to a parent pursuant to an action for dissolution or separation.

PENDENTE LITE A matter that is contingent on the disposition of a pending suit.

PUBLIC POLICY Policy administered by the state with respect to the health, safety and morals of its people in accordance with common notions of fairness and decency.

■=■

K.M. v. E.G.

Genetic mother (P) v. Gestational mother (D)

Cal. Sup. Ct., 37 Cal. 4th 130, 117 P.3d 673 (2005).

NATURE OF CASE: Appeal from parentage determination.

FACT SUMMARY: K.M. (P) donated her eggs to her lesbian partner, E.G. (D), who gave birth to the resulting twins. The relationship deteriorated and K.M. (P) sought a parentage determination and custody of the children while E.G. (D) objected on the basis that K.M. (P) was not the twins' parent and had no standing.

🏛 RULE OF LAW
Both the gestational mother and the genetic mother in a lesbian relationship are the parents of children produced through alternative reproductive techniques where the women intended to raise the children in their joint home.

FACTS: E.G. (D) and K.M. (P) began their romantic relationship in 1992 and began cohabitating in San Francisco in March 1994 when they registered as domestic partners. E.G. (D) had told K.M. (P) of her desire to be a mother, and she applied to adopt a child in 1993. She also underwent 13 artificial insemination attempts from July 1993 through November 1994. E.G. (D) claims that she always told K.M. (P) of her intention to be a single mother, and K.M. (P) testified that she believed the women would raise any child together. In December 1994, E.G. (D) and K.M. (P) agreed that K.M. (P) would provide E.G. (D) with her eggs for in vitro fertilization. E.G. (D) stated that she told K.M. (P) that she wanted any child to be hers alone, but that she would consider allowing K.M. (P) to adopt the child after five years if the relationship lasted. K.M. (P) denied knowledge of E.G.'s (D) wish to be a single parent and would not have donated her eggs had she known. Both women agreed not to disclose that K.M. (P) was the eggs' donor. In March 1995, K.M. (P) signed a four-page consent form which included language specifically disclaiming K.M.'s (P) parental rights to any child resulting from the donated ova. E.G. (D) signed a consent form acknowledging her parental responsibility for any child resulting from the in vitro technique. E.G. (D) testified that the two women received the forms in the mail and discussed them in February 1995. K.M. (P) testified that she did not see her consent form until 10 minutes prior to signing it and that she felt some of the language did not apply to her. For example, the form included a statement that K.M. (P) would not seek to learn the identity of the recipient of her donation. K.M. (P) testified that she wanted the women to have children together and believed she would also be a parent. The in vitro was successful, and E.G. (D) gave birth to twin girls in December 1995. E.G. (D) referred to

K.M.'s (P) family as the twins' family. K.M.'s (P) father was grandfather, her sister and brother were called aunt and uncle, and her nieces and nephews were considered the twins' cousins. E.G. (D) quickly added the twins to her insurance policies and named them as beneficiaries of other policies, but K.M. (P) did not. The nanny and the children's school considered both women to be the twins' parents. E.G. (D) and K.M. (P) split up in March 2001, and K.M. (P) filed a petition to establish her parental relationship to the five-year old girls. She also filed for custody and visitation. In September 2001, E.G. (D) and the twins moved to Massachusetts to live with E.G.'s (D) mother. E.G. (D) moved to dismiss K.M.'s (P) action on the basis that K.M. (P) explicitly relinquished all parental rights to the twins when she signed the ova donation consent form. The trial court granted the motion to dismiss, and the Court of Appeals affirmed. The courts compared K.M. (P) to a sperm donor who is not a legal father under the Family Code section 7613 if he donates sperm through a physician for reproductive use. The trial court further found that K.M. (P) is not the presumed parent because she failed to conclusively establish that she welcomed the twins into her home and held them out as her natural children. Neither party disclosed the twins' biological relationship to K.M. (P). The Court of Appeals found that only E.G. (D) intended to birth and raise a child as her own. K.M. (P) should have adopted the children. K.M. (P) appealed.

ISSUE: Are both the gestational mother and the genetic mother in a lesbian relationship the parents of children produced through alternative reproductive techniques where the women intended to raise the children in their joint home?

HOLDING AND DECISION: (Moreno, J.) Yes. Both the gestational mother and the genetic mother in a lesbian relationship are the parents of children produced through alternative reproductive techniques where the women intended to raise the children in their joint home. Family Code section 7613 does not apply to the facts of this case because the women intended to raise any child resulting from K.M.'s (P) ova donation in their joint home. The facts here are similar to those in *Johnson v. Calvert* in that the genetic parent(s) did not intend to "donate" their sperm and ova but intended to procreate and raise the child as their own after a surrogate mother gave birth. K.M. (P) did not intend to donate her eggs to a stranger

Continued on next page.

for procreation but intended to create a child with E.G. (D) and raise that child as their own. Further, the intent test is not applicable because the parentage claims are not mutually exclusive. The children can have two parents who are both women. The couple lived together at the time of conception, and K.M.'s (P) understanding was that the women would jointly raise the child. The Uniform Parentage Act governs parentage determinations and defines "mother." K.M. (P) has a mother-child relationship with the twins pursuant to the UPA because of their genetic relationship. The dissent argues that this area of the law requires predictability, but he would rely on the intent test, which is a court determination of party intent years after the fact and cannot be predictable. K.M. (P) did sign the consent form but she cannot waive her parentage of the children. Parties cannot agree to limit or abrogate the children's right to support. In any event, K.M. (P) did not intend to donate her ova, but intended to procreate with E.G. (D) and raise the children in their joint home. The court does not need to consider whether K.M. (P) is the presumptive parent. Reversed.

DISSENT: (Kennard, J.) The Family Code statutes are controlling here. K.M. (P) donated her ova similar to a sperm donation and knowingly and voluntarily signed the form relinquishing her parental rights. The Family Code sections should be applied to male and female donors equally, and E.G. (D) is the sole mother of the children. The statutory language and legislative history do not support the majority's determination here despite the majority's laudable attempt to provide the twins with a second legal parent. The statutes do not grant K.M. (P) a parent-child relationship, and the parties' intention is clearly demonstrated by the consent forms signed.

DISSENT: (Werdegar, J.) A child can theoretically have two mothers through adoption or pursuant to the UPA when one woman is the gestational mother and the other is the genetic mother. This area of the law requires predictability. In this fact situation, the intent of the parties should control under *Johnson*. E.G. (D) definitely intended to be the twins' sole mother. The evidence of K.M.'s (P) intention to be the twins' mother is disputed. The majority thus ignores *Johnson*'s intent test and creates a new law for egg donation despite demonstrable intent. Surrogacy agreements are now in jeopardy. Further, Family Code section 7613 excludes a possible parent rather than establishes a parent. The majority's interpretation requires a presumption that the section would not apply to a sperm donor who donates his sperm to a woman with whom he resides and that the women in this factual situation should be treated the same as that man. Ova donation is not similar enough to sperm donation. Proper application of the statute still leaves the question of intent, which would result in K.M. (P) not being the children's mother. This court in *Johnson* intended to avoid government intrusion into parentage under a "best interests" approach of parental determination. Here, the court forces E.G. (D) to accept

K.M. (P) as an unintentional parent because of their sexual orientation and private relationship. The legislature must restore predictability to this area.

ANALYSIS

Critics argue that this case establishes separate treatment for women. Women can use sperm donations without fear of the sperm donor being considered a legal parent or having the right to establish paternity. Egg donors, on the other hand, could be determined a legal parent. The parties here did not disclose the donor's identity, signed documents relinquishing K.M.'s parental rights, and E.G. made multiple solo attempts to have a child before resorting to K.M.'s donation. On the other hand, public policy encourages and can even legally require persons in a relationship to take on parental responsibility to children born of the relationship.

■=■

Quicknotes

BEST INTERESTS OF CHILD Standard used by courts when rendering decisions which involve a child or children.

CUSTODY The granting of care and control of a child or children to a parent pursuant to an action for dissolution or separation.

PUBLIC POLICY Policy administered by the state with respect to the health, safety and morals of its people in accordance with common notions of fairness and decency.

VISITATION Rights awarded by the court in a divorce or custody proceeding to a parent who does not have custody over the child or children, permitting that parent to visit with the child or children.

■=■

J.B. v. M.B.

Ex-wife (P) v. Ex-husband (D)

N.J. Sup. Ct., 170 N.J. 9, 783 A.2d 707 (2001).

NATURE OF CASE: Appeal from judgment that frozen preembryos of a divorced couple must be destroyed where one of the parties so desires and the other disagrees, but is still capable of having children.

FACT SUMMARY: J.B. (P) and M.B. (D), a divorced couple, disagreed about the disposition of frozen preembryos they created when they were married. J.B. (P) wanted the preembryos destroyed, but M.B. (D) wanted them implanted or donated to infertile couples. They also disagreed about whether they had entered, when they were still married, into an agreement governing the disposition of the preembryos.

🏛 RULE OF LAW
Absent an enforceable contract to the contrary, frozen preembryos of a divorced couple must be destroyed where one of the parties so desires and the other disagrees, but is still capable of having children.

FACTS: J.B. (P) and M.B. (D) were married. They had difficulty conceiving a child and went through in vitro fertilization (IVF) procedures that produced 11 preembryos that were the result of fertilizing J.B.'s (P) eggs with M.B.'s (D) sperm. Four were placed in J.B. (P), who became pregnant, and the remaining seven were cryopreserved—frozen at extremely low temperatures. J.B. (P) and M.B. (D) later divorced, but disagreed on the disposition of the preembryos, the only issue not resolved by the divorce. J.B. (P) wanted them destroyed, but M.B. (D) maintained that he and J.B. (P) had agreed that any unused preembryos would be used by J.B. (P) or donated to infertile couples. There was no clear evidence of such an agreement. A consent agreement that the couple had signed as part of the IVF program gave control over the preembryos to the IVF program (Cooper Center) upon the couple's divorce, unless a court specified otherwise. The trial court granted J.B. (P) summary judgment on the preembryo-disposition issue, the appellate division affirmed, and the New Jersey Supreme Court granted review.

ISSUE: Absent an enforceable contract to the contrary, must frozen preembryos of a divorced couple be destroyed where one of the parties so desires and the other disagrees, but is still capable of having children?

HOLDING AND DECISION: (Poritz, C.J.) Yes. M.B. (D) contended on appeal that judgment of the court below violated his constitutional rights to procreation and the care and companionship of his children, and that his rights outweighed J.B.'s (P) right not to procreate, because her right to bodily integrity was not implicated. He also argued that he and J.B. (P) had a clear agreement to give the preembryos a chance at life. J.B. (P) countered that any alleged agreement between the parties to use or donate the preembryos would be unenforceable as a matter of public policy, on the ground that individuals should not be bound by agreements requiring them to enter into family relationships or that seek to regulate personal intimate decisions relating to parenthood or family life. She also argued that absent an express contract, the court should not imply such an agreement. Finally, she argued that requiring the use or donation of the preembryos would violate her constitutional right not to procreate, but that destroying the preembryos would not significantly affect M.B.'s (D) right to procreate because he is fertile and capable of fathering other children.

As to whether there was an agreement between J.B. (P) and M.B. (D) regarding the disposition of the preembryos upon their divorce, a starting point is the consent agreement provided to J.B. (P) and M.B. (D) by the Cooper Center. That form does not manifest a clear intent by J.B. (P) and M.B. (D) as to the preembryo-disposition issue, because although it says that ownership of the preembryos will be relinquished to the Center if the couple divorces, it also carves out an exception that permits the parties to obtain a court order directing disposition. This conditional language stands in sharp contrast to language in other consents provided by other IVF facilities that have been upheld. In *Kass v. Kass*, 696 N.E.2d 174 (N.Y. 1998), New York's highest court enforced a couple's written decision to donate their preembryos for scientific research when they could not agree on disposition. That court found that the parties had signed an unambiguous contract to relinquish control of their preembryos to the facility in the event of a dispute. As opposed to the couple in *Kass*, the couple here is seeking another determination from the court. Here, a formal, unambiguous, memorialization of the parties' intentions would be required to confirm their joint determination. Because the lack of such a writing is not contested, the court holds that J.B. (P) and M.B. (D) never entered into a separate and binding agreement. Ordinarily, because both parties are contributors to the genetic material comprising the preembryos, the decision as to disposition is theirs to make. But here, where the parties disagree, the decision is left to the court. In the absence of legislative guidance, constitutional cases from other states and the federal judiciary, as well as cases in which the court

Continued on next page.

has recognized the fundamental nature of procreational rights, provide a framework within which disputes over the disposition of preembryos can be resolved. A case from the Tennessee Supreme Court, *Davis v. Davis*, 842 S.W.2d 588 (Tenn. 1992), for example, in a situation similar to the one in this case, balanced the right to procreate of the wife, who sought to donate the preembryos, against the right of the husband, who sought destruction of the preembryos, not to procreate, and concluded that the husband's right would be significantly affected by unwanted parenthood. Against that interest, the court weighed the wife's burden of knowing that the lengthy IVF procedures she underwent were futile. The court found that the wife's interest, although not insignificant, did not outweigh the father's interest. The court held that the scales ordinarily would tip in favor of the right not to procreate if the opposing party could still become a parent through other reasonable means, and this court agrees with the Tennessee court in this regard. M.B.'s (D) right to procreate is not lost if he is denied an opportunity to use or donate the preembryos; he only loses the right to procreate with his former wife's eggs. In contrast, J.B.'s (P) right not to procreate may be lost through attempted use or donation of the preembryos, which could have lifelong repercussions. The court will not force her to become a biological parent against her will. Additionally, the laws of the state evidence a policy against enforcing private contracts to enter into or terminate familial relationships, such as a surrogate mother agreement that required the biological mother to surrender her parental rights. This is consistent with the policy that consent to terminate parental rights is revocable in all but statutorily approved situations. Therefore, enforcement of an agreement that would allow the implantation of preembryos at a future date where one party has reconsidered his or her earlier assent raises similar issues—if implantation is successful, the party will have been forced to become a biological parent contrary to his or her will. There is disagreement among legal commentators and in the case law on the subject, and there are persuasive reasons for enforcing preembryo disposition agreements. Also, because IVF is in widespread use and there is a need for agreements between the participants and the IVF clinics, the better rule, and the one the court adopts, is to enforce agreements entered into at the time IVF is begun, subject to the right of either party to change his or her mind. This rule promotes the public policies that underlie limitations on contracts involving family relationships by permitting either party to object at a later date to provisions that that a party no longer subscribes to. In a large number of cases, the agreements will control, so that the clinics may reasonably rely on them, provided they are written in clear language and not signed in blank, and other similar safeguards are provided. If there is disagreement between the parties because one party has changed his or her position, the interest of both parties must be evaluated. Because ordinarily the party choosing not to become a biological parent

will prevail, this decision should not result in increased litigation. Affirmed.

CONCURRENCE: (Verniero, J.) An infertile party should be allowed to assert his or her right to use a preembryo against the objections of the other party, if such use is the only means of procreation. In that case, the balance arguably would weigh in the infertile party's favor absent other countervailing considerations.

▶ ANALYSIS

Despite the court's holding in this case that the couple did not enter into a binding contract directing the disposition of their preembryos, it nevertheless discusses at great length whether such agreements are enforceable and also discusses the rule that it adopts regarding enforcement of preembryo disposition agreements. It would seem, therefore, that much of the court's discussion is dicta, the main purpose of which is to anticipate and attempt to guide future cases. If there is one thing that all involved in this area seem to agree on is that the advances in reproductive technologies have outstripped the development of legal principles to resolve the inevitable disputes that accompany such reproductive opportunities, and that there is a need for general principles that will guide resolution of such future disputes.

Quicknotes

OBITER DICTA Statement by a judge in a legal opinion that is not necessary for the resolution of the action.

PUBLIC POLICY Policy administered by the state with respect to the health, safety and morals of its people in accordance with common notions of fairness and decency.

SUMMARY JUDGMENT Judgment rendered by a court in response to a motion made by one of the parties, claiming that the lack of a question of material fact in respect to an issue warrants disposition of the issue without consideration by the jury.

Parents and Children

Quick Reference Rules of Law

Roe v. Doe

Court-appointed guardian for daughter (P) v. Father (D)

N.Y. Ct. App., 29 N.Y.2d 188, 272 N.E.2d 567 (1971).

NATURE OF CASE: Action for an order of support.

FACT SUMMARY: Because his daughter refused to live in a dormitory while at college, the father (D) cut off her support and refused to pay her tuition bill.

🏛 RULE OF LAW
If a minor of employable age and in full possession of her faculties voluntarily and without cause abandons the parent's home against the will of the parents, then the parents' duty to support the child is terminated.

FACTS: The father (D), a prosperous attorney, supported his 20-year-old daughter in college but forbade her to live anywhere but in a dormitory. The daughter moved out of the dormitory and into an apartment. The father (D) cut off all support. The daughter refused to return home, and, instead, she sold her car and lived off the proceeds, but failed to pay the $2,000 tuition payment. The court appointed a guardian (P) for the daughter, and the guardian (P) instituted a support proceeding, alleging that the father (D) had refused and neglected to provide fair and reasonable support. The trial court ordered the father (D) to pay.

ISSUE: Does a father's duty to support his child continue when the child is employable, in control of her faculties, and has abandoned the father's home against his will?

HOLDING AND DECISION: (Scileppi, J.) No. Where, through no fault of the father, a child voluntarily abandons the home for the purpose of seeking her own way in the world, the child forfeits her claim to support. In return for support, a parent may demand adherence to reasonable restrictions. Here, the father's (D) demand that his daughter remain in a dormitory was not unreasonable or capricious. The daughter cannot enlist the aid of the court in frustrating her parent's authority. The daughter has forfeited her right to support. Affirmed.

CONCURRENCE: (Jasen, J.) The court is without power to interfere in family problems without a showing of grave harm to the child's health and welfare. Such a showing was absent here because the father (D) would have supported the daughter if she returned home or if she had moved back into a dormitory.

▶ ANALYSIS

It is the basic rule that the father is primarily liable for the support of the child while the wife is only secondarily liable. Where support is not given, one remedy is to have the child buy the necessities and then charge the father. Another remedy is to allow the child, or a guardian, to bring a direct, civil suit against the father. In addition, there is the possibility of criminal charges for neglect. At common law, there was no duty imposed on the father to support the children.

■═■

Quicknotes

CHILD SUPPORT Payments made by one parent to another in satisfaction of the non-custodial parent's legal obligation to provide for the sustenance of the child.

■═■

Prince v. Massachusetts

Mother (P) v. State (D)

321 U.S. 158 (1944).

NATURE OF CASE: Appeal from conviction for child labor law violation.

FACT SUMMARY: Prince (P) took her children with her to help her distribute religious publications, in violation of child labor laws.

RULE OF LAW
A state may prohibit children, under child labor laws, from hawking religious literature.

FACTS: Prince (P), a Jehovah's Witness, distributed religious literature in the street. Her children assisted her, in violation of state school attendance and child labor laws. Prince (P) was prosecuted under these laws and was convicted. Prince (P) appealed.

ISSUE: May a state prohibit children, under child labor laws, from hawking religious literature?

HOLDING AND DECISION: (Rutledge, J.) Yes. A state may prohibit children, under child labor laws, from hawking religious literature. The rights of children to exercise religion and parents to give them religious training is unquestioned. However, it is not absolute. Religious tenets that are contrary to the public welfare may be infringed upon. This is particularly true in the case of children. Children do not have the rational capacity of adults, and the state, therefore, has a greater interest in regulating their behavior. Here, the state has made a decision that the public good requires that children attend school and not work and has classified the hawking of religious literature as work. The obvious public policy of education plus the interest of the state in controlling the behavior of children validate the law. Affirmed.

DISSENT: (Murphy, J.) For the statute to be valid, Massachusetts (D) would have had to have shown an immediate danger to lawfully protectable interest, something it did not do.

▶ ANALYSIS

The problem encountered here was hardly a novel one. An inherent tension exists between state authority and free exercise of religion. Probably the most influential decision in this area was *Pierce v. Society of Sisters*, 268 U.S. 510 (1925), which upheld the right to religious schooling.

Parham v. J.R.

State agency (D) v. Institutionalized minor (P)

442 U.S. 584 (1979).

NATURE OF CASE: Appeal of constitutional challenge to state system of voluntary mental health institutionalization of minors.

FACT SUMMARY: A class action suit challenged Georgia's voluntary mental health institutionalization system, which permitted parents to place their minors in such institutions without a formal hearing.

🏛 **RULE OF LAW**
A state may permit parents to have their children institutionalized without a formal adversary hearing.

FACTS: Georgia had a statutory scheme for the institutionalization of minors which gave great deference to the wishes of the parents of the minor. Upon the request of a parent, a minor would be institutionalized provided a medical official connected to an institution agreed it was appropriate. No adversary hearing was provided for J.R., a minor who had been institutionalized by the state, of whom he was a ward, who filed a class action suit challenging the statutory framework. The district court and court of appeals held that the Due Process Clause required an adversary hearing prior to commitment.

ISSUE: May a state permit parents to have their children institutionalized without a formal adversary hearing?

HOLDING AND DECISION: (Burger, C.J.) Yes. A state may permit parents to have their children institutionalized without a formal adversary hearing. When official action is challenged, the interest of the individual affected by the action is balanced against the governmental interest and the chance of erroneous deprivation of such interest when the challenged procedures are used. While a child has a liberty interest at stake here, the long-standing Anglo-American respect for parental authority makes this interest much less compelling than in the case of an adult. The state has an obvious interest in institutionalizing minors that require it. The question then becomes whether the current procedures are adequate to ensure that only minors requiring such institutionalization are in fact committed. This Court is unconvinced that a quasi-judicial hearing would be any more appropriate than a decision by a neutral medical expert, as the statute currently requires. For this reason, the statutory scheme is constitutionally sufficient. Reversed.

▶ *ANALYSIS*

Although the opinion does not so state, it seems that the plaintiffs were arguing that a formal judicial hearing aided by counsel should be required. The majority disagreed by pointing out that that which is constitutionally due is determined by the nature of the issue. Since the issue here was medical, said the court, medical expertise was the important factor in the decision to institutionalize.

■━■

Quicknotes

DUE PROCESS CLAUSE Clauses found in the Fifth and Fourteenth Amendments to the United States Constitution providing that no person shall be deprived of "life, liberty, or property, without due process of law."

■━■

Goorland v. Continental Insurance and YMCA

Injured minor child (P) v. Insurance company (D) and gym (D)

Del. Super. Ct., 2003 WL 22321462 (2003).

NATURE OF CASE: Motion to bar action seeking contribution.

FACT SUMMARY: Unemancipated minor (P) exited gym (D) and was hit by a driver insured by automobile liability insurance company (D).

🏛 RULE OF LAW
Parental immunity applies to protect the negligent parent of an unemancipated minor from contribution when parental negligence results in injury to the child.

FACTS: Four-year-old Jacob Goorland (P) ran out of the YMCA (D) and entered the parking lot. Gloria Thomas hit Jacob (P) with her car resulting in injury to him. Jacob (P) sued Thomas's insurance company, Continental Insurance (D), and the YMCA (D) to recover for his injuries. Defendants sought contribution from Jacob's (P) mother (D) for her negligence in not supervising her unemancipated minor child. Goorland (D) filed a motion to bar the suit for contribution.

ISSUE: Does parental immunity apply to protect the negligent parent of an unemancipated minor from contribution when parental negligence results in injury to the child?

HOLDING AND DECISION: (Cooch, J.) Yes. Parental immunity applies to protect the negligent parent of an unemancipated minor from contribution when parental negligence results in injury to the child. Parental immunity arose originally as a doctrine to prohibit a child from suing a negligent parent. The issue of proximate cause remains a factual question because the child could have committed a supervening act of negligence resulting in the injury. Soon after the Delaware courts recognized the immunity doctrine, however, the Delaware Supreme Court recognized several exceptions and repudiations across jurisdictions. Exceptions included: "(1) suits by emancipated children; (2) suits against the estate of a deceased parent; (3) suits for willful or intentionally inflicted torts; (4) suits for reckless or grossly negligent conduct; (5) suits against a parent acting in the relation of an employer; and (6) suits by an unemancipated child against a parent for injury to his property interests." In cases involving automobile accidents, parental immunity applies except relating to the parent's automobile liability insurance because the parent and child are not true adversaries when seeking insurance coverage for the injury. The Delaware Supreme Court rejected the opportunity to abrogate parental immunity in 1993, and the Court opted to adhere to prior precedent.

The Delaware Supreme Court articulated first, that parental immunity survives in third party contribution claims and claims by a minor child, where parental control, authority, or discretion is involved; second, that a defendant may present evidence of parental negligence as a supervening cause of the child's injury if such evidence is relevant to the theory of liability; and third, parental negligence as a proximate but not supervening cause may not result in reduction of payment to the child or a contribution claim. In this case, Goorland (D) exercised parental authority over Jacob (P). The Supreme Court has therefore previously rejected defendants' arguments, so the contribution claim may not survive. Defendants may present evidence at trial that Goorland's (D) negligence is a supervening cause to Jacob's (P) injuries. The Court also rejects YMCA's (D) argument that abrogation of parental immunity is appropriate because the Supreme Court has previously rejected such a request and adheres to prior precedent despite the national trend of erosion of the doctrine.

▶ ANALYSIS

The parental immunity doctrine goes back to the 1800s. One of its main purposes was to protect family assets in the case of injury to an unemancipated minor child despite the potential negligence of the parent. Although the courts have developed exceptions to the doctrine over the years, the doctrine has also been expanded as the definition of "parent" has transformed. States now recognize foster parents and other cohabitants as persons standing *in loco parentis* and the doctrine applies to these persons as well. Some states also recognize the immunity doctrine for unintentional parental harm to an unborn child.

Quicknotes

CONTRIBUTION The right of a person or party who has compensated a victim for his injury to seek reimbursement from others who are equally responsible for the injury in proportional amounts.

EMANCIPATED MINOR A minor who is released from the control of his parents and who has the right to his own earnings and services, but not to continued parental support and maintenance.

Continued on next page.

IN LOCO PARENTIS A situation in which a person has assumed the responsibilities and obligations of a lawful parent without undergoing the legal adoption process.

PARENTAL IMMUNITY The immunity of a parent from liability in actions brought by his or her child claiming negligence.

PROXIMATE CAUSE The natural sequence of events without which an injury would not have been sustained.

SUPERVENING CAUSE An independent cause, which is the proximate cause of an act.

Popple v. Rose

Injured (P) v. Parents of tortfeasor (D)

Neb. Sup. Ct., 254 Neb. 1, 573 N.W.2d 765 (1998).

NATURE OF CASE: Appeal from summary judgment for defendants.

FACT SUMMARY: The Popples (P) sued the Roses (D) in negligence when their child sexually attacked the Popples' (P) son.

🏛 RULE OF LAW
A parental duty to warn third parties of their children's known dangerous sexual propensities may exist in certain limited situations.

FACTS: When the Roses' (D) thirteen-year-old son sexually assaulted the Popples' (P) six-year-old son while babysitting, the Popples (P) filed suit, claiming that the Roses (D) negligently failed to warn them of their son's allegedly known dangerous sexual propensity. The Roses (D) filed a motion for summary judgment, which was granted. The Popples (P) appealed.

ISSUE: Does a parental duty to warn third parties of their children's known dangerous sexual propensities exist in certain limited situations?

HOLDING AND DECISION: (White, C.J.) Yes. A parental duty to warn third parties of their children's known dangerous sexual propensities may exist in certain limited situations. The state parental vicarious liability statute does not abrogate common law liability. In this case, the record contains no evidence that the Roses (D), or anyone else, had prior knowledge of any dangerous sexual propensity. Therefore, no duty to warn arose because the conduct was not a known, habitual propensity. Affirmed.

▶ ANALYSIS

The court in this case also discussed the state parental vicarious liability statute. Under its terms, parents are jointly and severally liable for the willful and intentional infliction of personal injury to any person or destruction of real and personal property occasioned by their minor children. Recovery is limited to actual damages up to a limit of $1,000.

■━■

Quicknotes

DUTY TO WARN An obligation owed by an owner or occupier of land to persons who come onto the premises, to inform them of defects or active operations which may cause injury.

FORESEEABILITY A reasonable expectation that an act or omission would result in injury.

NEGLIGENCE Conduct falling below the standard of care that a reasonable person would demonstrate under similar conditions.

SUMMARY JUDGMENT Judgment rendered by a court in response to a motion made by one of the parties, claiming that the lack of a question of material fact in respect to an issue warrants disposition of the issue without consideration by the jury.

VICARIOUS LIABILITY The imputed liability of one party for the unlawful acts of another.

■━■

Giuliani v. Guiler

Husband (P) v. Doctor (D)

Ky. Sup. Ct., 951 S.W.2d 318 (1997).

NATURE OF CASE: Wrongful death suit.

FACT SUMMARY: Giuliani (P) brought suit against his wife's obstetrician (D) for wrongful death and loss of consortium on behalf of himself and his four minor children.

> ## 🏛 RULE OF LAW
> A minor child has a claim for loss of parental consortium against third parties responsible for the loss of a parent.

FACTS: Mary Giuliani died during the birth of her fourth child. Guiler (D), the obstetrician, was not present at the time of the delivery. He instructed the nurses to induce labor and then left the hospital. The nurses became increasingly concerned and attempted to reach the doctor. While other persons attempted to aid her, Mary suffered cardiac and respiratory collapse and died. The father (P) brought a claim for wrongful death and loss of consortium and also a claim for loss of consortium on behalf of their four minor children. The trial judge dismissed the claim of the three minor children and the court of appeals affirmed.

ISSUE: Does a minor child have a claim for loss of parental consortium against third parties responsible for the loss of a parent?

HOLDING AND DECISION: (Wintersheimer, J.) Yes. A minor child has a claim for loss of parental consortium against third parties responsible for the loss of a parent. Kentucky currently recognizes loss of consortium claims between husband and wife and a parent's claim for loss of a child's affection and companionship upon death of the child. Loss of consortium is a common law doctrine which the court has the authority to modify and conform to changing conditions of society. While a loss of consortium claim brought on behalf of children against a wrongdoer who has caused the harm does not currently exist, it should. This state has expressly recognized the public policy in protecting and caring for children in a nurturing home. It has also recognized the value of a child to the family by statutorily providing parents with a consortium claim for the loss of the love and affection of their child. It is a natural development of the common law to recognize a cause of action for children who lose the love and affection of a parent to the negligence of a third party. Reversed and remanded.

▶ ANALYSIS

The court here overturns the prior decision of *Brooks v. Burkeen*, 569 S.W.2d 91 (1977), in which it held that children do not have an individual identity separate from that of their family and thus a claim for loss of parental consortium could not lie. Since that decision a majority of jurisdictions have recognized the validity of such claims.

Quicknotes

LOSS OF CONSORTIUM An action brought based on willful interference with the marital relationship.

WRONGFUL DEATH An action brought by the beneficiaries of a deceased person, claiming that the deceased's death was the result of wrongful conduct by the defendant.

Gallimore v. Children's Hospital Medical Center

Parents (P) v. Hospital (D)

Ohio Sup. Ct., 67 Ohio St. 3d 244, 617 N.E.2d 1052 (1993).

NATURE OF CASE: Appeal from a judgment in an action for loss of filial consortium.

FACT SUMMARY: When the Gallimores (P), parents of a minor child who was injured by a third-party tortfeasor, sought damages in a derivative action for loss of filial consortium, the Hospital (D) raised a number of policy arguments against recognition of such a tort action.

> 🏛 **RULE OF LAW**
> The parents of a minor child may maintain a claim for loss of filial consortium.

FACTS: The Gallimores' (P) minor child was injured in an accident. They sued in a derivative action against a third party tortfeasor for loss of consortium. Consortium includes services, society, companionship, comfort, love and solace. The court ruled in their favor, and the appeals court affirmed. The Hospital (D) appealed.

ISSUE: May the parents of a minor child maintain a claim for loss of filial consortium?

HOLDING AND DECISION: (Douglas, J.) Yes. The parents of a minor child may maintain a claim for loss of filial consortium. A parent may recover damages against a third party tortfeasor who intentionally or negligently causes physical injury to the parents' minor child. Ohio's wrongful death statute has been amended to permit recovery for loss of earning capacity, services and society of the decedent as elements of compensable damage. It would be incongruous to deny parents recovery for loss of the society and companionship of a seriously injured child while recognizing that such losses are compensable in cases involving death. Affirmed.

▌ *ANALYSIS*

The court in this case discussed the common law right of parents to recover for the loss of any injured child's services. Children were once viewed as economic assets, and a child occupied the same status with regard to a parent as a servant occupied with regard to the master. In modern times, society and companionship between parents and their child are more important than any "services" a minor child is capable of rendering to parents.

Quicknotes

CONSORTIUM The right of a spouse to enjoy the benefits of association with the other.

COMMON LAW A body of law developed through the judicial decisions of the courts as opposed to the legislative process.

TORTFEASOR Party that commits a tort or wrongful act.

Connecticut v. Miranda

State (P) v. Convicted assaulter (D)

274 Conn. 727, 878 A.2d 118 (2005).

NATURE OF CASE: Appeal of conviction for assault to a child.

FACT SUMMARY: Defendant took on a parental role for his girlfriend's two children and accompanied the youngest to the hospital claiming she had choked on milk. The hospital found multiple serious injuries of which the defendant was aware. The defendant was convicted and sentenced for assault.

🏛 RULE OF LAW
A nonparent's inaction, despite actual knowledge of serious injury to a minor child in his care, cannot result in a first degree assault charge.

FACTS: Miranda (D), 21, lived with his girlfriend, 16, as well as her son, 2, and her daughter, 4 months. He took care of the family and considered himself the children's stepfather despite having no legal or biological relationship to the children. One evening he called 911 claiming the daughter was choking on milk, and he accompanied the child to the hospital. Hospital personnel found multiple serious injuries to the child, including weeks-old rib fractures, two skull fractures only days old, a rectal tear, and nasal bleeding. They determined that none of these injuries could have been caused by air blockage from choking on milk. It was further determined that Miranda (D) was aware of the injuries and also aware that they were life-threatening to the child. Miranda (D) failed to help the girl by notifying the authorities or taking her for medical treatment. At trial, Miranda (D) was convicted of first-degree assault and injury to a child. He appealed and the case was remanded for resentencing, at which time he was re-sentenced to thirty years' imprisonment. Miranda (D) appealed again.

ISSUE: May a nonparent's inaction, despite actual knowledge of serious injury to a minor child in his care, result in a first degree assault charge?

HOLDING AND DECISION: (Per curiam) No. A nonparent's inaction, despite actual knowledge of serious injury to a minor child in his care, cannot result in a first-degree assault charge. This court's determination of Miranda I should be overruled because Miranda (D) should not have been convicted of first-degree assault based on the facts presented. This court's judges arrive at this decision by different reasoning so the full reasoning is including in the two concurring opinions. Reversed in part and remanded to dismiss assault in first degree and to resentence on injury to a child.

CONCURRENCE: (Borden, J.) The Miranda I court determined that Miranda (D) had a duty to act because he had established a parent-like relationship with his girlfriend's daughter. Despite the statute establishing a duty on the part of a parent or legal guardian, the court felt that the decision was in line with public policy and the continuing trend of nontraditional families with various persons in a parent-like role. This case, however, does not present a person in a parent or legal guardian position. This case involves Miranda (D) who was in no legal relationship with the child and thus under no common law duty to act to protect her. As a matter of law, Miranda (D) cannot be convicted of assault in the first degree.

CONCURRENCE: (Vertefeuille, J.) Assault does not include a failure to act. The dictionary defines assault as "a violent attack with physical means" or a threat to be violent. Physicality is presumed to be a part of assault. The statute at issue and its legislative history does not include failure to act. Thus, Miranda's (D) inaction simply cannot constitute assault.

DISSENT: (Katz, J.) Had the legislature disagreed with this court's determination in Miranda I, it had every opportunity to act to refine the statute at issue. It did not do so, therefore, the legislative intent must have been to criminalize inaction under similar circumstances. Inaction in this case was reckless conduct resulting in a child's exposure to risk of death and actual serious physical injuries. The first plurality would not criminalize inaction even by a parent and the second plurality would not criminalize inaction by someone in defendant's situation because he was not a parent or legal guardian. The justices may have ruled differently had the mother not inflicted the injuries here, but had allowed the boyfriend to injure the child. The mother would have been criminally responsible for her negligence in that situation similar to allowing her child to nearly starve to death. The times are changing and more children will live with nonparents. Criminalizing inaction of those persons, such as Miranda (D), protects vulnerable children.

▶ ANALYSIS

The important element of the court's finding is the initial duty to aid. A person in Miranda's position, a caretaker with no legal or biological relationship to the children, is under no duty to aid. If the person is under no initial duty,

Continued on next page.

they cannot be found guilty of assault for failure to aid even with knowledge of serious physical injury. Some states, such as New York, may find "wanton indifference to human life" if the injuries are serious enough and the failure to act egregious enough.

■≡■

Quicknotes

ASSAULT The intentional placing of another in fear of immediate bodily injury.

DUTY TO PROTECT/AID A moral duty and not one imposed by law; no liability attaches to those persons who fail to undertake a rescue or otherwise aid a person in need, absent a special relationship between them.

■≡■

Diehl v. State

Convicted mother (D) v. State (P)

Tex. Ct. App., 698 S.W.2d 712 (1985).

NATURE OF CASE: Appeal from conviction for possession of marijuana.

FACT SUMMARY: Diehl (D) was arrested for marijuana possession after police were given a tip by Diehl's (D) juvenile daughter.

RULE OF LAW
A young child may give police reliable information regarding illegal marijuana possession in his household.

FACTS: Diehl (D) cultivated marijuana. Her 11-year-old daughter tipped the police regarding this. She gave the police no more information than who she was and that Diehl (D) was growing the plant. A warrant was issued, and Diehl (D) was arrested after a search. She was convicted. She appealed, contending that her daughter's tip was insufficient to establish probable cause.

ISSUE: May a young child give police reliable information regarding illegal marijuana possession in his household?

HOLDING AND DECISION: (Warren, J.) Yes. A young child may give police reliable information regarding marijuana possession in his household. Marijuana, unlike processed drugs, is easily recognizable, both in appearance and odor and in the secrecy with which it is normally grown and processed. A necessity for detailed information does not appear to exist in this context. Affirmed.

DISSENT: (Levy, J.) The integrity of the family unit is so deeply rooted in our nation's history that a parent-child privilege should be recognized, making tips such as those involved here invalid. Further, to encourage children to turn in their parents raises an Orwellian specter that is frightening in its implications.

▶ ANALYSIS

In terms of intrafamilial immunity, not much attention has been paid to the possibility of a parent-child privilege. It has not been discussed, let alone adopted, in most jurisdictions. Most of the attention given to intrafamilial immunity has concentrated on the spousal communication privilege.

Quicknotes

PROBABLE CAUSE A reasonable basis for believing that a crime has been committed.

SPOUSAL PRIVILEGE A common law doctrine precluding spouses from commencing actions against one another for their torts.

Henne v. Wright

Mother (P) v. Department of Health (D)

904 F.2d 1208 (8th Cir. 1990).

NATURE OF CASE: Appeal from invalidation of a health statute.

FACT SUMMARY: Wright (D) and the Department of Health (D) appealed from a decision ruling that a state statute which restricts the choice of surnames which can be recorded on a newborn child's birth certificate was unconstitutional in that it impermissibly infringed upon the parent's fundamental right to choose a surname for their daughters.

🏛 RULE OF LAW
There is no constitutionally protected, fundamental right of privacy which covers the right of a parent to give a child a surname to which the child has no legally recognized parental connection.

FACTS: When Henne's (P) daughter was born, she wished to give her daughter the surname Brinton, the surname of the girl's acknowledged father. Spindell (P) wished to name her daughter McKenzie, simply because her other children were surnamed McKenzie. They were informed by their respective hospitals that those surnames could not be entered on the newborn birth certificates because a statute restricted the surnames which could be entered on birth certificates. Wright (D) headed the Dept. of Health (D), which denied the requests by Spindell (P) and Henne (P). Henne (P) brought suit claiming the actions taken by the Department of Health (D) violated her constitutional right of privacy to name her child as she wished, and Spindell (P) intervened. The trial court held in their favor, and from that decision, the Department of Health (D) appealed.

ISSUE: Is there a constitutionally protected, fundamental right of privacy which covers the right of a parent to give a surname to which the child has no legally recognized parental connection?

HOLDING AND DECISION: (Bright, Sr. J.) No. There is no constitutionally protected, fundamental right to privacy which covers the right of a parent to give a child a surname to which the child has no legally recognized parental connection. The statute in question does not prevent either Henne (P) or Spindell (P) from ever giving their children the surnames they have selected. To determine whether a "fundamental" right is implicated, the court looks to whether the right is "deeply rooted in the nation's history and tradition." There is no American tradition which supports an extension of the right of privacy to cover the right to name their children as asserted by Henne (P) and Spindell (P) herein. Since a fundamental

right is not involved, the statute is analyzed under the highly deferential rational standard of review. [The court then concluded that the statute involved bore some rational relationship to legitimate state interests and upheld the statute.] Reversed.

CONCURRENCE AND DISSENT: (Arnold, J.) Family matters come within the reach of fundamental rights. The right to name children is clearly within the principles of prior cases. The court's analysis of "history and tradition" is unpersuasive.

▶ ANALYSIS

Problems regarding a child's surname often come up in divorce proceedings. The husband often places in custody and visitation documents a limitation on the mother's right to rename the child, even if the mother has remarried. Some states have abolished the common-law notion that a father has a primary right or protectable interest in having the minor children of the marriage bear his surname. See *Marriage of Schiffman*, 169 Cal. Rptr. 918 (1980).

Pierce v. Society of Sisters

State agency (D) v. Educational corporation (P)

268 U.S. 510 (1925).

NATURE OF CASE: Appeal from decision enjoining operation of compulsory attendance laws.

FACT SUMMARY: Pierce (D) appealed from a decision granting the Society of Sisters (P) injunctive relief against the operation of state law requiring the attendance of children between the ages of eight and 16 in public schools.

🏛 RULE OF LAW
Laws requiring attendance in public schools by school-age children impermissibly interfere with the liberty of parents to direct the upbringing and education of their children.

FACTS: Oregon (D) enacted compulsory attendance legislation, scheduled to go into effect in September 1926, requiring that school-age children between the ages of eight and 16 attend public schools. The Society of Sisters (P) is an Oregon corporation charged with the power to care for orphans and the power to establish and maintain academies and schools. The Society of Sisters (P) sought injunctive relief from the operation of the legislation, contending that the legislation impermissibly infringed on the rights of their patron parents to guide the upbringing and education of their children. From a decision in favor of the Society of Sisters (P), Pierce (D) appealed.

ISSUE: Do laws requiring attendance in public schools by school-age children impermissibly interfere with the liberty of parents to direct the upbringing and education of their children?

HOLDING AND DECISION: (McReynolds, J.) Yes. Laws requiring attendance in public schools by school-age children impermissibly interfere with the liberty of parents to direct the upbringing and education of their children. The right of the State (D) to regulate schools has not been challenged. Further, there is no question that institutions such as the Society of Sisters (P) do not discharge their duties with respect to the education of children placed in their charge. The effect of the legislation in this case would be the destruction of all primary private schools in the state. The theory of liberty underlying state government excludes from the State (D) any general power to standardize their children through the public education system. Parents have the constitutional right to direct the upbringing and education of their children under their control. [The Court then disposed of concerns that the Society of Sisters (P) could not claim for themselves the liberty guaranteed by the Fourteenth Amendment.] The Society of Sisters (P) has businesses and property worthy of protection, and its complaint for injunctive relief was not premature. Affirmed.

▶ ANALYSIS

Some commentators have raised the question as to whether the present case raises First Amendment freedom of religion concerns. Not explicit in the present case but important in the case cited by the Court, *Meyer v. Nebraska*, 262 U.S. 390 (1923), is the interest of the teachers in private schools in the pursuit of their occupation.

■══■

Quicknotes

FIRST AMENDMENT RIGHTS Rights conferred by the First Amendment to the United States Constitution prohibiting Congress from enacting any law respecting an establishment of religion, prohibiting the free exercise of religion, abridging freedom of speech or the press, the right of peaceful assembly and the right to petition for a redress of grievances.

■══■

Mozert v. Hawkins County Board of Education

Parent (P) v. School board (D)

827 F.2d 1058 (6th Cir. 1987).

NATURE OF CASE: Appeal from injunction against use of certain textbooks.

FACT SUMMARY: Frost (P) contended her children and other students could not be forced to read textbooks in school which suggested ideas antithetical to their religious beliefs.

🏛 RULE OF LAW
It is not a violation of the Establishment Clause to require reading particular subjects so long as students are not required to affirm or deny religious beliefs.

FACTS: Frost (P), Mozert (P), and others objected to Hawkins County's (D) use of school textbooks which they believed were contrary to their religious beliefs. They sued and obtained an injunction prohibiting the schools from forcing their children to read the books, contending such violated the Establishment Clause. Hawkins County (D) appealed.

ISSUE: Is it a violation of the Establishment Clause to require students to read books with ideas potentially in conflict with their religious beliefs?

HOLDING AND DECISION: (Lively, C.J.) No. It is not a violation of the Establishment Clause to require students to read books presenting ideas which may conflict with their religious beliefs. So long as they are not required to affirm or deny any religious beliefs, the students are not deprived of their freedom of religion. Education cannot be so constrained as to preclude the presentation of ideas which may infringe on religious beliefs. If this could be done, the educational system would be unreasonably burdened. Therefore, the injunction was improperly issued. Reversed.

▌ ANALYSIS

This case points out the conflict between a parent's right to educate a child in a particular manner and the state's responsibility to educate the child. Only direct attacks on religion will result in a narrowing of state power due to the availability of religious education in lieu of public education.

Quicknotes

ESTABLISHMENT CLAUSE The constitutional provision prohibiting the government from favoring any one religion over others, or engaging in religious activities or advocacy.

INJUNCTION A court order requiring a person to do, or prohibiting that person from doing, a specific act.

Zelman v. Simmons-Harris

Parties not identified.

536 U.S. 639 (2002).

NATURE OF CASE: Constitutional challenge to state-sponsored school-choice program.

FACT SUMMARY: Ohio offered a pilot program for school choice to parents of students within the Cleveland City School District. Challengers to the program claimed that it endorsed religious education and practices in violation of the Establishment Clause of the U.S. Constitution.

🏛 **RULE OF LAW**
The state-sponsored school-choice program does not violate the Establishment Clause of the U.S. Constitution.

FACTS: The Cleveland City School District (the "District") primarily educated low and middle income students but was an abject failure. The District failed all 18 minimum standards set for acceptable school districts. A federal court in 1995 even declared the District to be in an unprecedented crisis. The vast majority of the District students failed to complete their education, and the few who remained could not read, write, or compute at appropriate levels. In response to the crisis situation, the State of Ohio developed a pilot program for school choice. The program provided tuition assistance to parents wishing to select a private school or public school other than the school to which the child would otherwise be assigned, such as an inner-city school. An alternative is tutorial aid for children remaining in their assigned school within the District. Challengers to the program argued that the state-sponsored program appeared or actually did endorse religious training in violation of the Establishment Clause of the U.S. Constitution. The Court of Appeals held that the program was constitutionally impermissible. This appeal followed.

ISSUE: Does the state-sponsored school-choice program violate the Establishment Clause of the U.S. Constitution?

HOLDING AND DECISION: (Rehnquist, C.J.) No. The state-sponsored school choice program does not violate the Establishment Clause of the U.S. Constitution. The program is designed for all students within the District, regardless of religious persuasion. Nothing, such as financial incentive, encourages parents to select religious private schools over secular education, and parents are treated equally, regardless of the school selected. A neutral program such as this does not present the appearance of state-endorsed religious education. An impartial observer recognizes that this program seeks to aid failing public school students and does not improperly endorse religious education. Ohio offers multiple educational choices to its students, including private religious education. Nothing discourages secular educational institutions from participating in the program, and nothing discourages parents from selecting secular educational institutions. The vast majority of the District's participating private schools happen to be religious institutions, but it is a statistical fact that most private schools in the District simply are religious institutions. Determining the constitutionality of a school-choice program based on the number of participating religious private schools could lead to absurd results where one city is allowed to have school-choice programs because fewer religious private schools are located there but another city is not allowed because of the existence of "too many" private religious schools. This program is neutral and constitutionally permissible. Reversed.

▶ *ANALYSIS*

Challengers objected to Ohio's school voucher program because most of the participating children were sent to religious schools. This happened because few non-religious schools participated, and so many children signed up that the state had to hold a lottery to assign tuition vouchers. The statistics of over 80% of participating schools being religious institutions resulted in the majority of participating students being sent to religious schools. The court did not consider the end result, however, but the process by which students could participate. Nothing in the process forced students to attend religious schools because parents could choose not to participate at all, could accept tutorial assistance instead of alternate school assignment, and parents could select where they wanted their child to attend school. Parental selection of religious institutions, despite using governmental financial aid in the form of tuition vouchers, had no overtones of that government encouraging religious education.

Quicknotes

ESTABLISHMENT CLAUSE The constitutional provision prohibiting the government from favoring any one religion over others, or engaging in religious activities or advocacy.

Cedar Rapids Community School District v. Garret F.

School district (D) v. Disabled student (P)

526 U.S. 66 (1999).

NATURE OF CASE: Appeal from an order enforcing the Individuals with Disabilities Education Act (IDEA).

FACT SUMMARY: The Cedar Rapids Community School District (D) claimed that it would be too expensive to provide one-on-one nursing care on a continuous basis so that Garret (P) could attend public school.

🏛 RULE OF LAW
A school district must provide health services, but not "medical services" which must be performed by a physician.

FACTS: Garret (P) alleged that the definition of "related services" in § 1401(a)(17) of the IDEA required a public school district in a participating state to provide a ventilator-dependent student with certain nursing services during school hours. Cedar Rapids Community School District (D) contended that the statute did not require it to provide continuous one-on-one nursing services during the school day, even though Garret (P) could not remain in school without such care. When the Cedar Rapids Community School District (D) denied a request to accept financial responsibility for the health care services Garret (P) required during the school day, Garret's mother requested a hearing before the Iowa Department of Education. An Administrative Law Judge concluded that the IDEA required the School District (D) to bear financial responsibility for all of the services in dispute, including continuous nursing services. The School District (D) appealed, and the court of appeals ruled in favor of Garret (P). The School District (D) appealed.

ISSUE: Must a school district provide health services, but not "medical services," which must be performed by a physician?

HOLDING AND DECISION: (Stevens, J.) Yes. A school district must provide health services, but not "medical services," which must be performed by a physician. Most of the services Garret (P) requested are already provided by the School District (D) to other students, and the in-school care necessitated by Garret's (P) ventilator dependency does not demand the training, knowledge, and judgment of a licensed physician. The School District (D) attempted to establish a kind of undue burden exemption primarily based on cost of services. Given that § 1401(a)(17) does not employ cost in its definition of related services or excluded medical services, accepting the School District's (D) cost-based standard as the sole test for determining the scope of the provision would require us to engage in judicial lawmaking without any guidance from Congress. Under the statute, our precedents, and the purposes of the IDEA, the School District (D) must fund such related services in order to help guarantee that students like Garret (P) are integrated into the public schools. Affirmed.

▶ ANALYSIS

The court in this case relied on case precedent. In *Irving Independent School District v. Tatro* (468 U.S. 883 (1984)), the scope of the medical services exclusion was determined. The term "medical services" was held to apply only to services that must be performed by a physician.

■===■

Quicknotes

IDEA 20 U.S.C. § 1400 et seq. Enacted to assure that all children with disabilities have available to them a free appropriate public education which emphasizes special education and related services designed to meet their unique needs.

SEPARATION OF POWERS DOCTRINE Each branch of government is precluded from interfering with the authority of another.

UNDUE BURDEN A burden which is unlawfully oppressive or troublesome.

■===■

Guardianship of Phillip B.

Matter of nonparental guardianship

Cal. Ct. App., 139 Cal. App. 3d 407 (1983).

NATURE OF CASE: Appeal from grant of petition for appointment as guardians.

FACT SUMMARY: When Phillip became attached to the H. (P) family after they began caring for him at the facility where he was institutionalized and at their home, they petitioned the court for guardianship.

RULE OF LAW
Courts may appoint a nonparental guardian over the person of a minor without parental consent, if it appears necessary.

FACTS: When their son was born with Down's syndrome, Warren and Patricia B. (D) decided to institutionalize him. About the time Phillip was five, Patsy and Herbert H. (P) started working on a daily basis at the facility which cared for Phillip. Phillip became quite attached to Mr. and Mrs. H. (P), went home with them on the weekends, and was openly accepted as a member of their family. Phillip's parents' (D) pattern of physical and emotional detachment from him continued over the same period. Regressive and violent changes in Phillip's behavior occurred after his parents (D) forbade his spending any more weekends at the H.'s (P) home. The H.'s (P) petitioned to be appointed as Phillip's guardians, and the trial court determined that Phillip's best interest would be served if the H.'s (P) were his guardians.

ISSUE: May courts appoint a nonparental guardian over the person of a minor without parental consent if it appears necessary?

HOLDING AND DECISION: (Racanelli, J.) Yes. Courts may appoint a nonparental guardian over the person of a minor without parental consent if it appears necessary. The legislature requires that before a court may issue an order awarding custody of a child to a nonparent without consent of the parents, it shall find that an award of custody to a parent would be detrimental to the child and the award to a nonparent is required to serve the best interests of the child. The trial court expressly found that an award of custody to his parents (D) would be harmful to Phillip in light of the psychological or "de facto" parental relationship established between him and the H.'s (P). The record contains abundant evidence that retention of custody by his parents (D) would cause Phillip profound emotional harm, due to their emotional abandonment of him. No legal basis is shown for disturbing the trial court's carefully considered determination. Affirmed.

ANALYSIS

The right of parents to retain custody of a child is fundamental and may be disturbed only in extreme cases where parents' actions are incompatible with parenthood. As Justice Tobriner has observed, persons who assume the responsibility of parents have been characterized as psychological parents. Such characterization is based on day-to-day interaction, companionship, and shared experiences. The role can be fulfilled either by a biological parent, by an adoptive parent, or by any other caring adult—but never by an absent, inactive adult, whatever his biological or legal relationship to the child may be.

Bowen v. American Hospital Association

Government agency (D) v. Association (P)

476 U.S. 610 (1986).

NATURE OF CASE: Review of order invalidating federal regulation.

FACT SUMMARY: The Department of Health and Human Services (HHS) (D) adopted a rule under federal law prohibiting discrimination against the handicapped, mandating general guidelines for medical care of handicapped infants.

🏛 RULE OF LAW
HHS may not adopt a rule under federal law prohibiting discrimination against the handi-capped, mandating general guidelines for care of handicapped infants.

FACTS: Section 504 of the 1973 Rehabilitation Act (the Act) prohibited discrimination against individuals with handicaps by any entity receiving federal assistance. Pursuant to this law, HHS (D) promulgated a regulatory framework detailing, in comprehensive fashion, procedures for medical facilities to follow in treating handicapped infants. Various parties challenged the validity of these rules. A district court held the rules invalid as beyond the scope of the Act's power delegation, and the court of appeals affirmed. The Supreme Court granted certiorari.

ISSUE: May HHS (D) adopt a rule, under federal law prohibiting discrimination against the handicapped, mandating general guidelines for care of handicapped infants?

HOLDING AND DECISION: (Stevens, J.) No. HHS (D) may not adopt a rule, under federal law prohibiting discrimination against the handicapped, mandating general guidelines for care of handicapped infants. The Act was passed to deal with discrimination against the handicapped. Consequently, any regulation promulgated thereunder must deal with such discrimination. A general regulatory framework for dealing with the handicapped, whether or not discrimination is shown, is beyond the scope of the Act. Such is the case here. Affirmed.

▶ ANALYSIS

The rules struck down in this case were essentially enacted to deal with situations where medical treatment was withheld from handicapped infants. The perception was that the medical community was inclined to withhold treatment to a much greater extent in handicapped infants. Several high-profile cases had prompted HHS's (D) action in this area.

Quicknotes

CERTIORARI A discretionary writ issued by a superior court to an inferior court in order to review the lower court's decisions; the Supreme Court's writ ordering such review.

OCGA § 19-7-3 - Grants any grandparent the right to seek visitation of a minor grandchild.

■═■

Miller v. HCA

Mother (P) v. Party not identified (D)

Tex. Sup. Ct., 118 S.W.3d 758 (2003).

NATURE OF CASE: Claims for battery and negligence.

FACT SUMMARY: Parents of a premature child asserted battery and negligence claims against the hospital for providing life-saving measures without their consent. The child suffered serious mental and physical damage because she was so premature, and the parents had wanted nature to take its course rather than medical intervention to ensure she lived.

🏛 RULE OF LAW
Liability for battery or negligence is not imposed upon parties providing life-saving measures without parental consent to a minor child in emergent conditions.

FACTS: Karla Miller (P) went into labor at just twenty-three weeks pregnant. Doctors at Woman's Hospital of Texas attempted to halt labor, but determined that an infection posed a risk to Karla's (P) life and delivery had to occur. Dr. Jacob, obstetrician, and Dr. Kelley, neonatologist, informed Karla (P) and Mark (P) Miller that the infant would have serious deficiencies and would likely not live. After deliberation, the Millers informed the physicians not to perform life-saving measures upon the infant if Karla (P) had to deliver. Mark (P) understood life-saving measures to include resuscitation. The decision to forgo heroic measures was charted and communicated to hospital personnel. Also charted and communicated was the fact that a neonatologist would not need to be present at the delivery because of the decision to forgo heroic measures. Hospital personnel and administrators met about the issue and discussed the situation further with Mark (P), when he returned from making funeral arrangements for the infant. They informed Mark (P) that resuscitation was required as hospital policy for any infant weighing over 500 grams. The hospital's final decision was to have a neonatologist present at the birth to determine if resuscitation was necessary per the stated hospital policy. Physicians agreed that forgoing resuscitation efforts without evaluating the child would be substandard care. Mark (P) refused to sign a consent form allowing resuscitation and was informed that he could only avoid it by removing Karla (P) from the hospital. Dr. Jacobs soon had to induce delivery in Karla (P) to preserve her health, and Sidney, 615 grams, was born. Sidney had a heartbeat, breathed, and cried at birth, and resuscitation measures were provided. Neither Mark (P) nor Karla (P) objected at the time. Sidney initially responded well, but within days of her birth, suffered a brain hemorrhage. Typical in premature infants, the hemorrhage resulted in

massive, irreversible physical and mental damage to Sydney. The Millers (P) filed suit against the hospital and HCA (D) for battery and negligence. At trial, Sydney, 7, required 24-hour care, was legally blind, incontinent, and suffered severe mental retardation. The Millers (P) argued reasonable medical certainty that Sydney would not have survived. The jury found for the Millers (P), and the trial court awarded them a multi-million dollar damage award. HCA (D) appealed and the court of appeals reversed and awarded nothing to the Millers (P). The Millers (P) appealed and this court granted review.

ISSUE: Is liability for battery or negligence imposed upon parties providing life-saving measures without parental consent to a minor child in emergent conditions?

HOLDING AND DECISION: (Enoch, J.) No. Liability for battery or negligence is not imposed upon parties providing life-saving measures without parental consent to a minor child in emergent conditions. An exception exists to the general rule which would impose liability because physicians are encouraged to save lives, even if parental consent cannot be obtained. The determination is primarily the role of a healthcare provider versus that of a parent when an infant's uncertain health is at issue. Parents are the presumed decision-makers and have the legal right to refuse medical care for their child. Parental consent prior to medical treatment of a child is required so that parents can make informed decisions. Absent consent, a treating physician has indeed committed a battery unless an exception is applicable. Courts have held that a physician may not perform surgery upon a minor child without parental consent when the surgery can be delayed without danger to the life of the child for sufficient time to inform the parents fully and obtain the necessary consent. When death is imminent, absent physician action, an exception to liability exists. Treatment does not imply consent, but acts as an exception to the general rule of liability, so the Restatement rule about belief that consent would be forthcoming is inapplicable. In the instant case, the issue is whether the treating physician should have obtained court permission to treat when the parents refused consent. The Millers (P) argued that the multiple physicians' and administrators' meetings demonstrate that no emergent situation existed that prevented treating physicians from obtaining court permission in the absence of their permission. The Millers (P), however, overlook the fact that the situation could not be fully evaluated until

Continued on next page.

after Sydney's birth. Pre-birth decisions did provide the luxury of time. After Sydney's birth, though, the treating physician had to make an instant decision to provide life-sustaining treatment to the premature infant. The physicians here fulfilled their obligations for assessment and treatment and the life-sustaining treatment in an emergent situation was appropriate. This opinion does not consider whether such a ruling applies to adults. Affirmed.

▶ ANALYSIS

Mark Miller wrote a letter to the editor of the Hastings Center Report regarding the facts of this case in which he claimed that he and his wife opted for compassionate care for their daughter and the hospital had eleven hours prior to Sydney's birth in which to obtain court permission to override the parents' wishes. He also claimed that the physicians provided experimental and aggressive treatment to their daughter. Mr. Miller then goes on to claim that the Millers' complaint was not the life-saving treatment given Sidney but the fact that the treatment caused the physical and mental damage she now suffers. Challengers to the Millers' claim argue that children in Sydney's position deserve the opportunity to live despite parents' wishes for "compassionate care" which would almost certainly result in the child's death. Disabilities, according to them, are not worse than no existence at all.

■=■

Quicknotes

BATTERY Unlawful contact with the body of another person.

LIABILITY Any obligation or responsibility.

NEGLIGENCE Conduct falling below the standard of care that a reasonable person would demonstrate under similar conditions.

■=■

Curran v. Bosze

Mother (P) v. Father (D)

Ill. Sup. Ct., 141 Ill. 2d 473, 566 N.E.2d 1319 (1990).

NATURE OF CASE: Appeal from denial of emergency petition.

FACT SUMMARY: When Curran (P) refused to allow her twins (fathered by Bosze [D]) to be tested as possible bone marrow donors to their twelve-year-old half-brother, who was Bosze's (D) son, Bosze (D) petitioned the court to order Curran (P) to produce the twins for compatibility testing and bone marrow donation, if compatible.

> ## 🏛 RULE OF LAW
> A parent or guardian may give consent on behalf of a minor daughter or son for the child to donate bone marrow to a sibling, only when to do so would be in the minor's best interest.

FACTS: Curran (P) and Bosze (D), parents of three-and-a-half-year-old twins, were never married, and Curran (P), the mother, had sole custody. Bosze (D) also had a twelve-year-old son, half-brother to the twins, who suffered from leukemia, which doctors believed would cause his death unless he received a bone marrow transplant from a compatible donor. Bosze (D) wanted the twins to be tested for compatibility, but Curran (P) refused. Bosze (D) filed an emergency petition with the circuit court to order Curran (P) to produce the twins for testing and for bone marrow harvesting if both or either of them proved compatible. The court ruled that it did not have authority to grant Bosze's (D) petition.

ISSUE: May a parent or guardian give consent on behalf of a minor daughter or son for the child to donate bone marrow to a sibling, only when to do so would be in the minor's best interest?

HOLDING AND DECISION: (Calvo, J.) Yes. A parent or guardian may give consent on behalf of a minor daughter or son for the child to donate bone marrow to a sibling, only when to do so would be in the minor's best interest. Three critical factors determine that it will be in the best interests of a child to donate bone marrow to a sibling. First, the parent who consents must be informed of the risks and benefits to the child. Second, there must be emotional support available to the child from the person or persons who take care of the child. Third, there must be an existing, close relationship between the donor and recipient. Curran (P) is aware that while the risks involved are small, they may be life-threatening if they occur. Because she opposes the procedure, Curran (P) would not be able to provide the twins with the emotional support necessary to enable them to undergo all that is involved with that procedure. Although the twins and Bosze's (D) son share the same biological father, no evidence indicates they are known to each other as family. Affirmed.

▶ ANALYSIS

The court stated that the benefit to a child who donates bone marrow to a sibling will be a psychological benefit, and such benefit is grounded firmly in the fact that the donor and recipient are known to each other as family. It is the existing sibling relationship which forms the context in which it may be determined that it will be in the best interests of the child to undergo a bone marrow harvesting procedure for a sibling. Thus, although the court sympathized with the tragedy of the situation, it agreed with the circuit court and the recommendation of the guardian ad litem for the twins that it was not in their best interests to undergo the proposed procedure.

■=■

Lalli v. Lalli

Illegitimate son (P) v. Estate of father (D)

439 U.S. 259 (1978).

NATURE OF CASE: Appeal of the denial of an accounting of an estate.

FACT SUMMARY: Lalli (P) contended that a New York statute which required an illegitimate child to establish paternity prior to the death of the father to be entitled to inherit from his estate violated equal protection.

🏛 **RULE OF LAW**
▬▬▬ A statute requiring the issue of paternity be settled during the lifetime of the father substantially relates to the legitimate state interest in facilitating the orderly disposition of property upon death and is therefore constitutional.

FACTS: Lalli (P), claiming to be Mario Lalli's illegitimate son, petitioned the court for a compulsory accounting, claiming he was entitled to inherit from Mario's estate. Rosamond Lalli (D), administratrix of the estate, claimed that Lalli (P) was not entitled to inherit because he had not obtained a judicial declaration of paternity prior to Mario's death. Under a New York statute, this was a prerequisite to an illegitimate child's right to inherit. Lalli (P) admitted he had not established paternity prior to Mario's death yet contended the statute discriminated against him because of his illegitimate birth, in violation of equal protection. The trial court upheld the constitutionality of the statute, the appellate court affirmed, and Lalli (P) appealed.

ISSUE: Is a statute requiring the issue of paternity to be settled during the father's lifetime to allow an illegitimate child to inherit from the father's estate constitutional?

HOLDING AND DECISION: (Powell, J.) Yes. A statute requiring the issue of paternity be settled prior to the father's death substantially relates to the legitimate state interest in facilitating the orderly disposition of property upon the father's death and is therefore constitutional. Because of the substantial state interest in the prompt and proper distribution of property upon death, a requirement that the father be available to ensure the accurate resolution of a paternity action is valid to ensure accuracy. The administration of the estate is facilitated, and the possibility of uncertainty is greatly decreased. Therefore, this statute substantially relates to a legitimate state goal and therefore does not deny equal protection of the law. Affirmed.

▶ **ANALYSIS**

It is argued that had this case been decided differently, all males who were not sterile during their lifetime would have

to include in their wills a disclaimer in order to avoid fraudulent claims against their respective estates by children asserting paternity. This case also can be seen as not limited to the context of inheritance and applicable to all cases of paternity.

▬▬▬

Quicknotes

EQUAL PROTECTION CLAUSE A constitutional provision that each person be guaranteed the same protection of the laws enjoyed by other persons in like circumstances.

LEGITIMATE STATE INTEREST Under a rational basis standard of review, a court will not strike down a statute as unconstitutional if it bears a reasonable relationship to the furtherance of a legitimate governmental objective.

▬▬▬

Clark v. Jeter

Illegitimate child (P) v. Father (D)

486 U.S. 456 (1988).

NATURE OF CASE: Review of dismissal of paternity action.

FACT SUMMARY: Pennsylvania had adopted a six-year statute of limitations on paternity actions seeking support of illegitimate children.

🏛 RULE OF LAW
A six-year statute of limitations on paternity actions by illegitimate children raises equal protection considerations.

FACTS: Pennsylvania adopted a statute providing that an action by an illegitimate child against the father for support had to be brought within six years of birth. No such requirement existed to legitimate children. In other contexts, such as intestacy controversies, no such statute existed. Clark (P) brought a paternity action on behalf of her daughter against Jeter (D) 10 years after she was born. The trial court dismissed based on the statute. This was affirmed on appeal. The Supreme Court accepted review.

ISSUE: Does a six-year statute of limitations on paternity actions by illegitimate children raise equal protection considerations?

HOLDING AND DECISION: (O'Connor, J.) Yes. A six-year statute of limitations on paternity actions by illegitimate children raises equal protection considerations. Disparate treatment of support actions based on legitimacy are subjected to heightened scrutiny not amounting to strict scrutiny. This Court's prior cases make it clear that statutes classifying on the basis of legitimacy in regards to when a support action may be brought must (1) give the illegitimate child a reasonable opportunity to seek support, and (2) be substantially related to the state's interest in preventing state claims. Here, it is evident that the statute in question does not satisfy the latter requirement, as the state permits the issue of paternity to be litigated in other contexts, such as probate. If the evidence bearing on paternity is legitimate at such a proceeding, it is also legitimate at a paternity hearing. This being so, the statute violates equal protection. Reversed.

▶ ANALYSIS

The Court had earlier struck down a one-year and a two-year statute. The Court held these periods not to have met the first criterion above. In the instant action, the Court stated that the period in issue, six years, might satisfy the reasonableness requirement. It would seem that a valid statute in this area would have to be at least six years long and be uniform in all areas dealing with legitimacy.

■=■

Quicknotes

EQUAL PROTECTION A constitutional guarantee that no person shall be denied the same protection of the laws enjoyed by other persons in life circumstances.

■=■

People in Interest of S.P.B.

Mother (P) v. Father (D)

Colo. Sup. Ct., 651 P.2d 1213 (1982).

NATURE OF CASE: Appeal from order to pay child support.

FACT SUMMARY: Although P.D.G. (D) acknowledged paternity of C.F.B.'s (P) baby, he denied an obligation to support the child because he wanted C.F.B. (P) to have an abortion for which he offered to pay, but she refused.

🏛 RULE OF LAW
The duty to support a child falls upon both parents, regardless of their marital status.

FACTS: P.D.G. (D) admitted paternity of S.P.B. but contended that he had no obligation to support the child because he did not want C.F.B. (P) to have the baby and offered to pay for an abortion. They never married, and C.F.B. (P) had custody of the child from birth. P.D.G. (D) asserted that the child support provision of the Uniform Parentage Act (UPA) violated his constitutional rights to due process and equal protection of the laws. The district court ordered him to pay one-half the birth expenses for the child and child support in the amount of $150 per month.

ISSUE: Does the duty to support a child fall upon both parents, regardless of their marital status?

HOLDING AND DECISION: (Dubofsky, J.) Yes. The duty to support a child falls upon both parents, regardless of their marital status. The state has an important interest in promoting the welfare of the child, but because a woman has a fundamental right to decide whether to terminate her pregnancy, the state has little choice in the means employed to achieve its objective. Here, the equal treatment which P.D.G. (D) seeks could only be achieved by according a father the right to compel the mother of his child to procure an abortion. P.D.G.'s (D) right is thus overridden prior to childbirth by the state's interest in protecting C.F.B.'s (P) fundamental right to make decisions relating to her pregnancy, and thereafter by the state's interest in ensuring that children receive adequate support. In addition, the statute creates a presumption that parents share an obligation of child support. The presumption furthers the substantial interests which the state has in protecting the respective rights of children, of parents, and of itself, and does not deny due process to P.D.G. (D). [Disposition not stated in the casebook excerpt.]

▶ ANALYSIS

The court stated that the UPA imposes a duty for support without according the father a right either to decide that the fetus should be aborted or to later avoid child support obligations by showing that he offered to pay for an abortion. Gender-based distinctions must serve important governmental objectives, and a discriminatory classification must be substantially related to the achievement of those objectives in order to withstand judicial scrutiny under the equal protection clause. This is an intermediate scrutiny level and may result in a decision either in favor of or against the statute at issue.

■≡■

Quicknotes

CHILD SUPPORT Payments made by one parent to another in satisfaction of the non-custodial parent's legal obligation to provide for the sustenance of the child.

DUE PROCESS RIGHTS The constitutional mandate requiring the courts to protect and enforce individuals' rights and liberties consistent with prevailing principles of fairness and justice, and prohibiting the federal and state governments from such activities that deprive its citizens of a life, liberty or property interest.

DUTY TO SUPPORT FAMILY Duty imposed by statute requiring a spouse to provide for the sustenance of his or her spouse and children.

EQUAL PROTECTION CLAUSE A constitutional provision that each person be guaranteed the same protection of the laws enjoyed by other persons in like circumstances.

UNIFORM PARENTAGE ACT Imposes duty of child support upon both parents without according the father a right to decide the fetus should be aborted or to avoid child support obligations by showing he offered to pay for an abortion.

■≡■

Moore v. City of East Cleveland

Grandmother (D) v. Housing authority (P)

431 U.S. 494 (1977).

NATURE OF CASE: Appeal from conviction of a misdemeanor.

FACT SUMMARY: By having two of her grandsons live with her, Mrs. Moore (D) violated an ordinance limiting occupancy of a dwelling unit to members of a single "family."

RULE OF LAW
It is unconstitutional for an ordinance to force citizens to live in certain narrowly defined family patterns.

FACTS: The City of East Cleveland (P) had a housing ordinance limiting occupancy of a dwelling unit to members of a single "family," that word being limited to a few categories of related individuals. Mrs. Moore (D) was convicted of violating the ordinance, a misdemeanor, because she had two small grandsons living with her who were first cousins to each other rather than brothers. The one grandson had come to live with Mrs. Moore (D), her son, and that son's child when his mother died. When the court of appeals affirmed the conviction and the Ohio Supreme Court denied review, Mrs. Moore (D) appealed to the U.S. Supreme Court. She argued that the ordinance was unconstitutional under the Due Process Clause.

ISSUE: Does the Constitution allow citizens to be forced into living in certain narrowly defined family patterns?

HOLDING AND DECISION: (Powell, J.) No. It is unconstitutional for an ordinance to force citizens to live in certain narrowly defined family patterns, as this one does. In the face of such interference with family life, which is a protected "liberty," the usual judicial deference to the legislature is inappropriate. Although preventing overcrowding, minimizing traffic, avoiding an undue burden on schools, etc., are legitimate goals, the ordinance at issue serves them marginally at best. It permits one large "properly" related family to move in but denies a smaller "improperly" related family that same privilege. Reversed.

CONCURRENCE: (Brennan, J.) This ordinance reflects cultural myopia by ignoring the fact that a large part of the population has traditionally lived in "extended family" units.

CONCURRENCE: (Stevens, J.) This ordinance has no "substantial relation to the public health, safety, morals, or general" welfare and cuts deeply into an owner's fundamental right to decide who may reside on her property. So,

it must fall under the limited standard of review of zoning decisions.

DISSENT: (Stewart, J.) Any substantive limitation on the power to regulate arises only if the interests at issue are "implicit in the concept of ordered liberty," and they are not in this case.

ANALYSIS

Initially, the court began raising the issue of substantive due process in cases dealing with traditional families. Moore and other cases have succeeded in extending that protection, although in a somewhat limited manner, to problems associated with nontraditional families. However, *Village of Belle Terre v. Boraas*, 416 U.S. 1 (1974) upheld an ordinance limiting the number of unrelated individuals who could live together in a dwelling unit.

Quicknotes

DUE PROCESS CLAUSE Clauses found in the Fifth and Fourteenth Amendments to the United States Constitution providing that no person shall be deprived of "life, liberty, or property, without due process of law."

Americana Healthcare Center v. Randall

Nursing home (P) v. Son of patient (D)

S.D. Sup. Ct., 513 N.W.2d 566 (1994).

NATURE OF CASE: Appeal from verdict ordering parental support.

FACT SUMMARY: After admitting his mother to Americana Healthcare Center (P), Randall (D) refused to pay for her care.

RULE OF LAW

Adult children who have the financial ability to do so may be ordered to provide support for an indigent parent.

FACTS: Randall (D) admitted his mother, Juanita, to Americana Healthcare Center (P), a nursing home specializing in mental problems. After signing the admission documents, Randall (D) applied for financial assistance from Medicaid, but was rejected. At the time of the rejection, Juanita's bills were two months overdue. Americana (P) contacted Randall (D) for payment, but Randall (D) refused and filed for bankruptcy instead. Americana (P) filed suit for breach of contract while also making a claim for payment under a state statute that required financially able, adult children to provide support for indigent parents. The trial court found in favor of Randall (D) as to the claims for breach of contract, but ruled in favor of Americana (P) on the claims for statutory relief. Randall (D) appealed, claiming the statute violated equal protection laws because it discriminated against adult children of indigent parents.

ISSUE: May a court order an adult child who is financially capable of providing for an indigent parent to do so?

HOLDING AND DECISION: (Amundson, J.) Yes. Adult children who have the financial ability to do so may be ordered to provide support for an indigent parent. An adult child has received and benefited from the support, care, comfort, and guidance of their parents. As a result, the adult child should bear the burden of reciprocating in the event a parent needs support in her later years. Placing this obligation on an adult child is not an arbitrary decision. No fundamental right has been implicated in this case, nor has any quasi-suspect class been created. Obligating Randall (D) or any adult child to support his indigent parent is rationally related to legitimate state interests in providing for the welfare and care of the elderly. The statute does not violate Equal Protection laws. Affirmed.

ANALYSIS

This case represents an excellent example of the growing concern over insuring care for the elderly. Many adult children do, however, voluntarily provide support for their parents. According to the Census Bureau, the number of parents receiving support increased by about 40% from 1986 to 1988. See *Bureau of Census, United States Dept. of Commerce, Who's Helping Out? Support Networks Among American Families: 1988* (1992).

Quicknotes

EQUAL PROTECTION CLAUSE A constitutional provision that each person be guaranteed the same protection of the laws enjoyed by other persons in like circumstances.

Growing up in the Law

Quick Reference Rules of Law

Tyler v. Weed

Child (P) v. Driver of car (D)

Mich. Sup. Ct., 285 Mich. 460, 280 N.W. 827 (1938).

NATURE OF CASE: Appeal from denial of damages for negligence.

FACT SUMMARY: Tyler (P), an infant, contended it was reversible error for the trial court to submit the issue of his comparative negligence to the jury, as he was under seven years old and presumed incapable of negligence.

🏛 RULE OF LAW
A child under the age of seven is conclusively presumed to be incapable of negligence.

FACTS: Tyler (P), when he was six years, eight months old, was struck by a car driven by Weed (D). He sued, and Weed (D) contended Tyler (P) was contributorily negligent. The trial court held the issue of contributory negligence was one of fact and submitted it to the jury. The verdict found no cause of action. Tyler (P) appealed, contending that, as an infant under seven, he was legally incapable of negligence.

ISSUE: Is a child under seven conclusively presumed to be incapable of negligence?

HOLDING AND DECISION: (McAllister, J.) Yes. A child under seven is conclusively presumed to be incapable of negligence. Research indicates thought and reason are not sufficiently developed prior to seven years to warrant holding an infant culpable for his own conduct. Thus, it was reversible error to submit the issue to the jury. Reversed.

CONCURRENCE: (Wiest, J.) Reversal was proper, yet the question of infant negligence is one of fact.

DISSENT: (Potter, J.) The senses of the individual child are the dispositive issues regarding negligence, not age.

▶ ANALYSIS

This case illustrates the common law rule regarding infant negligence. It points out one important aspect in which children and adults are treated differently under the law. Some states treat the issue as a question of fact; others allow a presumed incapacity but one which is rebuttable.

Quicknotes

CONTRIBUTORY NEGLIGENCE Behavior on the part of an injured plaintiff falling below the standard of ordinary care that contributes to the defendant's negligence, resulting in the plaintiff's injury.

REVERSIBLE ERROR A substantial error that might reasonably have prejudiced the party complaining.

Shields v. Gross

Child model (P) v. Photographer (D)

N.Y. Ct. App., 58 N.Y.2d 338, 448 N.E.2d 108 (1983).

NATURE OF CASE: Appeal from denial of rejection of contract.

FACT SUMMARY: Shields (P) contended she could disavow a contract consented to by her guardian while she was a minor.

> ## 🏛 RULE OF LAW
> Guardian consent to a minor's contract cannot be revoked on the basis of minority in the presence of a statute authorizing such guardian consent.

FACTS: Shields's (P) mother and guardian signed a consent form in favor of Gross (D), a photographer, granting him ownership of certain photographs taken of Shields (P) by Gross (D). Such consent was made pursuant to a state statute allowing for guardian consent on behalf of minor models to the commercial use of photographs. Shields (P) subsequently sued to reject the contract on the basis of minority. The trial court enjoined the use of the photos in some respects but held the consents valid. Shields (P) appealed.

ISSUE: May a minor disavow parental consent to a contract?

HOLDING AND DECISION: (Simons, J.) No. Guardian consent to a minor's contract cannot be revoked on the basis of minority in the presence of a statute authorizing such guardian consent to a contract. Thus, the guardian has agreed, on behalf of the minor, to the contract. The rationale behind allowing rejection on the basis of minority is eliminated. Thus, the contract was enforceable. Affirmed.

DISSENT: (Jasen, J.) A child's best interest must be considered more valuable than commercial or trade relations.

▌ ANALYSIS

The court indicated that in the absence of the statute, the contract was voidable on the basis of minority. Minors are considered to lack the capacity to formulate a meeting of the minds essential to contract theory. Contracts with minors are not void but are voidable at the minor's option.

∎▬∎

Quicknotes

BEST INTERESTS OF CHILD Standard used by courts when rendering decisions which involve a child or children.

GUARDIANSHIP A legal relationship whereby one party is responsible for the care and control over another and his property due to some legal incapacity on the part of the ward.

∎▬∎

Kreigh v. Cogswell

Minor property owner (P) v. Creditor of parent (D)

Wyo. Sup. Ct., 45 Wyo. 531, 21 P.2d 831 (1933).

NATURE OF CASE: Appeal from award of damages for conversion.

FACT SUMMARY: Kreigh (P) contended property owned by Cogswell (D) and her sisters was owned by their father, and, therefore, Cogswell (D) could execute upon such in satisfaction of the father's debt.

RULE OF LAW
Property acquired by a child belongs to the child, not the parents.

FACTS: Kreigh (P) and her minor sisters received certain sheep as gifts, which they raised on their father's land. Cogswell (D), a creditor of the father, executed upon and sold the sheep in satisfaction of the father's debt. Kreigh (P) sued in conversion and was awarded damages. Cogswell (D) appealed, contending property owned by minors was legally owned by the parent.

ISSUE: Does property acquired by a minor belong to his parent?

HOLDING AND DECISION: (Blume, J.) No. Property acquired by a minor child belongs to the child, not the parent. Therefore, the sheep belonged to the children and were not subject to execution by the father's creditors. Affirmed.

ANALYSIS

The common law recognized that the fruit of a child's labor belonged to its father rather than to the child. Other property, however, is the child's, and a creditor of the father has no greater interest than the father. Thus, the sale in this case was a conversion.

■══■

Quicknotes

CONVERSION The act of depriving an owner of his property without permission or justification.

■══■

Radakovich v. Radakovich

Ex-wife (P) v. Ex-husband (D)

Pa. Super. Ct., 2004 Pa. Super. 82, 846 A.2d 709 (2004).

NATURE OF CASE: Appeal from marital property determination.

FACT SUMMARY: During divorce proceedings, the wife (P) claimed the balance of a PNC brokerage account was marital property subject to equitable distribution. The husband (D) claimed it was intended for their son's post-graduate education. The trial court determined that the account belonged entirely to the son but only a portion of it was necessary for his education and the rest constituted marital property subject to equitable distribution.

🏛 RULE OF LAW
An account set up pursuant to the Uniform Transfers to Minors Act may not be disclaimed due to donor's lack of intent or lack of full understanding that the property transferred may not be reclaimed by the donor.

FACTS: Bonnie (P) and Richard Radakovich (D) set up a PNC brokerage account for their minor son to be used for his post-graduate education. Richard (D) was named custodian of the account and both parents signed all of the necessary paperwork. Bonnie (P) was aware of the account, its purpose, and the fact that deposits were made into the account from the joint marital checking account. In 1997, when their son was 17, Bonnie (P) filed for divorce and sought equitable distribution of the marital property, including the $113,000.00 balance of the PNC account. Richard (D) claimed the PNC account was not marital property because he was the custodian of the account for his son's benefit. The court appointed a master in 1999 who determined that the account should be turned over the son when he reached majority and should be placed into trust for him until then. Bonnie (P) and Richard (D) each filed exceptions to the master's findings. Bonnie (P) claimed the PNC account was marital property, and Richard (D) claimed it should not be held in trust for the son. In 2000, the trial court granted the exceptions in part and denied in part. The trial court ordered that the account was the son's property but that only $48,000.00 was necessary for his education, and the balance was marital property subject to equitable distribution. In 2002, the son, now 21, successfully intervened in the matter. In 2003, the trial court held that the son was not barred as an intervenor and that the PNC account was his property pursuant to the Pennsylvania Uniform Transfers to Minors Act [PUTMA]. The court did not, however, rule whether any portion of the account could be considered marital property. Bonnie (P) appealed.

ISSUE: May an account set up pursuant to the Uniform Transfers to Minors Act be disclaimed due to donor's lack of intent or lack of full understanding that the property transferred may not be reclaimed by the donor?

HOLDING AND DECISION: (Stevens, J.) No. An account set up pursuant to the Uniform Transfers to Minors Act may not be disclaimed due to donor's lack of intent or lack of full understanding that the property transferred may not be reclaimed by the donor. Bonnie (P) claimed that their son failed to prove that his parents made him an *inter vivos* gift of the PNC account, thus the account could not be analyzed under the PUTMA. The trial court, however, was correct in finding clear intent to establish the account under PUTMA, and that the property in the account could not be reclaimed by the parents. The language of the PUTMA statute is unambiguous and allows for an inexpensive method of transferring assets to minors. Such a transfer occurs when a donor places money into a brokerage account and designates a custodian for the minor under the PUTMA. The plain statutory language states that such transfer is irrevocable. Here, the financial consultant who set up the account testified that he established a UGMA (the predecessor act to PUTMA) account for the son with Richard (D) as the custodian. Richard (D) testified that he and Bonnie (P) intended to create such an account for their son's educational needs and that Bonnie (P) was aware of the intent and the source of the funds in the account. Bonnie (P) testified that she knew of the account's establishment, she executed the necessary documents, she did not object to the deposits made from the marital joint checking account, and she was aware of Richard's (D) custodial role. Her claim rests on her testimony that she was unaware of the full magnitude of the transfer, and that she never intended to make a gift of the PNC account funds to her son. Her lack of donative intent or understanding of the consequences of her actions, however, does not void the PUTMA transfer. Affirmed.

▶ ANALYSIS

The Pennsylvania statute is quite clear in requiring that all transferred property *must* be turned over to the minor in its entirety when the minor reaches age 21. Critics of the statute argue that the ease of the transfer is negated by the final nature of the transfer and of the inability to change custodians. Other transfer statutes exist in many states that enable parents to provide for a child's

Continued on next page.

educational needs, but financial analysts say the UTMA statutory transfers may be the easiest and most cost-effective if done correctly.

■═■

Quicknotes

CUSTODIAN Person having responsibility for a person or his property pursuant to law.

INTER VIVOS GIFT A gift that is made, and is to take effect, while the parties are living.

INTERVENTION The method by which a party, not an initial party to the action, is admitted to the action in order to assert an interest in the subject matter of a lawsuit.

MARITAL PROPERTY Property accumulated by a married couple during the term of their marriage.

■═■

Tinker v. Des Moines School District

Student (P) v. School (D)

393 U.S. 503 (1969).

NATURE OF CASE: Appeal from denial of injunctive relief.

FACT SUMMARY: Tinker (P) contended school officials could not constitutionally discipline him for wearing an armband in protest of the Vietnam War.

🏛 RULE OF LAW
School officials may not infringe a student's First Amendment rights.

FACTS: Tinker (P) and others, all minor high school students, were suspended from school for wearing black armbands in protest of the Vietnam War. They sued, seeking injunctive relief on the basis that the suspension violated their right to free speech. The trial court found the school's action reasonable in order to prevent the disturbance of school discipline. The court of appeals affirmed, and the Supreme Court granted certiorari.

ISSUE: May school officials infringe upon the First Amendment rights of their minor students?

HOLDING AND DECISION: (Fortas, J.) No. School officials may not infringe upon their minor students' First Amendment rights. Freedom of speech is shared by all citizens, regardless of age. In this case, the behavior regulated was pure speech and not threatening to the discipline of the school environment. Therefore, the actions in suspending the students violated the Constitution. Reversed and remanded.

DISSENT: (Black, J.) The armbands in fact caused disruption of the school environment, and the officials acted constitutionally in disciplining the students.

▶ ANALYSIS

This case raised many more problems than it solved. The problems were in determining what level of disruption justified an infringement on speech rights. It did, however, lead to a liberalization of school policies regarding passive expressions of opinion.

━━━

Quicknotes

CERTIORARI A discretionary writ issued by a superior court to an inferior court in order to review the lower court's decisions; the Supreme Court's writ ordering such review.

FIRST AMENDMENT Prohibits Congress from enacting any law respecting an establishment of religion, prohibiting the free exercise of religion, abridging freedom of speech or the press, the right of peaceful assembly and the right to petition for a redress of grievances.

FREEDOM OF SPEECH The right to express oneself without governmental restrictions on the content of that expression.

INJUNCTIVE RELIEF A court order issued as a remedy, requiring a person to do, or prohibiting that person from doing, a specific act.

━━━

Hosty v. Carter

Student newspaper editor (P) v. University dean (D)

412 F.3d 731 (7th Cir. 2005).

NATURE OF CASE: Appeal from determination that student newspapers cannot be subject to prepublication review by school officials.

FACT SUMMARY: An undergraduate newspaper supported by student activities fees published several articles critical of the school's administration and specific administrators. School officials required prepublication editorial review, but the paper's staff refused and shut the paper down.

RULE OF LAW

School officials at any educational level may regulate the content of a publicly funded student newspaper.

FACTS: *Innovator*, the student newspaper at Governors State University, elected to print stories of substance. Margaret Hosty (P) wrote several articles critical of the Dean of the College of Arts and Sciences primarily because of the school's decision to let go the paper's faculty advisor. The Dean and the University President accused the *Innovator* of publishing defamatory and inaccurate content, but the *Innovator*'s editorial staff refused to publish the University administration's response or rebuttals. The *Innovator* particularly refused to publish a retraction of the articles. Eventually, Patricia Carter (D), the Dean of Student Affairs and Services, informed the *Innovator*'s printer that she needed to review and approve all editions prior to printing. The printer feared losing payments and the *Innovator*'s editorial staff refused to submit to prepublication review. The *Innovator* ceased publishing in November 2000. Several *Innovator* staffers, including Hosty (P), filed suit against the University's administration, trustees, and several administrators, including Carter (D). The District Court held that no post-secondary student newspapers may be made subject to prepublication review and approval. Carter (D) appealed.

ISSUE: May school officials at any educational level regulate the content of a publicly funded student newspaper?

HOLDING AND DECISION: (Easterbrook, J.) Yes. School officials at any educational level may regulate the content of a publicly funded student newspaper. *Hazelwood School District v. Kuhlmeier*, 484 U.S. 260 (1988), is the applicable case for this issue. The Supreme Court set out the requirement that a court must first inquire whether the student newspaper was a public forum. If not, then the issue becomes whether the "actions are reasonable related to legitimate pedagogical concerns." A footnote stated that the Court was not addressing whether *Hazelwood* might apply to college and university level papers. This footnote is the primary focus of Harty's (P) claim and the basis for the District Court's holding that *Hazelwood* definitely does not apply to the university paper. The reasoning is wrong because *Hazelwood* certainly did not draw such a distinct line between lower grades and post-graduate education. The first question must still be asked and the requirement for that question does not vary with the students' ages. If the paper is a non-public forum, the school has an interest in ensuring it is portrayed as neutral in divisive issues and that the readers will be reading age-appropriate material, so prepublication review may be appropriate and permissible. The other end of the spectrum is protected private speech in a public forum, such as religious speech in a classroom used for extracurricular activities. If that speech is allowed as of right, then non-public forum speech may be subject to some regulation even if the speech is at a university level. Thus, *Hazelwood* applies to all educational levels, including college and university levels. Reversed.

DISSENT: (Evans, J.) The restriction in this case is an example of the worst form of First Amendment violation. The majority now allows school administrators to censor student speech merely by developing a "legitimate pedagogical reason." No other jurisdictions, even after *Hazelwood*, have permitted university-level prepublication review and approval. *Hazelwood* should not apply here.

▶ ANALYSIS

Many university student-run newspapers operated under the belief that they were exempt from the review and approval process to which high school papers could be subjected. After this decision, many student editorials decried the loss of the balance of First Amendment powers and feared school administrators censoring thoughtlessly. The U.S. Supreme Court decided not to accept this case on appeal. Many papers subsequently began campaigns to be designated "public forums" and to encourage administrators to support non-censorship of the papers.

■■■■

Quicknotes

RIGHT OF FREE SPEECH Right guaranteed by the First Amendment to the United States Constitution prohibiting Congress from enacting any law abridging freedom of speech or the press.

■■■■

Peterson v. Sorlien

Student cult member (P) v. Former minister (D)

Minn. Sup. Ct., 299 N.W.2d 123 (1980).

NATURE OF CASE: Appeal from a denial of damages for false imprisonment.

FACT SUMMARY: Peterson (P) contended efforts to deprogram her from her religious-cult lifestyle constituted false imprisonment.

🏛 RULE OF LAW
Voluntary participation or acquiescence to deprogramming precludes any action for false imprisonment.

FACTS: Peterson (P) was a member of a religious cult while attending college. Her parents employed a deprogrammer to bring her out of the cult, and Peterson (P) spent 16 days at this person's home. She remained there without making any attempt to leave or contact authorities, although she had several opportunities to do both. She subsequently sued Sorlien (D), her former minister, and her parents for false imprisonment. The trial court jury denied recovery, and she appealed.

ISSUE: Does voluntary participation in deprogramming preclude actions for false imprisonment?

HOLDING AND DECISION: (Sheran, C.J.) Yes. Voluntary participation in deprogramming precludes actions for false imprisonment. Peterson (P) was never held in a situation where she lacked a reasonable avenue of escape. As a result, she cannot now contend she was held against her will and falsely imprisoned. Affirmed.

CONCURRENCE AND DISSENT: (Wahl, J.) Many parents may view their child's religious beliefs with dismay but that is no reason to alter tort law to allow parents to infringe upon the First Amendment. The evidence presented was relevant to the issue of punitive damages but not to liability for false imprisonment. The plaintiff was not merely seeking monetary damages, however, but an injunction prohibiting her parents from interfering with her religious rights and freedoms. While the trial court rightly paid little attention to the minimal monetary damages sought, the majority here should have paid greater attention to the import of the injunction. It is inexplicable that plaintiff's later "acquiescence" to her deprogramming should relate back to abrogate her father's initial false imprisonment.

DISSENT: (Otis, J.) A parent should not have the right or ability to limit an adult child's freedoms because of a subjective determination that the child's freedoms are a result of "impaired judgmental capacity." The child's preference for an unusual religion or faith does not in and of itself constitute impaired judgmental capacity. The 21-year-old plaintiff suffered humiliation at the hands of her parents, however well-intentioned those parents may have been, and her rights should have been upheld by the majority.

▶ ANALYSIS

There have been cases holding that attempts to deprogram cult members violate civil rights. A different conflict exists between parental authority and a child's religious freedom. If the child is a minor, it is more difficult to ignore the parental interest involved.

■=■

Quicknotes

ABROGATE Annul; cancel; void.

FALSE IMPRISONMENT Intentional tort whereby the victim is unlawfully restrained.

FIRST AMENDMENT RIGHTS Rights conferred by the First Amendment to the United States Constitution prohibiting Congress from enacting any law respecting an establishment of religion, prohibiting the free exercise of religion, abridging freedom of speech or the press, the right of peaceful assembly and the right to petition for a redress of grievances.

FREEDOM OF RELIGION The guarantee of the First Amendment to the United States Constitution prohibiting Congress from enacting laws regarding the establishment of religion or prohibiting the free exercise thereof.

■=■

Roper v. Simmons

Party not identified (P) v. Convicted juvenile murderer (D)

543 U.S. 551 (2005).

NATURE OF CASE: Appeal from judgment setting aside death sentence.

FACT SUMMARY: Simmons (D) was 17 when he committed an intentional murder. A jury convicted him and, even considering his age as a mitigating factor, recommended that the judge impose the death penalty. The judge did so, and Simmons filed a petition for post-conviction relief.

🏛 RULE OF LAW
The death penalty may not be imposed upon offenders who were under the age of 18 when they committed their crime.

FACTS: Christopher Simmons (D), 17 and a junior in a Missouri high school, wanted to kill someone, and he talked to his teenage friends about his desire. He intended to kidnap someone, tie them up, and throw them over a bridge. Simmons (D) believed he would not be harshly punished because he was a minor. Simmons (D) then committed his planned murder, was arrested, and a jury convicted him for the murder. The judge instructed the jury to consider age as a mitigating factor and both defense counsel and the prosecutor mentioned Simmons's (D) age in closing statements. The jury recommended the death penalty, and the judge imposed it nine months later when Simmons (D) was 18. The Supreme Court then held in *Atkins v. Virginia*, 536 U.S. 304 (2002), that the death sentence could not be imposed upon a mentally retarded offender because it violated the Eighth and Fourteenth Amendments. Simmons (D) filed a petition for post-conviction relief claiming that *Atkins* could be extended to juvenile offenders. The Missouri Supreme Court agreed and overturned Simmons's (D) death sentence. The Missouri Supreme Court resentenced Simmons (D) to life imprisonment. The U.S. Supreme Court granted certiorari.

ISSUE: May the death penalty be imposed upon offenders who were under the age of 18 when they committed their crime?

HOLDING AND DECISION: (Kennedy, J.) No. The death penalty may not be imposed upon offenders who were under the age of 18 when they committed their crime. The Court first considered this precise issue in *Stanford v. Kentucky*, 492 U.S. 361 (1989), where it determined that the Eighth and Fourteenth Amendments did not proscribe execution of juvenile offenders 15–18 years old. Upon reconsideration of this issue, we find first that the Eighth

Amendment requires states to forbid execution of juvenile offenders. Objective indicia of a national consensus show the majority of states reject juvenile execution, and it is rarely imposed even where permitted. Juvenile offenders cannot be classified with adult offenders because of three general differences. First, juveniles are psychologically immature and have a demonstrable lack of responsibility. This immaturity and irresponsibility encouraged this country to proscribe juveniles from voting, marrying without parental consent, or serving on juries. Second, juveniles are heavily influenced by peers and negative influences. Third, the character of a juvenile is still forming. An adult offender is more morally responsible. A minor could learn to appreciate the gravity of his actions as his character develops as an adult. Psychologists do not diagnose juveniles as having sociopath or psychopath disorders because of the difficulty of diagnosing an immature personality. The court is certainly in no better position. Some may argue that the age of 18 is an arbitrary line, but that is the age this country uses to separate childhood from adulthood. Given this reconsideration, *Stanford* is no longer followed. Today's holding follows the international rejection of juvenile executions. The United States and Somalia are the only countries to refuse to ratify Article 37 of the United Nations Convention on the Rights of the Child, which specifically prohibits juvenile execution. Few other countries permit juvenile executions but only the United States actually applies the penalty. International precedent has no bearing on this decision, but confirms that this decision is appropriate. Affirmed.

DISSENT: (Scalia, J.) Today's decision states that the Constitution has changed requiring a change in precedent. The Court does not rely on the language of the Eighth Amendment, but instead relies on the "evolving standards of decency" in this country. The majority, however, fails to evaluate this country's standards and instead imposes standards upon it. Five justices cite to international support to set forth law for the entire population. "By what conceivable warrant can nine lawyers presume to be the authoritative conscience of the Nation?" The Court presumably relies on the international support, but ignores the clear fact that the United States has not ratified the Article 37 treaty. Not only has the majority set moral standards for the nation, it has ratified a treaty on behalf of the country. The United States does not have to conform to international law.

Continued on next page.

▶ *ANALYSIS*

This was a highly contested case that began with a divided Missouri Supreme Court and ended with a 5-4 decision in the U.S. Supreme Court. The Missouri Supreme Court had taken the unusual, and the dissenters argued improper, step of ignoring existing U.S. Supreme Court precedent and forging new law. The U.S. Supreme Court agreed with the state supreme court and brought the United States in line with international precedent. The justices may have intended to draft a bright-line ruling, but many questions arose after this case. Determining the existence of a "national consensus" is difficult without further guidance of where to find indicia of such a consensus. Also, the significance of international law on American jurisprudence may vary from case to case and now takes on a greater import for future cases.

■══■

Quicknotes

CERTIORARI A discretionary writ issued by a superior court to an inferior court in order to review the lower court's decisions; the Supreme Court's writ ordering such review.

EIGHTH AMENDMENT The Eighth Amendment to the federal Constitution prohibits the imposition of excessive bail, fines, and cruel and unusual punishment.

FOURTEENTH AMENDMENT Declares that no state shall make or enforce any law that shall abridge the privileges and immunities of citizens of the United States. No state shall deny to any person within its jurisdiction the equal protection of the laws.

■══■

Meyer v. Meyer

Mother of emancipated daughter (P) v. Ex-husband (D)

Mo. Ct. App., 493 S.W.2d 42 (1973).

NATURE OF CASE: Appeal from denial of future child support.

FACT SUMMARY: Mrs. Meyer (P) contended she should be awarded future child support for her daughter, who was divorced and living with her while pregnant, even though she had been emancipated.

RULE OF LAW
A child's marriage acts to emancipate her and end her parents' duty to supply support.

FACTS: Mrs. Meyer (P) was granted custody of her four children, and Mr. Meyer (D) was ordered to pay child support. One child left Mrs. Meyer (P), married, became pregnant, and divorced. She then moved back into Mrs. Meyer's (P) home. Mrs. Meyer (P) sought to hold Mr. Meyer (D) responsible for future support, as he failed to petition for a modification of the support order upon the child's marriage. The trial court denied the future support order, and Mrs. Meyer (P) appealed.

ISSUE: Does a child's marriage automatically emancipate her and end a parent's duty of support?

HOLDING AND DECISION: (Wasserstrom, J.) Yes. A child's marriage acts to emancipate her and ends the parents' duty to support her. The marriage represents a new familial relationship. The husband assumes the support obligation from the parents. Affirmed.

ANALYSIS

Several actions by minors will grant them the legal status of emancipation. One is the entering into military service. Another is living separate and apart from the parents at an appropriate age. Emancipation alters only the parent-child relationship. No other privileges of majority are bestowed.

■═■

Quicknotes

CHILD SUPPORT Payments made by one parent to another in satisfaction of the non-custodial parent's legal obligation to provide for the sustenance of the child.

EMANCIPATION A parent's surrender of all rights and duties regarding the care and control of a child.

■═■

In re Sumey

Juvenile (P) v. Parents (D)

Wash. Sup. Ct., 94 Wash. 2d 757, 621 P.2d 108 (1980).

NATURE OF CASE: Appeal from order of alternative placement.

FACT SUMMARY: Mr. and Mrs. Sumey (D) contended a state statute allowing for an order of alternative placement without a prior hearing on parental fitness was unconstitutional.

🏛 RULE OF LAW
The state's constitutionally protected interest in the welfare of the child outweighs the limited infringement upon parental constitutional rights to justify alterative placement without a prior hearing on parental fitness.

FACTS: Sheila (P), a juvenile, petitioned for alternative placement after her mother had her placed in a receiving home, and state crisis intervention failed to bring her family back together. The trial court granted the petition, and her parents appealed, contending the statute authorizing the alternative placement was unconstitutional. They contended they were entitled to a prior hearing on parental fitness.

ISSUE: Must a hearing on parental fitness be held prior to a court's issuance of an order of alternative placement?

HOLDING AND DECISION: (Utter, C.J.) No. The state's constitutionally protected interest in the welfare of the child outweighs the limited infringement upon parental constitutional rights to justify alternative placement without a prior hearing on parental fitness. The *parens patriae* interest of the state far outweighs the parents' right to care, custody, and companionship of the child. Thus, the statute was constitutional. Affirmed.

DISSENT: (Brachtenbach, J.) The majority opinion now allows any child to claim a "communication gap" as a reason to permit the Department of Social and Health Services to intrude into the sacred parent-child relationship. The "communication gap" testified to in this case was the sole basis for the child's removal from the home over her parents' objections. The court did not require a claim or proof of unfitness of the parents, or a claim or proof of harm or danger to the 15-year-old. The teenager threatened to run away as she had before, but this is insufficient to deprive a parent of his or her child for six months or longer. The legislative intent supports the argument that compelling evidence must be required when intervening in the parent-child relationship.

▶ ANALYSIS

Some states, such as Alabama, Arkansas, and California, have adopted emancipation statutes which allow minors of 14 to petition for emancipation upon showing they can manage their own financial affairs and are living separate and apart from their parents. Other acts of emancipation include military service and marriage.

■=■

Quicknotes

EMANCIPATION A parent's surrender of all rights and duties regarding the care and control of a child.

PARENS PATRIAE Maxim that the government as sovereign is conferred with the duty to act as guardian on behalf of those citizens under legal disability.

■=■

Burt v. Burt

Daughter (P) v. Father (D)

Miss. Sup. Ct., 841 So. 2d 108 (2001).

NATURE OF CASE: Appeal from order requiring payment of overdue child support.

FACT SUMMARY: A 21-year-old daughter sued her father for back child support. The father claimed the daughter had been emancipated and was not owed any child support.

🏛 RULE OF LAW
A minor remains entitled to court-ordered child support unless the minor has unequivocally satisfied the statutory requirements for emancipation.

FACTS: Bruce Burt (D) and Gloria Burt had two minor children, Amber (P) and Todd, when they divorced. The court ordered Bruce (D) to pay $275 monthly for the children's support. Gloria died soon after the divorce, and Amber (P) began living with friends, grandparents, and then her boyfriend. Bruce (D) stopped paying child support after Gloria's death. At one point, Amber (P) lived with her father but soon left because of his drinking. Amber (P) and Bruce (D) had no relationship during the next seven years. When she turned 21, Amber (P) sued Bruce (D) for back child support. Todd did not join the case nor seek a money award. The parties stipulated to an expert-determined support award although Bruce's (D) attorney added a handwritten note disavowing any assumption that support was in fact owed. The trial court awarded Amber (P) $29,795 in back child support and $13,882 in interest. Bruce (D) appealed.

ISSUE: Does a minor remain entitled to court-ordered child support unless the minor has unequivocally satisfied the statutory requirements for emancipation?

HOLDING AND DECISION: (Cobb, J.) Yes. A minor remains entitled to court-ordered child support unless the minor has unequivocally satisfied the statutory requirements for emancipation. Bruce (D) argued that Amber (P) emancipated herself by maintaining an independent life, living with others of her own choosing. He claimed that he wanted Amber (P) to live with him, and she chose not to do so, so she was emancipated. The emancipation statute sets out four standards resulting in the emancipation of a minor: (1) reaching age 21; (2) marrying; (3) ending education and working full-time before age 21; or (4) voluntarily live with persons other than the custodial parent and work full-time before age 21. Amber (P) did not have full-time work prior to reaching age 21, she was not married, and she thus did not fulfill any one of the statutory requirements for emancipation. Bruce (D) next argued that the chancellor's findings were against the weight of the evidence. First, he claims that Amber (P) lived with her boyfriend longer than the chancellor found, but this is insufficient to overturn the findings as a whole. Second, he claims that the evidence of his drinking was insufficient to support a finding that his intoxication was the basis for Amber (P) leaving his home. Testimony of Amber (P) and Bruce's (D) second ex-wife supported such a finding. Finally, Bruce (D) argued that Amber (P) lacked "clean hands" before the court because she failed to maintain a relationship with her father for seven years. The chancellor had the best opportunity to evaluate the witnesses, and she sided with Amber (P). None of Bruce's (D) claims are sufficient to overturn her findings or result in him not having to pay back child support. Affirmed.

▶ ANALYSIS

A minor is not emancipated merely because she is forced by circumstance to lead the life of an adult. The statutory requirements are unambiguous and relatively easy to apply to any given case. A parent cannot escape legal obligations to his child by claiming that she is an emancipated minor. Even when emancipated, a minor does not have all the rights and privileges of an adult. Emancipated minors are often still required to attend school and may not be able to marry without parental consent depending on the minor's age. Children having adult legal rights became a particularly hot topic when a young boy sought to "divorce" his biological parents rather than become emancipated so that he could become the legally adopted child of his foster parents.

Quicknotes

CHILD SUPPORT Payments made by one parent to another in satisfaction of the non-custodial parent's legal obligation to provide for the sustenance of the child.

CLEAN HANDS DOCTRINE Equitable doctrine denying relief to a party who seeks a remedy in relation to an action in which he did not act fairly.

EMANCIPATED MINOR A minor who is released from the control of his parents and who has the right to his own earnings and services, but not to continued parental support and maintenance.

Child Abuse and Neglect

Quick Reference Rules of Law

State v. Moorman

State (P) v. Convicted child abuser (D)

286 N.J. Super. 648, 670 A.2d 81 (1996).

NATURE OF CASE: Appeal from conviction for second-degree manslaughter.

FACT SUMMARY: Moorman (D) was convicted of second-degree manslaughter for the death of her toddler daughter. Experts testified at trial concerning battered child syndrome.

🏛 RULE OF LAW
Battered child syndrome is a reliable scientific basis for expert testimony of intentional abuse.

FACTS: Emergency medical personnel arrived at Moorman's (D) home to find Labria Moorman, 22 months, lying cold and still on the living room floor. She did not respond to resuscitation prior to or after her arrival at the hospital. Her treating physician discovered multiple contusions and scarring all over her body. Tests also showed blood in her stool. The physician questioned Moorman (D) who stated that Labria had fallen down a flight of stairs two days earlier but seemed fine. She also said that Labria fell down a flight of stairs approximately two weeks earlier and was taken to a different emergency room, treated, and released. The doctor then informed Moorman (D) that her daughter had died. The police interviewed Moorman (D) at her home after the county medical examiner was informed of the physician's suspicions. Moorman (D) told them the same story she had told the doctor. Then she added information about a fight between her and her live-in boyfriend resulting in her falling asleep on her couch with Labria. She awoke to find Labria unresponsive on the floor, but with a heartbeat. That's when Moorman (D) went to a neighbor to call the police. The medical examiner's office performed an autopsy and took photographs. The autopsy revealed blunt force trauma to the child's abdomen inconsistent with a fall down the stairs. It further revealed a tear in her bowel resulting in eventual heart failure. The examiner ruled Labria's death a homicide. The next day the police conducted a follow-up interview with Moorman (D) after advising her of her Miranda rights. Moorman (D) admitted that she had shaken Labria by the waist as a punishment for disobedience. Moorman (D) provided a tape-recorded statement and was charged with first-degree murder. The State (P) requested a Rule 104 hearing to permit its evidence of battered child syndrome at trial. The judge allowed the testimony as well as the autopsy photos. The judge recognized the assistant county medical examiner as an expert to testify on the issue of battered child syndrome (BCS). He testified about the classic BCS case, which is the existence of injuries due to continued abuse of a child, and the similarities in Labria Moorman's death. The judge gave jury instructions that the jury could only consider the BCS testimony as evidence that Labria's injuries could not have been caused by a fall down the stairs and not as evidence of any predisposition of Moorman (D) to commit the crime. Moorman's (D) expert testified that Labria's injuries were not consistent with the typical BCS case but he conceded he had not previously reviewed the autopsy photos. The jury convicted Moorman (D) of the lesser-included offense of second-degree manslaughter.

ISSUE: Is battered child syndrome a reliable scientific basis for expert testimony of intentional abuse?

HOLDING AND DECISION: (Petrella, J.) Yes. Battered child syndrome is a reliable scientific basis for expert testimony of intentional abuse. Expert testimony is reliable if it is generally accepted by the relevant scientific community. The trial judge properly admitted the BCS testimony because the experts testified that BCS has been accepted within the scientific community since the 1960s, it is supported by relevant literature, and other jurisdictions have accepted it. In any event, the evidence of prior injury was admissible to show absence of accident or mistake. Affirmed.

▶ ANALYSIS

Battered child syndrome does not address any one specific form of child abuse but addresses a pattern of abuse. Sufferers from battered child syndrome may develop similar abuse scarring and fractures but the best use of testimony regarding the syndrome is to demonstrate the lack of accident or mistake. Abusers often report that a child is clumsy or accident-prone to explain away contusions and fractures. Greater education on the signs of battered child syndrome can increase reporting which could save children's lives.

■=■

Quicknotes

CHILD ABUSE Conduct harmful to a child's physical or mental health.

■=■

Chronister v. Brenneman

Daughter's sister (P) v. Father (D)

Pa. Super. Ct., 742 A.2d 190 (1999).

NATURE OF CASE: Appeal from entry of a Protection from Abuse Order.

FACT SUMMARY: A father (D) administered corporal punishment to his daughter. The victim told her older half-sister (P) who contacted a child services agency and reported the incident. A Petition for Protection from Abuse was filed and the court granted it. The father (D) appealed.

RULE OF LAW
Parents have a "privilege" under the law to administer corporal punishment to their children under certain circumstances.

FACTS: A father (D) hit his sixteen-year-old daughter four or five times across her buttocks with a belt after she admitted lying to him (D). The daughter reported the strapping to her guidance counselor and her older half-sister (P) who contacted a child services agency. Later that same evening, the father (D) had a conversation about the rules of the house with the victim. The father left the table, retrieved a gun, looked at it, walked by the victim, and put the gun upstairs. The victim testified that she had eye contact with her father (D) as he walked by her with the gun. The next day, the court granted the victim's Petition for Protection From Abuse. The father (D) appealed.

ISSUE: Does hitting a child four or five times on the buttocks with a belt fall within a parent's right to administer corporal punishment to a child?

HOLDING AND DECISION: (Brosky, J.) Yes. The father's (D) choice of discipline here is neither being criticized nor condoned. His (D) motivation appears to be sound in that there is no evidence that his acts were anything but punishment. Abuse is defined as an attempt to cause bodily injury or serious bodily injury. Bodily injury is defined as the impairment of physical condition or substantial pain. The victim testified that the strapping was painful, but there was no evidence of anything other than temporary pain. In fact, the strapping did not leave bruises. Further, parents have a privilege to administer corporal punishment under certain circumstances. The force here was not designed to create a substantial risk of death or serious bodily injury. The order of protection is inappropriate in this case. Reversed.

DISSENT: (Melvin, J.) The record indicates that the father (D) beat his daughter with a belt that left bruises and finger imprints on her body. He (D) also removed a gun while in his daughter's presence right after discussing the rules of the house. Under these circumstances, the

Protection from Abuse Order was appropriate. I agree that parents in this Commonwealth have the right to discipline their children, but the defendant's behavior in this case rose to the level of abuse.

▶ ANALYSIS

States recognize a parent's right to use reasonable force to discipline a disobedient child. The largest group of child victims, however, is young, usually under age three. Among these children, head injuries are particularly common. Shaken baby syndrome and Munchausen's syndrome by proxy are now nationally recognized as child abuse.

Quicknotes

CHILD ABUSE Conduct harmful to a child's physical or mental health.

Walker v. Superior Court

Christian Science parent (D) v. State (P)

Cal. Sup. Ct., 47 Cal. 3d 112 (1988).

NATURE OF CASE: Appeal of denial of motion to dismiss.

FACT SUMMARY: Laurie Walker (D), a Christian Scientist, was charged with involuntary manslaughter when her four-year-old daughter died of meningitis after receiving no medical treatment.

🏛 RULE OF LAW
Neither the First Amendment nor its California counterparts bar the criminal prosecution of parents who refuse medical care to a gravely ill child on religious grounds.

FACTS: Laurie Walker's (D) four-year-old daughter was ill for 17 days before she died of meningitis. During this time, Walker (D), consistent with her Christian Science religion, chose to treat the child with prayer rather than medical care. Walker (D) engaged an accredited Christian Science prayer practitioner and a Christian Science nurse to attend the child. After the child's death, Walker (D) was charged with involuntary manslaughter and felony child endangerment. Walker (D) moved to dismiss on the basis that her conduct was specifically protected by law, arguing that § 270 of the California Penal Code, which made it a misdemeanor for a parent to fail to provide a child with, among other things, medical care, specifically provided that, when necessary, spiritual treatment such as prayer may substitute for medical care. Walker (D) also argued that her conduct was absolutely protected from criminal liability by the First Amendment to the U.S. Constitution and Article 1, § 4 of the California constitution. The trial court rejected these arguments.

ISSUE: Does the First Amendment or its California counterparts bar the criminal prosecution of parents who refuse medical care to a gravely ill child on religious grounds?

HOLDING AND DECISION: (Mosk, J.) No. The prosecution of parents charged with having killed or endangered the lives of their children by providing prayer in lieu of medical care violates neither statutory law nor the California or U.S. Constitutions. The legislative history of § 270 does not address whether parents are to be exempted from felony liability if physiological harm is caused by their choice to treat their children with prayer alone. And, while such liability seriously infringes on the religious practices of certain individuals, this infringement must be weighed against the compelling state interest in protecting the lives of children. The impingement on Walker's (D) practice of her religion is outweighed by the state's compelling

interest, and there is no adequately effective and less restrictive alternative available to further this interest. Affirmed.

▶ ANALYSIS

In a similar case, *In re E.G.*, 133 Ill. 2d 98 (1989), the Supreme Court of Illinois held that a 17-year-old had the right to refuse lifesaving medical treatment. The holding in that case was based on Illinois common law and not constitutional grounds. However, the critical factor in that case was that E.G. was adjudged a mature minor and capable of making the choice for herself—a choice a four-year-old would hardly be considered competent to make. In recent years, the trend has been toward conviction of Christian Scientist parents who refuse their children medical treatment.

Quicknotes

CALIFORNIA PENAL CODE § 270 Provides that "every parent of any child who willfully omits, without lawful excuse, to perform any duty imposed upon him by law, to furnish necessary food, clothing, shelter, or medical attendance or other remedial care for such child, is guilty of a misdemeanor."

FIRST AMENDMENT Prohibits Congress from enacting any law respecting an establishment of religion, prohibiting the free exercise of religion, abridging freedom of speech or the press, the right of peaceful assembly and the right to petition for a redress of grievances.

INVOLUNTARY MANSLAUGHTER The killing of another person without premeditation or deliberation or with the intent to kill or to commit a felony, which may be reasonably expected to result in death or serious bodily injury; involuntary manslaughter is characterized by reckless conduct in the commission of a lawful act, or by the commission of an unlawful act that is not a felony, but which leads to the killing of another.

Hermanson v. State

Decedent's parents (D) v. State (P)

Fla. Sup. Ct., 604 So. 2d 775 (1992).

NATURE OF CASE: Appeal from conviction for child abuse resulting in third-degree murder.

FACT SUMMARY: The Hermansons (D) were convicted of child abuse resulting in third-degree murder upon the death from juvenile diabetes of their daughter, whom they denied medical therapy in accordance with the teachings of their religion.

🏛 RULE OF LAW
The legislature must clearly indicate the point at which parents' reliance on their religious beliefs in the treatment of their children becomes criminal conduct.

FACTS: The Hermansons' (D) daughter died as a result of juvenile diabetes, which they were treating according to the dictates of Christian Science Church. Christian Scientists believe in healing by spiritual means rather than through the use of traditional medical practice. In accord with their beliefs, the Hermansons (D) sought the assistance of a Christian Science practitioner and a Christian Science nurse. They did not provide their daughter medical treatment. Their daughter died, and the Hermansons (D) were tried for and convicted of child abuse resulting in third-degree murder under Florida Statute § 827.04(1). They received four-year suspended prison sentences and were ordered to serve fifteen years' probation. The district court affirmed. The Hermansons (D) appealed, raising four issues, but the Florida Supreme Court only addressed the issue of due process, which it considered dispositive.

ISSUE: Must the legislature clearly indicate the point at which parents' reliance on their religious beliefs in the treatment of their children becomes criminal conduct?

HOLDING AND DECISION: (Overton, J.) Yes. The legislature must clearly indicate the point at which parents' reliance on their religious beliefs in the treatment of their children becomes criminal conduct. If the legislature decides to provide for religious accommodation while protecting the children of the state, it must clearly indicate when parents' conduct becomes criminal. One of the purposes of due process is "to insure that no individual is convicted unless 'a fair warning [has first been] given to the world in language that the common world will understand, of what the law intends to do if a certain line is passed.'" *Mourning v. Family Publications Serv., Inc.*, 411 U.S. 356 (1973). In the statutes in question, the point at which parents' actions become criminal is not clear. Therefore, no standard existed against which to determine when (and if)

the Hermansons' (D) conduct became criminal. Adjudication of guilt and sentence vacated; defendants discharged.

▶ ANALYSIS

In *State v. McKown*, 461 N.W. 2d 720 (Minn. Ct. App. 1990), aff'd, 475 N.W. 2d 63 (Minn. 1991), cert. denied, 112 S. Ct. 882, a child's parents utilized a Christian Science practitioner and a Christian Science nurse and did not seek conventional medical treatment. The parents were indicted for second-degree manslaughter when their child died of untreated diabetes. The issue in that case was whether the child abuse statute, which contained an exception for spiritual treatment similar to the Florida statute in the instant case, was to be construed in conjunction with a manslaughter statue that was based on culpable negligence resulting in death. In finding a violation of due process, the Minnesota Court concluded that there was a "lack of clarity in the relationship between the two statutes." Here, the statues in question did not establish a line of demarcation at which a person of common intelligence would know their conduct became criminal, thus denying the parents due process.

■■■

Quicknotes

DUE PROCESS The constitutional mandate requiring the courts to protect and enforce individuals' rights and liberties consistent with prevailing principles of fairness and justice and prohibiting the federal and state governments from such activities that deprive its citizens of life, liberty, or property interest.

■■■

Doe v. O'Brien

Parents (P) v. Social worker (D)

329 F.3d 1286 (11th Cir. 2003).

NATURE OF CASE: Appeal from case dismissal.

FACT SUMMARY: John Doe's (P) niece accused him of molesting her and Florida Department of Children and Family Services assigned Deborah O'Brien (D) to the case. After investigation, O'Brien (D) removed Jane and John Doe's (P) three children into emergency protective custody. After regaining custody of their children, the Doe family (P) sued for a declaration that the removal statute is unconstitutional.

🏛 **RULE OF LAW**
It is not a violation of a family's due process rights if child protective services removes children from parental custody based on potential abuse merely because time existed to obtain judicial authorization.

FACTS: John Doe's (P) hearing-impaired niece, age nine, filed a complaint with the Florida Department of Children and Family Services (DCF) that John Doe (P) sexually molested her when she was five. DCF learned that John Doe (P) resided in Hillsborough County with Jane Doe (P) and their three minor children, D.M. (P), N.O. (P), and B.O. (P). DCF then assigned Deborah O'Brien (D) to the case. O'Brien (D) opened an investigation and learned that John Doe (P) had a history of abuse reports, including another report of sexual abuse of a minor, and criminal sexual behavior, including a conviction for lewd and lascivious behavior toward children. O'Brien (D) met with her supervisor and the DCF legal department and was advised to remove the children. O'Brien (D) separately interviewed John and Jane Doe (P) and their three children (P). After the interviews, O'Brien (P) believed that the children were in danger from John Doe (P), and that Jane Doe (P) could not protect them. She removed them to the emergency custody of their maternal grandmother. The next day, a judge ordered them returned to their parents for lack of probable cause to keep the family apart. The Doe family (P) filed a suit seeking a declaration that the emergency removal statute is unconstitutional facially and as applied to them, specifically that it violates their Fourteenth Amendment due process rights and Fourth Amendment right to be free from unlawful search and seizure. The district court dismissed the action against O'Brien (D) and the Doe family (P) appeals.

ISSUE: Is it a violation of a family's due process rights if child protective services removes children from parental custody based on potential abuse merely because time existed to obtain judicial authorization?

HOLDING AND DECISION: (Black, J.) No. It is not a violation of a family's due process rights if child protective services removes children from parental custody based on potential abuse merely because time existed to obtain judicial authorization. The removal statute permits DCF to remove a child from her home without judicial authorization if probable cause exists that abuse is an imminent threat or has occurred. A hearing must be held within 24 hours. Doe (P) asserts that DCF routinely uses the emergency removal statute without first determining if obtaining a court order would be more appropriate. O'Brien (D) concedes she did not first consider obtaining a court order. The Doe (P) claim is that emergency removal is never appropriate if time exists to obtain a court order and the child is not in imminent danger. Only the Second Circuit has agreed with the Doe (P) position in *Tenenbaum v. Williams* where it held that judicial authorization should be obtained prior to emergency removal of a child if it can be done so timely and without endangering the child. Due process does not demand such an inflexible rule, and courts must be permitted to consider the individual circumstances of each case as well as the need for the contested government action. This is a subtle balancing test, and a bright-line question of time to obtain judicial authorization cannot be a substitute. Given the circumstances of this case, O'Brien (D) properly removed the children as they were in imminent danger of abuse from a father who previously allegedly abused two other children, including a disabled family member. O'Brien (D) did not act rashly but consulted with her supervisor and the DCF legal department prior to interviewing each Doe (P) family member. Only then did she remove the children for their safety. O'Brien's (D) actions did not violate the Doe (P) family's rights to due process. Affirmed.

▶ **ANALYSIS**

Most states recommend a determination if time exists to obtain judicial authorization prior to removing children from their parents' custody. If a child is in imminent or substantial danger, however, the judicial authorization is more properly obtained retroactively at the required hearing within so many hours of removal, typically 24-72 hours. No state allows a child to be removed without a timely hearing for the parents to contest removal. The

Continued on next page.

primary focus is on the child's well-being and not on the insult to the parents.

■=■

Quicknotes

CHILD ABUSE Conduct harmful to a child's physical or mental health.

DUE PROCESS RIGHTS The constitutional mandate requiring the courts to protect and enforce individuals' rights and liberties consistent with prevailing principles of fairness and justice, and prohibiting the federal and state governments from such activities that deprive its citizens of a life, liberty or property interest.

FOURTH AMENDMENT Provides that persons be secure as to their person and private belongings against unreasonable searches and seizures.

PROBABLE CAUSE A reasonable basis for believing that a crime has been committed.

■=■

People v. Carroll

State (P) v. Stepmother (D)

N.Y. Ct. App., 93 N.Y.2d 564, 71 N.E.2d 500 (1999).

NATURE OF CASE: Appeal from reversal of motion dismissing indictment.

FACT SUMMARY: Carroll (D) was indicted by the Grand Jury for endangering the welfare of a child when she witnessed the beating death of her three-year-old stepdaughter. She claimed a lack of evidence showing she had legal responsibility for the child.

> ## RULE OF LAW
> Any person legally responsible for a child may be criminally charged with endangering that child's welfare.

FACTS: Shanaya Jones's father beat her to death over a period of several days. Shanaya, 3, had come for a visit with her father and his wife, Carroll (D). Carroll (D) referred to herself as Shanaya's primary caretaker and mother during her visit. Shanaya stopped eating, which apparently precipitated days of severe beatings. Carroll (D) witnessed her husband punching Shanaya and throwing her into a wall, but did nothing for two days until an ambulance was called. Shanaya was declared dead in the emergency room. The autopsy showed the damage inflicted upon Shanaya, including that she was starving and dehydrated. The People (P) charged Carroll (D) with endangering the welfare of a child. Carroll (D) moved to dismiss the indictment for insufficient evidence that she was "legally charged" with Shanaya's care. The trial court granted her motion and the People (P) appealed. The Appellate Division reversed based on Carroll's (D) legal responsibility for the child making her legally charged with her care and based on her standing *in loco parentis* to Shanaya. Carroll (D) appealed.

ISSUE: May any person legally responsible for a child be criminally charged with endangering that child's welfare?

HOLDING AND DECISION: (Kaye, C.J.) Yes. Any person legally responsible for a child may be criminally charged with endangering that child's welfare. A person must be "legally charged" with the care of a child prior to being liable for endangering the welfare of that child. Carroll (D) argues that she was not Shanaya's mother, legal guardian, or hired caretaker, so she was not "legally charged" with her care. She asserts that her own statements to the contrary did not assume permanent, legal status. The statute does not define "legally charged," so the courts must consider legislative intent, statutory language, and Penal Law directive when interpreting the term. A person must have legal responsibility for a child to be "legally charged" with her care. The Family Court Act defines

legal responsibility to include any person responsible for the child's care at the relevant time. Such a person can liable for the abuse or neglect of that child. Viewed most favorably to the People (P), the People (P) presented evidence to the Grand Jury that Carroll (D) was legally responsible for Shanaya pursuant to the Family Court Act and thus was legally charged with her care pursuant to the Penal Law. Biological parents and legal guardians are no longer the only persons assuming responsibility for the care of a child. Any person acting as the primary caretaker can certainly be charged with endangering the welfare of a child. The People (P) do not have to prove Carroll's permanent intent to take on Shanaya's care because a person can be the functional equivalent of a parent without standing *in loco parentis* to the child. The People's (P) evidence would support a conviction and certainly support the indictment. Affirmed.

ANALYSIS

New York Penal Law has two sections regarding endangering the welfare of a child. One applies to any person and one applies to a person legally charged with the care for that child. The People could not charge Carroll under the first section because she did not participate in the abuse. The second section defines endangerment as a failure to prevent a child from becoming an abused or neglected person, which was appropriate for this tragic situation. Some critics of the endangering statutes fear their too broad application because of the lack of definition. Judges do not want to appear soft on child abuse and tend to support endangerment cases for everything from arguing in front of minor children to actual physical abuse. While the court in this case did not want to narrow of a reading of the statute, others are saying that narrower readings are a necessity.

Quicknotes

IN LOCO PARENTIS A situation in which a person has assumed the responsibilities and obligations of a lawful parent without undergoing the legal adoption process.

In re Pope
Minor child

N.C. Ct. App., 144 N.C. App. 32, 547 S.E.2d 153 (2001).

NATURE OF CASE: Appeal from termination of parental rights.

FACT SUMMARY: Rachel Pope's parental rights of Eva Pope were terminated. Rachel appealed on the basis of insufficient evidence of likelihood of repeated neglect.

🏛 **RULE OF LAW**
Parental rights may be terminated upon clear and convincing evidence of a likelihood of repetition of neglect when a past adjudication of neglect exists.

FACTS: The Buncombe County Department of Social Services (DSS) petitioned to terminate Rachel Emily Pope's parental rights as mother of Eva Leonia Grace Pope for willfully leaving Eva in foster care for over one year. The trial court made multiple findings of fact. DSS initially became involved because Eva was not thriving or meeting any developmental markers due to Rachel's lack of proper care. Eva never saw a physician, but only saw chiropractors and naturopathic doctors. Rachel's sister took Eva for a visit and brought Eva to a doctor out of concern for her condition. The physician immediately admitted Eva for failure to thrive. The hospital made multiple attempts to communicate the issues to Rachel, but Rachel was not interested in Eva's condition or the fact that Eva was starving to death. At trial, Rachel testified that Eva was healthy until her sister took her to a new environment. DSS developed a case plan for Rachel, which included psychological care and parenting classes, but Rachel did not progress. She continued to blame her sister for Eva's involvement with DSS. The trial court also found that Rachel has a psychological disorder, but Rachel did not accept the diagnosis. During Rachel's supervised visits with Eva, she would bring her inappropriate foods and attempt to feed her improperly. She also permitted Eva to engage in dangerous activities, such as standing unassisted in a windowsill in a room with concrete floors. The court further found that Rachel dearly loved Eva, but was simply unable to ever properly care for her. Eva had been in foster care for 24 months and Rachel was making no progress. Rachel testified that her only change in Eva's care would be to obtain a pediatrician for her. The trial court then terminated Rachel's parental rights. Rachel appeals on the basis of lack of probable cause of a repetition of neglect if she regained custody of Eva.

ISSUE: May a court terminate parental rights upon clear and convincing evidence of a likelihood of repetition of neglect when a past adjudication of neglect exists?

HOLDING AND DECISION: (Greene, J.) Yes. Parental rights may be terminated upon clear and convincing evidence of a likelihood of repetition of neglect when a past adjudication of neglect exists. Rachel argues that she has made progress in therapy and complied with her case plan, so the trial court incorrectly found a likelihood that Eva would experience neglect again in her custody. The court had to find clear and convincing evidence of past adjudication of neglect and a likelihood of repetition of that neglect. The trial court found no current neglect because Rachel did not have custody of Eva at the time of trial. The previous adjudication, however, was based upon Eva's starving and failure to thrive under Rachel's care. Rachel denied her neglect at the time and continued to deny Eva was unwell. Rachel would not change her care for Eva other than getting a pediatrician. Additionally, the trial court found that Rachel's behavior towards and care for Eva during her supervised visits was improper. The likelihood of a repetition of neglect exists. Affirmed.

DISSENT: (Tyson, J.) The purpose of the Juvenile Code is to reunite parent and child. The prior neglect adjudication cannot be the sole basis for termination of parental rights. DSS reported that Rachel was complying with her therapy and improving. The record further shows Rachel's willingness in completing her care plan requirements and moving forward with the DSS mandates. The record does not show clear and convincing evidence of a likelihood of neglect or of a willful failure to progress. Rachel never missed a visit with Eva despite her sister's unwillingness to foster a continuing relationship with Eva has been in her custody. It upset Rachel that Eva called Rachel's sister and husband "Mama" and "Daddy." Finally, the record does not show a willful failure to support Eva when Rachel was never under an order to pay support, Rachel's sister offered to help with expenses, and Rachel provided Eva with food and clothing. The goal should be reunification rather than termination.

▶ **ANALYSIS**

The original goal of children services agencies is reunification of parent and child. The parent, however, must be capable of complying with service plans and understanding prior mistakes. Termination of parental rights is never taken lightly and cannot happen overnight. Even in this case, the agency attempted to work with Rachel for two years before moving to terminate her rights. In all cases,

Continued on next page.

the court must consider the best interests of the child and not the best intentions of the parent.

■═■

Quicknotes

CLEAR AND CONVINCING EVIDENCE An evidentiary standard requiring a demonstration that the fact sought to be proven is reasonably certain.

PROBABLE CAUSE A reasonable basis for believing that a crime has been committed.

TERMINATION OF PARENTAL RIGHTS The purposeful cessation of lawfully recognized rights between a child and its parents and of the parent to the child, including physical possession of the child, companionship and support, the right to discipline the child, and control over the child's property.

■═■

Nicholson v. Scoppetta

Mother (P) v. Party not identified (D)

N.Y. Ct. App., 3 N.Y.3d 357, 820 N.E.2d 840 (2004).

NATURE OF CASE: Certification of three federal questions in class action.

FACT SUMMARY: A federal class action was filed for mothers charged with neglect because they were victims of domestic violence and their children were witnesses. The court certified three questions to this court.

RULE OF LAW
Emergency removal of children based on neglect allegations against the mother is not proper when the sole allegation is that the children witnessed an act of domestic violence against the mother.

FACTS: Sharwline Nicholson (P) filed a 42 USC § 1983 action against the New York City Administration for Children's Services (ACS) for removing her children because they witnessed acts of domestic violence committed against her. ACS alleged neglect on her part for subjecting them to the domestic violence environment. Nicholson's (P) action was consolidated with two other similar complaints. The court recognized two subclasses: the abused women and their children. The district court granted an injunction against ACS preventing them from removing children from a battered woman otherwise a fit parent as a violation of the women's substantive due process rights. ACS appealed and the Second Circuit affirmed except it did not reach the constitutional questions. These questions are certified to this court.

ISSUE: Is emergency removal of children based on neglect allegations against the mother proper when the sole allegation is that the children witnessed an act of domestic violence against the mother?

HOLDING AND DECISION: (Kaye, C.J.) No. Emergency removal of children based on neglect allegations against the mother is not proper when the sole allegation is that the children witnessed an act of domestic violence against the mother. The first question is whether a "neglected child" may include a child who merely witnessed an act of domestic violence? Clearly additional evidence is necessary to support a finding of neglect. A parent who is the victim of domestic violence cannot be considered to neglect her child solely on that basis. A court must find the necessary elements for neglect, namely that the preponderance of evidence shows impairment to the child's physical, emotional, or mental health or imminent danger of such impairment based on the caretaker's failure. Each element requires a link between the actions resulting in the child's impairment and the basis for the neglect petition. Neglect also requires evidence of the parent or caretaker's failure to exercise a minimum degree of care, which requires the court's objective assessment of the parent's failure to act. In cases involving battered women, the court should consider the facts of individual cases, including the risk to the woman if she leaves, the intensity of the violence, and risks if she seeks criminal prosecution of her batterer. The sole allegation cannot be that she was battered and her child witnessed it. If a court finds that the mother's actions did constitute failure to act given her individual circumstances, neglect is appropriate. The second question is whether witnessing domestic violence can constitute "danger" or "risk" to the child pursuant to the defined terms in the Family Court Act? The two legislative findings on the issue can be in conflict. The first stated goal is to reunite parents and children rather than focus on removals. The second stated goal is to protect children of families suffering from domestic violence because witnessing such violence is so detrimental to the children. Absent emergency circumstances as outlined in the Family Court Act, ACS should first file a petition. Presumptive removal is certainly not preferred. ACS must perform a fact-intensive investigation to justify removal and the Act's plain language supports this. Absent time to file a petition, then ACS should seek ex parte court authorization and the court must engage in the fact-finding inquiry. Emergency removals are the last step in the continuum of ACS recourse. It would be a rare circumstance where the emotional injury from witnessing domestic violence would be so great as to justify emergency removal. Finally, the third question is whether additional evidence must be presented to justify removal beyond the fact of the witnessing the violence? No blanket presumption of removal exists, so particularized evidence must be presented for removal justification. Evidence of efforts to avoid removal is also appropriate.

ANALYSIS

Advocates for victims of domestic violence were outraged by the increasing ACS removals and the further victimization of the battered mothers. Some of the cases had prior judicial authorization, however, and those did not raise such an outcry. This follows the court's decision that conceded that some circumstances with battered mothers may rise to the level of neglect. The result of this case, which settled after this opinion, was that ACS workers received additional training in recognizing domestic violence situations and a greater increase in judicial

Continued on next page.

authorization prior to removal of children in non-emergency situations.

∎▬∎

Quicknotes

CHILD NEGLECT Conduct on the part of a parent or guardian that demonstrates unfitness on the part of that individual to provide the proper care and control over the child, resulting in harm or potential harm to the child's physical or mental health.

CLASS CERTIFICATION Certification by a court's granting of a motion to allow individual litigants to join as one plaintiff in a class action against the defendant.

EX PARTE A proceeding commenced by one party.

∎▬∎

In re M.F. v. Florida Dept. of Children & Families

In the interests of abused child (P) v. State agency (D)

Fla. Sup. Ct., 770 So. 2d 1189 (2000).

NATURE OF CASE: Appeal from adjudication of dependency.

FACT SUMMARY: The Florida Department of Children & Families (D) filed a petition to have the three children of L.F. and R.F. (P) declared dependent and temporary custody transferred to the children's grandparents. R.F. (P) appealed as to his two biological children based on insufficient findings of potential abuse for those two.

RULE OF LAW
Evidence of sexual abuse of one child is sufficient to support an adjudication of dependency as to the siblings of that child.

FACTS: R.F. (P) was convicted and sentenced to prison for a capital sexual battery against one of his children, K.F., who was not R.F.'s biological child. The Florida Department of Children & Families (DCF) (D) petitioned to remove all three children, K.F., 8, M.F., 5, and M.F., 3, from their mother's care and placed them with the children's grandparents. DCF (D) filed an amended petition to have the children declared dependent and have temporary custody awarded to the grandparents. At the hearing, the court heard evidence of the potential abuse facing the children from R.F. (P) based on his criminal sexual conviction. The court adjudicated M.F. and M.F. dependent as to the father based on prospective abuse because of his criminal conviction and prospective neglect because of his fifteen-year incarceration. R.F. (P) appealed. The Second Circuit found the conviction for child sex offense was alone sufficient to support the adjudication, but certified a split among the jurisdictions because the Fifth Circuit and Third Circuits came to different conclusions.

ISSUE: Is evidence of sexual abuse of one child sufficient to support an adjudication of dependency as to the siblings of that child?

HOLDING AND DECISION: (Per curiam) Yes. Evidence of sexual abuse of one child is sufficient to support an adjudication of dependency as to the siblings of that child. This issue has not been previously considered by the court but this court has previously decided that parental rights may be terminated for similar reasons. DCF (D) has the burden to establish its case by a preponderance of the evidence. The Florida Juvenile Justice Act's intention is to protect children and strengthen family ties when possible. The dependency proceeding is a furtherance of this intent by protecting the child rather than punishing the parent. The Third Circuit found abuse against one child

to be sufficient basis for removal of all children. The Fifth Circuit required additional proof of risk to the other children. The plain language of the Act is more consistent with the Fifth Circuit's more flexible ruling. The statute requires a showing of substantial risk to the child and this is not accomplished with a per se rule that abuse of one child automatically places the other children at risk. R.F.'s (P) conviction alone is insufficient to support the district court's finding. The totality of the circumstances, however, is sufficient to support the finding. Affirmed.

CONCURRENCE: (Pariente, J.) The record does not show the circumstances surrounding R.F.'s (P) conviction or how the siblings will be at risk when he is incarcerated for fifteen years. The conviction alone is therefore insufficient to support the adjudication of dependency. The Legislature also does not offer a per se rule. The court should adopt a rebuttable presumption of dependency when the parent has a sexual abuse conviction.

ANALYSIS

Most states do not allow for termination of parental rights on the showing that a sibling was subject to sexual abuse by the parent. The parent typically has an opportunity to regain custody and another abuse allegation is substantiated resulting in removal of the child. After a previous adjudication of dependency even based on the sibling's abuse, the second removal may certainly lead to a termination of the parental rights. Here, given that R.F. was serving a fifteen-year prison sentence, it was unlikely he would ever regain custody of the minor children. Even the youngest would be an adult by the time he got out.

Quicknotes

BATTERY Unlawful contact with the body of another person.

DEPENDENT One who depends upon another person for support.

PER CURIAM Denotes a decision that represents the opinion of the entire court.

PER SE By itself; not requiring additional evidence for proof.

PREPONDERANCE OF THE EVIDENCE A standard of proof requiring the trier of fact to determine whether the fact sought to be established is more probable than not.

Stecker v. First Commer. Trust Co.

Physician (D) v. Estate administrator (P)

Ark. Sup. Ct., 331 Ark. 452, 962 S.W.2d 792 (1998).

NATURE OF CASE: Appeal of liability determination for child's death.

FACT SUMMARY: The estate of a deceased toddler sued the child's physician for malpractice and failure to report suspected child abuse in violation of statutory law. The physician claimed insufficient evidence to support a verdict against her.

> **RULE OF LAW**
> A violation of the child-abuse reporting statute can support a finding of proximate cause resulting in a child's death.

FACTS: Dr. Rheeta Stecker (D) was 16-month-old Laura Fulbright's treating physician. Stecker (D) saw Fulbright at 12 months old for her well-baby checkup. Stecker (D) was friends with Fulbright's mother, Mary Ellen Robbins. Robbins's boyfriend, Joseph Rank, lived with Robbins and Fulbright. At the well-baby visit, Stecker (D) alerted Robbins and Rank to a fracture of the child's arm, and the couple disclaimed knowledge of it. Stecker (D) was concerned about abuse and neglect so referred Fulbright to an orthopedist who did not find signs of parental neglect. Stecker (D) remained concerned but did not report her concerns to authorities, Fulbright's biological father, nor did she confront Robbins and Rank. Approximately one month later, Stecker (D) again examined Fulbright because of the couple's concerns that the toddler was clumsy. Stecker (D) noted Fulbright's symptoms could be from drinking too much juice or were consistent with head trauma. Two weeks later, Stecker's (D) physician husband treated Fulbright for swollen eyes after Robbins reported the toddler fell down stairs. Stecker (D) treated Fulbright the next day with Robbins reporting additional falls just since the day before. Stecker (D) confronted Robbins with her concerns and Robbins was adamant that Rank was not violent. Stecker (D) did not notify the authorities. No abuse occurred when a visitor was staying with Robbins and Rank. Two months later, Robbins left Fulbright alone in Rank's care and returned home to find Fulbright dead. The administrator of 16-month-old Laura Fulbright's estate, First Commercial Trust Co. (the Administrator) (P) sued Stecker (D) for malpractice and failure to report child abuse on behalf of the estate and several Fulbright relatives. The Administrator (P) also sued Robbins Rank. Rank was convicted of murder in Fulbright's death. At the first trial, Stecker (D) was found not liable for Fulbright's death, found not liable for civil penalties under the child-abuse reporting statute, and she was granted a directed verdict on the malpractice claim. The Administrator (P) had sought to introduce the expert testimony of a witness

who was found not qualified to testify to the Hot Springs standard of care on child abuse. This court reversed and remanded on appeal based on the trial court's error in excluding the expert testimony. A jury in the second trial found for the Administrator (P) on the malpractice claim. Stecker (D) appealed on the basis that her motion for a directed verdict should have been granted.

ISSUE: Can a violation of the child-abuse reporting statute support a finding of proximate cause resulting in a child's death?

HOLDING AND DECISION: (Newbern, J.) Yes. A violation of the child-abuse reporting statute can support a finding of proximate cause resulting in a child's death. Proximate cause must be proved by more than mere conjecture but by evidence such that a reasonable person would find defendant more likely than not caused the result. Stecker's (D) expert testified that Stecker (D) did not violate the applicable standard of care under the circumstances. He did testify, however, that he would have reported his suspicions. The Administrator's (P) first witness testified that Stecker (D) should have contacted the authorities. Stecker (D) argues that insufficient evidence was presented to support a finding that her failure to report was a proximate cause for Fulbright's death. To the contrary, her own witness stated he would have reported the suspected abuse and that such a report could have saved Fulbright's life. The Administrator's (P) witness testified that a report would have resulted in an alert to anyone who knew Fulbright. Stecker (D) did not rebut the testimony that a third person in the home prevented abuse occurring to Fulbright. The jury made a factual determination. Affirmed.

> **ANALYSIS**
>
> Physicians are mandatory reporters for child abuse statutes. Under the mandatory reporting laws, suspicions of child abuse must be reported regardless of the source of those suspicions or the relationship between the mandatory reporter and the suspected abuser. The mandatory reporter does need a reasonable belief that the suspicions are well-founded, but it is always preferable to err on the side of the child and to report suspected abuse. All states have mandatory reporting acts to qualify for federal funding under Child Abuse Prevention and Treatment Act.

Continued on next page.

Quicknotes

CHILD ABUSE Conduct harmful to a child's physical or mental health.

MALPRACTICE A failure to perform one's professional duties during the course of a client relationship, either intentionally or negligently, or the poor or improper discharge of one's professional obligations.

REASONABLE PERSON STANDARD The standard of case exercised by one who possesses the intelligence, education, knowledge, attention, and judgment required by society of its members when governing behavior; the standard applies to a person's judgment when determining breach of a duty under the theory of negligence.

■━━■

Idaho v. Wright

State (P) v. Mother (D)

497 U.S. 805 (1990).

NATURE OF CASE: Appeal from conviction for lewd conduct.

FACT SUMMARY: Laura Lee Wright (D) appealed her conviction of lewd conduct with a minor on the ground that the admission of a hearsay statement at trial violated her rights under the Confrontation Clause.

🏛 RULE OF LAW
The admission of a hearsay statement violates the Confrontation Clause when the statement does not bear "particularized guarantees of trustworthiness."

FACTS: Laura Lee Wright (D) and her husband, Robert L. Giles, were each convicted of two counts of lewd conduct with a minor under 16 years of age. The minors were Wright's (D) two daughters, aged five and two at the time the crimes were charged. Wright (D) appealed only from the conviction involving the younger daughter. Wright (D) contended that the admission, at trial, of certain hearsay statements made by the younger child to a pediatrician violated Wright's (D) rights under the Confrontation Clause of the Sixth Amendment, made applicable to the states by the Fourteenth Amendment. The trial court admitted the statements under Idaho's (P) residual hearsay exception. This exception provided that a hearsay statement not specifically covered by other hearsay exceptions but having equivalent circumstantial guarantees of trustworthiness can be admitted if it is the most probative evidence on point and if the best interests of justice will be served by its admission. The Idaho Supreme Court ruled that the younger daughter's hearsay statement was barred by the Confrontation Clause.

ISSUE: Will the admission at trial of a child's hearsay statement violate a defendant's rights under the Confrontation Clause?

HOLDING AND DECISION: (O'Connor, J.) Yes. A defendant's rights under the Confrontation Clause will be violated by admission of a child declarant's hearsay statement unless that statement bears "particularized guarantees of trustworthiness." The Confrontation Clause bars admission of some evidence that would otherwise be admissible under an exception to the hearsay rule. Admission under a firmly rooted hearsay exception satisfies the constitutional requirement of reliability because of the weight accorded long-standing judicial and legislative experience in assessing the trustworthiness of certain types of out-of-court statements. In order for a hearsay statement to withstand scrutiny under the Confrontation Clause, the

circumstances surrounding the making of the statement must demonstrate "particularized guarantees of trustworthiness" such as are indicated by the firmly rooted hearsay exceptions. Corroborating evidence may not be used to bolster the inherent untrustworthiness of hearsay statements. The State (P) did not demonstrate the existence of such "particularized guarantees of trustworthiness" in the circumstances surrounding the making of the hearsay statement in this case. Affirmed.

▶ ANALYSIS

The Court pointed to a number of factors as indicative of whether hearsay statements made by a child witness in sexual abuse cases are reliable. These factors include spontaneity and consistent repetition, lack of motive to fabricate, and use of terminology unexpected of a child of similar age. Nevertheless, while not completely precluding, under the Confrontation Clause, the admission of hearsay statements that do not fit into a traditional hearsay exception, the Court's ruling makes it extremely difficult for such statements to be admitted.

■=■

Quicknotes

CONFRONTATION CLAUSE A provision in the Sixth Amendment to the United States Constitution that an accused in a criminal action has the right to confront the witnesses against him, including the right to attend the trial and to cross-examine witnesses called on behalf of the prosecution.

HEARSAY EXCEPTION Out-of-court statement made by a person other than the witness testifying at trial that is offered in order to prove the truth of the matter asserted, and is admissible at trial notwithstanding the fact that it is hearsay.

■=■

Baltimore City Dept. of Social Services v. Bouknight

Social service agency (P) v. Mother of abused child (D)

493 U.S. 549 (1990).

NATURE OF CASE: Appeal from ruling permitting Fifth Amendment defense.

FACT SUMMARY: Bouknight (D), who was ordered by Baltimore City Department of Social Services (P) to produce Maurice M., an abused child over whom she had custody, refused, pleading the Fifth Amendment.

🏛 RULE OF LAW
The custodian of a child may not invoke the Fifth Amendment to resist a court order to produce the child.

FACTS: Maurice M. was adjudged an abused child by the juvenile court, which asserted jurisdiction and placed Maurice under the supervision of Baltimore City Dept. of Social Services (BCDSS) (P). BCDSS (P) agreed to let Bouknight (D), Maurice's mother, have custody of Maurice under certain conditions contained in a court-approved protective supervision order. Later, claiming that Bouknight (D) had violated the terms of the supervision order, BCDSS (P) petitioned for, and was granted, an order removing Maurice from Bouknight's (D) custody. The court held Bouknight (D) in contempt for failing to produce Maurice and ordered her imprisoned until she either produced Maurice or revealed his whereabouts. Bouknight (D) invoked the Fifth Amendment, arguing that the act of production of Maurice would amount to testimony regarding her control over and possession of Maurice, which might aid the state in prosecuting her.

ISSUE: May a custodian of a child invoke the Fifth Amendment to resist a court order to produce the child?

HOLDING AND DECISION: (O'Connor, J.) No. The Fifth Amendment applies only to testimonial communications. A person may not claim the Amendment's protections based upon the incrimination that may result from inspection of a thing sought to be produced. While the Fifth Amendment may be available to a person who complies with a requirement (e.g., order to produce) after invoking the privilege and subsequently facing prosecution, it does not justify refusal to comply with an order to produce. Reversed.

▶ ANALYSIS

While this case excerpt makes it clear that the Fifth Amendment may not be invoked to resist an order to produce, it does not address to what extent the amendment may be used to shield a defendant from subsequent prosecution. The Court specifically left this question for another day: "We are not called upon to define the precise limitations that may exist upon the state's ability to use the testimonial aspects of Bouknight's [D] act of production in subsequent criminal proceedings."

■■■

Quicknotes

CHILD ABUSE Conduct harmful to a child's physical or mental health.

FIFTH AMENDMENT Provides that no person shall be compelled to serve as a witness against himself, or be subject to trial for the same offense twice, or be deprived of life, liberty, or property without due process of law.

■■■

In re Eden F.

Minor child

Conn. Sup. Ct., 250 Conn. 674, 741 A.2d 873 (1999).

NATURE OF CASE: Appeal from reversal of termination of parental rights.

FACT SUMMARY: Ann F.'s parental rights were terminated as to her two minor daughters, Eden F. and Joann F. based primarily on her repeated inability to care properly for Eden's special needs or to provide a safe, stable environment for either daughter. Ann appealed the termination on the basis that the department failed to make reasonable reunification attempts.

RULE OF LAW
The statutory requirement of clear and convincing evidence of reunification attempts prior to termination of parental rights is not retroactive.

FACTS: Ann F. spent her childhood in foster care and was admitted on multiple occasions to a psychiatric hospital. Her diagnoses included schizophrenia and bipolar disorder. Ann met Thomas F. at the hospital, married him, and they had Eden F. in 1988. The department of children and families services (DCF) removed Eden at five days old because of Ann's psychiatric state. Eden remained in foster care until she was three years old. In February 1991, Eden returned to Ann's care despite remaining in the legal custody of DCF. Eden's commitment to the state was revoked in August 1991. In 1992, Ann became the subject of multiple reports because she often complained about "strange goings on" in her home, sexual abuse, and others reported her conduct toward Eden. Ann was pregnant with her boyfriend's child, Joann. Another report was made in March 1993 that Ann left seven-month-old Joann in the care of four-year-old Eden at a hospital emergency room. DCF placed a 96-hour hold on the children, and Ann was admitted to the hospital. Eden and Joann remained in foster care and/or DCF custody from that date on. Ann continued inpatient and outpatient psychiatric treatment while participating in regular visits with her girls. The girls were committed to DCF custody, and Ann worked with DCF on her expectations. In 1994, Eden returned to Ann's care after a series of unsupervised visits leading to overnight visits and then a full return. The reunification quickly deteriorated, and Eden was undergoing a full series of evaluations at DCF's request. Eden's results came in 1995 with a diagnosis of Reaction Attachment Disorder and other behavioral and psychological issues. Ann had trouble enrolling Eden in school, and the family therapist moved, so the two were not in therapy for a number of months. Ann had a crisis telephone line enabling her to reach DCF in an emergency, but she once left a message that was not returned for five days. In March 2005, Eden returned to

foster care after Ann left her in the care of two men who broke apart their home. DCF petitioned to terminate the parental rights of Ann, Thomas, and Joann's father, Randy, in June 1995. The grounds for termination included Ann's failure to progress, the men's abandonment of their children, and prior adjudications of neglect. Thomas consented to termination. The trial court found, *inter alia*, that DCF made reasonable attempts at reunification. The appellate court reversed the termination of Ann's parental rights to both girls on the basis that the facts did not support such a finding with clear and convincing evidence. The appellate court remanded with instructions to dismiss the petitions. DCF appealed.

ISSUE: Is the statutory requirement of clear and convincing evidence of reunification attempts prior to termination of parental rights retroactive?

HOLDING AND DECISION: (Palmer, J.) No. The statutory requirement of clear and convincing evidence of reunification attempts prior to termination of parental rights is not retroactive. DCF claims that the appellate court wrongly included an element for proving by clear and convincing evidence that reasonable attempts at reunification were made because no such element existed in the statute at the date the petitions were filed. Ann claims that DCF was required to prove such an element, or alternatively, that the statutory amendments are retroactive. A trial court must first adjudicate a proper statutory ground for termination of parental rights in the adjudicatory phase and then determine whether termination is in the child's best interests in the dispositional phase. Language requiring attempts at reunification was not part of the termination statute at the time the petitions were filed. The court was merely required to make a written finding as to any attempts that were made for reunification. Ann claims that the appellate court's interpretation is supported by public policy. Ann also claims support is found in the federal Adoption Assistance and Child Welfare Act of 1980, but the Act merely sets forth eligibility requirements for federal assistance to state foster care rather than individual guidance in termination cases. Finally, Ann makes a due process claim, but reunification attempts were not constitutionally mandated prior to termination. The legislature could have made such a requirement prior to 1995, but did not. Nothing indicates that the legislature intended the added language to apply retroactively despite legislative comments during the bill debate. Substantive protections are presumptively prospective and the requirement for reunification efforts is certainly substantive. Finally, the

Continued on next page.

additional amendments to the act cannot be applied retro-actively and Ann makes no attempt to distinguish the amendments. Ann certainly made some progress during these past years, and she clearly loves her children. Her ongoing psychiatric issues, however, and the expert testimony during the trial support the trial court's finding that she has failed to make satisfactory progress. The trial court also reasonably found termination to be in Eden's best interests despite the lack of a presently available adoptive home. Adoption is a preferred outcome, but termination may still be in a child's best interests even if adoption is not immediately possible. Reversed and remanded to affirm the trial court's findings.

DISSENT: (McDonald, J.) The trial court should be required to find on clear and convincing evidence that reasonable reunification attempts were made and any finding that this was accomplished is clearly erroneous. Further, the trial court erred in finding Ann had not rehabilitated herself and that termination was in Eden's best interests. The U.S. Supreme Court case of *Santosky* requires courts to find a basis for termination on at least clear and convincing evidence because of the severity of the result. The federal Adoption Assistance and Child Welfare Act of 1980 requires reunification attempts before federal money will be approved. Finally, public policy supports a requirement of reunification attempts. Eden was still being assessed herself when she was returned to her mother's care, which handicapped the relationship from the start. The crisis phone line was a message line and Ann's message was not returned for five days. Eden's inability to be enrolled in school resulted in Ann caring for her full-time for three weeks without respite. And no attempts were made to reunify Ann with Joann. The termination should be reversed.

ANALYSIS

The U.S. Supreme Court set the standard for termination of parental rights at clear and convincing evidence. *Santosky v. Kramer*, 455 U.S. 745 (1982). Reasonable efforts to reunite the family now fall under that standard, but only to the extent that states require the efforts as a prerequisite to termination. The Adoption and Safe Families Act of 1997 further clouded the issue because it places primary importance on the safety and security of the children rather than reunification with the family of origin.

Quicknotes

BEST INTERESTS OF CHILD Standard used by courts when rendering decisions which involve a child or children.

CHILD NEGLECT Conduct on the part of a parent or guardian that demonstrates unfitness on the part of that individual to provide the proper care and control over the child, resulting in harm or potential harm to the child's physical or mental health.

CLEAR AND CONVINCING EVIDENCE An evidentiary standard requiring a demonstration that the fact sought to be proven is reasonably certain.

DUE PROCESS RIGHTS The constitutional mandate requiring the courts to protect and enforce individuals' rights and liberties consistent with prevailing principles of fairness and justice, and prohibiting the federal and state governments from such activities that deprive its citizens of a life, liberty or property interest.

INTER ALIA Among other things.

PUBLIC POLICY Policy administered by the state with respect to the health, safety and morals of its people in accordance with common notions of fairness and decency.

TERMINATION OF PARENTAL RIGHTS The purposeful cessation of lawfully recognized rights between a child and its parents and of the parent to the child, including physical possession of the child, companionship and support, the right to discipline the child, and control over the child's property.

In re Michael B.

Minor child

N.Y. Ct. App., 80 N.Y.2d 299, 604 N.E.2d 122 (1992).

NATURE OF CASE: Appeal from custody determination.

FACT SUMMARY: Michael B. was in foster care with Maggie from infancy to early elementary school. His biological father was never declared unfit but fought a "best interests of the child" determination that the bond between the foster family and Michael had grown too strong for him to regain custody.

🏛 RULE OF LAW
Foster parents are not placed on equal footing with biological parents when considering the "best interests of the child" for custody determinations.

FACTS: Michael B. was born in July 1985 addicted to cocaine. His unwed mother voluntarily placed him in foster care. His four siblings were also in different foster homes. Michael needed extraordinary care and was placed in a preadoptive home with Maggie W. L. Michael's biological father was not listed on the birth certificate, but was identified by May 1987. The Catholic Child Care Society (Agency) sought to terminate the parental rights of both of Michael's biological parents on the basis that neither parent maintained contact or responsibility for Michael for more than a year despite the ability to do so. Michael's mother never appeared and was now deceased. Father consented to a finding of permanent neglect and commitment and custody to the Agency. He requested that the children be placed with their two godmothers, however. The Agency did not do so, and Father withdrew his plea and sought to obtain custody. In late May, he entered a residential drug rehabilitation program and began visitation with Michael. The parties agreed to a suspended finding of permanent neglect in August 1988 with Father to meet certain conditions to parent the children within 12 months. Near the end of the 12 months, the court held a hearing and found Father was in substantial compliance with his program despite not undergoing drug testing or finding employment. The Law Guardian requested a hearing in December 1989 for a best interests hearing for Michael based on his bonding with Maggie and lack of bonding with Father. Michael's siblings were released to Father in June and July of 1990. The court determined in November 1990 that it lacked jurisdiction to reconsider Michael's custody, and that he was wrongly in foster care. The court ordered increased visitation between Michael and Father and released Michael to Father in December 1990. The Agency and Law Guardian appealed, and the Appellate Division reversed and remanded for a new custody determination on the basis that the Family Court

retained jurisdiction to determine the best interests of the child despite the dismissed permanent neglect petition. The bonding issue was also relevant because of the possible impact on Michael. Michael remained with Father during the appeal. Testimony on remand overwhelmingly favored continued foster care, but the trial court affirmed custody to Father. The Appellate Division again reversed, awarded custody to Maggie, and remanded to a different Family Court judge to determine Father's visitation. The Appellate Division did not find Father unfit but considered the bonding between Michael and Maggie and Maggie's ability to better provide for Michael's needs. Michael remained with Maggie since early 1992. Father sought leave to appeal, which this court granted.

ISSUE: Are foster parents placed on equal footing with biological parents when considering the "best interests of the child" for custody determinations?

HOLDING AND DECISION: (Kaye, J.) No. Foster parents are not placed on equal footing with biological parents when considering the "best interests of the child" for custody determinations. No parties further contend that the Family Court failed to retain jurisdiction over the child's best interests until final disposition. Father claims that, absent a finding of unfitness, the court's inquiry is merely into whether the child will suffer "grievous injury" in a custody transfer. Agency argues that the extraordinary circumstances here require a determination of the more appropriate placement for the child. Voluntary foster placement is available to parents without the threat of losing custody of their children to a state-preferred home. Legal custody of voluntarily placed children remains with the state agency and not with the selected foster parents. Extended foster care is not preferred because permanent homes are best for children. Regular reviews of a parent's fitness after a finding of permanent neglect and regular reviews of the foster care are required and are not meant to result in permanent foster placements. Father's argument against a deeper inquiry into the bond of an extended foster placement is apt, because a biological parent will always lose despite an ability to care for the child. Agency argues that Father created this current situation and that the extraordinary circumstances allow for a look at the bond of the foster family. Both sides claim that their version of the appropriate inquiry is the definition of considering the "best interests of the child." The statute at issue, § 392(b), has a legislative history supporting temporary foster care and reunification with the biological parents if fit. The biological and foster parents are not on

Continued on next page.

equal footing with the court to determine the "better" parent. Pursuant to the statute, when the child is not free to be adopted, the inquiry is whether temporary foster care should continue or a return to the biological parent is appropriate. The biological parent's fitness is the primary concern for the best interests of the child inquiry. The court then considers the agency's support plan and the impact of custody change on the child. The child may well have bonded with the foster family after an extended placement, but the child is not free to be adopted, and this is not the goal of the child services agencies. The Appellate Division erred in granting custody to the foster parents because they are not "suitable persons" for custody under the statute. The agency also brings a petition to terminate parental rights, not the child's foster parents. Foster parent arrangements are addressed elsewhere within the statute. As to the current circumstances, new allegations have arisen as to Father's fitness because his children have once again been removed from his custody. Legal custody of Michael is returned to the Agency and physical custody will remain with Maggie. The case is remanded to Family Court for a new trial as to Father's fitness.

CONCURRENCE: (Bellacosa, J.) The statute is not appropriate to grant permanent custody to foster parents. The majority should not have limited the best interests analysis as it did because a broader inquiry is permissible under the court's *parens patriae* powers and precedent. The Appellate Division appropriately considered Michael's best interests and such an inquiry should be permissible and encouraged as a better method of obtaining finality and just results.

▶ ANALYSIS

Michael was seven and a half at the time of this opinion. He had lived with Maggie for the vast majority of his young life and every court agreed that the situation had become tragic. The psychological impact to Michael after a transfer of custody could be immeasurable. More foster care programs are now looking for permanency planning which provides for adoption if reunification is not possible. Taking human nature into account, however, it is difficult to surmise that foster parents are truly making the greatest effort to reunite the family after years of bonding with a potential adoptive child.

■■■

Quicknotes

BEST INTERESTS OF CHILD Standard used by courts when rendering decisions which involve a child or children.

PARENS PATRIAE Maxim that the government as sovereign is conferred with the duty to act as guardian on behalf of those citizens under legal disability.

TERMINATION OF PARENTAL RIGHTS The purposeful cessation of lawfully recognized rights between a child and its parents and of the parent to the child, including physical possession of the child, companionship and support, the right to discipline the child, and control over the child's property.

■■■

Kingsley v. Kingsley

Minor child (P) v. Parent (D)

Fla. Dist. Ct. App., 623 So. 2d 780 (1993).

NATURE OF CASE: Appeal from a court order terminating parental rights and granting a petition for adoption by a child's foster parents.

FACT SUMMARY: Gregory Kingsley (P) petitioned for termination of the parental rights of his natural parents and for adoption by his foster parents.

⚖ RULE OF LAW
A minor does not have legal standing to sue on his own behalf.

FACTS: At the age of 11, Gregory Kingsley (P) filed a petition in the juvenile division of the circuit court for termination of the parental rights of his natural parents. He filed a separate complaint, in the civil division of the circuit court, for declaration of rights and adoption by his foster parents, George and Elizabeth Russ. Before trial, Gregory's (P) foster parents, the guardian ad litem, and the Department of Health and Rehabilitative Services (HRS) filed additional petitions for termination of parental rights on Gregory's (P) behalf. Over Rachel Kingsley's (D) objection, the court tried the termination and adoption proceedings at the same time. After denying George Russ's (P) motion for summary judgment, the court terminated Rachel's (D) parental rights, granting the adoption petition. Rachel (D) appealed, arguing that Gregory (P) did not have the capacity to sue.

ISSUE: Does a minor have legal standing to sue on his own behalf?

HOLDING AND DECISION: (Diamantis, J.) No. A legal minor does not have legal standing to sue on his own behalf. However, although the trial court erred in allowing Gregory (P) to file the petition in his own name, the error was rendered harmless by the fact that separate petitions for termination of parental rights were filed on his behalf by his foster parents and HRS. Trying the two cases together also constituted error, but such error was harmless for two reasons. First, a great deal of the testimony concerning the relationship between Gregory (P) and his foster parents was admissible in the termination proceeding. Second, Rachel (D) has not shown that any comparisons between her parenting skills and those of the Russes (P) affected the trial court's decision regarding the determination of the issues of abandonment and neglect. The orders terminating parental rights and denying the motion for summary judgment are affirmed. However, the order granting adoption is reversed.

CONCURRENCE AND DISSENT: (Harris, C.J.) The majority is correct that so long as parents do nothing

to forfeit their fundamental liberty interest in the care, custody, and management of their child, no one, including the child, can interfere with that interest. However, the evidence here could have supported either a showing of abandonment or a showing of no abandonment. Thus, the errors cannot be considered harmless. The most egregious error was to try the adoption case along with the termination case. Because the procedural errors may well have affected the outcome of this case, the mother is entitled to a new hearing on the issue of abandonment under proper pleadings and confronted only by the proper parties.

▶ ANALYSIS

Because Gregory Kingsley brought this suit in his own name, it drew the attention of the public in a way no other parental rights termination case ever had. The media proceeded to mischaracterize the case as a boy seeking to "divorce" his parents. Rightists like Patrick Buchanan saw the lower court's grant of standing as a threat to family integrity. The appellate court's decision defused some of the controversy, but does not necessarily undo the benefits flowing from media focus on children's rights.

Quicknotes

GUARDIAN AD LITEM Person designated by the court to represent an infant or ward in a particular legal proceeding.

MOTION FOR SUMMARY JUDGMENT Judgment rendered by a court in response to a motion by one of the parties, claiming that the lack of a question of material fact in respect to an issue warrants disposition of the issue without consideration by the jury.

STANDING TO SUE Plaintiff must allege that he has a legally predictable interest at stake in the litigation.

TERMINATION OF PARENTAL RIGHTS The purposeful cessation of lawfully recognized rights between a child and its parents and of the parent to the child, including physical possession of the child, companionship and support, the right to discipline the child, and control over the child's property.

Adoption of Gregory

Minor child

Mass. Sup. Jud. Ct., 434 Mass. 117, 747 N.E.2d 120 (2001).

NATURE OF CASE: Appeal from termination of parental rights.

FACT SUMMARY: A father claimed the department of social services failed to accommodate his disability and thus wrongly obtained a termination of his parental rights. Both parents appealed the termination of their rights despite a history of disinterest in the child and inability to provide a safe, stable environment.

🏛 RULE OF LAW
The Americans with Disabilities Act does not serve as a defense to termination of parental rights.

FACTS: Gregory was born March 3, 1997, to Mother and Father. Mother immediately displayed a disinterest in caring for Gregory, and Father was unable to provide sufficient care and support. Gregory has a condition making him overly sensitive to loud noises, and both parents fought loudly in front of him, upsetting him. The hospital filed a mandated report of suspected potential neglect. The Department of Social Services (DSS) filed a petition on March 11, 1997 and received temporary custody of Gregory. DSS moved to dispense with Mother and Father's consent to adopt, and the court granted that motion. Gregory has extraordinary needs due to a panoply of medical conditions and cognitive delays. His foster parents provide physical and concentrated therapy for Gregory for hours each day. Attempting to reunite the family, DSS provided services to Mother and Father to improve their parenting skills regarding Gregory, but neither parent took advantage of the services. After a hearing, the trial court found both parents unfit, granted custody to DSS, and dispensed with parental consent to adopt. Mother and Father appealed.

ISSUE: Does the Americans with Disabilities Act serve as a defense to termination of parental rights?

HOLDING AND DECISION: (Ireland, J.) No. The Americans with Disabilities Act does not serve as a defense to termination of parental rights. Father claims that DSS did not make accommodations for his disability, Attention Deficit Hyperactivity Disorder, in violation of the Americans with Disabilities Act (ADA). The ADA requires public agencies to make reasonable accommodations to persons utilizing the agency services. The ADA does not apply to termination proceedings because such proceedings do not constitute "services, programs or activities," so the ADA cannot be a defense to a termination. The ADA does, however, require DSS to accommodate Father's disability for its offered services prior to seeking termination. DSS

did so here. DSS provided a social worker experienced in working with cognitively limited persons such as Father, and it rearranged visitation to better suit Father's schedule. The parenting instructions were also provided with input from experts in cognitively limited persons. Father did not take advantage of these accommodations and consistently demonstrated a decided lack of interest in participating in parenting classes or Gregory's life. Father also failed to raise his ADA concern until now despite being represented by counsel throughout this process. The parents also claim unsubstantiated findings of unfitness, but the trial court made ninety detailed findings to support the determination of unfitness. Mother was unable to provide basic care to Gregory if she became upset and Father once threatened to kill a social worker in a fit of frustration. Neither parent remained for the entire three-hour parenting classes or exhibited any interest in Gregory's medical appointments. The parents finally requested post-termination and post-adoption visitation, but the trial court appropriately left that decision up to the adoptive parents. Affirmed.

▶ ANALYSIS

Government agencies are required to provide accommodations to patrons with disabilities seeking to use the agency services. Such services include those provided by child welfare agencies in an attempt to reunify families who have temporarily lost custody. Despite the father's claims in this case, the agency actively provided accommodations for the parents' limitations even absent an explicit request for such accommodations. The final determination has to be the child's safety and welfare and not whether the parent received every possible accommodation despite a notable disinterest in improving parenting skills.

Quicknotes

AMERICANS WITH DISABILITIES ACT Prohibits discrimination in employment, housing, transportation and other services on the basis of an individual's physical or mental disabilities.

CHILD NEGLECT Conduct on the part of a parent or guardian that demonstrates unfitness on the part of that individual to provide the proper care and control over the child, resulting in harm or potential harm to the child's physical or mental health.

Continued on next page.

TERMINATION OF PARENTAL RIGHTS The purposeful cessation of lawfully recognized rights between a child and its parents and of the parent to the child, including physical possession of the child, companionship and support, the right to discipline the child, and control over the child's property.

Smith, Administrator, New York City Human Resources Administration, et al. v. Organization of Foster Families for Equality & Reform et al.

Foster parent organization (P) v. State agency (D)

431 U.S. 816 (1977).

NATURE OF CASE: Appeal from a judgment declaring a state foster-care statute unconstitutional.

FACT SUMMARY: The district court held that a New York statute allowing agency removal of children from foster homes without a hearing was a denial of the constitutional right to due process.

🏛 RULE OF LAW
A state foster-care statute which allows an agency to remove children from foster homes after notifying the foster parents in advance and allowing them an opportunity to contest the decision does not violate due process requirements.

FACTS: The Organization of Foster Families for Equality and Reform (Organization) (P) challenged a New York statute which allowed the state Department of Social Services (D) to remove children from foster homes, contending it constituted a denial of due process. The statute provided that the Department (D) could, in its discretion, remove a child from a foster home. It required that the agency give the foster parents ten-day written notice, and gave the foster parents the right to request a conference where they could be represented by counsel and informed of the reasons for the removal, and to contest the removal. The foster parents could then seek a full hearing and then judicial review. The district court held that due process required a child be afforded a hearing at which all relevant parties could testify prior to removal. The Department (D) appealed.

ISSUE: Does due process require that a child be afforded a hearing prior to his removal from a foster home?

HOLDING AND DECISION: (Brennan, J.) No. A state foster-care statute which allows an agency to remove children from a foster home after notifying the foster parents and affording them an opportunity to contest the removal does not violate due process. Foster-parent rights are created by the state. As a result, any relationship between foster parents and children includes the state as a partner. Therefore, the state may prescribe removal procedures. In this case, the procedures involved adequately protected the public and private interests and did not present an unsatisfactory potential for error. Reversed.

▶ ANALYSIS

In *Rivera v. Marcus*, 696 F.2d 1016 (2d Cir. 1982), the federal court held that due process was denied when a state removed one of two siblings from a foster parent who was a half sister. The sister did not waive any familial interest protected by due process when she consented to be a foster parent.

Quicknotes

DUE PROCESS RIGHTS The constitutional mandate requiring the courts to protect and enforce individuals' rights and liberties consistent with prevailing principles of fairness and justice, and prohibiting the federal and state governments from such activities that deprive its citizens of a life, liberty or property interest.

Wilder v. Bernstein

Parties not identified.

848 F.2d 1338 (2d Cir. 1988).

NATURE OF CASE: Appeal from settlement of class action.

FACT SUMMARY: Appellants appealed from the settlement of a class action suit that was initially brought to challenge the state law provisions regarding religious matching in connection with publicly funded childcare placements.

RULE OF LAW
The state-sponsored scheme for child placement must be racially and religiously free of discrimination.

FACTS: New York children may enter the foster care system by being voluntarily placed or through a Family Court finding of abuse and neglect resulting in involuntary placement. New York may care for the children in its own agencies or contract with private agencies. The preference has long been for private agencies, most of which are religiously affiliated. 90% of the per diem costs for each child are paid with federal, state, and city funds. Statutory law requires a child to be placed with a placement of similar faith when practicable. Religious placement is one of many relevant factors and is not determinative. A challenge, *Wilder I*, to the religious placement statute occurred because of the use of public funds in the placements. The court determined that the statute could be found to "impermissibly inculcate religion" but the State had an obligation to enforce the biological parents' religious choices when placing the child. The court upheld the statute. The fourth amended complaint was filed at the time of the settlement now at issue. Among the claims was that Black children were placed less often in the better-funded Catholic and Jewish agencies; that Protestant children are not placed as often as children in the Catholic and Jewish programs; that the Establishment Clause is violated; and that Protestant children face limited ability to practice their faith when placed in Catholic and Jewish agencies.

ISSUE: Must the state-sponsored scheme for child placement be racially and religiously free of discrimination?

HOLDING AND DECISION: (Newman, J.) The settlement's stated purpose was the assurance of placement of children without racial and religious discrimination in a manner consistent with state and federal constitutions. The city would place children on a first-come, first-served basis with a preference for religious matching honored only to the extent that it does not give a child greater access to a program over other similarly situated children. The appellants set forth four objections to the settlement: (1) it should not have been approved in the absence of a prima facie case of discrimination because it adopts race-conscious remedies; (2) it violates state requirements for religious matching; (3) it infringes on the free exercise rights of children and parents; and (4) it will foster excessive entanglement between government and religion in violation of the Establishment Clause. The first claim with respect to race-conscious remedies is based on the requirement that statistics be maintained as to the race and religion of each child placed with the agency; however, such statistics are not intended to force each agency to take its proportionate share of each group only to determine whether discrimination is in fact occurring. With respect to the third argument, so long as the state makes reasonable efforts to assure that the religious needs of the children are met during the interval in which the state assumes parental responsibilities, the free exercise rights of the children and their parents are not violated. Last the appellants contend that the settlement violates the Establishment Clause because it will foster excessive entanglement between the state and religion. In the childcare context the state has a responsibility to act in the place of parents when they cannot discharge their own responsibilities, including assuring that the religious needs of the children are met. Toward this end there will be some degree of entanglement, but the entanglement standard cannot be applied as rigorously here as in the context of aid to private religious schools. The settlement on its face does not exceed that which is appropriate in the context of state-sponsored childcare in substitution of the responsibilities of parents. Affirmed.

ANALYSIS

The court here adopts a less stringent standard with respect to Establishment Clause analysis in the childcare context where the state assumes the responsibilities of parents and therefore is obliged to also meet the children's religious needs in some manner. The court states that in the childcare context it is permissible to accept some risks of entanglement and to assess such entanglement on the basis of what actually occurs, not what might occur, so that certain arrangements that may be permissible will not be invalidated.

Continued on next page.

Quicknotes

CLASS ACTION A suit commenced by a representative on behalf of an ascertainable group that is too large to appear in court, who share a commonality of interests and who will benefit from a successful result.

■━━■

DeShaney v. Winnebago County Dept. of Social Services

Abused child (P) v. State agency (D)

489 U.S. 189 (1989).

NATURE OF CASE: Appeal of a child abuse case based on due process grounds.

FACT SUMMARY: Winnebago County Department of Social Services (D) had reason to suspect that DeShaney (P) was repeatedly abused by his father but took no steps to remove DeShaney (P) from his father's custody.

RULE OF LAW

The Due Process Clause does not confer an affirmative right to state protection from child abuse, nor does it create a duty to protect against such abuse.

FACTS: In 1980, when DeShaney (P) was one year old, his parents divorced, and custody was granted to his father. Beginning in 1982, Winnebago (D) learned that DeShaney (P) received medical attention for suspicious injuries. Over a period of several months, a caseworker visited DeShaney (P) and recorded several more instances of suspicious injuries but did nothing else. In 1984, DeShaney (P) was beaten so severely by his father that he fell into a coma and required emergency brain surgery that left him profoundly retarded. DeShaney (P) and his mother sought redress under 42 U.S.C. § 1983, alleging a deprivation of liberty without due process of law by Winnebago's (D) failure to protect DeShaney from known child abuse. The lower courts rejected this claim on the basis that no duty to protect against private violence existed and that an attenuated causal connection was insufficient to establish constitutional deprivation. DeShaney (P) appealed.

ISSUE: Does the Due Process Clause confer an affirmative right to state protection from child abuse or create a duty to protect against such abuse?

HOLDING AND DECISION: (Rehnquist, C.J.) No. The Due Process Clause does not confer an affirmative right to government protection from child abuse, nor does it create an affirmative duty to protect against such abuse. The Due Process Clause clearly provides that states shall not "deprive any person of life, liberty, or property, without due process of law." There is no requirement that the Due Process Clause extends to imposing an affirmative obligation to ensure safety from private violence. Instead, the Due Process Clause was intended "to protect the people from the state, not to ensure that the state protected them from each other." Thus, no affirmative right to government protection exists under the Due Process Clause. Moreover, the Due Process Clause does not create a duty arising from "special relationships" to protect against known dangers. Prior cases recognizing duties created by special relationships involved the provision of medical care to incarcerated prisoners and ensuring the safety of involuntarily committed mental patients. Here, DeShaney (P) was in his father's custody, not in state custody. Even though Winnebago (D) was aware of the abuse, the state took no part in its creation. Thus, Winnebago's (D) failure to protect DeShaney (P) from known abuse by his father does not violate the Due Process Clause. Although not asserted here, there may be a claim for redress under state tort law. Affirmed.

DISSENT: (Blackmun, J.) The fact that Winnebago (D) took active state intervention in DeShaney's (P) life should trigger the fundamental duty to protect DeShaney (P) once the danger of abuse became clear. Moreover, the court should not retreat into formalistic line-drawing between state action and inaction in interpreting the applicability of the Due Process Clause.

ANALYSIS

Generally, abuse reporting statutes require that physicians and other professionals like teachers and social workers report suspected incidents of child abuse. To encourage such reporting, most statutes provide immunity, in the absence of malice, from tort actions. However, much abuse still goes undiscovered for varying reasons. Physicians, for instance, may be reluctant to disrupt friendly relations with parents of the child or may not desire to spend the time required by juvenile court proceedings. Reporting statutes can also discourage parents from seeking medical attention for their children who have been abused.

Quicknotes

CHILD ABUSE Conduct that is harmful to a child's physical or mental health.

DUE PROCESS CLAUSE Clauses found in the Fifth and Fourteenth Amendments to the United States Constitution providing that no person shall be deprived of "life, liberty, or property, without due process of law."

Nichol v. Stass

Biological parents (P) v. Foster parents (D)

Ill. Sup. Ct., 192 Ill. 2d 233, 735 N.E.2d 582 (2000).

NATURE OF CASE: Appeal from dismissal of petition.

FACT SUMMARY: Jonathan Nichol, 2, died while in foster care with the Stasses (D). His parents sued the Stasses (D) who claimed sovereign immunity as state actors.

RULE OF LAW
Sovereign immunity does not apply to foster parents.

FACTS: Jonathan Nichol, 2, was placed into temporary foster care through the Human Enrichment and Development Association (HEDA) with the Stasses (D). He drowned in their toilet while in their care. The Nichols (P) sued the Stasses (D) on several grounds and later amended their petition to allege that HEDA was supervising the Stasses (D) and failed to provide adequate oversight. The Stasses (D) filed a motion to dismiss on the basis of sovereign immunity, which the trial court initially stated it intended to deny but then stayed order until a similar case in the appellate court was ruled upon. That case held that a foster parent was a state employee subject to sovereign immunity. The trial court granted the Stass (D) motion and gave immediate leave for plaintiffs to appeal. The appellate court affirmed on the basis that the Stasses (D) acted as agents for the state. The Nichols (P) appealed.

ISSUE: Does sovereign immunity apply to foster parents?

HOLDING AND DECISION: (Miller, J.) No. Case law conflicts on the issue of foster parents being state agents or employees. The Foster Parent Law does not deem them as such, the State Employee Indemnification Act identifies foster parents as employees for indemnification purposes only, and no statutes provide for state employment of foster parents. The Stasses (D) should have included their contract with HEDA with their motion to dismiss, but they did not, and the court must consider them independent contractors in the absence of any evidence to the contrary. The Stasses (D) argue that the state regulations with which they must comply to be foster parents cement their status as state agents or employees. To the contrary, these are merely licensing requirements. The Stasses (D) have not demonstrated they are state agents or employees. The appellate court determined that the state had a non-delegable duty to Jonathan and could be vicariously liable for injuries occurring to Jonathan while in foster care. The Nichols (P) are not seeking to recover from the state, and the state imposed its administrative regulations rather than its duty of care upon the Stasses (D). A non-delegable duty includes a right to physical details of performance, which is not included in the administrative regulations

of foster parents. The Stasses (D) alternatively argue that they stand *in loco parentis* to Jonathan and are shielded from liability by parental immunity. A limited form of parental immunity is available to foster parents in negligence actions. The limited immunity is similar to that afforded educators who are also paid person working in parent-like roles with children. Immunity does not extend to violations of the foster care regulations or findings of neglect. A material fact exists as to whether the plaintiffs' claim is barred by parental immunity. Reversed and remanded.

DISSENT: (Heiple, J.) Parental immunity should not be extended to foster parents because the foster parent relationship is intended to be temporary, the relationship is contractual and paid, and the state extensively regulates the foster parent conduct in a manner unprecedented in biological families. Immunizing foster parents from liability removes the encouragement to abide by the regulations. Immunity here would protect conduct which left Jonathan Nichol dead.

ANALYSIS

A similar case after this one involved an institution seeking parental immunity for its care of a foster child. The Illinois Supreme Court did not extend immunity to the institution on the basis that its staff exercised professional rather than parental judgment which resulted in the death of a child. The parental immunity in foster care is now effectively limited to cases involving a foster parent and a foster child in a quasi-parent relationship. Most child advocates argue that immunity for foster parents is a terrible idea because it further blurs the already murky status of a foster parent—parent or employee?

Quicknotes

IN LOCO PARENTIS A situation in which a person has assumed the responsibilities and obligations of a lawful parent without undergoing the legal adoption process.

PARENTAL IMMUNITY The immunity of a parent from liability in actions brought by his or her child claiming negligence.

SOVEREIGN IMMUNITY Immunity of government from suit without its consent.

CHAPTER 1

Adoption

Quick Reference Rules of Law

Florida Department of Children & Families v. Adoption of B.G.J.

State agency (P) v. Consent order (D)

Fla. Ct. App., 819 So. 2d 984 (2002).

NATURE OF CASE: Appeal from order granting consent to adoption.

FACT SUMMARY: Foster parents wished to adopt their foster child, but the state agency had already approved another set of adoptive parents. The foster parents sought the trial court's consent to adopt based on the existing bond between the parents and child and the trial court granted the consent order.

> ## RULE OF LAW
> The trial court does not have jurisdiction to grant adoption consent to a family when DCF has approved a different adoptive family.

FACTS: B.G.J. was born in 2000 to a cocaine-addicted mother and placed into foster care with J.M. and G.M. Custody was later granted to the Florida Department of Children & Families (DCF) (P) after termination of the biological parents' rights in 2001. J.M. and G.M. contacted DCF (P) about adopting B.G.J. but the DCF policy is to keep sibling groups together and B.G.J.'s siblings were adopted by K.W. and M.W. in March 2001. Hearings were held regarding adoption options for B.G.J. A DCF administrator testified to a personal preference to keep B.G.J. with his foster parents but stated that DCF (P) was still considering placement with K.W. and M.W. After another hearing and an evaluation of each family, DCF (P) determined not to place B.G.J. with J.M. and G.M. permanently. In September 2001, DCF (P) approved K.W. and M.W. to adopt B.G.J. and B.G.J.'s Guardian Ad Litem objected based on the bond between the child and his foster parents. The trial court found it in B.G.J.'s best interests to remain with J.M. and G.M. and further found that DCF (P) consented at the prior hearing to the adoption when the administrator expressed a preference for J.M. and G.M. DCF (P) appealed.

ISSUE: Does the trial court have jurisdiction to grant adoption consent to a family when DCF has approved a different adoptive family?

HOLDING AND DECISION: (Stevenson, J.) No. The trial court does not have jurisdiction to grant adoption consent to a family when DCF has approved a different adoptive family. DCF (P) is in the best position to select and approve adoptive families for the children in its custody. This court stated as much in a prior case where the court sided with DCF in its selection rather than the trial court's determination. DCF policy to keep siblings together and its match selection process resulted in DCF determining K.W. and M.W. to be the most appropriate adoption selection. The trial court did not find DCF's selection to be

of inappropriate parents, and it cannot then interfere with DCF's decision. Further, the DCF administrator testimony was oral, equivocal, and not binding upon DCF. Reversed and remanded to allow K.W. and M.W. to adopt B.G.J.

ANALYSIS

The trial court retains jurisdiction to determine the best interests of the child until final disposition of a termination and adoption case. The court cannot, however, substitute its individual judgment for that of the experienced child welfare agency absent a finding that the agency selected an unfit family. To permit otherwise would bring an unacceptable level of uncertainty into the adoption process because the court could always undermine the DCF selection.

Quicknotes

BEST INTERESTS OF CHILD Standard used by courts when rendering decisions which involve a child or children.

GUARDIAN AD LITEM Person designated by the court to represent an infant or ward in a particular legal proceeding.

TERMINATION OF PARENTAL RIGHTS The purposeful cessation of lawfully recognized rights between a child and its parents and of the parent to the child, including physical possession of the child, companionship and support, the right to discipline the child, and control over the child's property.

Vela v. Marywood

Mother (P) v. Child-placement agency (D)

Tex. Ct. App., 17 S.W.3d 750 (2000).

NATURE OF CASE: Appeal from termination of parental rights.

FACT SUMMARY: Corina Vela (P), unmarried and pregnant, sought guidance and information from Marywood (D), a licensed child-placement agency. Vela (P) signed a relinquishment document, and the court subsequently terminated her parental rights. Vela (P) appealed, stating she did not voluntarily sign the relinquishment form.

> 🏛 **RULE OF LAW**
> A child-placement agency must provide full disclosure to an expectant mother before a court terminates parental rights according to a signed relinquishment document.

FACTS: Vela (P) was a nineteen-year-old, unmarried, pregnant woman, who sought guidance and information from Marywood (D), a licensed child-placement agency. Aundra Moore, a Marywood (D) counselor, met with Vela (P) several times, and they discussed the benefits of an open adoption. Vela (P) felt assured that she would have contact with her baby after the adoption took place, and she subsequently signed a relinquishment form. The day after the birth of her son, Vela (P) changed her mind and contacted Moore about terminating the adoption process. Moore informed Vela (P) that the relinquishment was irrevocable. The court terminated Vela's (P) parental rights, and Vela (P) appealed.

ISSUE: Must a child-placement agency provide full disclosure to an expectant mother before a court terminates parental rights according to a signed relinquishment document?

HOLDING AND DECISION: (Yeakel, J.) Yes. A child placement agency must provide full disclosure to an expectant mother before a court terminates parental rights according to a signed relinquishment document. Moore assured Vela (P) that the adoption would be an open one, and Vela (P) relied on those representations. Marywood (D) disclosed part of the process and its consequences to Vela (P) and thus had a duty to make a complete disclosure that the open adoption plan would not be legally binding after termination of Vela's (P) parental rights. Moore also placed herself in a confidential relationship with Vela (P) and had a duty to act in good faith. No evidence exists that Vela (P) would have moved forward in the adoption process if the open adoption plan were not allowed. The relinquishment affidavit was procured through Marywood's (P) misrepresentations and was thus not voluntarily signed. Reversed.

▌ **ANALYSIS**

A birth parent has a specific period of time in which to change her mind, which change can greatly and detrimentally affect adoptive parents. Birth parents, however, must be able to make the difficult choice to enter the adoption process voluntarily without misrepresentations and interference from supposedly helpful agencies. Some courts, however, disagree with the *Vela* court that coercive influence may be sufficient to revoke a relinquishment affidavit.

■=■

Quicknotes

GOOD FAITH An honest intention to abstain from taking advantage of another.

TERMINATION OF PARENTAL RIGHTS The purposeful cessation of lawfully recognized rights between a child and its parents and of the parent to the child, including physical possession of the child, companionship and support, the right to discipline the child, and control over the child's property.

■=■

Matter of Petrie

Retention of counsel for adoption proceedings

Ariz. Sup. Ct., 154 Ariz. 295, 742 P.2d 796 (1987).

NATURE OF CASE: Appeal from disciplinary proceeding.

FACT SUMMARY: Petrie (D) contended that he had no attorney-client relationship with the Pietzes and, therefore, did not violate disciplinary rules by representing another couple in the same adoption.

🏛 RULE OF LAW
An attorney cannot represent two competing couples in the adoption of a child.

FACTS: The Pietzes consulted with attorney Petrie (D) on the adoption of a child. Petrie (D) agreed to represent them when they found a suitable child. After 1½ years, the Pietzes contacted Petrie (D) through a third party and informed him of the availability of a child. Petrie (D) wrote to the Pietzes asking them if they were interested in the adoption. They indicated they were. Petrie (D) subsequently arranged the adoption for another couple, after recommending them to the real mother. The Pietzes brought a complaint with the State Bar (P), contending Petrie (D) violated professional ethics. Petrie (D) appealed the Bar's (P) disciplinary findings, contending he had no attorney-client relationship with the Pietzes.

ISSUE: Can an attorney represent competing couples in an adoption?

HOLDING AND DECISION: (Holohan, J.) No. An attorney cannot represent competing couples in an adoption. Petrie (D) established an attorney-client relationship with the Pietzes at his first meeting with them. His subsequent representation of the second couple created a conflict of interest. His recommendation to the natural mother that the second couple be selected clearly breached the duty between attorney-client. Thus, the disciplinary order of a 30-day suspension was proper.

▶ ANALYSIS

Adoptions may be arranged through one attorney under the right circumstances. If there is simply the natural mother and the adoptive parents involved, no conflicting interests usually arise. However, if such interests do conflict, separate counsel should be retained.

■===■

Quicknotes

ATTORNEY-CLIENT RELATIONSHIP The confidential relationship established when a lawyer enters into employment with a client.

CONFLICT OF INTEREST Refers to ethical problems that arise, or may be anticipated to arise, between an attorney and his client if the interests of the attorney, another client or a third party conflict with those of the present client.

■===■

Ferdinand v. Department for Children and Their Families

Mother (P) v. State agency (D)

768 F. Supp. 401 (D.R.I. 1991).

NATURE OF CASE: Motion for a permanent injunction.

FACT SUMMARY: When the Department for Children and Their Families (D) refused Rose Ferdinand's (P) request for an adoption subsidy because it had been waived at the time of adoption, the court issued a temporary restraining order to qualify Ferdinand (P) for adoption assistance payment and other related benefits.

🏛 RULE OF LAW
The state has an affirmative duty to fully explain all available assistance programs so that potential adoptive parents can make an informed decision.

FACTS: The Ferdinands were both employed when they adopted Nia, a black child. The Ferdinands later divorced. Rose Ferdinand (P) received no child support and had to support Nia, as well as another younger child. When she requested adoption assistance, the Department (D) denied the "belated" request, contending that the Ferdinands were offered and declined such at the time of the adoption and any further entitlement had been waived. Rose (P) moved for a preliminary injunction, alleging that proper benefits were not explained and the case should be re-opened based on extenuating circumstances. The court issued a temporary restraining order, and Rose (P) sought a permanent injunction that the Department (D) grant her the requested benefits and services.

ISSUE: Does the state have an affirmative duty to fully explain all available assistance programs so that potential adoptive parents can make an informed decision?

HOLDING AND DECISION: (Pettine, Sr. J.) Yes. The state has an affirmative duty to fully explain all available assistance programs so that potential adoptive parents can make an informed decision. The fact that Mrs. Ferdinand (P) was never made aware of her ability to qualify for nominal assistance that would leave the door open for later recalculations despite her earlier waiver of a subsidy. constitutes an extenuating circumstance. In fact, the Department's (D) own procedures regarding adoption subsidies indicate that it is not the adoptive parents' needs, but rather the child's needs that determine eligibility for assistance. The Ferdinands' out-of-state residency did not and does not affect their eligibility for the Adoption Assistance Program. Motion granted.

▶ ANALYSIS

Some form of subsidized adoption has been adopted in all states. The Adoption and Safe Families Act of 1997 revised federal child welfare law. Reasonable efforts to reunite families are mandated by this law.

Quicknotes

PERMANENT INJUNCTION A remedy imposed by the court ordering a party to cease the conduct of a specific activity until the final disposition of the cause of action.

TEMPORARY RESTRAINING ORDER A court order preserving the status quo pending a hearing regarding injunctive relief.

In the Matter of the Adoption of K.J.B., L.D.B., and R.J.B.

Minor children

Kan. Sup. Ct., 265 Kan. 90, 959 P.2d 853 (1998).

NATURE OF CASE: Appeal from granted petition for stepparent adoption.

FACT SUMMARY: The children's stepfather sought to adopt them and claimed no need for the biological father's consent, because the father had not met his parental responsibilities for two years. The biological father argued his consent was certainly necessary based on his financial support during the relevant time period.

> ### 🏛 RULE OF LAW
> A parent's social security payments for the benefit of minor children qualify as credits to the parent's child support liability and constitute the assumption of parental duties.

FACTS: After their parents' divorce in 1989, L.D.B. and R.J.B. lived with their mother and K.J.B. lived with their father. Father was under a monthly child support order of $254 for L.D.B. and R.J.B., but he only made a single $98 payment in June 1996. K.J.B. was soon determined to be a child in need of services, so K.J.B. joined the siblings with the mother. The mother married Stepfather in 1991. Father began receiving social security disability benefits with portions paid to his children's benefit in 1991 with benefits backdated to 1990. The children received $255 monthly. Father visited the children for one year, and then custody of all three was adjudicated to the mother, and the court ordered supervised visitation because of Father's mental problems. Father saw the children four times in the following three months. In 1992, Father moved for specific visitation rights, which were granted and he followed until September 1993. The mother moved to alter the visitation schedule in October 1993, and Father had no contact with the children since. Father did not appear at the January hearing on mother's motion, so the court stayed its grant of visitation rights until Father requested them. Father later testified he was involuntarily committed to a state hospital from October–December 1993. Father further testified that Stepfather informed him the children were no longer his and to stop calling, so Father stopped contacting them. Father spent additional time in hospital care and in jail for Driving Under the Influence. Stepfather filed a petition before the magistrate judge to adopt the children in November 1995 with the claim that Father's consent was unnecessary, because he had failed or refused to assume parental duties for two years. The issue was removed to federal court, and the district court determined that father's social security benefits payments and incidental contacts were insufficient assumption of parental duties. The magistrate judge then granted Stepfather's petition and

Father filed a motion to stay pending appeal of the district court decision.

ISSUE: Do a parent's social security payments for the benefit of minor children qualify as credits to the parent's child support liability and constitute the assumption of parental duties?

HOLDING AND DECISION: (Six, J.) Yes. A parent's social security payments for the benefit of minor children qualify as credits to the parent's child support liability and constitute the assumption of parental duties. The court first considers the appropriate standard of review. First, the evidence is reviewed favoring the prevailing party below with a conclusion Father did not assume parental duties. Next, Father's fitness is not controlling and neither are the best interests of the child. Third, adoption statutes are to be strictly construed in favor of the biological parent's rights. Finally, the court must determine Father's efforts to take advantage of all parenting opportunities when he was incarcerated and unable to fulfill parental obligations. In consideration of the district court's finding, the court may disregard all incidental parental contact. The issue is whether Father met a substantial portion of his child support obligation. Father's monthly social security benefits were more than the court-ordered obligation, and he thus financially provided for his children. The stepparent adoption cannot move forward absent parental consent when that parent has provided a substantial portion of judicially decreed child support. Father may not have met his emotional responsibilities, but he met his financial ones. Reviewing Father's duties of love and affection toward his children, one must conclude that he failed to assume parental duties. The lack of love and affection, however, does not override the meeting of his financial obligations. The statute must be strictly construed in Father's favor, so Father has not "failed or refused" to assume parental duties. Reversed.

DISSENT: (Abbott, J.) The legislature intended for the courts to consider the entire picture when determining the failure of a parent to meet his responsibilities. The Court of Appeals opinion should be affirmed.

▶ ANALYSIS

Stepparent adoption can be time-consuming and costly when the biological parent is missing or refuses to consent. States have different requirements to proceed with

Continued on next page.

stepparent adoption, but the biological parents are always given an opportunity to object.

Quicknotes

BEST INTERESTS OF CHILD Standard used by courts when rendering decisions which involve a child or children.

CUSTODY The granting of care and control of a child or children to a parent pursuant to an action for dissolution or separation.

STAY An order by a court requiring a party to refrain from a specific activity until the happening of an event or upon further action by the court.

STAY OF PROCEEDINGS The temporary cessation of proceedings by the court until one of the parties has performed an action required by the court pertaining to the suit.

VISITATION Rights awarded by the court in a divorce or custody proceeding to a parent who does not have custody over the child or children, permitting that parent to visit with the child or children.

In the Matter of the Adoption of C.D.M.

Minor child

Okla. Sup. Ct., 39 P.3d 802 (2001).

NATURE OF CASE: Appeal from grant of stepparent adoption petition.

FACT SUMMARY: The stepfather sought to adopt C.D.M. without the biological father's consent based on the lack of relationship between the father and child. The father argued that court orders and imprisonment prevented him from having the relationship and his consent was thus still required.

🏛 RULE OF LAW
A parent may not rely on court orders to excuse lack of relationship with his child and thus attempt to block a stepparent adoption proceeding.

FACTS: Kori Rene Wyman and Chad Louis Maxwell had C.D.M. on January 8, 1996. Maxwell has had no relationship with C.D.M. since July 1996. A court entered a permanent protective order against Maxwell for Kori and C.D.M. in August 1996. Maxwell was arrested in March 1997 for stalking Kori and violating the protective order. He pled guilty and was sentenced to a five-year sentence with the final two years suspended. In June 1997, Maxwell petitioned to determine paternity and for visitation with C.D.M. The court denied visitation and ordered monthly child support of $141.80. Maxwell then pled guilty to assault and battery of Kori when he also attempted to take C.D.M. He was sentenced to one year, and he began serving his sentences in November 1998. Paternity was decreed and visitation denied in December 1999 and child support ordered at $125.00 monthly. Maxwell never sent money for the support but his mother did send a few hundred dollars during the fall of 1999. Kori and her husband, David Lee Wyman, filed a petition for David to adopt C.D.M. without Maxwell's consent. The parties argued Maxwell's consent was unnecessary, because he willfully lacked a relationship with his child for 12 of the preceding 14 months and failed to comply substantially with a support order for the child.

ISSUE: May a parent rely on court orders to excuse lack of relationship with his child and thus attempt to block a stepparent adoption proceeding?

HOLDING AND DECISION: (Kauger, J.) No. A parent may not rely on court orders to excuse lack of relationship with his child and thus attempt to block a stepparent adoption proceeding. Maxwell argues that his violations of the protective order were an attempt to see his child and that his involuntary incarceration should not be construed as a willful lack of relationship. The Wymans must prove that Maxwell's consent is not necessary by clear and convincing evidence, because consent by the biological parents is presumed necessary. Maxwell has had no contact with C.D.M. since the child was an infant and excuses the lack of contact based on the protective order, the no-visitation paternity order, and the incarceration. Incarceration cannot serve as the sole basis for termination of parental rights, but the reason for the incarceration is certainly relevant. Other jurisdictions also consider the reason, the behavior before and after incarceration, and the parent's regard for his parental responsibilities. Maxwell never assumed his parental responsibilities or attempted to foster a loving, affectionate relationship with C.D.M. To the contrary, he has acted in total disregard for the child's well-being. The trial court properly determined that father's lack of relationship for the past 12 months was willful and negated the need for his consent to David's adoption of C.D.M. The trial court also did not err in finding adoption to be in C.D.M.'s best interests. Reversed and trial court decision affirmed.

DISSENT: (Opala, J.) The father was involuntarily incarcerated and had a court-ordered prohibition against visitation but the majority allows this to support a mother's claim of willful lack of relationship with the child. Today's ruling is constitutionally infirm and violates Maxwell's due process rights.

▶ ANALYSIS

Most states are hesitant to abridge the rights of biological parents, but this court clearly considered the totality of the circumstances in finding that the father intentionally lacked a relationship with his child. At first blush, it does seem that the court used its own orders against the biological father, but the father intentionally engaged in the conduct which placed him in prison and under a protective order. The father may not have intentionally lacked a relationship with the child after being punished for his conduct, but the intentional conduct from the beginning evidenced an intent to avoid a relationship.

■=■

Quicknotes

ASSAULT AND BATTERY Any unlawful touching of another person without justification or excuse.

BEST INTERESTS OF CHILD Standard used by courts when rendering decisions which involve a child or children.

Continued on next page.

CHILD SUPPORT Payments made by one parent to another in satisfaction of the non-custodial parent's legal obligation to provide for the sustenance of the child.

CLEAR AND CONVINCING EVIDENCE An evidentiary standard requiring a demonstration that the fact sought to be proven is reasonably certain.

DUE PROCESS RIGHTS The constitutional mandate requiring the courts to protect and enforce individuals' rights and liberties consistent with prevailing principles of fairness and justice, and prohibiting the federal and state governments from such activities that deprive its citizens of a life, liberty or property interest.

PROTECTIVE ORDER Court order protecting a party against potential abusive treatment through use of the legal process.

TERMINATION OF PARENTAL RIGHTS The purposeful cessation of lawfully recognized rights between a child and its parents and of the parent to the child, including physical possession of the child, companionship and support, the right to discipline the child, and control over the child's property.

Groves v. Clark

Birth mother (P) v. Adoptive parents (D)

Mont. Sup. Ct., 277 Mont. 179, 920 P.2d 981 (1996).

NATURE OF CASE: Appeal from denial of a petition for specific performance.

FACT SUMMARY: When Groves (P), the birth mother, was denied visitation rights agreed to before the adoption, she sued for specific performance of the agreement.

RULE OF LAW
Birth parents and prospective adoptive parents are free to contract for post-adoption visitation and trial courts must give effect to such contracts when continued visitation is in the best interest of the child.

FACTS: Groves (P) gave her child up for an "open adoption" by the Clarks (D) after the Clarks (D) had signed an agreement granting Groves (P) continued visitation rights. The Clarks (D) later refused Groves's (P) request to visit her daughter on her birthday. Groves (P) filed a petition for specific performance of her visitation agreement which the court denied, after holding that the agreement was void and unenforceable. Groves (P) appealed.

ISSUE: Are birth parents and prospective adoptive parents free to contract for post-adoption visitation and must trial courts give effect to such contracts when continued visitation is in the best interest of the child?

HOLDING AND DECISION: (Trieweiler, J.) Yes. Birth parents and prospective adoptive parents are free to contract for post-adoption visitation and trial courts must give effect to such contracts when continued visitation is in the best interest of the child. In this case, the parties did bargain for the right of visitation, and Groves insisted on such an agreement before consenting to the adoption. Furthermore, Montana has a new statutory provision recognizing agreements entered into between birth parents and prospective adoptive parents. Reversed and remanded.

ANALYSIS

The court in this case ruled that there be a hearing. If the district court concludes that the visitation agreement is in the child's best interests, there is no reason that such an agreement should not be enforced by the court. There has been a recent trend to allow the birth parents continued contact with their child after adoption.

Quicknotes

BEST INTERESTS OF CHILD Standard used by courts when rendering decisions which involve a child or children.

SPECIFIC PERFORMANCE An equitable remedy whereby the court requires the parties to perform their obligations pursuant to a contract.

Lankford v. Wright

Adoptee (P) v. Party not identified (D)

N.C. Sup. Ct., 347 N.C. 115, 489 S.E.2d 604 (1997).

NATURE OF CASE: Appeal from denial of equitable adoption.

FACT SUMMARY: The Newtons died intestate and without legally adopting their foster daughter, Barbara, despite a stated intention of doing so and a lifetime of holding her out as their only child. Barbara sought a declaration of her rights as an heir to the estate, but North Carolina did not recognize the doctrine of equitable adoption.

🏛 RULE OF LAW
North Carolina does recognize the doctrine of equitable adoption.

FACTS: Barbara Ann Newton Lankford lived with Clarence and Lula Newton pursuant to the Newtons' agreement with her birth mother. The Newtons held Barbara out to be her child, she took their last name, and she obtained a social security number as Barbara Ann Newton. Clarence Newton passed away, but Lulu and Barbara maintained a typical mother-daughter relationship throughout Barbara's adult years. At Lulu's death, her will, which named Barbara as co-administrator and provided specific bequests to her, could not be probated because an unknown person defaced a portion of it. The result was that Lulu died intestate. Barbara filed a declaratory action to determine her rights as heir to the estate, but administrators and named heirs moved for summary judgment. The trial court granted the motion as Barbara was never legally adopted. The Court of Appeals affirmed on the basis that North Carolina does not recognize equitable adoption. Barbara petitioned this court for discretionary review.

ISSUE: Does North Carolina recognize the doctrine of equitable adoption?

HOLDING AND DECISION: (Frye, J.) Yes. North Carolina does recognize the doctrine of equitable adoption. Equitable adoption exists to give legal force to the adoptive parent's intent when appropriate legal steps were never taken. Equitable adoption is not the equivalent to legal adoption, because it merely confers inheritance rights upon the adoptee. A foster child acting as a biological child is placed into the position she would be in had she been legally adopted. Necessary elements include: (1) Express or implied agreement to adopt the child; (2) reliance on that agreement; (3) biological parents' relinquishing custody; (4) the child lives with and acts toward the foster parents as a natural child; (5) foster parents taking the child into their home and treating her as a natural child; and (6) intestacy of the foster parents. This case presents clear and convincing evidence of each element. Equitable

adoption does not interfere with legal adoption and has been accepted by the majority of states. Reversed and remanded.

DISSENT: (Mitchell, C.J.) An equitable remedy should not be fashioned where statutory and legal rights exist to control inheritance. The legislative scheme to control intestate succession regarding adopted children is comprehensive and unambiguous. The foster parents here may have held the child out as their own, but they never legally adopted her. Equity cannot overrule statutory schemes.

▶ ANALYSIS

The states that recognize equitable adoption do so solely for inheritance purposes and not to avoid the legal requirements of termination of biological parents' rights and legal adoption by adoptive parents. Equitably adopted children typically have no additional rights other than a determination as to rights to the intestate estate of a foster parent. No one can establish custody through equitable adoption.

■=■

Quicknotes

EQUITABLE ADOPTION An oral contract to adopt a child, not executed in accordance with statutory requirements, giving rise to rights of inheritance in the child upon the death of the promisor.

INTESTATE To die without leaving a valid testamentary instrument.

MOTION FOR SUMMARY JUDGMENT Judgment rendered by a court in response to a motion by one of the parties, claiming that the lack of a question of material fact in respect to an issue warrants disposition of the issue without consideration by the jury.

■=■

Chambers v. Chambers

Virtual adoptee (P) v. Decedent's estate (D)

Ga. Sup. Ct., 260 Ga. 610, 398 S.E.2d 200 (1990).

NATURE OF CASE: Appeal from grant of summary judgment.

FACT SUMMARY: Pete Chambers (P) claimed to have been equitably adopted by Ethel Chambers and thus entitled to claim under her estate. Ethel's heirs (D) claimed that no equitable adoption or intent to adopt existed.

🏛 RULE OF LAW
Equitable adoption may not exist in the absence of an agreement and consent between the natural parent and the adoptive parent.

FACTS: Pete Carlton Chambers (P) was removed from his birth mother's care because she was in a mental institution when she gave birth. The mother consented to him being adopted by a Jones County couple, but it was learned that the wife was terminally ill. As Pete's (P) birth mother was originally another county's resident, she was requested to pick him up. She did so and later placed Pete (P) with Ethel Louise Chambers. Ethel raised Pete (P) from infancy, named him Pete Carlton Chambers, and held him out as her son. They later filed a petition to have his name legally changed, but the petition specifically stated that Ethel was not adopting him. Adopting him would have stopped foster care payments made to her for her care of Pete (P). After Ethel's death, Pete (P) sued Ethel's administrator, biological son Harold Gaines Chambers (D), and another biological son, George David Chambers (D), to have his status recognized as an equitable adoptee. Defendants filed a motion for partial summary judgment accompanied by Pete's (P) biological mother's affidavit that she never consented to an adoption, never had her parental rights terminated, and she did not surrender her parental rights to Ethel. The trial court granted the motion and Pete (P) appealed.

ISSUE: May equitable adoption exist in the absence of an agreement and consent between the natural parent and the adoptive parent?

HOLDING AND DECISION: (Fletcher, J.) No. Equitable adoption may not exist in the absence of an agreement and consent between the natural parent and the adoptive parent. Pete (P) must demonstrate the existence of an agreement between his biological mother and Ethel for adoption to make out his claim for equitable adoption. Another required element for an equitable adoption claim is his natural mother's consent to the adoption, which was negated by the mother's affidavit. Pete (P) simply fails to make out a case. Affirmed.

▶ ANALYSIS

Equitable adoption requires an agreement between the adoptive parents and the natural parents, performance from all parties, and the intestacy of the foster parents. The states that recognize equitable adoption do so solely for inheritance purposes and not to avoid the legal requirements of termination of biological parents' rights and legal adoption by adoptive parents. Equitably adopted children typically have no additional rights other than a determination as to rights to the intestate estate of a foster parent.

Quicknotes

EQUITABLE ADOPTION An oral contract to adopt a child, not executed in accordance with statutory requirements, giving rise to rights of inheritance in the child upon the death of the promisor.

INTESTATE ESTATE The property of an individual who dies without executing a valid will.

PARTIAL SUMMARY JUDGMENT Judgment rendered by a court in response to a motion by one of the parties, claiming that the lack of a question of material fact in respect to one of the issues warrants disposition of that issue without going to the jury.

Sonet v. Unknown Father

Adoptive parents (P) v. Biological father (D)

Tenn. Ct. App., 797 S.W.2d 1 (1990).

NATURE OF CASE: Appeal from dismissal of adoption petition.

FACT SUMMARY: An older mother sought to adopt an infant, but the infant was not thriving in her care. She appealed when the trial court denied her adoption petition.

> ## 🏛 RULE OF LAW
> Age is a relevant consideration for the child's best interests in an adoption petition.

FACTS: Harry Sonet, 62, married Mary Elizabeth, 65, in June 1987. That fall, the unwed teenaged daughter of the Sonets' (P) workman gave birth to Joseph Daniel Hasty. The mother surrendered the infant to the Sonets (P). In the spring of 1988, the Sonets (P) filed a petition to adopt Joseph. Mary and Joseph moved out in 1989, and Harry no longer pursued the petition. The protective services worker assigned to the Sonet case testified at trial to five reports of neglect, failure to thrive, and lack of electricity. The Florida authorities removed Joseph from Mary's (P) care in 1989, when strangers reported her for asking a stranger to watch Joseph at a park. Authorities became suspicious that she was kidnapping Joseph because of her age, out-of-state car registration, and lack of custody papers. The Florida Department of Health and Human Services took custody of Joseph for a couple of months, during which time he contracted several infections. In May 1989, legal custody was temporarily granted to the Department, and Joseph was placed in foster care. Mary (P) regained custody in June 1989 and claimed that Joseph was missing two fingernails and had bleeding toes from too-small shoes. On evaluation, Joseph was determined to be environmentally deprived and developmentally delayed, and the evaluator recommended against him being returned to Mary's (P) custody. Joseph's treating physician, however, felt that Joseph should be returned to Mary (P), and that his deficiencies were not related to his environment but to genetics. The trial court denied Mary's (P) petition and returned legal custody of Joseph to the Department for placement in a permanent home.

ISSUE: Is age a relevant consideration for the child's best interests in an adoption petition?

HOLDING AND DECISION: (Cantrell, J.) Yes. Age is a relevant consideration for the child's best interests in an adoption petition. Mary (P) had both negative and positive factors presented as evidence. Her age is certainly taken into account as it is relevant to the child's welfare. Mary (P) is now seventy years old and Joseph is three.

He has bonded with Mary (P), but she has only unrelated family members for help with his care. Joseph also had failed to thrive while in Mary's (P) care. The trial court did not err in denying the adoption petition.

▶ ANALYSIS

Most states have age limits on potential adoptive parents. Older persons may elect to adopt foreign-born children, but most international countries are also placing upper age limits for adoption as well. As the population continues to live longer, more couples put off having or adopting children until after careers are established, and the age limits are continually being reevaluated. Age is a relevant factor when considering the best placement for a child.

■▬■

Quicknotes

BEST INTERESTS OF CHILD Standard used by courts when rendering decisions which involve a child or children.

■▬■

Petition of R.M.G.

White foster parents (P) v. Black grandparents (D)

D.C. Ct. App., 454 A.2d 776 (1982).

NATURE OF CASE: Appeal of adoption hearing.

FACT SUMMARY: Adoptive custody of a black child was given to her natural grandparents rather than her white foster parents, and race was a factor in the making of this decision.

RULE OF LAW
Race is a legitimate factor in deciding upon the propriety of an adoption.

FACTS: D., a black, was born to an unwed, teenage mother. The mother put her up for adoption. In the meantime, D. was placed with Mr. and Mrs. H., who were white. The H.s petitioned to adopt D. However, D.'s natural grandparents also petitioned to adopt her. Both households appeared to be stable and capable of caring for D. The trial court found that although the H. household may have been slightly more appropriate for D. if the race issue were ignored, the court took the racial issue into account, as the statute governing adoptions permitted. The trial court awarded D. to the grandparents, and the H.s appealed.

ISSUE: Is race a legitimate factor in deciding upon the propriety of an adoption?

HOLDING AND DECISION: (Ferren, Assoc. J.) Yes. Race is a legitimate factor in deciding upon the propriety of an adoption. For the statute allowing race to be a factor to be valid, a compelling interest must be shown. The interest here is the welfare of the adoptive child, which the court holds to be compelling. The statute also must be precisely tailored to meet the interest. Here, the statute, rather than conferring any sort of stigma of invidious classification, merely permits a court to use it as a factor when appropriate to achieve the goal of serving the best interests of the child. [The court went on to hold that in evaluating race the trial court must evaluate the extent that the adoptive parents' race will affect the child's development, how the competing adoptive parents compare in this regard, and how significant the racial differences are when all other relevant factors are taken into consideration. Since the trial court did not use this analysis, the decision was reversed and remanded.]

CONCURRENCE: (Mack, Assoc. J.) The trial court impermissibly presumed that the race of the H.s would adversely affect D., without making supported factual findings in this regard.

DISSENT: (Newman, C.J.) Since using race as a factor is permissible and that is what the trial court did, its decision should be upheld.

ANALYSIS

As the years go by, more and more previously taken-for-granted classifications become disfavored. In areas such as employment and schooling, the classifications have tended to be held invalid. Allowing the use of race, the most suspect classification of all, to be a factor in a governmental decision presents itself as something of an anomaly. It would seem that the overriding interest of providing the child in question with the best home possible provides the impetus for this exception to the general rule.

Quicknotes

BEST INTERESTS OF CHILD Standard used today in consideration of adoption.

FOSTER PARENTS Parents appointed by law to serve as guardians of the child by virtue of their voluntary assumption of parental rights and responsibilities, and otherwise acting as the child's advocate in place of the child's natural parents.

Mississippi Band of Choctaw Indians v. Holyfield

Native American tribe (P) v. Adoptive parent (D)

490 U.S. 30 (1989).

NATURE OF CASE: Appeal from adoption order.

FACT SUMMARY: The trial court held that because the minor children were not born on, nor had they ever lived on, the reservation, the Tribe (P) had no jurisdiction over their adoption.

🏛 RULE OF LAW
Indian tribes have exclusive jurisdiction over child custody and adoption of Indian children domiciled on the reservation.

FACTS: Twin babies were born to members and domiciliaries of the Choctaw Tribe (P) and reservation. The children were born off the reservation and immediately placed for adoption with Holyfield (D), a non-Indian. The state court confirmed the adoption pursuant to a consent decree signed by the parents. The Tribe (P) moved to vacate the adoption order on the basis that it had exclusive jurisdiction over the adoption under the Indian Child Welfare Act of 1978 (I.C.W.A.). The court denied the motion on the basis that because the children were not born on, nor had they ever resided on, the reservation, they were not domiciliaries of the reservation, and thus the Tribe (P) did not have exclusive jurisdiction over the adoption. The court of appeals affirmed, and the Supreme Court granted review.

ISSUE: Do Indian tribes have exclusive jurisdiction over child adoptions where the children are domiciled on the reservation?

HOLDING AND DECISION: (Brennan, J.) Yes. Indian tribes have exclusive jurisdiction over child adoption where the children are domiciled on the reservation. The definition of domicile under the I.C.W.A. must be interpreted in light of national Indian policy; thus, a federal definition providing uniformity must be used. While the children were not born on the reservation and never resided there, they are still domiciliaries because their parents were domiciliaries at the time of birth. Thus, as domiciliaries, their adoption came under the exclusive jurisdiction of the Tribe (P). The state court had no jurisdiction in the matter. Reversed.

DISSENT: (Stevens, J.) The parents' unambiguous wish was to have the children adopted and to invoke the jurisdiction of the state court. Thus, this avenue should have been available to them.

▶ ANALYSIS

The adoption of Indian children presents a unique problem. Statistics have shown a remarkably high incidence of the removal of such children from natural parents. Along with this has been an unusual placement of such children in non-Indian homes. This was thought to threaten the Indian culture and led to passage of the I.C.W.A. The I.C.W.A. is not an all-encompassing statute, and courts are required to supplement its provisions by analogizing from state and federal law.

Quicknotes

CONSENT DECREE A decree issued by a court of equity ratifying an agreement between the parties to a lawsuit; an agreement by a defendant to cease illegal activity.

Lofton v. Department of Children and Family Services

Foster parent (P) v. State agency (D)

358 F.3d 804 (11th Cir. 2004).

NATURE OF CASE: Appeal from grant of summary judgment.

FACT SUMMARY: Steven Lofton (P) is a homosexual seeking to adopt in Florida, but who is prevented by Florida statute § 63.042(3). He and six other homosexual, prospective adoptive parents challenged the constitutionality of the statute.

RULE OF LAW

The Florida statute does not impermissibly violate homosexuals' fundamental and equal protection rights by denying them the legal ability to adopt.

FACTS: Lofton (P) was the foster parent to three HIV-positive foster children. He sought to apply to adopt one of his foster children through the Department of Children and Family Services (DSS) (D), but refused to specify his sexual orientation on the application. Lofton (P) also did not note his live-in homosexual partner on the form. DSS (D) rejected Lofton's (P) application, because of his refusal to respond to their repeated queries about his homosexuality. The other plaintiffs are also homosexuals who sought to adopt specific children but were rejected under the Florida statute. The plaintiffs argue that the statute unconstitutionally violates their fundamental and equal protection rights. The district court granted summary judgment to Florida, and plaintiffs appealed.

ISSUE: Does the Florida statute impermissibly violate homosexuals' fundamental and equal protection rights by denying them the legal ability to adopt?

HOLDING AND DECISION: (Birch, J.) No. The Florida statute does not impermissibly violate homosexuals' fundamental and equal protection rights by denying them the legal ability to adopt. Adoption is a statutory privilege rather than a right in Florida, and the state is permitted to make otherwise-suspect classifications to protect the welfare of adoptable children. There are no fundamental rights to adopt, be adopted, or to apply for adoption. Nor is there a right to family integrity. Plaintiffs also argue that the statute impermissibly burdens a right to private sexual intimacy contending that *Lawrence v. Texas*, 539 U.S. 558 (2003), deemed that right a fundamental one. The *Lawrence* case is not particularly applicable here because no such right was identified in *Lawrence*, minor children are involved, and the state action in the case is statutory privilege rather than criminal sanction. The Florida legislature could also have determined under equal protection analysis that homosexuals are not similarly situated to unmarried individuals because unmarried individuals could eventually provide a married household for the child. Finally, plaintiffs misconstrue Florida's interest in placing adoptable foster children into permanent homes, because Florida may still place restrictions on the homes even when there is a backlog of adoptable children. It is not any home that will do just because it is a permanent one. The duty of the court is not to determine whether the Florida legislature is making the right decision in passing the statute, but whether the statute is rational. The statute is reasonable, rational, and does not exist merely because of animus toward homosexuals. Affirmed.

▶ ANALYSIS

This case received national attention because of celebrity support and media spotlights. The *Lofton* court employed highly deferential rational basis review and the burden for homosexuals seeking to adopt becomes nearly insurmountable. It is arguable that the *Lofton* decision is inconsistent with the *Lawrence* decision and contrary to the analysis of the *Lofton* court. The *Lawrence* decision stated that morality may not be the only reason behind constitutional decisions, and morality played such a large role behind the statute at issue in *Lofton*. States continue to alter their laws addressing rights affecting homosexuals, and adoption laws may evolve again, even in Florida.

Quicknotes

EQUAL PROTECTION CLAUSE A constitutional provision that each person be guaranteed the same protection of the laws enjoyed by other persons in like circumstances.

FUNDAMENTAL RIGHT A liberty that is either expressly or impliedly provided for in the United States Constitution, the deprivation or burdening of which is subject to a heightened standard of review.

RATIONAL BASIS REVIEW A test employed by the court to determine the validity of a statute in equal protection actions, whereby the court determines whether the challenged statute is rationally related to the achievement of a legitimate state interest.

RIGHT TO PRIVACY Those personal liberties or relationships that are protected against unwarranted governmental interference.

SUMMARY JUDGMENT Judgment rendered by a court in response to a motion made by one of the parties, claiming that the lack of a question of material fact in respect to an issue warrants disposition of the issue without consideration by the jury.

In re M.M.D.

Matter of both partners adopting child

D.C. Ct. App., 662 A.2d 837 (1995).

NATURE OF CASE: Appeal of denied participation in an adoption proceeding.

FACT SUMMARY: After one member of a gay couple had adopted a child, the other member of the couple sought to adopt as well, becoming a second "natural" parent.

🏛 RULE OF LAW
(1) A same-sex couple can adopt a child.
(2) If one member of an unmarried couple has adopted a child, the relationship will not be cut off if the other member of the couple adopts the child.

FACTS: A young pregnant woman responded to an ad in which a gay couple sought to adopt a child. Bruce (P), one member of the couple, adopted Hillary. Later, both Bruce (P) and his partner Mark (P) jointly petitioned to adopt Hillary. However, the same court that approved the original adoption ruled that the statute would terminate Bruce's (P) rights if Mark (P) were to adopt. Bruce (P) and Mark (P) appealed.

ISSUE:
(1) Can a same-sex couple adopt a child?
(2) If one member of an unmarried couple has adopted a child, will the relationship be cut off if the other member of the couple adopts the child?

HOLDING AND DECISION: (Ferren, Assoc. J.)
(1) Yes. A same-sex couple can adopt a child. The statute authorizing adoption does not specifically mention unmarried couples. However, the statute does include both singular and plural use of the word "parent," implying that any person or persons may adopt. The focus of applicable case law has consistently remained the best interests of the child. If the unmarried couple is fit, whether of the same sex or opposite sexes, there is no apparent reason why a member of the couple cannot adopt. Here, the couple is stable and successful. The trial judge had previously determined that Bruce's (P) adoption of Hillary was in her best interest. There appears to be no reason why Hillary should not be adopted by this couple.
(2) No. If one member of an unmarried couple has adopted a child, the relationship will not be cut off if the other member of the couple adopts the child. The purposes behind cutting off the rights of natural parents in an adoption include the need to clarify inheritance and establish a permanent relationship with the adoptive parent. Neither purpose is served by cutting off Bruce's (P) rights as the initial adoptive parent. Since the statute

authorizes adoption by a "spouse" where consent of the natural parent is given, it seems reasonable to allow Bruce (P) to consent to the adoption of Hillary by Mark (P). Bruce (P) can retain his parental relationship with Hillary when Mark (P) adopts. Reversed.

DISSENT: (Steadman, Assoc. J.) The statute in question only contemplated adoption by married parents. The only exception to the cut-off provision is where the husband or wife is also a natural parent of the child. It is the legislature's job, not the court's, to extend adoption rights to cover alternative family schemes.

▶ ANALYSIS

Should gay marriage ever be recognized, then the debate in this case would become academic. Once a gay couple were married, then the adoption statutes that refer to married couples would include them, and legislatures would have to act to specifically exclude gay couples from the provisions. In that case as well, the cut-off exception where one member of a gay couple was a natural parent would operate without any confusion.

■■■

Quicknotes

BEST INTERESTS OF CHILD Standard used by courts when rendering decisions which involve a child or children.

■■■

State ex rel. Torres v. Mason

Natural father (P) v. Judge in adoption proceeding (D)

Or. Sup. Ct., 315 Or. 386, 848 P.2d 592 (1993).

NATURE OF CASE: Petition for a writ of mandamus after denial of a motion to dismiss an adoption proceeding.

FACT SUMMARY: After Torres (P) and Wing were divorced, Wing agreed to allow their child to be adopted by an Oregon couple who took the child from the child's home in Washington state to the couple's Oregon home, but Torres (P) challenged the Oregon adoption proceeding for lack of jurisdiction.

RULE OF LAW
Jurisdiction for purposes of adoption exists if a child and at least one contestant have a significant connection to the state and substantial evidence exists in the state.

FACTS: A few years after Torres (P) and Wing, residents of the state of Washington, had a child, the couple divorced and custody of the child was awarded to Wing, the mother. They all continued to live in Washington state. Wing later consented to the adoption of the child by an Oregon couple, the Rays, who took the child from Washington to their home in Oregon. One month later, the Rays filed a petition to adopt the child. Mason (D), the circuit court judge, appointed the couple temporary guardians of the child. Torres (P) moved to dismiss the adoption proceeding, arguing that the Oregon court lacked subject-matter jurisdiction. After a hearing, Mason (D) denied Torres' (P) motion to dismiss. Torres (P) then filed this petition for an alternative writ of mandamus, which the supreme court granted.

ISSUE: Does jurisdiction for purposes of adoption exist if a child and at least one contestant have a significant connection to the state and substantial evidence exists in the state?

HOLDING AND DECISION: (Peterson, J.) Yes. Jurisdiction for purposes of adoption exists if a child and at least one contestant have a significant connection to the state and substantial evidence exists in the state. Oregon's Uniform Child Custody Jurisdiction Act (UCCJA) explicitly applies to a child custody determination, but unless adoptions are also covered, the purposes of the UCCJA are only partially achieved. Thus, the UCCJA applies to adoption proceedings. Whether it confers jurisdiction on the Oregon court in this proceeding is another matter, however. The Act does not say when a child's connection to a state becomes "significant." Here, the child had lived his whole life in Washington until one month before the adoption proceeding was commenced. Under the facts of this case, one month is not a sufficient passage of time to develop a significant connection under the UCCJA. Because the Oregon court lacked jurisdiction, the adoption proceeding should be dismissed.

ANALYSIS

Oregon did not qualify for default jurisdiction, either, since Washington had also adopted the uniform act, RCW 26.27 et seq. and actually had jurisdiction at the time of the adoption proceedings. RCW 26.27.030(1)(a) created Washington jurisdiction if, within six months before the commencement of the proceeding, a child has lived with a parent for six consecutive months in Washington.

Quicknotes

SUBJECT MATTER JURISDICTION A court's ability to adjudicate a specific category of cases based on the subject matter of the dispute.

WRIT OF MANDAMUS A court order issued commanding a public or private entity, or an official thereof, to perform a duty required by law.

McKinney v. State

Parents (P) v. State agency (D)

Wash. Sup. Ct., 134 Wash. 2d 388, 950 P.2d 461 (1998).

NATURE OF CASE: Appeal from a defense jury verdict.

FACT SUMMARY: When the McKinneys (P), adoptive parents, were not provided with all medical and social records of an adopted child until after formal adoption, they claimed the state adoption agency (D) was negligent.

🏛 RULE OF LAW
Adoptive parents may state a cause of action against an adoption placement agency for the negligent failure to meet the statutory disclosure requirements.

FACTS: The McKinneys (P) adopted a little girl that had been placed with them as a foster child. Although they knew she had behavior problems, had been in several other foster homes, was removed from the biological mother due to neglect, and that she was developmentally disabled, they adopted her. They later alleged that the adoption placement agency, the Department of Social and Health Services (DSHS) (D), was negligent when it failed to provide the baby's medical and social records when requested to do so before the formal adoption. The jury found that DSHS (D) was negligent, but that such negligence was not the proximate cause of damages to the McKinneys (P). The McKinneys (P) appealed.

ISSUE: May adoptive parents state a cause of action against an adoption placement agency for the negligent failure to meet the statutory disclosure requirements?

HOLDING AND DECISION: (Talmadge, J.) Yes. Adoptive parents may state a cause of action against an adoption placement agency for the negligent failure to meet the statutory disclosure requirements. The status of prospective adoptive parent attaches when the child is eligible for adoption under the statute, the persons interested in adopting the child have manifested a formal intent to adopt, and the adoption agency has formally acknowledged the eligibility of such persons to adopt the child. In the present case, the trial court properly instructed the jury on the duty of the DSHS (D) to disclose information to the McKinneys (P). Substantial evidence supported the jury's determination that DSHS (D) was negligent, but such negligence was not the proximate cause of damages to the McKinneys (P). Affirmed.

▶ ANALYSIS

The McKinneys (P) had originally alleged violation of 42 U.S.C. § 1983, outrage, fraud, and breach of contract in their amended complaint. Only the negligence claims were sent to the jury. The McKinneys (P) had also alleged that their status of prospective parents should have begun when they were foster parents.

Quicknotes

NEGLIGENCE Conduct falling below the standard of care that a reasonable person would demonstrate under similar conditions.

Doe v. Sundquist

Birth mother (P) v. Party not identified (D)

106 F.3d 702 (6th Cir. 1997).

NATURE OF CASE: Appeal from denial of injunction to block statutory disclosure of adoption records.

FACT SUMMARY: Tennessee passed a statute that would potentially disclose adoption records to certain interested parties. Plaintiffs sought to enjoin its enforcement as a violation of their privacy rights.

🏛 RULE OF LAW
The production of adoption records pursuant to statute is not a violation of constitutionally protected privacy rights.

FACTS: Sealed adoption records were only available by court order from 1951-1996 and only if in the best interests of the child or the public. A 1996 statute was to make adoption records available to a defined set of persons with provisions for an elective "contact veto" to prevent adoptee contact of birth families. Promise Doe (birth mother), Jane Roe (birth mother), Kimberly C. (adoptive mother), Russ C. (adoptive father), and Small World Ministries, Inc. (a Tennessee child-placement agency) (P) filed a petition for a preliminary injunction to prevent the enforcement of the statute as a violation of their privacy rights. The district court denied the injunction and plaintiffs appeal.

ISSUE: Is the production of adoption records pursuant to statute a violation of constitutionally protected privacy rights?

HOLDING AND DECISION: (Engle, J.) No. The production of adoption records pursuant to statute is not a violation of constitutionally protected privacy rights. The plaintiffs claim a violation of their familial privacy, reproductive privacy, and privacy against disclosure of confidential information if the proposed statute is enforced. It is skeptical that disclosure of adoption records violates a constitutional right unless Congress elevates records disclosure above the right to know the identity of one's parents. First, the familial privacy right is not violated because citizens may still marry, give birth, adopt, and be adopted. Second, the statute's restrictions are not at all analogous to laws struck down for restricting abortion. Third, no general right to nondisclosure of confidential information exists in the Constitution, and adoption-related rights have not been recognized as fundamental. In any event, the statute does not infringe upon when, how, or by whom a child may be adopted. The plaintiffs must also realize that their chances of success on their federal claims are slim and a preliminary injunction is thus not appropriate. Affirmed.

▶ ANALYSIS

Tennessee was the first state to pass such an open records law after years of adoption records being sealed. The plaintiffs in this case opted to pursue their state court claims instead of the federal claims but lost again. The state court judge held no constitutional right existed for nondisclosure of a person's identity.

■=■

Quicknotes

BEST INTERESTS OF CHILD Standard used by courts when rendering decisions which involve a child or children.

PRELIMINARY INJUNCTION A judicial mandate issued to require or restrain a party from certain conduct; used to preserve a trial's subject matter or to prevent threatened injury.

RIGHT TO PRIVACY An individual's right to be protected against unwarranted interference in his personal affairs, falling into one of four categories: (1) appropriating the individual's likeness or name for commercial benefit; (2) intrusion into the individual's seclusion; (3) public disclosure of private facts regarding the individual; and (4) disclosure of facts placing the individual in a false light.

■=■

Joslyn v. Reynolds

Ex-husband (P) v. Ex-wife (D)

Ohio Ct. App., 2001 WL 1194869 (2001).

NATURE OF CASE: Appeal from dismissal of complaint to vacate adoptions.

FACT SUMMARY: An adoptive father sought to vacate the adoptions of his stepchildren based on a claim that the marriage to their mother was fraud. The mother sought to dismiss the petition for failure to state a claim for which relief can be granted.

> ## RULE OF LAW
> A marriage based on fraud does not give rise to a claim for vacation of adoptions arising out of that marriage.

FACTS: Robert B. Joslyn (P) married Michelle A. Reynolds (D) and adopted her three children from a prior marriage. The couple divorced and Joslyn (P) was ordered to pay child support for all three children. Joslyn (P) filed a petition to vacate the adoptions on the ground of fraud and he sought compensation for all previously paid child support. Reynolds (D) filed a motion to dismiss for failure to state a claim upon which relief could be granted. The trial court found that Joslyn's (P) claim was barred by the applicable one-year statute of limitations and that he impermissibly sought to enforce a claim arising out of a marriage promise. The court granted Reynolds's (D) motion and Joslyn (P) appeals.

ISSUE: Does a marriage based on fraud give rise to a claim for vacation of adoptions arising out of that marriage?

HOLDING AND DECISION: (Whitmore, J.) No. A marriage based on fraud does not give rise to a claim for vacation of adoptions arising out of that marriage. Joslyn's (P) fraud claim is based on a claim that Reynolds (D) induced him to marry her to provide for her and her children. Their relationship began when Reynolds (D), married at the time, was hired to care for Joslyn (P), a quadriplegic. Joslyn (P) had a $10,000 monthly annuity payment, which Reynolds (D) began to manage. Reynolds (D) left her husband, initiated a sexual relationship with Joslyn (P), and expressed great interest in marrying him. She and her children moved in, and the couple wed two years later. Joslyn (P) then adopted Reynolds' (D) three children. Shortly thereafter, Joslyn (P) claims that Reynolds (D) ended any sexual relationship, became unfaithful, spent significant sums of money, and claimed only to have married him for his money. The relationship became worse, and Joslyn (D) feared for his life. His family took him to a hospital, and Reynolds (D) proceeded to vandalize the home with one of her paramours. Joslyn (P) moved in with his family, and Reynolds (D) denied him access to the children. The couple

divorced, and Joslyn (D) was ordered to pay $2354.00 in monthly child support. Four years after the entry of the adoption decrees, Joslyn (P) filed the petition to vacate the decrees. The court must take these allegations as true in considering Reynolds's (D) motion to dismiss, and the allegations are heartbreaking. Joslyn's (P) claim, however, does arise out of a marriage obligation and cannot be recognized. The fraud here goes to the basis for the marriage rather than the basis for the adoptions, and the court will not expand the definition of fraud in stepparent adoptions. No relief is available for the claims of this petition, and the trial court did not err in dismissing the petition. Affirmed.

ANALYSIS

The inducement to enter into the relationship with the parent does not necessarily equate to an inducement to enter into an adoptive relationship with children although the two seem to be intimately related. The inducing party must have made material misrepresentations upon which the other party relied in going through with the adoptions.

Quicknotes

CHILD SUPPORT Payments made by one parent to another in satisfaction of the non-custodial parent's legal obligation to provide for the sustenance of the child.

FRAUD A false representation of facts with the intent that another will rely on the misrepresentation to his detriment.

STATUTE OF LIMITATIONS A law prescribing the period in which a legal action may be commenced.

In re Petition of Otakar Kirchner

Birth father

Ill. Sup. Ct., 164 Ill. 2d 468, 649 N.E.2d 324 (1995).

NATURE OF CASE: Appeal from order of writ of habeas corpus.

FACT SUMMARY: An unwed father was deceived by his girlfriend into believing that his child died at birth. The birth mother arranged for the child to be adopted, and the adoptive family participated in her deceit. When he discovered the truth, he initiated proceedings to gain custody of his son. His parental rights were restored, but the adoptive family refused to give him physical custody of his son. He sought a writ of habeas corpus while the adoptive family petitioned for a custody hearing.

🏛 RULE OF LAW
An unwed, fit father is entitled to the care, custody, and control of his child upon the vacatur of an invalid adoption based on deceit and an invalid adoption proceeding.

FACTS: Otakar Kirchner (Otto) and his girlfriend, Daniella, intended to marry after learning she was pregnant with his child. During the pregnancy, Otto returned to his native Czechoslovakia for a visit, and Daniella was informed he had resumed a relationship with a former girlfriend. She moved out of their home into a women's shelter and made arrangements to place the baby with an adoptive family. She informed the adoptive parents, the Does, and their attorney that she intended to tell Otto that the baby died at birth. The Does and the attorney agreed to the plan. Upon Otto's return, he located Daniella, and the couple reconciled. She did not inform him of the intended adoption, however. When she gave birth, Otto could not contact her, and mutual friends told him that the baby had died. Daniella gave birth to Baby Richard and placed him with the Does. Otto and Daniella again reconciled, and Otto became suspicious of Daniella's story. She confessed the truth to him 57 days after Richard's birth. Otto began efforts to gain custody of his son. Otto and Daniella married, and Otto continued his quest. At trial, the court found him to be an unfit parent, because he was an unwed father who made no efforts to locate his son within thirty days of the birth which was one statutory definition of unfitness. The appellate court affirmed, and Otto appealed to this court. This court reversed and held that Otto's parental rights were never properly terminated. This court further held that the appellate court's focus on the best interests of the child was improper, because it first had to find clear and convincing evidence of unfitness. The Does also never made a good faith effort to locate Otto despite knowing of his existence and Daniella's plan to deceive him. They were also aware that he would not

consent to adoption. After this court's order to vacate the adoption and to return Richard to Otto, the General Assembly passed a statute requiring a custody determination based on the child's best interests after all pending adoption vacation proceedings. The Does accordingly did not return Richard to Otto and petitioned the court for a custody hearing. Otto filed this petition for writ of habeas corpus on the basis that he was entitled to custody of Richard immediately upon vacation of the adoption proceeding, and the Does therefore had no standing to petition for a custody hearing. This court granted the writ and the Does appealed.

ISSUE: Is an unwed, fit father entitled to the care, custody, and control of his child upon the vacatur of an invalid adoption based on deceit and an invalid adoption proceeding?

HOLDING AND DECISION: (Per curiam) Yes. An unwed, fit father is entitled to the care, custody, and control of his child upon the vacatur of an invalid adoption based on deceit and an invalid adoption proceeding. The Does claim standing pursuant to the Marriage and Dissolution of Marriage Act. Unwed and married fathers have the same rights and opportunities to develop a relationship with their children. The Adoption Act grants an unwed father rights to the care, custody, and control of his child subject only to the rights of the birth mother. An unwed father's consent is crucial to an adoption proceeding unless he has been declared unfit after a showing of clear and convincing evidence. The Does now seek a custody hearing under the Marriage and Dissolution of Marriage Act as a method of circumventing the rights granted to Otto under the Adoption Act. A person may obtain custody pursuant to this Act without an initial finding of unfitness, so the Act must be narrowly construed to protect natural parents' rights. A hearing pursuant to this Act would contravene the protections afforded unwed fathers in the Adoption Act. The Does and Richard's guardian ad litem next argue that Richard has a liberty interest in his relationship with the Does, but Richard also has a liberty interest in his relationship with his biological father. Psychological attachments to nonparents are not recognized as a child's liberty interest. The writ is affirmed.

DISSENT: (Miller, J.) The Does may petition for a custody hearing because they have physical custody of Richard, and any person so situated may petition. The court then determines custody in the best interests of the child. The majority is requiring voluntary relinquishment

Continued on next page.

on the part of the unwed father or adoptions are near impossible. The question of whether the Does were complicit in the deception is a fact question to be determined in the hearing. The majority finds the facts without an adequate record.

DISSENT: (McMorrow, J.) Richard is now four years old and has just been removed from his home and taken from his parents, the Does. The majority ignores Richard's rights and orders a change in custody completely void of any determination of the child's best interests. The granted writ violates Richard's procedural due process rights by ignoring the rights afforded him pursuant to the child custody procedures in the Marriage Act and in the Adoption Act. Otto is an unwed, noncustodial, biological father to Richard with no emotional ties and his constitutional rights are not impinged by the requirement of a best-interests-of-the-child custody hearing. Custody is not automatically vested in Otto merely because his parental rights were restored. Custody is only granted after a hearing on the child's best interests. The majority fails Baby Richard.

▶ *ANALYSIS*

The tragedy is for the child because, as the dissent notes, he is now four and will be suddenly taken from the only home and parents he knows and placed with two strangers in a foreign home. Challenges to adoption decrees are typically limited to six months in an effort to avoid situations like this.

■━■

Quicknotes

BEST INTERESTS OF CHILD Standard used by courts when rendering decisions which involve a child or children.

CLEAR AND CONVINCING EVIDENCE An evidentiary standard requiring a demonstration that the fact sought to be proven is reasonably certain.

DUE PROCESS RIGHTS The constitutional mandate requiring the courts to protect and enforce individuals' rights and liberties consistent with prevailing principles of fairness and justice, and prohibiting the federal and state governments from such activities that deprive its citizens of a life, liberty or property interest.

GOOD FAITH An honest intention to abstain from taking advantage of another.

GUARDIAN AD LITEM Person designated by the court to represent an infant or ward in a particular legal proceeding.

LIBERTY INTEREST A right conferred by the Due Process Clauses of the state and federal constitutions.

TERMINATION OF PARENTAL RIGHTS The purposeful cessation of lawfully recognized rights between a child and its parents and of the parent to the child, including physical possession of the child, companionship and support, the right to discipline the child, and control over the child's property.

WRIT OF HABEAS CORPUS A proceeding in which a defendant brings a writ to compel a judicial determination of whether he is lawfully being held in custody.

■━■

Common Latin Words and Phrases Encountered in the Law

A FORTIORI: Because one fact exists or has been proven, therefore a second fact that is related to the first fact must also exist.

A PRIORI: From the cause to the effect. A term of logic used to denote that when one generally accepted truth is shown to be a cause, another particular effect must necessarily follow.

AB INITIO: From the beginning; a condition which has existed throughout, as in a marriage which was void ab initio.

ACTUS REUS: The wrongful act; in criminal law, such action sufficient to trigger criminal liability.

AD VALOREM: According to value; an ad valorem tax is imposed upon an item located within the taxing jurisdiction calculated by the value of such item.

AMICUS CURIAE: Friend of the court. Its most common usage takes the form of an amicus curiae brief, filed by a person who is not a party to an action but is nonetheless allowed to offer an argument supporting his legal interests.

ARGUENDO: In arguing. A statement, possibly hypothetical, made for the purpose of argument, is one made arguendo.

BILL QUIA TIMET: A bill to quiet title (establish ownership) to real property.

BONA FIDE: True, honest, or genuine. May refer to a person's legal position based on good faith or lacking notice of fraud (such as a bona fide purchaser for value) or to the authenticity of a particular document (such as a bona fide last will and testament).

CAUSA MORTIS: With approaching death in mind. A gift causa mortis is a gift given by a party who feels certain that death is imminent.

CAVEAT EMPTOR: Let the buyer beware. This maxim is reflected in the rule of law that a buyer purchases at his own risk because it is his responsibility to examine, judge, test, and otherwise inspect what he is buying.

CERTIORARI: A writ of review. Petitions for review of a case by the United States Supreme Court are most often done by means of a writ of certiorari.

CONTRA: On the other hand. Opposite. Contrary to.

CORAM NOBIS: Before us; writs of error directed to the court that originally rendered the judgment.

CORAM VOBIS: Before you; writs of error directed by an appellate court to a lower court to correct a factual error.

CORPUS DELICTI: The body of the crime; the requisite elements of a crime amounting to objective proof that a crime has been committed.

CUM TESTAMENTO ANNEXO, ADMINISTRATOR (ADMINISTRATOR C.T.A.): With will annexed; an administrator c.t.a. settles an estate pursuant to a will in which he is not appointed.

DE BONIS NON, ADMINISTRATOR (ADMINISTRATOR D.B.N.): Of goods not administered; an administrator d.b.n. settles a partially settled estate.

DE FACTO: In fact; in reality; actually. Existing in fact but not officially approved or engendered.

DE JURE: By right; lawful. Describes a condition that is legitimate "as a matter of law," in contrast to the term "de facto," which connotes something existing in fact but not legally sanctioned or authorized. For example, de facto segregation refers to segregation brought about by housing patterns, etc., whereas de jure segregation refers to segregation created by law.

DE MINIMIS: Of minimal importance; insignificant; a trifle; not worth bothering about.

DE NOVO: Anew; a second time; afresh. A trial de novo is a new trial held at the appellate level as if the case originated there and the trial at a lower level had not taken place.

DICTA: Generally used as an abbreviated form of obiter dicta, a term describing those portions of a judicial opinion incidental or not necessary to resolution of the specific question before the court. Such nonessential statements and remarks are not considered to be binding precedent.

DUCES TECUM: Refers to a particular type of writ or subpoena requesting a party or organization to produce certain documents in their possession.

EN BANC: Full bench. Where a court sits with all justices present rather than the usual quorum.

EX PARTE: For one side or one party only. An ex parte proceeding is one undertaken for the benefit of only one party, without notice to, or an appearance by, an adverse party.

EX POST FACTO: After the fact. An ex post facto law is a law that retroactively changes the consequences of a prior act.

EX REL.: Abbreviated form of the term ex relatione, meaning upon relation or information. When the state brings an action in which it has no interest against an individual at the instigation of one who has a private interest in the matter.

FORUM NON CONVENIENS: Inconvenient forum. Although a court may have jurisdiction over the case, the action should be tried in a more conveniently located court, one to which parties and witnesses may more easily travel, for example.

GUARDIAN AD LITEM: A guardian of an infant as to litigation, appointed to represent the infant and pursue his/her rights.

HABEAS CORPUS: You have the body. The modern writ of habeas corpus is a writ directing that a person (body) being detained (such as a prisoner) be brought before the court so that the legality of his detention can be judicially ascertained.

IN CAMERA: In private, in chambers. When a hearing is held before a judge in his chambers or when all spectators are excluded from the courtroom.

IN FORMA PAUPERIS: In the manner of a pauper. A party who proceeds in forma pauperis because of his poverty is one who is allowed to bring suit without liability for costs.

INFRA: Below, under. A word referring the reader to a later part of a book. (The opposite of supra.)

IN LOCO PARENTIS: In the place of a parent.

IN PARI DELICTO: Equally wrong; a court of equity will not grant requested relief to an applicant who is in pari delicto, or as much at fault in the transactions giving rise to the controversy as is the opponent of the applicant.

IN PARI MATERIA: On like subject matter or upon the same matter. Statutes relating to the same person or things are said to be in pari materia. It is a general rule of statutory construction that such statutes should be construed together, i.e., looked at as if they together constituted one law.

IN PERSONAM: Against the person. Jurisdiction over the person of an individual.

IN RE: In the matter of. Used to designate a proceeding involving an estate or other property.

IN REM: A term that signifies an action against the res, or thing. An action in rem is basically one that is taken directly against property, as distinguished from an action in personam, i.e., against the person.

INTER ALIA: Among other things. Used to show that the whole of a statement, pleading, list, statute, etc., has not been set forth in its entirety.

INTER PARTES: Between the parties. May refer to contracts, conveyances or other transactions having legal significance.

INTER VIVOS: Between the living. An inter vivos gift is a gift made by a living grantor, as distinguished from bequests contained in a will, which pass upon the death of the testator.

IPSO FACTO: By the mere fact itself.

JUS: Law or the entire body of law.

LEX LOCI: The law of the place; the notion that the rights of parties to a legal proceeding are governed by the law of the place where those rights arose.

MALUM IN SE: Evil or wrong in and of itself; inherently wrong. This term describes an act that is wrong by its very nature, as opposed to one which would not be wrong but for the fact that there is a specific legal prohibition against it (malum prohibitum).

MALUM PROHIBITUM: Wrong because prohibited, but not inherently evil. Used to describe something that is wrong because it is expressly forbidden by law but that is not in and of itself evil, e.g., speeding.

MANDAMUS: We command. A writ directing an official to take a certain action.

MENS REA: A guilty mind; a criminal intent. A term used to signify the mental state that accompanies a crime or other prohibited act. Some crimes require only a general mens rea (general intent to do the prohibited act), but others, like assault with intent to murder, require the existence of a specific mens rea.

MODUS OPERANDI: Method of operating; generally refers to the manner or style of a criminal in committing crimes, admissible in appropriate cases as evidence of the identity of a defendant.

NEXUS: A connection to.

NISI PRIUS: A court of first impression. A nisi prius court is one where issues of fact are tried before a judge or jury.

N.O.V. (NON OBSTANTE VEREDICTO): Notwithstanding the verdict. A judgment n.o.v. is a judgment given in favor of one party despite the fact that a verdict was returned in favor of the other party, the justification being that the verdict either had no reasonable support in fact or was contrary to law.

NUNC PRO TUNC: Now for then. This phrase refers to actions that may be taken and will then have full retroactive effect.

PENDENTE LITE: Pending the suit; pending litigation underway.

PER CAPITA: By head; beneficiaries of an estate, if they take in equal shares, take per capita.

PER CURIAM: By the court; signifies an opinion ostensibly written "by the whole court" and with no identified author.

PER SE: By itself, in itself; inherently.

PER STIRPES: By representation. Used primarily in the law of wills to describe the method of distribution where a person, generally because of death, is unable to take that which is left to him by the will of another, and therefore his heirs divide such property between them rather than take under the will individually.

PRIMA FACIE: On its face, at first sight. A prima facie case is one that is sufficient on its face, meaning that the evidence supporting it is adequate to establish the case until contradicted or overcome by other evidence.

PRO TANTO: For so much; as far as it goes. Often used in eminent domain cases when a property owner receives partial payment for his land without prejudice to his right to bring suit for the full amount he claims his land to be worth.

QUANTUM MERUIT: As much as he deserves. Refers to recovery based on the doctrine of unjust enrichment in those cases in which a party has rendered valuable services or furnished materials that were accepted and enjoyed by another under circumstances that would reasonably notify the recipient that the rendering party expected to be paid. In essence, the law implies a contract to pay the reasonable value of the services or materials furnished.

QUASI: Almost like; as if; nearly. This term is essentially used to signify that one subject or thing is almost analogous to another but that material differences between them do exist. For example, a quasi-criminal proceeding is one that is not strictly criminal but shares enough of the same characteristics to require some of the same safeguards (e.g., procedural due process must be followed in a parole hearing).

QUID PRO QUO: Something for something. In contract law, the consideration, something of value, passed between the parties to render the contract binding.

RES GESTAE: Things done; in evidence law, this principle justifies the admission of a statement that would otherwise be hearsay when it is made so closely to the event in question as to be said to be a part of it, or with such spontaneity as not to have the possibility of falsehood.

RES IPSA LOQUITUR: The thing speaks for itself. This doctrine gives rise to a rebuttable presumption of negligence when the instrumentality causing the injury was within the exclusive control of the defendant, and the injury was one that does not normally occur unless a person has been negligent.

RES JUDICATA: A matter adjudged. Doctrine which provides that once a court of competent jurisdiction has rendered a final judgment or decree on the merits, that judgment or decree is conclusive upon the parties to the case and prevents them from engaging in any other litigation on the points and issues determined therein.

RESPONDEAT SUPERIOR: Let the master reply. This doctrine holds the master liable for the wrongful acts of his servant (or the principal for his agent) in those cases in which the servant (or agent) was acting within the scope of his authority at the time of the injury.

STARE DECISIS: To stand by or adhere to that which has been decided. The common law doctrine of stare decisis attempts to give security and certainty to the law by following the policy that once a principle of law as applicable to a certain set of facts has been set forth in a decision, it forms a precedent which will subsequently be followed, even though a different decision might be made were it the first time the question had arisen. Of course, stare decisis is not an inviolable principle and is departed from in instances where there is good cause (e.g., considerations of public policy led the Supreme Court to disregard prior decisions sanctioning segregation).

SUPRA: Above. A word referring a reader to an earlier part of a book.

ULTRA VIRES: Beyond the power. This phrase is most commonly used to refer to actions taken by a corporation that are beyond the power or legal authority of the corporation.

Addendum of French Derivatives

IN PAIS: Not pursuant to legal proceedings.

CHATTEL: Tangible personal property.

CY PRES: Doctrine permitting courts to apply trust funds to purposes not expressed in the trust but necessary to carry out the settlor's intent.

PER AUTRE VIE: For another's life; during another's life. In property law, an estate may be granted that will terminate upon the death of someone other than the grantee.

PROFIT A PRENDRE: A license to remove minerals or other produce from land.

VOIR DIRE: Process of questioning jurors as to their predispositions about the case or parties to a proceeding in order to identify those jurors displaying bias or prejudice.

Casenote Legal Briefs